Same

Synonyms - <u>almost</u> same meaning

sleep - doze     start - begin

Antonyms - ~~opposite~~ meaning

sleep - wake
laugh - cry          Crystal C.

# HBJ
# LANGUAGE

5

Dorothy S. Strickland
Richard F. Abrahamson
Roger C. Farr
Nancy R. McGee
Nancy L. Roser

**5**

Karen S. Kutiper
Patricia Smith

# HBJ
# LANGUAGE

**HBJ** **HARCOURT BRACE JOVANOVICH, PUBLISHERS**
Orlando   San Diego   Chicago   Dallas

Printed in the United States of America

ISBN 0-15-316415-8

# Acknowledgments

For permission to reprint copyrighted material, grateful acknowledgment is made to the following sources:

*Associated Press:* From "Humphrey Lured Back to Ocean By Whale Calls" in *Monterey Peninsula Herald,* November 5, 1985.

*Children's Better Health Institute, Indianapolis, IN:* "Benjamin Franklin: Prominent Signer of the Constitution" by Matt Neapolitan from *Children's Digest* Magazine, August/September 1986. Copyright © 1986 by Children's Better Health Institute, Benjamin Franklin Literary & Medical Society, Inc.

*Harcourt Brace Jovanovich, Inc.:* Short pronunciation key and entries from *HBJ School Dictionary.* Copyright © 1985 by Harcourt Brace Jovanovich, Inc. "Study Steps to Learn a Word" from *HBJ Spelling,* Signature Edition, Level 5 (Purple) by Thorsten Carlson and Richard Madden. Copyright © 1988, 1983 by Harcourt Brace Jovanovich, Inc.

*Harper & Row, Publishers, Inc.:* Text from pp. 76–80 and two illustrations in *By the Shores of Silver Lake* by Laura Ingalls Wilder, illustrated by Garth Williams. Text copyright 1939 by Laura Ingalls Wilder; copyright renewed © 1967 by Roger L. MacBride. Pictures copyright 1953 by Garth Williams; copyright renewed © 1981 by Garth Williams.

*Macmillan Publishing Company:* "Searching for Aladdin" from *Puppeteer* by Kathryn Lasky, illustrated by Christopher G. Knight. Copyright © 1985 by Kathryn Lasky and Christopher G. Knight.

*Morrow Junior Books, a division of William Morrow and Company, Inc.:* Text and illustrations from "Ramona to the Rescue" in *Ramona and Her Father* by Beverly Cleary, illustrated by Alan Tiegreen. Copyright © 1975, 1977 by Beverly Cleary.

*The New York Times Company:* From "A Winning .300 Hitter From His Wheelchair" by Jack Cavanaugh in *The New York Times,* July 10, 1988. Copyright © 1988 by The New York Times Company.

*The Sacramento Bee:* From "Fluke Appearance: Whale Surfaces in Delta" by Jon Engellenner in *The Sacramento Bee,* October 15, 1985. From "Delta Whale Taking a Doomed Course" by Jon Engellenner in *The Sacramento Bee,* October 16, 1985. From "Slough to Get Noisy for Whale" by Jon Engellenner in *The Sacramento Bee,* October 24, 1985.

*Sacramento Union:* Untitled poem by Richard Fonbuena to honor Humphrey the humpback whale from *Sacramento Union,* February 1, 1986.

## Art Acknowledgments

Anthony Accardo: 42; M. Adams: 288, 289; Alec Block: 96; Tom Bobroski: 146; Randy Chewning: 56 (top), 56 (bottom), 106 (top), 106 (bottom), 106 (bottom left), 107, 118 (top), 118 (bottom), 119 (top), 119 (bottom), 232, 244, 245, 290, 291, 454; Suzanne Clee: 94, 322; R. Collier: 104, 105, 370; Rick Cooley: 138; Carolyn Croll: 274; Susan David: 34; Gail deLuca: 98, 331; Pat and Robin DeWitt: 2, 19, 88, 100, 140, 150, 162, 163, 164, 165, 184, 194, 276, 278, 286, 366, Glossary 2, 4, 7, 8; Eldon Doty: 320, 332; Don Dyen: 196, 234, 244; George Ford: 368, 328; Simon Galkin: 230, 306, 347, 426; R. Gauer: 208–209, 242; Meryl Henderson: 10, 11, 12, 13, 14, 15; Jan Naimo Jones: 50; Susanna Luckey: 57, 192, 197, 412, 416; L. Lustig: 240, 282; Turi MacCombie: 236; Diana Magnuson: 46, 54, 152, 153; Laurie Marks: 40, 155, 346; J. McCreary: 312, 243; James Needham: 144; R. Olsen: 216; Jan Palmer: 56, 102; Marcia Perry: 372; Steve Petruccio: 90, 378, 379; R. Remkiewicz: 154; Eileen Rosen: 284; D. Roy: 154 (top), 154 (middle), 154 (bottom); Ed Sauk: 238; Dennis Schofield: 188; Pat Stewart: 410; Wayne Still: 148, 190, 328, 390, 391; M. Tisdale: 209; Mou-sien Tseng: 374; George Ulrich: 228, 324; Gary Undercuffler: 92, 432 (top), 432 (bottom), 433; Lane Yerkes: 36, 48, 194, 195, 330, 376, 377, 430.

*Cover:* Tom Vroman

*Production and Layout:* Helena Frost Assoc., Ltd.

## Photo Acknowledgments

PHOTOGRAPHS: Pages 3, HBJ Photo/Rob Downey; 6(t), HBJ Photo/Rob Downey; (b), HBJ Photo/Rob Downey; 7(t), HBJ Photo/Rob Downey; (b), HBJ Photo/Rob Downey.

UNIT 1:8, HBJ Photo/Charlie Burton; 9, Ed Mahan; 20, HBJ Photo; 29 (t), HBJ Photo; (b), HBJ Photo; 30(t), HBJ Photo; (b), HBJ Photo; 31, HBJ Photo; 38, HBJ Photo/Rodney Jones; 52, NBJ Photo/Rodney Jones.

UNIT 2: 62, HBJ Photo; 63(t), Christopher G. Knight/Macmillan Publishing, Co.; 65, Christopher G. Knight/The New Film Company, Inc./ Macmillan Publishing, Co.; 66, Christopher G. Knight/The New Film Company, Inc./Macmillan Publishing, Co.; 67, Christopher G. Knight/The New Film Company, Inc./Macmillan Publishing, Co.; 68, Christopher G. Knight/The New Film Company, Inc./Macmillan Publishing, Co.: 74, HBJ Photo; 83(l), HBJ Photo; (r), HBJ Photo; 84(l), HBJ Photo; (r), HBJ Photo; 85, HBJ Photo.

*continued at the end of the book*

iv

# Contents

## 1 | Telling About Your Experiences    8

### Reading ⬌ Writing Connection

### Composition Focus: Personal Narrative

### Language Focus: Sentences

# 2 | Explaining Facts

## Reading ◆ Writing Connection

## Composition Focus: Expository Paragraph

## Language Focus: Nouns

# **3** Giving Directions

## Reading ⬌ Writing Connection

## **Composition Focus: How-to Paragraph**

## **Language Focus: Verbs**

**4** **Comparing and Contrasting** 160

# 5 Reporting Events 206

## Reading ⬌ Writing Connection

## Composition Focus: News Story

## Language Focus: Pronouns

# 6  Painting Pictures with Words

## Reading ⟷ Writing Connection

## Composition Focus: Descriptive Paragraph

## Language Focus: Adjectives

# 7 Communicating Your Opinions

**Informing Others**

## Reading ◂▸ Writing Connection

## Composition Focus: Research Report

## Language Focus: Prepositions, Conjunctions, Interjections

# 9 Entertaining Others

## Reading ↔ Writing Connection

## Composition Focus: Tall Tale

## Language Focus: Mechanics Wrap-up

# Extra Practice 1

Dear Student,

Imagine what would happen if language disappeared. What would you do for entertainment? How would you explain your ideas and feelings? How would you learn?

Since language is so important to your life, it is also important to learn more about it. <u>HBJ Language</u> will help you learn more about your language, English. This book will help you learn to use English more effectively when you listen, speak, read, and write.

We hope that you enjoy learning about English, the language that is such a big part of your life.

Sincerely,

The Editors

# Understanding the Writing Process

Writing a story, an article, or a poem is like learning, practicing, and performing a new movement in figure skating. The skater follows a plan to learn and practice the new movement. If the skater follows the plan, he or she will be able to master the movement and give a good performance.

A writer also follows a plan to produce a piece of writing for an audience. This plan is called the **writing process.** The process has five stages:

1. Prewriting
2. Drafting
3. Responding and Revising
4. Proofreading
5. Publishing

Just as a skater may have to try several times before a new movement is right, a writer may have to go back and forth through the stages of the writing process. The diagram shows how a writer may move through the five stages.

| Prewriting | Drafting | Responding and Revising | Proofreading | Publishing |
|---|---|---|---|---|
| | | | | |

# 1 Prewriting

The prewriting stage helps you through the hardest part of the writing process—getting started. During this stage, you

- identify your audience, the person or persons for whom you are writing.
- define your purpose, or reason for writing, and decide on a form for your writing.
- brainstorm a list of possible topics for writing.
- select one topic that is best for your audience and your purpose.
- gather and organize information about your topic.

The chart shows some different forms of writing, some audiences, and some purposes for writing.

| Writing Form | Audience | Purpose |
|---|---|---|
| news story | community | **to inform** readers about a school event |
| thank-you note | friend | **to express** appreciation |
| tall tale | parent | **to entertain** by telling a humorous story |
| business letter | company representative | **to persuade** representative to refund money |

## Graphic Organizers

Graphic organizers are tools that you can use in the prewriting stage. They will help you think of ideas and organize your information.

**Cluster**   Use a cluster to help you think of details about your topic. A cluster can be very helpful when you are planning to write a description.

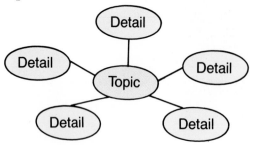

**Chart**   Use a chart to explain the steps in a process. For example, you may need to list a set of actions that must be carried out in a certain order. A chart can help you when you are planning to write a how-to paragraph.

| How to _____ | ── Title |
|---|---|
| Materials: | ── Materials |
| 1. | |
| 2. | ── Steps |
| 3. | |
| 4. | |
| 5. | |

**Venn Diagram**   Use a Venn diagram when you want to find the similarities and differences between two objects. A Venn diagram can be helpful when you are planning to write a paragraph of comparison and contrast.

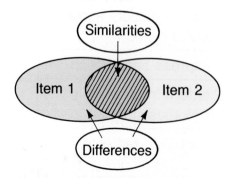

**Story Map**   Use a story map when you are planning a story. A story map reminds you to introduce the characters and setting of your story and to tell what problem starts the story. A story map also helps you remember to include additional events and a turning point before the ending of your story.

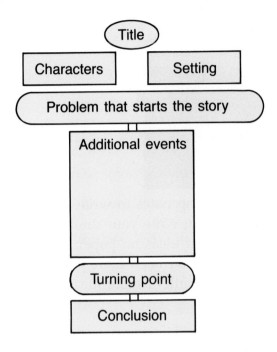

**Diagram**   Use a diagram when you are planning to write a paragraph of cause and effect. A diagram helps you to understand relationships and to make them clear.

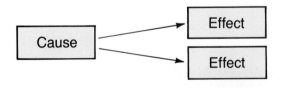

**Outline**   Use an outline to help you organize information for a research report. An outline is most helpful when you are writing about a broad topic that includes many main ideas and details.

Topic
I. Main idea
  A. Detail
  B. Detail
  C. Detail
II. Main idea
  A. Detail
  B. Detail

## 2 Drafting

In the drafting stage, you use your prewriting notes to write a first, rough version of your composition. As you write your draft, do not worry about making errors. Just get your ideas on paper. If you run into problems, such as finding that you need more material, go back to the prewriting stage and think of more ideas.

## 3 Responding and Revising

The responding and revising stage is a real challenge. In this stage, you work with a partner or a group to respond to your draft by checking to see if it is right for your audience and purpose. You think about the organization and language of your draft. You think about the information you have included. Then you revise your writing by making changes that will improve it.

## 4 Proofreading

In the proofreading stage, you make your work shine. You check your work to find and correct errors in grammar, spelling, capitalization, and punctuation.

## 5 Publishing

The last stage of the writing process is publishing. In this stage you present your work to your audience. You can publish your work orally or in writing. Thinking about your audience and your purpose will help you decide the best way to publish your work.

# UNIT

## 1

# Telling About Your Experiences

◆ **COMPOSITION FOCUS:** Personal Narrative
◆ **LANGUAGE FOCUS:** Sentences

When was the last time something funny, scary, or exciting happened to you? Did you tell your friends about what happened? Did you write about it in a diary, a journal, or a letter? If you did, you wrote a personal narrative. A personal narrative tells a story about something that really happened to you.

When you read an autobiography (a person's life story told by the person himself or herself), you are reading a personal narrative. Also, when you read magazine articles or nonfiction books that are told from the first-person or "I" point of view, you are reading personal narratives.

In the following pages you will read a personal narrative by newspaper reporter Hans Knight. In it, Mr. Knight describes some sad yet exciting events in his own life. He tells the very personal story of how he came to be a writer. In this unit you will study the elements that make up a good personal narrative.

Hans Knight wrote "The Man in the Trench Coat" *to express* his own thoughts about writing.

# Reading with a Writer's Eye
## Personal Narrative

As a writer, Hans Knight has interviewed many famous people. The tables were turned, however, when he interviewed a former prime minister of Great Britain. Suddenly it was Mr. Knight who was answering a question; the question was "How did you become a writer?" The question started him thinking—and remembering. The following personal narrative is the result. As you read this personal narrative, notice how this writer has organized and presented the events in his story.

### The Man in the Trench Coat
#### by Hans Knight

In the lives of most of us, there is one person who points a path to our future. Sometimes that person is a favorite teacher, sometimes a great ball player, singer, painter, or scientist. It all depends on what your dream is.

My own dream was to be a writer. I always loved words. For as long as I can remember, I've had the urge to put my words on paper so they wouldn't get lost. But my inspiration was not a famous poet or novelist. He was just a man in a trench coat. Strictly speaking, he didn't even exist. Yet I owe him much.

I thought of this man not long ago when my newspaper sent me out to interview Harold Wilson, the former prime minister of Great Britain. He had come to a small college in Pennsylvania to give a talk on world affairs. After his formal speech, we sat down at a wooden table on the campus lawn. A student brought him a bottle of lemonade, and Mr. Wilson poured me a glass, too. In his rumpled tweed jacket, this burly white-haired man with friendly blue eyes hardly looked like a captain who had once steered a ship of state. He patiently answered my questions. I finally said, "Thank you, Mr. Prime Minister," and prepared to leave.

Then something strange happened. He gently put his hand on my arm. "Just a moment," the former prime minister said. "You've asked me many questions. Now it's my turn. Tell me, how did you become a writer?"

I was stunned. Over the years, people had often asked me that question, but none of them had been a prime minister of England. "Sir," I stammered, "why would you be interested in my career?"

Mr. Wilson raised one bushy eyebrow. "Well," he chuckled, "one never learns anything unless one asks, does one? Beside, I noticed your accent. I'm a Yorkshireman, and you talk a bit like me . . ."

"Mr. Prime Minister," I said, "you have a keen ear. I did live in Yorkshire, during the war. But I wasn't born in England. I came to your country from Austria, as a refugee."

"Aye," Mr. Wilson said, "Hitler and his gang. A bad lot, weren't they? A very bad lot."

My mind flashed back to my boyhood in a small country town near Vienna. It was close to paradise for a boy: swimming in a pine-framed lake in summer; playing hockey on its frozen surface in winter; listening to great music on scratchy records in my father's tiny radio store; floating down a narrow brook in a wash-tub, like Tom Sawyer and Huckleberry Finn braving terrible dangers on the Mississippi. I wasn't what anyone would call a good student, but one day I won an essay competition. My teacher wrote on the paper, "Promising, keep writing." I went home and told everybody that I was going to be a famous author. Very soon.

On March 12, 1938, the Nazis took over Austria. They hated many people. Most of all, they hated Jews. They blamed them for everything bad that happened in the world. I had two Jewish grandparents who had died before I was born. It made no difference to the Nazis. The Nazis took my father's store. They threatened us and chased us in the streets. Even some of our friends turned against us. That hurt the most.

So it happened that on a blustery winter night, I became a refugee. I found myself on a boat crossing the English Channel, clutching my little sister Lilly's hand. There were some 40 kids, huddled together under damp blankets. We could smell the heavy, salty air that seemed to press down upon us in our makeshift cabins. Few of us would ever see our parents again, but we didn't know that at the time. As children will, we thought of our escape as a great adventure. I imagined that I was Long John Silver sailing to Treasure Island. Perhaps, too, I sensed that there was indeed a treasure awaiting us in England: our freedom.

The Second World War broke out six months later. I was now fifteen years old, too old to become an English schoolchild as Lilly had done. I found work as a laborer in a textile mill in Halifax, a

foggy industrial town. Often, we heard the drone of the Nazi bombers in the clouds. The air raid sirens would wail, and we'd go to our shelters. (These were merely holes dug in the back yard, covered with corrugated iron sheets.) Since few bombs actually dropped on Halifax, everybody soon ignored the murmuring planes and just carried on with their jobs.

The work in the mill was hard and monotonous. The people around me had more important things on their minds than my lost chance at a writing career. My grand visions began to seem pretty foolish to me, too. Remember, my native language was German. I'd picked up enough English to get by in a textile mill, but how could I ever hope to write for a living in this strange, new tongue?

It would take a miracle to unseal my fate, and suddenly one night, a kind of miracle occurred. I had gone to see a movie at the Odeon Theater in Halifax. It was called *This Man Is News*. The hero was a writer, a newspaper reporter, played by a little-known actor. His name was Barry K. Barnes. He was rather thin and not terribly handsome, but watching him in the darkness I was entranced. There on the screen unfolded a life of high adventure. One moment, Mr. Barnes was covering a big story in London. The next, he was chasing Nazi spies in Paris. He dodged bullets in dark alleys with the greatest of ease. And always, always, he wore that magnificent trench coat, its belt not buckled but tied in a casual knot. When I walked out at the end of that movie, groping my way home through the pitch-black streets, I knew my destiny. I wanted to be like Barry K. Barnes, a newspaper reporter.

From that night on, my course was set. With the dashing image of Mr. Barnes in my mind, I stopped feeling sorry for myself. Instead, I started to turn my dream into substance. After a weary day at the mill, I haunted the public library, a German-English dictionary in hand. I carefully read about Tom Sawyer and Huck Finn—this time in English. I even read some Shakespeare. I didn't understand much of that, but what little I did understand was enough to show me the true beauty and power of words—words that make you feel the deepest sadness, and the highest happiness, and everything in between. After a while, magically, I found I didn't need the dictionary anymore.

When Barry K. Barnes and his trench coat returned to the Odeon in the sequel, *This Man in Paris,* I was waiting for him. No longer was I a poor mill boy with no hope of escape. I watched him this time with my shattered dream back in one piece. Yes, I would be a writer, in whatever language I had to use.

Soon after the war ended I moved to the United States. One joyous day, I was hired by the great *New York Times* as a copy boy. Was it trench coat time at last? No, not quite. A copy boy lugs paste pots, gets coffee, and runs errands for the editors. He does not act at all like Barry K. Barnes. There is a difference between real life and the movies.

But . . . so what? I did learn to string words together—not as well as I had dreamed, I doubt that any writer ever does, but not so badly as to cause nightmares either. And along the way, I was lucky to taste some of the writer's sweet rewards. I have met people from all walks of life, from the unsung heroes who seldom make the headlines to celebrities who make them too often. On a very good day—who knows?—the words I write might form bridges where there were none before. They might touch someone the way a little-known actor in a forgotten movie once touched me.

That was why, on a sunny afternoon, when a former prime minister of England sat down with me and shared a lemonade and some talk, I couldn't help thinking, "You may never reach the top of the ladder, but maybe you have hold of the bottom rung." And that was also why, as Mr. Wilson waved a cheery goodbye from his car, I sent a silent message to a man in a trench coat.

Thank you, Barry K. Barnes, wherever you are.

## Respond

1. The man in the trench coat was not even real, yet he changed a lonely boy's life. Why did he mean so much to Hans Knight?

## Discuss

2. Does the writer organize all the major events from the earliest to the latest? If not, describe how the events are presented.

3. A good personal narrative should give details that make you feel as if you are experiencing the event yourself. Which details in Hans Knight's personal narrative make it come alive?

# Thinking As a Writer
## Analyzing a Personal Narrative

A personal narrative is a true story that a writer tells about himself or herself. It is written in the first person, using the word *I*. In a personal narrative the writer describes not only events, but how he or she feels about those events.

Each personal narrative has a beginning, a middle, and an ending. Notice how Hans Knight mixes events and feelings in these excerpts from "The Man in the Trench Coat."

> In the lives of most of us, there is one person who points a path to our future.

The **beginning** tells what the personal narrative will be about.

> There on the screen unfolded a life of high adventure. One moment, Mr. Barnes was covering a big story in London. The next, he was chasing Nazi spies in Paris. He dodged bullets in dark alleys with the greatest of ease. And always, always, he wore that magnificent trench coat, its belt not buckled but tied in a casual knot. When I walked out at the end of that movie, groping my way home through the pitch-black streets, I knew my destiny. I wanted to be like Barry K. Barnes, a newspaper reporter.

The **middle** describes events in time order, using words such as *first* and *next*.

**Causes and effects** are often part of a personal narrative. An effect is what happened. A cause is the reason it happened.

> And that was also why, as Mr. Wilson waved a cheery goodbye from his car, I sent a silent message to a man in a trench coat.
> Thank you, Barry K. Barnes, wherever you are.

The **ending** tells what happened to the writer as a result of the events described.

## Discuss

1. What time-order words does the writer use?
2. What cause and effect does the writer describe?
3. What words or phrases reveal the writer's feelings?

# Try Your Hand

**A. Analyze a Personal Narrative**  Read part of a personal narrative. Write the words that describe the main event.

> To tell you the truth, I didn't like having my baby sister around until the day I almost lost her. That fateful afternoon, my mother drove Minnie and me to the Breezeway Mall so that she could buy a new washing machine. She bought drinks for us and told us to stay at the table with the red umbrella. I did sit, drawing with Minnie and hating every minute of it. I considered what we were doing "baby stuff." Was I thrilled when my friend Annie came by! We left Minnie for only five minutes so that we could check the records at Brant's. Imagine my horror at returning to the table with the red umbrella and finding it empty! I looked all around the area in panic. Just minutes before my mother appeared, I spied Minnie and a security guard approaching me. My relief was intense.

**B. Make a Diagram**  Make a diagram of the personal narrative above. Begin by writing the topic sentence and drawing a rectangle around it. Then, underneath, write only *events*. Number the events in the order in which they are presented.

**C. Add to the Narrative**  Find and list words from the narrative that reveal the writer's feelings. Then write a new sentence that expresses what the writer's feelings might be.

**D. Read Personal Narratives**  Look at Hans Knight's personal narrative on pages 10–15, or find another personal narrative in a magazine or a book. Then work with a partner to identify the events being described, the order of events, and the writer's thoughts and feelings.

## Writer's Notebook

**Collecting Words with Feeling**  Look again at Hans Knight's personal narrative and any personal narratives you found in magazines or books. Record in your *Writer's Notebook* the words and phrases that writers use to tell about their feelings. Also, listen to the words and phrases people use in their everyday conversations to tell how they feel. Record these words and phrases in your *Writer's Notebook*.

# Thinking As a Writer
## Connecting Cause and Effect

**Writer's Guide**

To write a personal narrative, good writers
- tell what happened.
- tell the causes or the effects of the major events.

When you write a personal narrative, you describe events, such as fleeing to England on a boat. You also describe feelings, such as being discouraged about your dream. Sometimes events and feelings are the causes of things that happen.

| Cause | Effect |
|---|---|
| Hans was entranced by what he saw on the movie screen. | He made up his mind to become a writer. |

At other times, events and feelings are the *effects* of things that happen.

| Cause | Effect |
|---|---|
| Hans went to see *This Man Is News.* | Hans was entranced by what he saw on the movie screen. |

As you write a personal narrative, be sure to connect causes and effects so that your reader will have a better understanding of what happened.

## Discuss

1. Look back at the selection on pages 10–15. Identify some of the cause-and-effect relationships.
2. Imagine a personal narrative by Hans Knight about the effects of writing "The Man in the Trench Coat." What possible effects might he describe?

## Try Your Hand

**Write Cause-and-Effect Statements**  Write cause-and-effect statements like the ones above about an event that you experienced. For example, you could write about what happened when you helped your father make dinner or when you planned a trip with your family.

# Developing the Writer's Craft
## Using Details to Explain

For the reader to see how events are related, the writer must give enough details that tell the cause or the effect of an event. Read these sentences from "The Man in the Trench Coat."

> The Nazis took over Austria.
> Most of all, they hated Jews.
> They threatened us and chased us in the streets.
> So it happened that I became a refugee.

The writer gives the cause (the Nazis) that leads up to the final effect (becoming a refugee). The word *so* in the last sentence helps signal this as an effect. Writers often use the words *so* and *because* when they give causes and effects. Sometimes the writer gives a cause first, and sometimes an effect.

When you write your personal narrative, give reasons for the events you describe. Use words like *so* and *because* to alert the reader to events or feelings that were caused by earlier events.

## Discuss

1. The fact that people in Halifax soon ignored the bomber planes is an effect. What is the cause?
2. Was Hans Knight's viewing of *This Man Is News* a cause or an effect? Can an event be both things? Give an example.

## Try Your Hand

**Identify Cause and Effect**   Look at the pictures of the girl and the refrigerator. Write a sentence telling what is happening to her. Then add three more sentences that add details to your explanation.

# 1 Prewriting
## Personal Narrative

The students in Andrew's class at Mission Elementary School were going to put together a collection of personal narratives. Andrew used the checklist in the **Writer's Guide** to help plan his personal narrative. Look at what he did.

### Writer's Guide

**Prewriting Checklist**

- ☑ Brainstorm topics or look through your journal for a topic.
- ☑ Select a topic.
- ☑ Think about your audience and your purpose.
- ☑ Gather information.
- ☑ Organize the information in the correct time order.

### ◆ Brainstorming and Selecting a Topic

Andrew had been keeping a journal for the past month, so he decided to look through his journal for possible topics. He made a list of the general subjects of his journal entries. Look at Andrew's list.

Next, Andrew looked over his list and crossed out topics that might be hard to use for a personal narrative. Since a narrative is almost always given in time order, he crossed out topics he could not easily present that way. Remembering that his class was making a collection of *personal* narratives, Andrew also crossed out topics that did not really include him.

Finally, Andrew circled the topic that would make the best narrative, a trip to Channel Islands National Park.

*what I like about school*

*Grandmother's stories about growing up in Scotland*

*the jokes my friends told on the camping trip*

*our trip to Channel Islands National Park*

*presents I would like for my birthday*

### Discuss

1. Look at the topics Andrew crossed off his list. Which would have been hard to present in time order? Which do not really include Andrew?
2. Suppose that instead of "what I like about school," Andrew had written "my first week at my new school." Might that be a good topic for a personal narrative? Why or why not?

## ◆ Gathering Information

After Andrew chose his topic, he carefully read the entries in his journal about his family's trip to the Channel Islands. Andrew had written three entries in his journal about the trip. Andrew realized that he would need to *select* and *organize* the information from his journal before he could write his personal narrative.

In his three journal entries, Andrew had written about more than just the trip to the Channel Islands. Andrew decided that the best way to select the information from his journal would be to put check marks by everything that was about the trip.

Here is some of what he did.

*Journal Entry 1*
We almost overslept this morning because Dad's alarm didn't go off. Then Julie nearly forgot her camera. We finally got going by 8:00. ✓We left for the Channel Islands from a dock near the National Park Headquarters in Ventura.

*Journal Entry 2*
✓The sun was just starting to shine through the fog when we got to the islands.✓ We only went to Anacapa Island, but we could see other islands around us.✓ I'm glad the sun came out on this trip so we could see more of the scenery.

*Journal Entry 3*
✓The ocean was rough when we docked at the island.✓ We had to be careful getting out of the boat.✓ From the top of the stairs we could see most of the island. We had to climb 154 stairs from the dock.✓ All around us were baby seagulls that had been born just three or four weeks ago.

## Discuss

1. When Andrew was selecting information for his personal narrative, why didn't he put checks next to the first three sentences in Journal Entry 1?

2. Suppose Andrew wanted to write a personal narrative about things going wrong on family vacations. Might he be able to use the sentences he didn't check in his narrative? Explain why or why not.

◆ **Organizing Information**

After Andrew put a check mark by all the sentences in his journal about his trip to the Channel Islands, he read the sentences again. He decided not to use the information about getting to the islands. He chose instead to use only the information about what happened once he got to the islands.

Andrew knew he would next have to organize what he had chosen. He began by writing on a sheet of paper all the information that he wanted to use from his journal. Then he put the events in correct time order. Here is some of what he did.

1. The ocean was rough when we docked at the island.
2. We had to be careful getting out of the boat.
3. We had to climb 154 stairs from the dock.
4. From the top of the stairs we could see most of the island.

## Discuss

1. When Andrew was organizing the information from Journal Entry 3, why did he order the sentences as he did?

2. What other cause and effect from Journal Entry 3 will appear on Andrew's cause-and-effect chart?

Andrew also noticed that some of his information told about causes and effects. To make sure he would correctly explain the cause-and-effect relationships, he made a chart. Here is part of Andrew's chart.

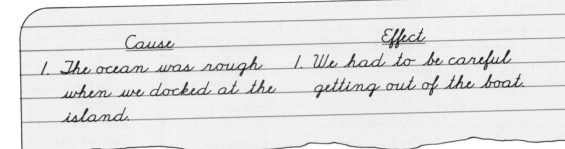

*Cause*

1. The ocean was rough when we docked at the island.

*Effect*

1. We had to be careful getting out of the boat.

## Try Your Hand

Now plan a personal narrative of your own.

**A. Brainstorm and Select a Topic**   If you are keeping a journal, look through it and make a list of topics that you might use for a personal narrative. If you are not keeping a journal, write three journal entries about recent events in your life. Think about each topic and about your audience.
   ◆ Cross out topics that cannot be presented in time order.
   ◆ Cross out topics that do not directly include you or that you do not want to share.
   ◆ Among the remaining topics, circle the one that would make the best personal narrative.

**B. Gather Your Material**   Once you have decided on your topic, read through your journal entries and put checks next to the information that is about your topic.

**C. Organize the Information**   Look over your notes.
   ◆ Make sure the information you choose is in time order. If necessary, move sentences into correct time order.
   ◆ Look for any information or ideas in your journal entries that are connected by cause and effect. Put them in a chart so that you will remember to explain the cause-and-effect relationships clearly to your readers.

 **Save your chart and sentences in your *Writer's Notebook*. You will use them when you draft your personal narrative.**

# 2 Drafting
## Personal Narrative

**Writer's Guide**

**Drafting Checklist**

☑ Use your chart and sentences for ideas.

☑ Plan a beginning, a middle, and an ending for your narrative.

☑ Tell your narrative in time order.

☑ Show cause-and-effect connections when they will help your audience.

Using the material he had selected and organized from his journal and the cause-and-effect chart, Andrew followed the checklist in the **Writer's Guide** to draft his personal narrative. Look at what he did.

> *My Trip to the Channel Islands*
> *My trip to Channel Islands National Park last month was full of surprises. I saw many new animals and learned many things. As soon as we had walked up the 154 stairs to the main part of Anacapa Island, we saw dozens of seagull chicks just three or four weeks old. I was surprised. They were brown and spotted.*

## Discuss

1. Andrew's first sentence tells his audience that his trip was full of surprises. What does Andrew's second sentence lead his audience to expect?
2. Is "My Trip to the Channel Islands" a better title than "A Family Vacation Trip" would have been? Why or why not?

## Try Your Hand

Now you are ready to write a personal narrative.

A. **Review Your Information** Think about the information you selected and organized in the last lesson. Decide whether you want to include any more of it in your personal narrative.

B. **Think About Your TAP** Remember that your task is to write a personal narrative. Your purpose is to tell your audience about something you did.

**TAP**

**Task:** What?
**Audience:** Who?
**Purpose:** Why?

C. **Write Your First Draft** Follow the steps in the **Drafting Checklist** to write your personal narrative.
   When you write your draft, just put all your ideas on paper. Do not worry about spelling, punctuation, or grammar. You can correct the draft later.

**Save your first draft in your** *Writer's Notebook.* **You will use it when you revise your personal narrative.**

# 3 Responding and Revising
## Personal Narrative

Andrew used the checklist in the **Writer's Guide** to revise his personal narrative. Look at what he did.

### ◆ Checking Information

When Andrew read over his draft, he decided to add a description of the adult gulls. To show his change, Andrew used this mark ∧ . Andrew took out a sentence about the ranger's uniform. To show the change, he used this mark ✍ .

### ◆ Checking Organization

Andrew decided to move the last sentence so that it followed a related sentence. To show that the sentence should be moved, he used this mark ↻ .

### ◆ Checking Language

When Andrew checked the sentences in his personal narrative, he added the cause-and-effect word *because* to make a clearer connection between ideas. He also decided that the word *walked* should be clearer and more vivid. After using his thesaurus, Andrew crossed out *walked* and replaced it with the word *trudged*. Andrew used this mark ∧ to make his change.

> **Writer's Guide**
>
> **Revising Checklist**
> - ☑ Read your personal narrative to yourself or to a partner.
> - ☑ Think about your audience and your purpose. Add or cut information.
> - ☑ Check to see that you have organized events in time order.
> - ☑ Check for clear cause-and-effect connections. Add cause-and-effect words if necessary.

My Trip to the Channel Islands

My trip to Channel Islands National Park last month was full of surprises. I saw many new animals and learned many things. As

**Replace —** soon as we had ~~walked~~ *trudged* up the 154 stairs to the main part of Anacapa Island, we saw dozens of seagull chicks just three or four weeks

**Add —** old. I was surprised *because* They were brown and spotted. *adult gulls are white.* The ranger told us the chicks will need to learn to fly soon. ~~The ranger wore a brown~~

**Cut —** ~~uniform.~~ I had never seen so many baby

**Move —** animals before!

## Discuss

1. Why did Andrew add information about the adult gulls' color?
2. Why did Andrew take out the information about the ranger?
3. Why did Andrew move the last sentence?
4. How is Andrew's personal narrative better than his draft? Explain your answer.

## Try Your Hand

Now revise your first draft.

**A. Read Your First Draft** As you read your personal narrative, think about your audience and your purpose. Read your draft silently or to a partner to see if it is complete. Ask yourself or your partner the questions in the box.

### Responding and Revising Strategies

| ✔ **Respond** Ask yourself or a partner: | ✔ **Revise** Try these solutions: |
|---|---|
| ◆ Have I kept information in time order? | ◆ **Move** information into time order. |
| ◆ Have I used cause-and-effect words when they will help my reader? | ◆ **Add** cause-and-effect words if necessary. |
| ◆ Have I included enough information related to my topic? | ◆ **Take out** any unrelated information. **Add** details that tell why. |
| ◆ Have I chosen the most exact and vivid words to say what I mean? | ◆ Use the **Writer's Thesaurus** to help you replace vague or overused words. |

**B. Make Your Changes** If the answer to any question in the box is *no*, try the solution. Use the **Editor's Marks** to show your changes.

**C. Review Your Personal Narrative Again** Decide whether there is anything else you want to revise. Keep revising your personal narrative until you feel it is well organized and complete.

> **EDITOR'S MARKS**
> ∧ Add something.
> ⤴ Cut something.
> ◯ Move something.
> ∧ Replace something.

 Save your revised personal narrative in your *Writer's Notebook.* You will use it when you proofread your personal narrative.

WRITING PROCESS

# Revising Workshop
## Using a Thesaurus

A **thesaurus** is a book that lists words and their synonyms. Good writers use a thesaurus to find synonyms that will make their writing interesting and give it variety. Look at the underlined words in these sentences.

1. My mind <u>went</u> back to my boyhood.
2. My mind <u>flashed</u> back to my boyhood.
3. We could smell the <u>sea</u> air in our <u>rooms</u>.
4. We could smell the <u>heavy, salty</u> air in our <u>makeshift cabins</u>.

In all four sentences, the writer tells about his boyhood. In the second and fourth sentences, however, plain words have been replaced with more vivid words that create a clearer picture and express the writer's feelings more exactly. *Makeshift cabins* describes the same place as *rooms,* but *makeshift cabins* gives a much more colorful image of where the children slept.

## Practice

Rewrite each sentence. Replace the word or words in parentheses with words that express the meaning in a more exact and vivid way. For some words, you may want to refer to a thesaurus or to the **Writer's Thesaurus** at the back of the book.

1. When I was a little (child), I lived on a (busy) chicken farm in New Jersey.
2. Early each morning, my uncle (walked) down to the chicken coop to (get) the eggs the hens had laid.
3. Although I usually (stayed away from) the (noisy) chickens, some mornings I went with my uncle.
4. The chickens would (jump) up and (tap their beaks) against my ankles.
5. Then I would get (scared) and would (run) around in a state of (fear).
6. My (yells) would make the chickens (go) off in all directions, and my uncle would get (angry).
7. Finally, he sat me down for a good (talk). We both decided that my (job) on the farm could be to make the pigs (happy) by giving them extra attention from the other side of their fence!

# 4 Proofreading
## Personal Narrative

After Andrew revised his personal narrative, he used the checklist in the **Writer's Guide** and the **Editor's Marks** to proofread it. Look at what he did.

### Writer's Guide

**Proofreading Checklist**

- ☑ Check to see that you have capitalized the word *I*.
- ☑ Check for errors in punctuation.
- ☑ Check to see that all your paragraphs are indented.
- ☑ Circle any words you think are misspelled. Find out how to spell them correctly.
- ⇨ For proofreading help, use the **Writer's Handbook**.

The ranger told us an interesting story about a building on the island that i thought was a church. Actually it is for storring water. The guide explained to my family and Me that a long time ago people used to shoot at the old water tower. Later, the building like a church was constructed to store the water because the people on the island figured no one would shoot at a church. so far the water has been protected!

## Discuss

1. Look at Andrew's proofread paragraph. What kinds of mistakes did he make?
2. Andrew had to correct the words *I* and *me*. What kind of corrections did he make? Why?
3. What is the only time you would capitalize the word *my* in a sentence?

## Try Your Hand

**Proofread Your Personal Narrative** Now use the **Writer's Guide** and the **Editor's Marks** to proofread your personal narrative.

 **Save your corrected personal narrative in your** *Writer's Notebook.* **You will use it when you publish your narrative.**

### EDITOR'S MARKS

- ≡ Capitalize.
- ⊙ Add a period.
- ∧ Add something.
- ⋏ Add a comma.
- ⌄⌄ Add quotation marks.
- ✌ Cut something.
- ⋀ Replace something.
- ⁀ Transpose.
- ◯ Spell correctly.
- ⊓ Indent paragraph.
- / Make a lowercase letter.

WRITING PROCESS

# 5 Publishing
## Personal Narrative

Andrew made a clean copy of his personal narrative and checked it to make sure he had not left out anything. Then he and his classmates shared their personal narratives by reading them aloud and then binding them into a scrapbook. You can read Andrew's personal narrative on page 32 of the **Writer's Handbook** at the back of this book.

Here's how Andrew and his classmates published their personal narratives.

**Writer's Guide**

**Publishing Checklist**

☑ Make a clean copy of your personal narrative.

☑ Check to see that nothing has been left out.

☑ Check that there are no mistakes.

☑ Share your personal narrative in a special way.

1. First, Andrew got together with his classmates. They took turns reading aloud their personal narratives to each other. They followed the **Tips for Reading a Personal Narrative Aloud** on page 31.

2. Next, the students found photographs that illustrated their personal narratives. Those who did not have actual photographs made drawings or cut out pictures from old magazines.

3. Andrew and his classmates pasted clean copies of their compositions and their illustrations into a scrapbook of class narratives.

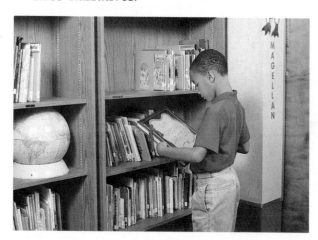

4. Then, they placed the scrapbook in the classroom library so that class members can read each other's personal narratives.

## Discuss

1. Why is it a good idea to read from a written personal narrative instead of telling the story without notes?
2. Look back at the parts of Andrew's personal narrative on pages 24 and 25. What questions would you have for Andrew?

## Try Your Hand

**Publish Your Personal Narrative**   Follow the checklist in the **Writer's Guide.** If possible, get together with your classmates and create a class scrapbook, or try one of these ideas for sharing your narrative.

◆ Record your personal narratives on audio tape. Then play the tape for another class. Give a copy of the tape to the school library.

◆ Post your personal narratives on a classroom bulletin board. Next to the narratives, place the photographs or other materials that illustrate the narratives.

WRITING PROCESS

# Listening and Speaking
## Tips for Reading a Personal Narrative Aloud

Reading a personal narrative aloud is an especially enjoyable way to share your writing. When you read your personal narrative aloud, try these suggestions to make your performance come alive.

1. Practice reading your personal narrative to yourself ahead of time so that you are comfortable with it.
2. Whether you are reading aloud or simply telling a personal narrative, speak clearly and loudly enough so that your listeners can hear you.
3. Use a lively tone of voice. Also, change your tone of voice to show different emotions, such as surprise or fear.
4. Look at your audience. If you follow tip number 1, you will be able to glance up at your audience while you are reading. This helps your audience to feel that you are talking directly to them.

# Writing in the Content Areas

**Writer's Guide**

When you write, remember the stages of the Writing Process.
- Prewriting
- Drafting
- Responding and Revising
- Proofreading
- Publishing

Use what you learned to write about something that has happened to you. You could write a journal entry or a narrative paragraph. One way to publish your writing is to display it on a bulletin board titled "A Day in Our Lives." Use one of these ideas or an idea of your own.

## Fine Arts

Let "A Funny Thing Happened on the Way to School" be the title of a paragraph you write about something real or imagined that happened to you. Tell when and where the funny thing took place. Turn the paragraph into a comic strip. Use one sentence for each frame of your strip.

## Science

Find an insect, a bird, a squirrel, a hamster, or another wild or caged animal to watch for five minutes. Write about what the animal does.

## Mathematics

Conduct a poll. First, think of a question related to something that is happening in your town or school. Then, ask at least ten people to answer your question. Make a graph that shows how many times you received certain answers. Write a paragraph that explains your results.

## Social Studies

Ask your librarian to help you find a biography of someone who interests you. Find a paragraph that tells about one event in the person's life. Imagine that you are the person. Retell the event in your own words as if it were happening to you. How is your version different from the one in the biography?

# CONNECTING
## WRITING ↔ LANGUAGE

A well-written personal narrative helps the reader understand what the writer thought and felt during an experience. What do you think and feel as you read this personal narrative?

---

### My First Skydive

Have you ever jumped from an airplane flying 12,000 feet above the ground? I did it last fall. It was an experience I'll never forget. At first I wasn't nervous at all. I stood confidently in the doorway of the plane. Then my knees began to shake. How terrified I was! I stepped through the door and dropped like a stone through the air. After what seemed like a year, my instructor signaled to me to pull my rip cord. RRRIP! The earth came slowly up to meet me. I landed gently in a grassy field. Right away I wanted to go up again. Skydiving is the world's greatest sport! Don't take my word for it. Try jumping from a sky near you.

---

◆ **The Four Types of Sentences in a Personal Narrative** Notice how the writer used different kinds of sentences to draw you into the experience. The sentence *I stood confidently in the doorway of the plane* is a declarative sentence. It makes a statement. The sentence *How terrified I was!* adds feeling to the narrative. It is an exclamatory sentence. *Have you ever jumped from an airplane flying 12,000 feet above the ground?* is an interrogative sentence. It asks the reader a question. *Try jumping from a sky near you* is an imperative sentence. It tells the reader to do something.

◆ **Language Focus: Sentences** The following lessons will help you use the four types of sentences in your own writing.

# 1 Sentences

◆ FOCUS   A **sentence** is a group of words that expresses a complete thought.

These word groups are sentences.

**1.** A reporter spoke to people at the fair.
**2.** The newspaper printed an article about the fair.

Each sentence names someone or something and tells what that person or thing did.

These word groups are not sentences. They do not express complete thoughts.

**3.** a local band
**4.** worked at the ticket booth

Word group 3 does not tell *what* a local band did. Word group 4 does not tell *who* worked at the ticket booth.

Begin a written sentence with a capital letter and end it with a mark of punctuation.

**5.** M any families ate lunch at the fair .

### Link to Speaking and Writing

Use complete sentences to make your meaning clear. What other words could you add to make a sentence?

*Tom,*
*Will meet you at the food*
*booths.*

## Guided Practice

**A.** Tell whether each word group is a *sentence* or *not a sentence*.

**1.** The ticket booth opened at 11:30 A.M.
**2.** Lined up for tickets.
**3.** Rode the Ferris wheel.
**4.** The younger children enjoyed the merry-go-round.
**5.** The food booths sold many different treats.

**B. 6.–7.** Add words to those word groups in **A** that are not sentences to make sentences.

## Independent Practice

**C. Identifying Sentences**  Read each group of words. Then write *sentence* or *not a sentence*.

**8.** The clowns arrived in a tiny red car.

MODEL ▷ sentence

**9.** Everybody laughed at the clown act.

**10.** All the clowns wore red rubber noses.

**11.** Threw a pie in the air.

**12.** Watched from the sidewalk.

**13.** The newspaper reporter spoke to the clowns.

**14.** A short clown sprayed the reporter with water.

**15.** A little boy.

**16.** The clowns drove off in a tiny red car.

**D. Proofreading Sentences**  Write each group of words that is a sentence. Begin each sentence with a capital letter and end it with a period. Write *not a sentence* for each group of words that is not a sentence.

**17.** newspaper readers want to know about their community

MODEL ▷ Newspaper readers want to know about their community.

**18.** many people in town

**19.** reporters interview community leaders

**20.** the classified ads tell about available jobs

**21.** the entertainment page lists neighborhood fairs

**22.** newspapers keep people in touch with their communities

**E. 23. – 26. Revising Sentences**  Find each group of words in **C** and **D** that is not a sentence. Add words to make a sentence.

**23.** Threw a pie in the air.

MODEL ▷ The clown in the baggy pants threw a pie in the air.

## Application — Writing and Speaking

**Radio Announcement**  Imagine that you are a radio announcer. Write a radio advertisement. Describe a street fair for your listeners. Be sure your sentences express complete thoughts. Read your radio announcement to your classmates.

# 2 Four Kinds of Sentences

◆ **FOCUS** The four kinds of sentences are declarative, interrogative, imperative, and exclamatory.

Remember that every sentence expresses a complete thought.

A **declarative sentence** makes a statement. It ends with a period.

**1.** The artist used color well .

An **interrogative sentence** asks a question. It ends with a question mark.

**2.** Where did the artist live ?

An **imperative sentence** gives a command or makes a request. It ends with a period.

**3.** Look at the colors in the painting .
**4.** Please tell me the name of the painting .

An **exclamatory sentence** expresses strong feeling or surprise. It ends with an exclamation point.

**5.** What bright colors the artist used !

> **Link to Speaking and Writing**
> Your voice tells your listeners whether you are making a statement, asking a question, making a request, or expressing strong feeling. Punctuation marks tell your readers the same thing.

## Guided Practice

**A.** Identify each sentence as *declarative, interrogative, imperative,* or *exclamatory.*

1. Picasso created many paintings and sculptures.
2. What unusual works they are!
3. When was he born?
4. Look up the information in an encyclopedia.
5. He lived in France from 1904 until his death.

## Independent Practice

**B. Identifying the Four Kinds of Sentences**   Read each sentence. Then write *declarative, interrogative, imperative,* or *exclamatory.*

6. Mary Cassatt was a famous American painter.

MODEL> declarative

7. How delicate and tender her paintings are!
8. Where was she born?
9. She was born in Pittsburgh, Pennsylvania, in 1845.
10. Cassatt lived in Paris, France, for many years.
11. She often painted mothers and children.
12. Does the library have a book about Cassatt's life?
13. Ask the librarian for help.

**C. Proofreading Sentences**   Write each sentence. Begin and end each sentence correctly.

14. who is Alexander Calder

MODEL> Who is Alexander Calder?

15. he is a famous American sculptor
16. he made fascinating mobiles
17. what is a mobile
18. it is a sculpture moved by air currents
19. look at the mobile sway in the breeze
20. what a beautiful sight it is

## Application — Writing

**Note**   Think about a trip you would like to go on with your class. Maybe you would like to visit an art museum or a state park. Write a note to your teacher. Tell where you would like to go. List questions and express feelings you have about the place. Use all four kinds of sentences. Be sure to begin and end each sentence correctly.

# 3 Subjects and Predicates

◆ **FOCUS** Each sentence is made up of two parts, the subject and the predicate.

The **subject** of a sentence is the part that tells whom or what the sentence is about. The **predicate** is the part that tells what the subject is or does.

| Subject | Predicate |
|---|---|
| **1.** Students | talk about their pets. |
| **2.** The oral reports | are enjoyable for everyone. |
| **3.** Some parents | attend. |

Sometimes the subject is only one word, as in sentence 1. The subject can also be more than one word, as in sentences 2 and 3.

Sometimes the predicate is only one word, as in sentence 3. The predicate can also be more than one word, as in sentences 1 and 2.

## Guided Practice

**A.** Identify whether the *subject* or the *predicate* of each sentence is underlined.

  1. Kevin talked about his Siamese cat.
  2. The cat disappeared suddenly one day.
  3. His whole family searched.
  4. They looked all through the house and in the garage.
  5. One car door was mysteriously open.
  6. That smart cat was in the car.
  7. The soft backseat made a good bed for new kittens.
  8. Everybody gathered around.
  9. Nobody bothered the babies.
  10. Mrs. Rodriguez rode her bicycle to work that morning.

---

**THINK AND REMEMBER**
◆ Be sure your sentences have two parts, a subject and a predicate.

---

## Independent Practice

**B. Identifying Subjects and Predicates**   Read each sentence. Study the underlined words. Write *subject* or *predicate*.

11. <u>Kim</u> reported on poodles.

MODEL ▷ subject

12. Poodles <u>are intelligent and friendly</u>.
13. <u>These smart dogs</u> often perform in circuses.
14. Their hair <u>is curly</u>.
15. <u>Many American families</u> own poodles.
16. Poodles <u>make good pets</u> for older people.

**C. Distinguishing Between Subjects and Predicates**   Write each sentence. Underline the subject once. Underline the predicate twice.

17. Roberto shared information about gerbils.

MODEL ▷ <u>Roberto</u> <u>shared information about gerbils</u>.

18. Gerbils are popular pets in the United States.
19. The class gerbil eats fruits, seeds, and vegetables.
20. A group of students presented a report on fish.
21. The most common tropical fish is the guppy.
22. A clean tank keeps fish healthy.

**D. Completing Sentences**   Add a subject or a predicate to each group of words. Write the new sentence.

23. Parakeets _____ .

MODEL ▷ Parakeets make excellent pets.

24. _____ enjoy parakeets.
25. _____ talked about his pet hamster.
26. Hamsters _____ .
27. _____ took a vote on whose pet they liked best.
28. The winner _____ .
29. _____ took photographs of the pets.
30. _____ thanked the parents for their help.

## Application — Writing

**News Item**   Imagine that the cat in the picture is yours. You want to write a news item for your class newsletter. Write sentences that tell about your cat. Tell what kind of cat it is, how you got it, and what name you plan to give it. Be sure your sentences express complete thoughts.

# 4 Complete and Simple Subjects

**FOCUS**
◆ The **complete subject** is all the words that make up the subject of a sentence.
◆ The **simple subject** is the main word or words in the complete subject.

Remember that every sentence has a subject. All the words in the subject are called the complete subject. The simple subject is the main word or words in the complete subject.

In each of the following sentences, the words in color are the complete subject. The underlined word is the simple subject.

1. The two girls communicate by telephone.

2. A telephone call to a distant place is easy to make.

Sometimes the simple subject is exactly the same as the complete subject.

3. Susan calls Karla often.

The simple subject may be several words that name a person or place.

4. Karla Brown lives across town from Susan.

## Guided Practice

**A.** The complete subject is underlined in each sentence. Identify the simple subject.

1. Alexander Graham Bell invented the telephone.
2. Bell perfected his invention in 1876.
3. Our country has many telephones.
4. Many American businesses depend on the telephone.
5. Push-button telephones are handy.
6. A cordless telephone is convenient too.
7. Long-distance operators help callers.
8. Many people have answering machines.
9. These machines take messages automatically.
10. Telephones are important tools of communication.

## Independent Practice

**B. Identifying Simple Subjects**   The complete subject is underlined in each sentence. Write the simple subject.

11. The telephone is helpful in an emergency.

MODEL ▷ telephone

12. My family has the emergency numbers by the phone.
13. One number is for the police department.
14. Another emergency number is for the fire department.
15. A neighbor of ours called the police about a burglary.

**C. Identifying Complete and Simple Subjects**   Write each sentence. Draw a line after the complete subject. Then underline the simple subject.

16. The telephone helps keep families in touch.

MODEL ▷ The telephone|helps keep families in touch.

17. We call our cousins in Iowa once a month.
18. My dad phones his aunt in Denmark on special holidays.
19. A long chat on the telephone is better than a letter.

**D. Completing Sentences**   Add a complete subject to each group of words. Write the new sentence. Underline the simple subject.

20. _____ performed a play about a telephone.

MODEL ▷ The students in our class performed a play about a telephone.

21. _____ could dial itself, think, and talk.
22. _____ were amazed by the fantastic phone.
23. _____ arrested the phone for not paying its bill!
24. _____ was funny and extremely unusual.

## Application — Writing

**Telephone Message**   Imagine that you are taking a telephone message for your sister, Karla, from her best friend, Susan. Write the message in sentences. Underline each simple subject.

# 5 Complete and Simple Predicates

**FOCUS**
◆ The **complete predicate** is all the words that make up the predicate of a sentence.
◆ The **simple predicate** is the key word or words in the complete predicate.

Remember that every sentence has a predicate. All the words in the predicate are called the complete predicate. The simple predicate is the main word or words in the complete predicate.

In each of the sentences below, the words in color are the complete predicate. The underlined word is the simple predicate, or verb.

1. Gymnastics team tryouts begin today .

2. The coach talks to the students about gymnastics .

3. Jamie listens to his advice and suggestions .

4. Good communication is important on any team .

The simple predicate can be one word or more than one word.

5. Coach Rivers coached Jamie last year .

6. He has coached many students over the years .

7. He will be coaching the team next year, too .

## Guided Practice

**A.** The complete predicate is underlined in each sentence. Identify the simple predicate.

1. Each gymnast had become a little nervous.
2. Coach Rivers gave the team a pep talk.
3. Emily was first in line.
4. Mr. Rivers watched carefully.
5. Emily slipped.
6. Her performance was still excellent.
7. The other gymnasts praised her performance.
8. The team received the highest score.

## Independent Practice

**B. Identifying Simple Predicates**   The complete predicate is underlined in each sentence. Write the simple predicate.

   9. A gymnast <u>develops balance and strength.</u>

MODEL ▷ develops

  10. A good gymnast <u>practices often.</u>
  11. American gymnasts <u>do well at the Olympics.</u>
  12. I <u>will practice my gymnastics routine every day.</u>
  13. I <u>have been training with my coach for two years.</u>
  14. She <u>gives helpful tips and encouragement.</u>

**C. Identifying Complete and Simple Predicates**   Write each sentence. Draw a line between the complete subject and the complete predicate. Underline the simple predicate.

  15. Gymnastics has been a popular sport for some time.

MODEL ▷ Gymnastics|<u>has been</u> a popular sport for some time.

  16. It is also a very demanding sport.
  17. Gymnastics contests can be very exciting.
  18. A perfect score for a gymnastics event is 10.00.
  19. Judges watch the performance of each gymnast closely.

**D. Completing Sentences**   Add a simple predicate to each group of words. Write the complete sentence.

  20. The gymnastics team _____ hard all year long.

MODEL ▷ The gymnastics team worked hard all year long.

  21. The team _____ in a state meet.
  22. The coach _____ to the team before the meet.
  23. The meet _____ at two o'clock.

## Application — Writing

**Sports Report**   Imagine that you are doing a sports report for your school newspaper about the gymnastics team. Write sentences telling about the activities of the athletes. Underline the simple predicate in each sentence.

# 6 Subject in Imperative Sentences

◆ **FOCUS** In an imperative sentence, *you* (understood) is always the subject.

Remember that the complete subject is all the words that make up the subject of a sentence. The simple subject is the main word or words in the complete subject.

In each of the following sentences, the word in color is the simple subject.

1. Tom started a club.
2. The members are writers.
3. They share their stories and poems.

In an imperative sentence, *you* is always the subject. It is not stated. Instead, *you* is "understood."

4. *You* (understood) Fill out this club application.
5. *You* (understood) Give it back as soon as possible.

## Guided Practice

**A.** Identify the simple subject of each sentence.

1. Lyle is the president of the writing club.
2. Say hello to him before the meeting.
3. The members read their writing aloud each week.
4. Read your poem about the butterfly.
5. The story about the black cat was very funny.
6. Ask the writer questions about her story.
7. Write down your ideas during the meeting.
8. Finish your poem about the night sky.
9. We can meet at my house next week.
10. Get permission from your parents first.

---

**THINK AND REMEMBER**

◆ Remember that in an imperative sentence, *you* (understood) is always the subject.

---

# Independent Practice

**B. Identifying the Subjects of Sentences** Write the simple subject of each sentence.

11. Call the meeting to order.

    MODEL ▷ *You* (understood)

12. The club needs a new sign.
13. Choose someone to design the sign.
14. Andrea is the best artist in the club.
15. Lend her your pencil, please.
16. Make sure you give it back.
17. The sign should be red and yellow.
18. Ask your mother for a paintbrush.
19. Each member must chip in fifty cents.
20. Let Denise hold all the money.
21. I will buy paint on sale.
22. Hang the finished sign on the door.

**C. Identifying Simple Subjects in Imperative and Declarative Sentences** Read each sentence. Write whether it is *declarative* or *imperative*. Then write the simple subject.

23. Pay attention to the club president.

    MODEL ▷ imperative; *You* (understood)

24. We will put our stories and poems in a book.
25. Choose your favorite piece of writing.
26. Give your stories and poems to Maureen.
27. Maureen will type each one.
28. Help her type them.
29. Add an illustration to your story or poem.
30. Be sure your illustration fits on a page in the book.
31. We will make copies of the book for each member.
32. Each person can have two copies.
33. The club officers will give a copy to the library.
34. Hand in your stories and poems by next Wednesday.
35. Ask Maureen or Lyle, if you have any questions.

## Application — Writing and Speaking

**Announcement** Imagine that you are a member of the writing club. You want other members to join the club. Write an announcement that could be read over the loudspeaker at school. Give information about the club. Use imperative sentences. Then read the announcement to your class.

# 7 Compound Subjects

◆ **FOCUS** A **compound subject** is two or more subjects that have the same predicate.

The simple subject is the main word or words in the complete subject of a sentence. The word in color in each of the following sentences is the simple subject.

1. Jen walked to the post office yesterday.
2. I walked to the post office yesterday.

Some sentences have more than one main word in the complete subject. Two or more subjects that have the same predicate are called a compound subject. The words in color in the following sentences are compound subjects.

3. Jen and I walked to the post office yesterday.
4. Hal or Marjorie will mail the letter for you.

The simple subjects in a compound subject are joined by *and* or *or*. Commas are also used to separate three or more simple subjects in a compound subject.

5. Letters , packages , and postcards arrive in a short time.

## Guided Practice

**A.** Identify the compound subject in each sentence.

1. Letters and newspapers come in the mail.
2. Mrs. Jensen, Mr. Hart, and Mr. Petry deliver our mail.
3. Rain or hot weather never stops them.
4. A raincoat or a poncho is the rainy-day uniform.
5. Shorts and safari hats keep mail carriers cool on hot days.
6. A thermos of juice or a glass of water helps, too.

---

**THINK AND REMEMBER**

◆ Remember that a **compound subject** is two or more simple subjects that have the same predicate.
◆ Join the two or more simple subjects in a compound subject with *and* or *or*.

---

# Independent Practice

**B. Identifying Compound Subjects**   Read each sentence. Write the compound subject and the joining word.

7. Jen and I write every week.

MODEL > Jen and I

8. Calls and visits are too expensive.
9. Jen and Billy moved away last fall.
10. Jeff, Anne, and I miss them both.
11. Jeff and Anne like to hear from our two old friends.
12. Postcards or letters arrive from them every Thursday.

**C. Proofreading Sentences with Compound Subjects**   Rewrite the following sentences. Add commas where they are needed.

13. The street the city and the ZIP code are parts of an address.

MODEL > The street, the city, and the ZIP code are parts of an address.

14. The stamp the address and the postmark appear on the outside of the envelope.
15. Boxes envelopes and stamps are available for sale.
16. Mr. Lee Ms. Abley or Mr. Conklin will sell you what you need for mailing.
17. Letters postcards and packages to foreign countries should be mailed early for the holidays.

**D. Completing Sentences**   Complete these sentences with compound subjects. Write the sentences.

18. _____ and _____ are the days I write letters.

MODEL > Monday and Friday are the days I write letters.

19. _____ and _____ help me check my spelling.
20. _____, _____, and _____ fill my writing drawer.
21. _____ and _____ often write letters to each other.
22. _____, _____, and _____ are among my favorite writing topics.
23. _____ and _____ arrive in my mailbox.

## Application — Writing

**Thank-You Note**   Imagine that your grandparents gave you a set of colored pens and writing paper for your birthday. Write a note thanking them for the gifts. Tell them how you will use them. Use compound subjects. If you need help writing a thank-you note, see page 46 of the **Writer's Handbook** at the back of this book.

# 8 Compound Predicates

> The library lends books and holds book sales.

◆ **FOCUS** A **compound predicate** is two or more predicates that have the same subject.

Remember that the simple predicate is the key word in the complete predicate of a sentence. It is the verb. The word in color in each of the following sentences is the simple predicate, or verb.

1. The library subscribes to many newspapers.
2. The library has a reading room.

Some sentences have more than one main word in the complete predicate. Two or more simple predicates that have the same subject are called a compound predicate. The words in color in the following sentence are a compound predicate.

3. I borrow books and listen to tapes.

The simple predicates in a compound predicate are often joined by *and* or *or.* Commas are also used to separate three or more simple predicates in a compound predicate.

4. Children read or listen to the storyteller.
5. People sit, read, and take notes in the library.

## Guided Practice

**A.** Identify the two simple predicates that make up the compound predicate in each sentence.

1. Good stories thrill and excite me.
2. I wrote and illustrated this one.
3. I finished and mailed it on the same day.
4. The magazine editors read and liked my story.
5. They praised my work and asked me for more.
6. My friends surprised and delighted me with a party.

---

**THINK AND REMEMBER**
- Remember that a **compound predicate** is two or more predicates that have the same subject.
- Join the two or more simple predicates in a compound predicate with *and* or *or.*

---

# Independent Practice

**B. Identifying Compound Predicates**  Read each sentence. Write the compound predicate and the joining word.

7. Editors select and buy books from writers.

> MODEL  select and buy

8. Artists design and plan books.
9. The printer prints and ships the books.
10. Bookstore workers unpack and display new books every day.
11. Customers browse, choose, and buy.
12. Sometimes a customer selects and orders a book from a catalogue.
13. The clerk smiles and wraps the book.

**C. Proofreading Sentences with Compound Predicates**  Rewrite these sentences. Add commas where they are needed.

14. I wrote illustrated and published a book.

> MODEL  I wrote, illustrated, and published a book.

15. First I researched brainstormed and organized my thoughts.
16. The characters in my story laugh dance and sing.
17. In each chapter the sun rises blazes and sets.
18. Clouds develop form and disappear.
19. My parents read enjoyed and praised my story to their friends.

**D. Completing Sentences**  Complete these sentences with compound predicates. Write the sentences.

20. A famous writer _____ and _____ her story.

> MODEL  A famous writer read and discussed her story.

21. Later she _____ and _____ at our school.
22. The principal and the teachers _____ and _____ .
23. Her books _____ and _____ .
24. In her spare time, the writer _____ , _____ , and _____ .
25. For her next project she _____ or _____ .

## Application — Writing

**Book Summary**  Pretend that you are writing part of a book review column for your school newspaper. Think of a favorite book or a book you read recently. Use sentences with compound predicates to tell what happens in one part of the book.

# 9 Compound Sentences

◆**FOCUS**  A **compound sentence** is two or more simple sentences joined by *and, or,* or *but.*

A simple sentence expresses only one complete thought. It has one complete subject and one complete predicate.

   **1.** The reporters arrived early.
   **2.** The athletes were ready for their interviews.

A compound sentence is two or more simple sentences joined by *and, or,* or *but.* Notice that a comma comes before *and, or,* or *but.*

   **3.** The reporters arrived early , and
      the athletes were ready for the interviews .

   **4.** The reporter may interview the skier , or
      he may talk to a skater .

   **5.** The skier was nervous , but
      the interview went well .

## Guided Practice

**A.** Identify each sentence as a *simple sentence* or a *compound sentence.*

   **1.** The racer waxes and sharpens his skis.
   **2.** He reaches the mountaintop, but it isn't his turn yet.
   **3.** He waits in line, and his stomach is in knots.
   **4.** The snow on the course is fresh and powdery.
   **5.** The skier stares into space, or he gazes at the course.
   **6.** His name is announced, and he stands at the starting line.
   **7.** The bell rings, and he takes off down the mountain.
   **8.** The crowd cheers and rings bells, but the skier hardly hears the noise.

---

**THINK AND REMEMBER**
◆ Join two simple sentences with *and, or,* or *but* to form a compound sentence.
◆ Place a comma before the joining word.

---

# Independent Practice

**B. Identifying Compound Sentences**   If the sentence is a compound sentence, write it, and draw a line under each simple sentence. If the sentence is not a compound sentence, write *simple sentence.*

9. We were late for the race, but it hadn't started yet.

MODEL  We were late for the race, but it hadn't started yet.

10. We took a bus to the mountain and climbed to the top.
11. It was crowded, but we found a good observation point.
12. Observers can stand at the top, or they can watch from the bottom.
13. You can shout, or you can ring a bell.
14. James is my favorite skier, but he didn't win a medal.
15. Someday I'll enter the Olympics and win a medal.
16. Peterson received a medal, and his eyes shone.
17. His family was waiting, but he gave an interview.
18. The television interview aired on Friday, and the radio interview was broadcast on Sunday.

**C. Proofreading Compound Sentences**   If the sentence is a compound sentence, write it. Add a comma where it is needed. If the sentence is not a compound sentence, write *simple sentence.*

19. My sister is a sports reporter and her articles have appeared in many sports magazines.

MODEL  My sister is a sports reporter, and her articles have appeared in many sports magazines.

20. She covers baseball games and reports on boxing.
21. Her favorite sport is ice hockey but she has never written an article about it.
22. Her next assignment might be a tennis match in Great Britain or it could be a skating contest in Canada.
23. Her typewriter is broken down but her computer is in good condition.
24. My parents miss her but she sends long letters home.

## Application — Writing and Speaking

**News Bulletin**   Imagine that you won a race or a contest. Write some sentences for a radio report. Describe what you did. Use compound sentences to tell about your thoughts, feelings, and actions. Deliver your bulletin to the class.

# 10 Avoiding Sentence Fragments and Run-on Sentences

◆ **FOCUS**   Two common sentence errors are sentence fragments and run-on sentences.

A **sentence fragment** is a group of words that does not have a subject and a predicate. A fragment does not express a complete thought.

1. draws pictures and sings songs   **no subject**
2. my sister's nursery school teacher   **no predicate**

You can make a sentence fragment into a sentence by adding a subject or a predicate.

3. My baby brother draws pictures and sings songs.
4. My sister's nursery school teacher lives next door to you.

A **run-on sentence** is two or more sentences not separated by correct punctuation or by connecting words.

5. My sister talks very well she learns words quickly.

You can correct a run-on sentence by making two simple sentences. You can also correct a run-on sentence by adding a comma and *and, or,* or *but.*

6. My sister talks very well. She learns words quickly.
7. My sister talks very well, and she learns words quickly.

## Guided Practice

**A.** Identify each group of words as a *simple sentence,* a *sentence fragment,* or a *run-on sentence.*

1. Jane chooses a book I read it to her.
2. Jane likes the book *Fox in Socks.*
3. Also likes fairy tales.
4. Many young children.
5. I write stories just for Jane she draws the pictures.
6. Jane sits quietly I watch her concentrate.

## Independent Practice

**B. Identifying Simple Sentences, Sentence Fragments, and Run-on Sentences**   Read each group of words. Write *simple sentence, sentence fragment,* or *run-on sentence.*

7. Scientists study animal language.

MODEL ▷ simple sentence

8. Dolphins send out sounds to communicate.
9. Whales make a kind of music a number of scientists have studied these strange songs for years.
10. Bees communicate through a kind of dance.
11. Shows the location of flowers.
12. A worker bee.
13. Chimpanzees communicate with grunts and screams they also use expressions, gestures, and body postures.

**C. Correcting Sentence Fragments and Run-on Sentences**   Make each sentence fragment a sentence by adding a subject or predicate. Correct each run-on sentence by writing two simple sentences or a compound sentence.

14. Koko the gorilla.

MODEL ▷ Koko the gorilla learned sign language.

15. Has a book about Koko.
16. Koko had a kitten it had no tail.
17. Koko and her kitten.
18. Many scientists studied Koko they watched her.
19. Has changed our understanding of language.
20. Some people speak two languages I don't.
21. Borrowed a Spanish cassette from Amy.
22. I listened to the cassette I didn't understand it.
23. Raúl explained the words I felt more confident.

## Application – Writing and Speaking

**Children's Story Beginning**   Write the opening sentences of a short, funny story for a young child. Avoid sentence fragments and run-on sentences. Read your story to a young child. If you need help writing a story beginning, see the **Writer's Handbook.**

# Building Vocabulary
## Context Clues

**Mother:** *Our little boy is saying his first sentence.*

**Junior:** *Grandma, I'm ecstatic that you're coming for a visit, and Mom and Dad are very happy too.*

When you discover a new word in your reading, how can you find out what it means? You can look up the word in a dictionary, of course. You can also try to figure out the meaning by looking at the *context*—the words that come before or after the unfamiliar word. Take this sentence, for example.

I'm ecstatic that you're coming for a visit, and Mom and Dad are very happy too.

If you don't know the word *ecstatic*, you can use context clues to help you guess its meaning. The words *very happy too* tell you the parents have the same feelings as the speaker, so the word *ecstatic* must mean "very happy."

Sometimes you will need to look ahead to the next sentence or back to the previous one. Try to figure out what *persistent* means in the first sentence below by reading the second sentence.

The persistent child wanted to talk to his grandmother.
He continued asking his parents if he could call her.

If you looked up *persistent* in the dictionary, it would probably not surprise you to learn that it means "continuing firmly despite opposition." The context clue *continued* helps make the meaning clear.

Be a good "word detective" as you read. Use context clues to help you figure out the meanings of unfamiliar words.

# Reading Practice

Read each numbered item. Use the context clues to figure out the correct meaning of the underlined word. Write the underlined word and its meaning.

1. A <u>linguist</u> is interested in how people learn to speak a language.
   **a.** person who studies language
   **b.** person who studies fish
2. Young children <u>comprehend</u> much of what is said in their presence. Even before they talk, they can make sense of what they hear.
   **a.** repeat          **b.** understand
3. For parents, a child's first word is a <u>noteworthy</u> event that they will always remember.
   **a.** everyday      **b.** important
4. As time passes, a child learns more words and develops an <u>extensive</u> vocabulary.
   **a.** large          **b.** small

# Writing Practice

Look up the meaning of each underlined word in a dictionary. Then rewrite each sentence, adding context clues to make the meaning clear.

5. The parents listened to their <u>toddler</u>.
6. He spoke <u>fluently</u> on the telephone.
7. They were <u>astounded</u> by his vocabulary.
8. The parents <u>lavished</u> praise on him.
9. The little boy <u>chortled</u> with pleasure.

# Project

Find and write down five unfamiliar words and their definitions. Write each word in a sentence, supplying context clues so a reader could guess the meaning. Then organize a "Context Clues Quiz." Divide into teams and take turns reading your sentences aloud. The team that guesses the most correct meanings wins.

# Language Enrichment
## Sentences

Use what you know about sentences to do these activities.

 **Cafeteria Commercial**

Get a copy of your school cafeteria's lunch menu for next week, and choose a meal. Then write a commercial that might be read to every classroom on the morning when that particular lunch will be served. Use the four kinds of sentences to describe the lunch and make people want to eat it. Read your commercial to the class.

 **Subject Scramble**

Enclose a dozen or more small objects in a shoe box. Cut a hole in the side of the box so that you cannot see what you are grabbing when you put in your hand. Then play "Subject Scramble" with a classmate. To begin, the first player reaches into the box and pulls out three things. The player must then create a sentence that uses the three things as a compound subject. Here's an example: *An eraser, a pencil sharpener, and a paper clip sit on a desk.* Then the player should put the three objects back into the box for the next player's turn. Players get one point for every reasonable sentence.

 **Lend an Ear**

Listen to a television show or radio show. As you listen, jot down one of each kind of sentence that you hear: declarative, interrogative, imperative, and exclamatory. Then share your sentences with your class. Tell how you knew what kind of sentence each was by just listening.

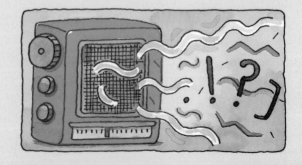

In this unit you learned how sentences are used to express ideas. Every sentence has a subject and a predicate. The subject of a sentence tells whom or what the sentence is about. The predicate tells what the subject is or does.

◆ **Using Sentences in Your Writing**  Knowing how to write sentences is one of the most important writing skills. Writing clear, correct sentences lets you share your ideas and helps your reader understand what you are saying. Pay special attention to sentences as you do these activities.

### What's the Good Word?

You learned how to use context clues to guess the meanings of unfamiliar words on the **Building Vocabulary** pages. Use what you learned to try this activity.

Read a newspaper story. Find three words you do not know. Use the context in which the words are used to make a good guess about their meanings. Then look up the words in a dictionary to see whether you are correct. Write a sentence using each new word.

### Sentence Poem

Write a rhymed or an unrhymed poem using the four kinds of sentences. First, decide what the topic of your poem will be. For example, it might be pets. Make each of the four lines of the poem a different kind of sentence: declarative, imperative, interrogative, or exclamatory. Here's an example:

> Please don't start to laugh.
> Here is my pet giraffe.
> Why would I laugh at you?
> How I love my pet gnu!

# **Unit Checkup**

**1**

| Think Back | Think Ahead |
|---|---|
| ◆ What did you learn about personal narratives in this unit? What did you do to write one? | ◆ How will what you learned help you when you read other narrative forms of writing?<br><br>◆ How will knowing the causes and effects of events help you write personal narratives? |
| ◆ What did you learn about complete sentences? How has that helped you in writing? | ◆ What is one way you can use different kinds of sentences to improve your writing? |

**Personal Narratives**   *pages 16–17*
Read the personal narrative. Then follow the directions.

> Last summer I received the best gift ever. My family had just moved to Tucson, Arizona. They bought me a camera, and they suggested I begin a photo album. At first I wasn't very excited about the idea. Then one day, we drove to the Saguaro National Monument. There were giant cacti as high as 50 feet! I was glad I had my camera because I saw lots of unusual plants. Now, I have some great photos of my new home state.

**1.** Write the main event.          **2.** List any time-order words used.
**3.** Write the words in the paragraph that reveal the writer's feelings.

**Connecting Cause and Effect**   *page 18*
Read these statements. Write *cause* if the statement tells the cause
of something that happened. Write *effect* if the statement tells the effect.

**4.** My mother got a job teaching journalism in San Antonio.
     We will move to San Antonio next month.
**5.** We decided not to go shopping.
     The gentle snowfall turned into a blizzard.
**6.** Angelita tripped over a crack in the sidewalk.
     She wished a warning sign had been placed there.

## Using Details to Explain   *page 19*

Read the following sentences. Write the sentences in the order that shows their cause-and-effect chain reaction.

7. Patrick, Henry, and Timothy planned a special birthday present for their grandparents.

8. The puppet show was a big success, and the boys were pleased.

9. They knew their grandparents enjoyed going to the theater.

10. They wanted the show to be perfect, so they rehearsed several times.

11. So the three boys put together a puppet show.

## The Writing Process   *pages 20−30*

12. Suppose you are selecting a topic for a personal narrative. Which of the following topics would be best to write about?
    a. your mother's job          b. imaginary animals
    c. recent events in your own life

13. After the writer gathers information, what is the next step?
    a. revising what was written          b. publishing the narrative
    c. putting the information in correct time order

14. Why are cause-and-effect words helpful in a personal narrative?
    a. A reader uses them to connect ideas.  b. The words are easy to spell.
    c. The words are interesting.

## Sentences √ *pages 34−35*

Read each group of words. Then write *sentence* or *not a sentence*.

15. Pepe likes to draw comic strips.

16. His favorite color.

17. Told Pepe to make a book of comic strips.

18. They laughed when they saw the talking cactus.

19. One of Pepe's comic strips won an art contest.

## Four Kinds of Sentences √ *pages 36−37*

Read each sentence. Then write *declarative, interrogative, imperative,* or *exclamatory*.

20. The news announcer warned them about the hurricane.

21. They were so scared when they heard the news!

22. Where could they go to escape the storm?

23. Go to the nearest emergency shelter.

24. They were glad to reach the shelter safely.

## Subjects and Predicates √ *pages 38–39*

Add a subject or a predicate to each group of words. Write the sentence.

25. Speedy's Delivery Service _____ .
26. _____ is owned by six young people.
27. _____ deliver packages all over the city.
28. Their many customers _____ .
29. The six young owners _____ .

## Complete and Simple Subjects √ *pages 40–41*

Add a complete subject to each group of words. Write the new sentence. Then underline the simple subject.

30. _____ works well enough when I use it.
31. _____ asked his father to fix his radio.
32. _____ is heard every hour on the radio.
33. _____ called a talk show being broadcast.
34. _____ listened to the talk show.

## Complete and Simple Predicates √ *pages 42–43*

Add a simple predicate to each group of words. Write the sentence.

35. The mail carrier _____ the magazine in the mailbox.
36. Shirley _____ the magazines with animal stories in them.
37. She _____ some of her magazines with her friends.
38. Shirley _____ some of the stories to her younger sister.
39. She _____ she is one of the characters in the story.

## Subjects in Imperative Sentences √ *pages 44–45*

Read each sentence. Write whether it is *declarative* or *imperative*. Then write the simple subject.

40. Hundreds of languages are spoken in the world.
41. Speak to me in the language of your family.
42. Please speak more slowly.
43. My family speaks Spanish and English.
44. Teach me to speak and read French.

## Compound Subjects √ *pages 46–47*

Rewrite the following sentences. Add commas if they are needed.

45. Dan Maria and Carlos read about the Southwest.
46. Texas Arizona and Oklahoma are part of the Southwest.
47. Deserts cities and ranches take up much of the land.
48. Cattle and wheat are raised by farmers there.
49. The sunshine scenery and mild climate attract tourists.

## Compound Predicates ✓ *pages 48–49*

Read each sentence. Write the compound predicate and the joining word.

**50.** Terry read the library book and returned it.
**51.** She wrote and reviewed her notes for homework.
**52.** Then she finished her homework and took it to class.
**53.** The teacher asked for her homework and graded it.
**54.** Terry read a story aloud and answered questions.

## Compound Sentences ✓ *pages 50–51*

If the sentence is a compound sentence, write it. Then draw a line under each simple sentence. If the sentence is not a compound sentence, write *simple sentence.*

**55.** We enjoyed the songs but didn't understand them.
**56.** A man played a guitar and sang about Mexico.
**57.** He asked us to sing along, and we sang the chorus.
**58.** The song was in Spanish and English.
**59.** We could sing aloud in Spanish, or we could just clap.

## Avoiding Sentence Fragments and Run-on Sentences ✓ *pages 52–53*

Make each sentence fragment a sentence by adding a subject or predicate. Make each run-on sentence a sentence by writing two simple sentences or a compound sentence.

**60.** Harriett's nickname.
**61.** Everyone calls her Hair she has gotten tired of that name.
**62.** Her thick, curly hair.
**63.** Harriett believes there might be a better nickname for her she has thought of several she would really prefer.
**64.** Are the names she wants her friends to use.

## Context Clues *pages 54–55*

Read each numbered item. Use the context clues to figure out the correct meaning of the underlined word.

**65.** We were not prepared for the abrupt ending of Pedro's story.
   **a.** sudden         **b.** satisfying
**66.** The weather announcer's warning of a torrent proved correct when everyone's homes were flooded.
   **a.** rush of rain     **b.** lack of rain
**67.** George was bashful, so he had trouble meeting new people.
   **a.** friendly         **b.** shy

# UNIT

## 2

# Explaining Facts

◆ COMPOSITION FOCUS: **Expository Paragraph**
◆ LANGUAGE FOCUS: **Nouns**

Suppose you are talking with a classmate about her visit to a local theater to watch rehearsals for a play. What questions might you ask your classmate? You might ask her to provide more information or to explain her comments about the theater more fully.

The writer of a selection is not usually there to answer your questions. The writer of an expository—or informative— paragraph must give readers all the information they will need to understand and appreciate the writing.

Author Kathryn Lasky and photographer Christopher G. Knight sometimes work together to inform their readers about unusual and interesting occupations and skills. In their work, they make sure their readers have all the information they will need.

In this unit you will learn how to write an expository paragraph. You will also learn how to inform readers better by connecting main ideas and details.

Kathryn Lasky and Christopher G. Knight work together *to inform* their readers. They have created several award-winning books.

# Reading with a Writer's Eye
## Information Article

Paul Vincent Davis is a performer and puppet maker whose art is the subject of Kathryn Lasky and Christopher G. Knight's book *Puppeteer.* As you read this selection from the book, notice that Kathryn Lasky gives information about how Paul creates his plot, characters, and scenery.

## Searching for Aladdin
### by Kathryn Lasky

The plot, adapted from the *Thousand and One Nights,* is simple enough: In Bagdad, a boy lives with his widowed mother. They are very poor. He meets a man who claims to be his uncle. But the man is really an evil magician who wants a magic lamp hidden deep in an underground cave. The magician gets the boy to retrieve the lamp through magic tricks and deceit. When the magician admits his true identity, the boy suddenly refuses to hand over the magic lamp, and the magician seals him in the cave. The boy soon discovers the djinn (or genie) of the lamp, escapes, becomes rich, marries the Sultan's daughter, loses her to the magician, gets her back, and lives happily ever after.

That is the plot, but it is not the whole story. It does not convey the bustle in the streets, the magnificence of the palaces, and the nature of the nine principal characters: Aladdin, his Mother, the Dwarf/Magician, the Sultan, the Princess, the Princess's Servant, a Royal Herald, a Rug Merchant, and the Djinn. In early summer, Paul begins by reading many versions of the tale. In one, Aladdin is described as a vicious, nasty boy, in another as a lazy, thoughtless one. But Paul is not satisfied with the notion of a good-for-nothing kid winding up with buckets of gold.

One of Paul's earliest decisions about the play is to make the boy poor, hard working, but unable to find a job. As Paul thinks about the characters he starts to sketch them. He draws several versions of all the puppets, especially Aladdin and the Sultan.

He is not altogether pleased with the rounded, bulbous nose of the Sultan and the cartoon look of some of the characters. He begins to move toward a line with a harder edge. Around him on his worktable are many books on Persian and Oriental art. He opens one and studies a miniature painting with jewellike colors. It shows men, their faces the shape of long O's, with neatly trimmed beards and curved mustaches. Their eyes are the shape of plump fish—tilted fish swimming at steep angles. There is a flatness to their faces. Everything exists within the same plane without shadows, hollows, or dimples. He begins to revise his sketches and moves toward these simpler forms for faces.

"It is not just like looking at a jewel, but being inside the jewel." Paul is looking at another book now, one on Islamic architecture. He has come across a dazzling series of photographs of mosque (mäsk) domes. Some are sheathed in gold leaf and are inlaid with jewels and precious stones. He soon realizes that for this show he will need a case of gold paint, and he might actually use up the entire contents of his glitz box with all its fake jewels and sequins and gold braid. After all, there are two palaces to build, and a jeweled orchard.

For a month Paul has been going through books on Persian and Oriental art and architecture studying paintings of people, plants, animals, clothing. The paintings have a unique perspective, an intriguing flatness, that has given Paul an idea. His production of *Aladdin and His Wonderful Lamp* will have a large cast of nonspeaking characters that, as hand puppets, would be impossible to move around the stage. Inspired by the work of medieval Persian artists,

Paul decides to make them flat, actually cut out from plywood and painted. Major puppets such as Aladdin and his Mother will, of course, be full-bodied, regular hand puppets. But the forty slaves, the elephants, the camels that must march across the stage in the dazzling procession will be "flats" cut out with an electric jigsaw. Immediately, Paul closes up the book and dashes out to his favorite hardware store to buy a jigsaw. That night he experiments with the saw, cutting all sorts of shapes.

The flatness becomes for Paul a key mechanical element in the design of the show. The city streets will be on flat pieces that can be lifted away to show a barren desert. The Sultan's palace will appear flat, but its two central doors will swing open to reveal a jeweled interior. Landscapes, cityscapes, and buildings will be illustrated on flat surfaces that will be able to lift, open, or slide—three basic movements to reveal other spaces and interiors. A stage plan has started to form in Paul's mind, and he has a clever idea. When the rock to the cave entrance must magically flip or slide away, Paul is considering using a puff of smoke. It is a handy device that he has used before to mask a trick.

By midsummer Paul knows how the scenery will change, which puppets will be flats, and which will be full-bodied. He knows

what alterations he must make to his puppet stage, and he has written thirteen pages of a script on his word processor. It is a beginning, he tells a friend, but there are still too many puffs of smoke.

By the end of the summer there has been progress. Paul has figured out how, at the Magician's bidding, the rock to the cave will open on a special pivoting hinge. He knows more about Aladdin's character. "He's a nice kid but not too nice—no Goody Two-Shoes. A little bit pushy, but full of humor."

And he has a completed script. There are twenty-eight pages of dialogue and a special role for him as al-Hariri. Al-Hariri was an actual historical figure, one of Arabia's foremost storytellers. As al-Hariri he will tell the tale of Aladdin and occasionally make appearances in front of the puppet stage in a turban and flowing gown. But there is something missing from this script. Paul has written words for the nine major characters, but he has yet to find voices for each of them. They must all sound very different in spite of the fact that all nine voices come from one throat—Paul's.

## Respond

1. What do you like best about "Searching for Aladdin"? Does any of the information surprise you?

## Discuss

2. What is the first paragraph in "Searching for Aladdin" about? What is the second paragraph about? Where in the selection does the writer tell about the scenery?

3. What would you expect the next section of *Puppeteer* to be about? (Hint: Look at the last paragraph of "Searching for Aladdin.") What kinds of information and examples would you expect in the next section?

# Thinking As a Writer
## Analyzing an Expository Paragraph

An **expository paragraph** gives readers information about a topic. The expository paragraph must have a clear topic sentence supported by details and examples.

When you read this paragraph from "Searching for Aladdin," identify the topic sentence. Then notice how the writer uses details to support her main idea.

> The flatness becomes for Paul a key mechanical element in the design of the show. The city streets will be on flat pieces that can be lifted away to show a barren desert. The Sultan's palace will appear flat, but its two central doors will swing open to reveal a jeweled interior. Landscapes, cityscapes, and buildings will be illustrated on flat surfaces that will be able to lift, open, or slide—three basic movements to reveal other spaces and interiors.

The **topic sentence** tells the main point of the expository paragraph.

The **body** provides details and examples that support and illustrate the topic sentence.

## Discuss

1. Look at the topic sentence of the expository paragraph above. What is the key word in the topic sentence?
2. How does Kathryn Lasky develop and illustrate the main idea in the topic sentence?

## Try Your Hand

A. **Analyze Topic Sentences**   Read the following topic sentences from expository paragraphs about other occupations. For each topic sentence, write what you would expect the rest of the paragraph to be about.

1. The computer terminal in the car gives the police officer access to important information.

2. Andre follows the same routine every day when he practices his guitar.

**3.** Each of the cues Ana receives during her newscast means something different.

**4.** Your school principal must pay attention to the needs of four different groups of people.

**B. Identify Key Words** Key words—like *flatness* in the paragraph on page 70—help the reader focus on the main idea of the paragraph. Write the *key words* in the previous topic sentences. As a writer, you can use key words to help focus your topic sentence.

**C. Identify Detail Sentences** Each of these details might follow a different topic sentence from **A.** Write each topic sentence from **A.** Then write the detail sentence from **C** that best follows it.

**a)** After playing scales for half an hour, he practices his own compositions for upcoming concerts.

**b)** By entering a license number into the computer, the officer can find out if the car is stolen or if its owner is wanted for any other violation.

**c)** For example, the floor manager might move his index finger in a clockwise circle to tell her to speed up.

**d)** The principal reports directly to the school board, whose directions and policies must be followed.

**D. Read Expository Paragraphs** Find an encyclopedia article on a topic that interests you. Identify an expository paragraph in the article. Then read aloud the paragraph to a partner, identifying the topic sentence and at least two supporting examples or details.

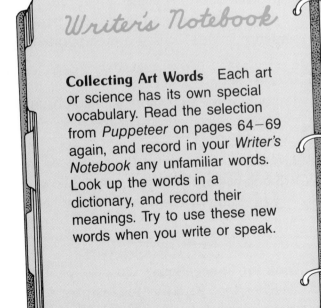

*Writer's Notebook*

**Collecting Art Words** Each art or science has its own special vocabulary. Read the selection from *Puppeteer* on pages 64–69 again, and record in your *Writer's Notebook* any unfamiliar words. Look up the words in a dictionary, and record their meanings. Try to use these new words when you write or speak.

# Thinking As a Writer
## Connecting a Main Idea and Details

**Writer's Guide**

In an expository paragraph, good writers

◆ express the main idea in a well-focused topic sentence.

◆ connect the details and examples in the paragraph to the topic sentence and to each other.

In a good expository paragraph, a writer expresses a main idea in a well-focused topic sentence. The topic sentence tells what the writer is going to inform the readers about. This topic sentence tells readers what kind of information to expect in the paragraph.

1. A magician must be able to distract the audience cleverly.

The writer of an expository paragraph must back up the topic sentence with details and examples that explain it. In a well-written expository paragraph, these details and examples are smoothly connected to each other and to the topic sentence.

2. The magician will often make a flamboyant gesture to draw the audience's attention.
3. While the audience is watching the gesture, the magician can make a subtle movement the audience will not notice.

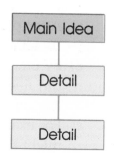

These sentences help explain how a magician can "distract the audience cleverly." Sentence 3 supports the topic sentence and is also connected to sentence 2.

When you write an expository paragraph, be sure your topic sentence is well-focused and supported by details.

## Discuss

1. Look at the expository paragraph on page 70. How does each sentence in the body of the paragraph support the topic sentence?
2. At first, the order of the sentences may not seem to matter. Look at page 68 to see what follows in the paragraph. Explain why Kathryn Lasky put the last sentence where she did.

## Try Your Hand

**Look for Connections**   On page 65, the author tells how Paul sketches the characters for his play. List all the words on the page that are about drawing or art. These words are one way Kathryn Lasky connects and develops her ideas.

# Developing the Writer's Craft
## Using Examples

Good writers want to make sure that their readers understand what they mean, so they give examples to explain each main point. Examples make an expository paragraph clearer and more interesting.

Notice that these two sentences illustrate how flatness became a key mechanical element of Paul's design.

1. The city streets will be on flat pieces that can be lifted away to show a barren desert.
2. The Sultan's palace will appear flat, but its two central doors will swing open to reveal a jeweled interior.

Without the examples above, we would never know what "flatness" meant to Paul's plan for the show. Like the sentences above do, the best examples often let readers form a mental picture of what the writer is explaining.

When you write your expository paragraph, give clear, specific examples to help your readers *see* what you have in mind.

## Discuss

1. Look at the first full paragraph on page 69. What examples does Kathryn Lasky use to illustrate the key word *progress* in the topic sentence?
2. If Paul's statement at the end of that paragraph had been the topic sentence, what kinds of examples would you have expected in the rest of the paragraph?

## Try Your Hand

**Use Examples** Think of a type of performing that interests you, such as playing in a band, reading the news on television, or dancing in a show. Write a topic sentence about the type of performing. Then write three examples to support your topic sentence.

# 1 Prewriting
## Expository Paragraph

Rosa, a student at Archer Elementary School, wanted to write an expository paragraph about an occupation for a magazine her class was putting together. She used the checklist in the **Writer's Guide** to plan her expository paragraph. Look at what she did.

## ◆ Brainstorming and Selecting a Topic

First, Rosa brainstormed a list of possible topics for her expository paragraph. Rosa included occupations of people she knew, as well as occupations she was interested in but did not know much about.

Next, Rosa looked over her list and crossed out topics that readers would already know about or for which she might have trouble finding information.

Finally, Rosa circled the topic she felt would make the most interesting expository paragraph. She decided to write about the occupation of advertising copywriter, because she always enjoyed hearing her Aunt Alicia discuss the ads she had written. Rosa knew she could ask her aunt for information and could find additional facts in the library.

> elementary school teacher
> ~~spy~~
> bus driver
> ~~fast food restaurant worker~~
> (advertising copywriter)
> vice president of Mexico

## Discuss

1. Look at each topic Rosa crossed off her list. Why do you think she didn't choose it?

2. Suppose Rosa knew people in each of those occupations. Might she have made a different choice? Why or why not?

# Gathering Information

After Rosa selected her topic, she gathered information for her expository paragraph. She read a description of an advertising copywriter's job in a library book about advertising. She also called her Aunt Alicia to get more information and to clarify some of the points in the article. Rosa made notes while reading the article and while talking to her aunt. Afterwards, she looked over her notes to make sure they were clear and easy to read.

> Advertising copywriter writes all words that appear in ads.
> Works with creative director, copy chief, art director, and artists.
> Two parts to ad: headline and body
> Body must stress benefits not features.
>
> Ask Aunt Alicia
> Who is creative director?
> Decides on overall slant and "look" of ad
>
> Who is copy chief?
> Copywriter's boss
>
> What is the difference between feature and benefit?
> Feature tells about product.
> Benefit shows how product appeals to buyer.
> "Battery-operated" is a feature. "Battery-operated so that you can take it anywhere" is a benefit.
>
> Where did you work before the job you have now?
> Worked as writer for mail-order catalogue

## Discuss

1. What points did Rosa clarify in her conversation with her aunt? What other points might she still need to clarify?
2. What information in her notes might Rosa not use in her paragraph? Explain your answer.

## ◆ Organizing the Facts

After Rosa had gathered all the information she needed for her expository paragraph, she was ready to organize her notes. She knew that the purpose of her paragraph was to inform her readers about the job of copywriter. Rosa chose the information from the article and from her conversation with her aunt that she thought would best explain the job of advertising copywriter to her readers.

She decided that the first sentence in her notes was the main idea for her paragraph. Under it she arranged the facts she thought would most interest and best inform her readers. She put related facts together in her notes so that she could easily connect them when she drafted her expository paragraph.

> *Advertising copywriter writes all words that appear in ads.*
>
> *Two parts to ad: headline and body*
> *Headline?*
> *Body must stress benefits instead of just features.*
> *Feature tells about product—"battery operated."*
> *Benefit shows how product appeals to buyer—"Battery-operated so that you can take it anywhere."*

When she organized her information, Rosa realized she did not know what a headline was supposed to do. She decided to call her aunt and ask her so that she could add that information to her expository paragraph.

## Discuss

1. According to Rosa's notes, where in her expository paragraph will she put her examples of features and benefits? Why did she decide to put the examples where she did?

**2.** What information from her notes did Rosa leave out? Why do you think she decided to leave it out?

**3.** Is it important for Rosa to explain what a headline is supposed to do? Why or why not?

## Try Your Hand

Now plan an expository paragraph of your own.

**A. Brainstorm and Select a Topic**   Brainstorm a list of possible topics. Include occupations you know about or would be interested in learning about. Think about each topic and about your audience.

- ◆ Cross out topics that do not interest you.
- ◆ Cross out topics that your audience might already know about.
- ◆ Cross out topics for which you might have trouble finding information.
- ◆ Circle the most interesting topic left on your list. This will be the topic of your expository paragraph.

**B. Gather Information**   When you are satisfied with your topic, plan how you can gather information about it. You may want to use an encyclopedia or a library book. You may also decide to interview someone who has the kind of job you are writing about. Be sure to take notes on both your reading and the interview. Use the interview to help answer any questions that occur to you in your reading.

**C. Organize the Facts**   Look over your notes.

- ◆ An expository paragraph should have a clearly focused main idea. Make sure that you have included the main idea in your notes.
- ◆ Think about your purpose. Cross out any information that does not explain your main idea.
- ◆ Think about your audience. Add any information your audience might need to better understand your main idea.
- ◆ Arrange your information so that the facts are clearly connected to each other and to the main idea.

 **Save your notes in your *Writer's Notebook*. You will use them when you draft your expository paragraph.**

COMPOSITION: PREWRITING   Expository Paragraph   **77**

# 2 Drafting
## Expository Paragraph

Using her notes and the material she had
organized, Rosa followed the **Writer's Guide** to draft
her expository paragraph. Look at what she did.

> *An advertising copywriter writes all*
> *the words that appear in the ads you*
> *see in newspapers, magazines,*
> *and even on billboards! Most ads*
> *have two parts. the headline and the*
> *body. The headline must get the*
> *reader's attention.*

### Writer's Guide
**Drafting Checklist**
- ☑ Use your notes for ideas.
- ☑ Write the topic sentence first.
- ☑ Write the body of the paragraph.
- ☑ Make sure that the sentences in the paragraph relate to each other and to the topic sentence.

## Discuss

1. Look at Rosa's topic sentence. What examples did she add to it? Are these examples helpful? Why or why not?
2. Is the part about a headline's purpose clear? Explain your answer.
3. What information might Rosa's readers expect next?

## Try Your Hand

Now you are ready to write an expository paragraph.

**A. Review Your Information**   Think about the information you gathered and organized in the last lesson. Decide whether you need more information. If so, gather it.

**B. Think About Your TAP**   Remember that your task is to write an expository paragraph. Your purpose is to inform your audience about your topic.

**C. Write Your First Draft**   Follow the steps in the **Drafting Checklist** to write your expository paragraph.
   When you write your draft, just put all your ideas on paper. Do not worry about spelling, punctuation, or grammar. You can correct the draft later.

**Task:** What?
**Audience:** Who?
**Purpose:** Why?

 Save your first draft in your *Writer's Notebook*. You will use it when you revise your expository paragraph.

# 3 Responding and Revising
## Expository Paragraph

Rosa used the checklist in the **Writer's Guide** to revise her expository paragraph. Look at what she did.

### ◆ Checking Information

Rosa decided to take out the fifth sentence because it gives information unconnected to her topic sentence. To show her change, she used this mark ✄.

### ◆ Checking Organization

Rosa moved the fourth sentence nearer to the beginning of the paragraph so that her readers would better understand the importance of the headline and the body of the ad. To show that the sentence should be moved, she used this mark ⌣.

### ◆ Checking Language

Rosa noticed that the pronoun *it* toward the end of the paragraph was unclear, so she replaced it with a noun. She used this mark ∧ to make her change.

**Move** — **Cut** — **Replace**

> An advertising copywriter writes all the words that appear in the ads you see in newspapers, magazines, and even on billboards! Most ads have two parts, the headline and the body. The headline must get the reader's attention. Good copywriters must understand their audience, which is the advertiser's customers. Some customers may want to buy many things and other customers may want to buy only one thing. The body must tell the audience about the features and the benefits of it the product. Product features, like "battery-operated," just tell about the product. Product benefits, like "battery-operated so you can take it anywhere," show how the product might appeal to the audience.

## Discuss

1. Rosa thought that the sentence about what customers might buy was unrelated to her topic sentence. Do you agree or disagree? Why?
2. How is Rosa's revised expository paragraph better than her draft? Explain your answer.
3. Are there other changes Rosa could have made? Explain your answer.

## Try Your Hand

Now revise your first draft.

A. **Read Your First Draft**  As you read your paragraph, think about your audience and purpose. Read your draft silently or to a partner to see if it is complete and well organized. Ask yourself or your partner the questions in the box.

---

### Responding and Revising Strategies

| ✔ Respond<br>**Ask yourself or a partner:** | ✔ Revise<br>**Try these solutions:** |
| --- | --- |
| ◆ Does my topic sentence express the main idea of the paragraph? | ◆ **Refocus** the topic sentence to state your main idea more clearly. |
| ◆ Have I supported my topic sentence with strong examples? | ◆ **Add** examples to make your paragraph clearer and more interesting. |
| ◆ Does each sentence in the body of the paragraph support the topic sentence? | ◆ **Cut** sentences that do not support the topic. See the **Revising Workshop** on page 81. |
| ◆ Are the sentences in a clear, logical order? | ◆ **Move** any sentences that seem out of place. |

---

B. **Make Your Changes**  If the answer to any question in the box is *no,* try the solution. Use the **Editor's Marks** to show your changes.

C. **Review Your Expository Paragraph Again**  Decide whether there is anything else you want to revise. Keep revising your paragraph until you feel it is well organized and complete.

> **EDITOR'S MARKS**
>
> ∧ Add something.
> ✗ Cut something.
> ⌒ Move something.
> ∧ Replace something.

 Save your revised expository paragraph in your *Writer's Notebook.* **You will use it when you proofread your paragraph.**

# Revising Workshop
## Keeping to the Topic

Good writers want their ideas to be clear to their audience. One way they do this is to make sure that each paragraph has a topic sentence and the other sentences in the paragraph are about the topic sentence.

For instance, suppose you were reading a paragraph with this topic sentence: "In Yellowstone National Park I saw every kind of scenery I could imagine." You would expect the rest of the sentences in the paragraph to describe the variety of scenery the writer saw at Yellowstone. You would be surprised if there were sentences in the paragraph about bears or a campfire sing-along.

In your paragraph, make sure that your topic sentence tells what the paragraph will be about and that the other sentences are about the topic sentence.

## Practice

Each of the following topic sentences is followed by two sentences that might appear in the rest of the paragraph. Write the sentence—**a.** or **b.**—that would best fit in the paragraph with that topic sentence.

1. The floats in the Thanksgiving Day Parade were colorful and exciting.
   **a.** One float used red, white, and blue flowers to make an American flag.
   **b.** I had watched the parade on television before, but I had never seen it in person.
2. I saw some interesting animals on my trip to the Everglades.
   **a.** I put on a lot of mosquito repellent so that I wouldn't get bitten.
   **b.** On one riverbank I saw some alligators that lay so still they almost didn't look real.
3. On our vacation at the dude ranch, I did some things I had never done before.
   **a.** At first I was scared to be on a horse, but I soon decided it was fun.
   **b.** Playing horseshoes by the corral reminded me of the time I played horseshoes on my uncle's farm.

# 4 Proofreading
## Expository Paragraph

After revising her expository paragraph, Rosa used the **Writer's Guide** and the **Editor's Marks** to proofread it. She also proofread an additional paragraph she had written explaining more about other jobs in the advertising agency. Look at what she did.

The creative director, art director, copy *chief* (cheif) and artist's are all part of the creative team, the creative director decides on the overall *look* and "slant" of the ad. The art director is *responsible* (responsable) for making sure the art creates just the right (affect). *effect*

## Discuss

1. Look at Rosa's proofread paragraph. What kinds of mistakes did she make?
2. Rosa inserted the correct spelling of *effect*. Is *affect* also a word? If so, how is it used?

## Try Your Hand

**Proofread Your Expository Paragraph**   Now use the **Writer's Guide** and the **Editor's Marks** to proofread your expository paragraph.

**Save your corrected expository paragraph in your *Writer's Notebook*. You will use it when you publish your paragraph.**

# 5 Publishing
## Expository Paragraph

Rosa made a clean copy of her expository paragraph and checked it to be sure she had not left out anything. Then she and her classmates published their expository paragraphs in a class magazine. You can find Rosa's paragraph on page 24 of the **Writer's Handbook.**

Here's how Rosa and her classmates published a magazine.

### Writer's Guide
**Publishing Checklist**
- ☑ Make a clean copy of your expository paragraph.
- ☑ Check to see that nothing has been left out.
- ☑ Check that there are no mistakes.
- ☑ Share your expository paragraph in a special way.

1. First, they decided which expository paragraphs to include in their magazine. They decided to include all the paragraphs from their class.

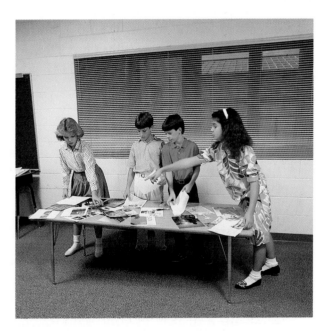

2. After they had chosen the paragraphs, they found magazine pictures that helped to illustrate the occupations described in the paragraphs.

3. Then, they decided in what order they wanted the paragraphs to appear in the magazine. Rosa and her classmates carefully glued the paragraphs and matching pictures onto heavy paper.

4. Last, they presented their finished magazine to their school principal.

## Discuss

1. What might be a good title for the magazine?
2. In what ways might you decide to arrange the paragraphs in the magazine?

## Try Your Hand

**Publish Your Expository Paragraph**   Follow the checklist in the **Writer's Guide.** If possible create a class magazine, or try one of these ideas for sharing your expository paragraph.

◆ Put up a display in your school library of the paragraphs and matching pictures. Ask your librarian to suggest books on different occupations for you to place near the display.

◆ Have a Jobs Fair in your classroom and invite other classes to visit. You and your classmates might station yourselves around the room and inform visitors about the occupations you've written about.

# Listening and Speaking
## Tips on How to Speak and Listen in a Response Group

### Speaking in a Response Group

1. Begin by making sure that all group members understand that the purpose of the response group is to improve writing.
2. Take turns speaking about each other's writing. Speak clearly so that everyone can hear you. Think about what you want to say before you speak.
3. Be polite when you respond. Do not interrupt while another person is speaking.
4. Describe what you liked about the other group members' writing. Ask questions about the parts you do not understand. Make suggestions.

### Listening in a Response Group

1. Listen carefully to the person speaking. Think about how the speaker's suggestions could improve your writing.
2. Wait until the speaker is finished before you respond.
3. Listen to discover ideas from other group members' writing.
4. Thank the group members for their help.

# Writing in the Content Areas

### Writer's Guide

When you write, remember the stages of the Writing Process.

◆ Prewriting
◆ Drafting
◆ Responding and Revising
◆ Proofreading
◆ Publishing

Use what you learned to write about things you know well. You could write an expository paragraph for someone who does not know much about a certain topic. One way to publish your writing is to organize your class's paragraphs by topics. You might then place them in a class booklet called "All About Everything." Use one of these ideas or an idea of your own.

## Science

Think of the animal that you know most about, or use a book to learn more about an animal that interests you. Without naming the animal, write about its habits, its habitat, its diet, and any other information you want to share. In the last sentence, ask the reader to identify the animal.

## Music

Do you like the sound the strum of a guitar makes or the tinkling sound of a piano? Write a paragraph giving information about your favorite musical instrument. Explain what it looks like, what it is made of, and why you think its sound is pleasing.

## Social Studies

Write a paragraph giving the most interesting details you know about your favorite person from history. You may want to focus on the person's childhood or on his or her greatest challenge.

## Physical Education

Write a paragraph telling about games you could play or exercises you could perform while waiting for a bus. Give information about the object of each game (how you win or what you try to do) or the purpose of each exercise. Also tell about any equipment needed and the amount of time it takes to do each activity.

Writers of expository paragraphs share facts they know with readers who may not know about certain topics. A well-written expository paragraph explains any difficult or technical words that readers might not know. How does the writer explain the difficult words in this paragraph?

---

## A Map of Shapes

How can you find your way through an unfamiliar area? A compass will help you find directions. A road map might show you landmarks such as buildings and parks. If you're exploring the wilderness though, try a map that shows an area's topography. Topography means "the physical features of a region or place." A topographical map shows natural features such as hills, boulders, smaller rocks, and bodies of water. This type of map also shows man-made features such as walls, fences, and docks. To get a topographical map of your area, ask your librarian for the address of an appropriate organization.

---

◆ **Nouns in an Expository Paragraph**   The words highlighted in color are nouns. They do the job of naming people, places, things, and ideas. Notice how the writer explained difficult nouns with simpler nouns.

◆ **Language Focus: Nouns**   The following lessons will help you use different kinds of nouns in your own writing.

# 1 Nouns

◆ **FOCUS**  A **noun** names a person, a place, a thing, or an idea.

The words in color in these sentences are nouns.
1. My favorite shirt has a decal of some cats .
2. My brother owns shirts that show a surfer and the symbol for peace .
3. My mother likes the shirt from Canada .

The words *brother, surfer,* and *mother* name people. *Canada* names a place. The words *shirt, decal, cats, shirts,* and *symbol* name things. *Peace* names an idea.

> **Link to Speaking and Writing**
> Use exact nouns to paint a clear picture. Why is the revised sentence clearer?

> The ~raccoon~ animal ran toward the water. ~stream~

## Guided Practice

**A.** Identify the nouns in each sentence.
1. My pals started a club one rainy day.
2. All the members live in Riverton.
3. James wore his favorite T-shirt to the meeting.
4. The shirt has a picture of a brontosaurus.
5. An artist painted the dinosaur with red ink.
6. Maria is president of the group.
7. My brother has never had so much fun.

**B.** Replace the underlined noun in each sentence with a more exact noun.
8. Erica's T-shirt shows pets.
9. Juan bought his shirt in town.
10. The T-shirt is a dark color.
11. Robbie's shirt shows that he loves sports.
12. The club members held the meeting in the room.
13. They chose the animal as their mascot.

## Independent Practice

**C. Identifying Nouns**   Read each sentence. Write the nouns.

14. The members raised money for a trip to Orlando.

> MODEL   members, money, trip, Orlando

15. Each member traced a picture onto a piece of paper.
16. The clerks at the store helped each person.
17. The manager made the designs into stencils.
18. Jenna placed a stencil over the fabric.
19. Kelly decorated the shirt with ink.
20. Each T-shirt showed a picture or a word.
21. Bob sent a sample to Amy Greenspan in Kalamazoo.
22. The trip to Florida created excitement for weeks.

**D. 23. – 31. Classifying Nouns**   Beside each noun you listed in **C**, write *person, place, thing,* or *idea.*

> MODEL   23. members—persons       money—thing
>            trip—thing or idea     Orlando—place

**E. Revising Sentences**   Use your **Writer's Thesaurus** to replace each underlined noun with a more exact noun. Write the sentence.

32. This group is for hikers.

> MODEL   This club is for hikers.

33. The club hiked through the wilderness.
34. A storm washed away the road.
35. The wind knocked down many trees.
36. The faces of the hikers showed their feelings.
37. Some members rested near the building.
38. A vehicle carried the hikers down the mountain.

## Application — Writing

**Club Report**   Imagine that you are a member of a club. Write a report that tells what the club did last Saturday. Use exact nouns to name the people you met, the places you visited, the things you used or saw, and the ideas you discussed.

# 2 Singular and Plural Nouns

## FOCUS

◆ A **singular noun** names one person, place, thing, or idea.
◆ A **plural noun** names more than one person, place, thing, or idea.

...one moon...

two moons...

Remember that a noun is a naming word. The plural form of most nouns ends in s or *es*. Notice how each noun in color ends.

1. Earth has one moon. Mars has two moons .
2. Look at that star in the sky. The skies are usually full of stars .
3. I could see a cluster of stars through my telescope. Several fuzzy bunches of stars are overhead.

The plurals of the nouns *moon* and *star* are formed by adding s. The noun *sky* is made plural by changing the y to an i and adding *es*. The noun *bunch* is made plural by adding *es*.

The chart shows rules for forming plurals.

| |
|---|
| Add s to most singular nouns: star—stars, moon—moons. |
| Add *es* to nouns ending in s, ss, x, ch, or sh: lens—lenses, class—classes, box—boxes, bunch—bunches, dish—dishes. |
| Add s to nouns that end in a vowel plus y: day—days. |
| Change the y to i and add *es* with nouns that end in a consonant and y: sky—skies, reply—replies. |

## Guided Practice

**A.** Identify each noun as *singular* or *plural*.

1. beach
2. foxes
3. mess
4. hairbrushes
5. pony
6. alleys
7. circus
8. bush
9. bones

**B. 10.–14.** Give the plural form of each singular noun in **A.**

## Independent Practice

**C. Identifying Nouns**   Write each underlined noun. Then write *singular* or *plural* after the noun.

15. <u>Rockets</u> were in a <u>display</u> at the space <u>center</u>.

    rockets—plural
    display—singular
    center—singular

16. Visitors crowd into the <u>place</u> on a <u>holiday</u>.
17. We boarded a <u>bus</u> for a <u>tour</u>.
18. From the <u>valley</u> we could see the distant <u>hills</u>.
19. The <u>driver</u> gave a <u>speech</u> about the space <u>program</u>.
20. I learned that there might be more <u>planets</u>.
21. After the <u>trip</u> the <u>tourists</u> ate <u>lunch</u>.

**D. 22.–27. Spelling Plural Nouns**   Write the plural form of each singular noun in **C.**

22. displays, centers

**E. Writing Original Sentences**   Write the plural form of each of these nouns in a sentence.

28. beach

    The beaches at the Canaveral Seashore are sandy and wide.

| | | |
|---|---|---|
| 29. ferry | 33. boss | 37. crutch |
| 30. business | 34. mess | 38. highway |
| 31. candle | 35. porch | 39. dress |
| 32. baby | 36. pancake | 40. bunch |

## Application — Writing

**Science Log**   Imagine that you are an astronomer watching the planets and the stars through a telescope. Write an entry in your science log. Use plural nouns that follow each of the spelling rules in this lesson.

# 3 More Plural Nouns

◆ **FOCUS**   The plural forms of some nouns follow special rules.

The words in color in these sentences are plural nouns. Notice how they are spelled.

1. The rangers saved the lives of five deer .
2. They used their radios to get help.
3. The brave men and women were heroes .

The singular nouns *life, deer, radio, man, woman,* and *hero* do not follow the regular rules for spelling the plural forms. This chart shows the rules for nouns like these.

---

When a noun ends in *f* or *fe*, change the *f* to *v* and add *es*: life—lives, loaf—loaves. Some nouns that end in *f* add only an *s*: belief—beliefs.

---

When a noun ends with a vowel plus *o*, add *s*: radio—radios. When a noun ends with a consonant plus *o*, add *es*: hero—heroes. With some nouns that end in a consonant plus *o*, add only an *s*: piano—pianos.

---

Some singular nouns have irregular plural forms:

| | | |
|---|---|---|
| woman—women | tooth—teeth | ox—oxen |
| man—men | foot—feet | mouse—mice |
| child—children | goose—geese | |

---

Some nouns have the same singular and plural form:

| | | |
|---|---|---|
| sheep—sheep | trout—trout | moose—moose |
| deer—deer | fish—fish | series—series |

---

## Guided Practice

**A.** Name the plural form of each noun.

1. loaf
2. tooth
3. radio
4. hero
5. life
6. child
7. man
8. sheep
9. woman

## Independent Practice

**B. Writing Plural Nouns**   Write the plural form of each noun.
If necessary, use a dictionary to check your spelling.

**10.** wolf

MODEL  wolves

| | | |
|---|---|---|
| **11.** giraffe | **17.** fish | **23.** moose |
| **12.** knife | **18.** ratio | **24.** half |
| **13.** stereo | **19.** zero | **25.** elk |
| **14.** self | **20.** chief | **26.** solo |
| **15.** hoof | **21.** mouse | **27.** shelf |
| **16.** calf | **22.** goose | **28.** staff |

**C. Changing Singular Nouns to Plural Nouns**   Write the plural
form of the noun in parentheses ( ) to complete each sentence.
If necessary, use a dictionary to check your spelling.

**29.** Two (man) stood on the cliff.

MODEL  Two men stood on the cliff.

**30.** They heard (echo) from the canyon floor.
**31.** Their (wife) called to them from the other side.
**32.** The campers listened to their (radio).
**33.** Rangers found strange (deer) in the canyon.
**34.** The (child) saw them near the river.
**35.** Do the animals have purple (foot)?
**36.** Yes, their (hoof) are purple.
**37.** Their voices sound like (piano).
**38.** The strange creatures love (tomato).
**39.** Their (tooth) are long and silver.
**40.** These unusual deer are afraid of (mouse).
**41.** The rangers also discovered several blue (goose).

## Application — Writing

**Science Fiction**   Write the beginning sentences of a science
fiction story for young children. Write about an imaginary animal.
Use plural nouns from this lesson to name the animal, where
it lives, and what it does. If you need help writing a story
beginning, see page 33 of the **Writer's Handbook.**

# 4 Common and Proper Nouns

**FOCUS**
◆ A **common noun** names any person, place, thing, or idea.
◆ A **proper noun** names a particular person, place, or thing.

Remember that a noun names a person, a place, a thing, or an idea. The words in color in these sentences are nouns. The nouns that begin with capital letters are proper nouns.

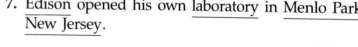

1. Benjamin Franklin invented a lightning conductor .
2. He became a popular statesman of the United States .
3. Franklin Institute of Boston is a school in Massachusetts .
4. This school on Berkeley Street was named after him.

Notice that a proper noun may be one word, as in *Massachusetts*. A proper noun may also be more than one word, as in *Franklin Institute of Boston*. Only the important words in a proper noun are capitalized.

## Guided Practice

**A.** Identify each underlined noun as a *common noun* or a *proper noun*.

1. Thomas Edison invented the electric light and the phonograph.
2. This inventor was born in the month of February.
3. The Edisons once lived in Milan, Ohio.
4. Young Thomas was called Alva or Al by his family.
5. Al sold newspapers on the Grand Trunk Railway.
6. Later, this young man worked in Canada.
7. Edison opened his own laboratory in Menlo Park, New Jersey.

## THINK AND REMEMBER

- Remember that a **common noun** names any person, place, thing, or idea.
- Remember that a **proper noun** names a particular person, place, or thing.

## Independent Practice

**B. Identifying Common and Proper Nouns**  In each sentence the nouns are underlined. Write each noun. Then write *common* or *proper*.

8. Mr. Samms took the class to an exhibit.

MODEL > Mr. Samms—proper, class—common, exhibit—common

9. The students visited the exhibit on a Wednesday.
10. The director of the Science Museum greeted the class.
11. The inventions came from Asia, Europe, and North America.
12. China has given the world many inventions.
13. Ts'ai Lun of China invented paper.

**C. Proofreading Sentences**  Write each sentence correctly. Capitalize all proper nouns.

14. chris did her report on the invention of the car.

MODEL > Chris did her report on the invention of the car.

15. An electric car was built by william morrison.

16. Morrison lived in des moines, iowa.

17. The first bicycle was invented in france.

18. J. K. starley of england made improvements.

19. In march, bob gave a safety speech for young riders.

20. He spoke to the saturday class at walt whitman school.

## Application — Writing

**Journal Entry**  Imagine that you have just invented a new kind of camera. Write a journal entry that tells what your invention is called, how it works, who will use it, and where and when you invented it. Use common and proper nouns. If you need help writing a journal entry, see page 31 of the **Writer's Handbook.**

# 5 Capitalization of Proper Nouns

◆ **FOCUS**   Each important word in a proper noun begins with a capital letter.

Remember that a proper noun names a particular person, place, or thing. Notice the proper nouns in color in these sentences.

1. Our class visited the White House on a Monday in May .
2. We were there on Memorial Day .
3. President Bush arrived by helicopter.

Proper nouns are used to name a particular person, place, day, month, or holiday. Remember that each important word in a proper noun begins with a capital letter.

**Link to Speaking and Writing**
You can sometimes make your writing more exact by using proper nouns. Why is the revised sentence better?

We visited *Aunt Bess* ~~my relative~~ on ~~a holiday~~ *Mother's Day*.

## Guided Practice

**A.** Identify the proper noun or nouns in each sentence. Tell which letters should be capitalized.

1. The class traveled to washington.
2. Their teacher, lee carmody, made the arrangements.
3. My uncle works for the department of the treasury.
4. His birthday is in july on independence day.

**B.** Replace each underlined person or place with a proper noun.

5. At the <u>zoo</u> <u>a student</u> saw pandas from <u>another country</u>.
6. The tour of the <u>museum</u> was enjoyable.
7. <u>My brother</u> enjoyed the tour of the <u>building</u>.

## Independent Practice

**C. Identifying Proper Nouns**   Write the proper nouns in each sentence correctly. Be sure to capitalize each important word.

8. We spent our vacation in new orleans, louisiana.

MODEL> New Orleans, Louisiana

9. The city borders the mississippi river.

10. The river leads to the gulf of mexico.

11. Author mark twain wrote stories about the river.

12. Every february tourists travel to new orleans.

13. Visitors enjoy a holiday called mardi gras.

14. People in costumes parade on bourbon street.

15. The university of new orleans is the largest university in the city.

16. My friend janet visited the city with her family last tuesday.

**D. Revising Sentences**   Replace each underlined word or phrase with a more specific proper noun. Then write the sentence so that it makes sense.

17. During a summer month my family goes swimming.

MODEL> During July my family goes swimming.

18. We travel to the ocean.

19. The ocean is near a large city.

20. On a weekend day the beach is crowded.

21. Large sand dunes rise up beside the road.

22. We usually go to the beach on a holiday.

23. Then my cousin comes with us.

## Application — Writing

**List**   Make a list of ten places you would like to see. You can list bodies of water, cities, countries, or buildings. Write the proper nouns carefully. Capitalize the important words.

# 6 Abbreviations

## FOCUS

♦ An **abbreviation** is a shortened form of a word.
♦ Many abbreviations begin with a capital letter and end with a period.

Bus Tour: Mon., Oct. 13
Meet at Coy Rd. terminal
Depart at 9:30 A.M.
Arrive at Olvera St.
at 1:00 P.M.

Abbreviations are often used in writing people's names or addresses, in journals, and in notes or announcements. Most abbreviations are not used in other kinds of writing.

The chart lists some frequently used abbreviations.

| Ms. a woman | Mr. a man | Mrs. a married |
| Dr. Doctor | Jr. Junior | woman |
| Rev. Reverend | | Sr. Senior |
| Ave. Avenue | St. Street | Rd. Road |
| Dr. Drive | Rt./Rte. Route | Blvd. Boulevard |
| Co. Company | Inc. Incorporated | |
| Dept. Department | Corp. Corporation | |
| Sun. Sunday | Wed. Wednesday | Fri. Friday |
| Mon. Monday | Thurs. Thursday | Sat. Saturday |
| Tues. Tuesday | | |
| Jan. January | Apr. April | Oct. October |
| Feb. February | Aug. August | Nov. November |
| Mar. March | Sept. September | Dec. December |
| A.M. before noon | P.M. after noon | |
| mo. month | yr. year | |

Initials are a special kind of abbreviation that stands for a person's name. An initial is the first letter of a word in a person's name. Initials are capitalized, and each letter is followed by a period.

A. A. Milne wrote *Winnie-the-Pooh*.

## Guided Practice

**A.** Identify the abbreviations for the underlined words.
   1. The Bay Fish <u>Company</u>
   2. 730 Broad <u>Street</u>
   3. <u>Monday, December</u> 7
   4. <u>Reverend</u> John Black
   5. (<u>married woman</u>) Jones
   6. <u>Doctor</u> Arthur J. O'Connor

> **THINK AND REMEMBER**
> ◆ Remember that an **abbreviation** is a shortened form of a word.
> ◆ Begin most abbreviations with a capital letter and end them with a period.

## Independent Practice

**B. Identifying Abbreviations**  Write each item. Abbreviate the underlined word.

7. Cushman <u>Drive</u>

MODEL> Cushman Dr.

8. George Adams, <u>Junior</u>
9. (<u>man</u>) John Muir
10. 10 Downing <u>Street</u>
11. <u>Route</u> 6A
12. <u>Department</u> 3049

13. 7:43 (<u>after noon</u>)
14. 5:00 (<u>before noon</u>)
15. Frank Padilla, <u>Senior</u>
16. (<u>woman</u>) Sally Ride
17. 411 Blue Hill <u>Avenue</u>

**C. Proofreading Abbreviations**  These sentences and notes contain incorrectly written abbreviations. Rewrite each item with the correct abbreviation.

18. Dtr. Kathleen P Robinson is my family's doctor.

MODEL> Dr. Kathleen P. Robinson is my family's doctor.

19. office at 67 Villa rd.
20. will not be in on wed.
21. next appointment on Aug 16 at 3:30 pm
22. at the corner of rt. 4
23. in the jj Welch Comp. building
24. Her brother is Frank k Serra, jnr
25. works for Able Disks, Incd.
26. will visit mon., sept 15
27. rev. n. R. Ruiz lives nearby.
28. will meet for lunch at 11:45 am on tue.

## Application — Writing

**Mailing List**  Make a birthday-card list. Use abbreviations of the months of the year to divide the list into twelve sections. Write the names, addresses, and birthdays of people to whom you would like to send cards. Use abbreviations and initials.

# 7 Singular Possessive Nouns

◆ **FOCUS** A **singular possessive noun** shows ownership by one person or thing.

Sometimes nouns tell what someone or something owns or has. The words in color in these sentences are singular possessive nouns.

**1.** The student's idea was a good one.

**2.** The mural's colors will be bright.

To form the possessive of a singular noun, add an apostrophe and *s* (ˢ).

**3.** Carrie's teacher supplied the paints.

**4.** Dennis's paintbrush was too thin.

**Link to Speaking and Writing**
Use possessive nouns to make your writing and speaking shorter and smoother. Why is the revised sentence better?

*The paints belonging to Kyle are on the table.* (Kyle's)

## Guided Practice

**A.** Give the singular possessive form of each noun.

**1.** Amy    **3.** Mr. Jacoby    **5.** Charles    **7.** mural    **9.** paint

**2.** school    **4.** class        **6.** Beth      **8.** Janis

**B.** Change the underlined words to include a singular possessive noun.

**10.** The boat of Joseph looks real.

**11.** The roof of the building is colorful.

**12.** The paints that belong to Chris are missing.

**THINK AND REMEMBER**
◆ Remember that a **singular possessive noun** shows ownership by one person or thing.
◆ Add an apostrophe and *s* to a singular noun to form a possessive noun.

# Independent Practice

**C. Making Singular Nouns Possessive**  Write the singular possessive form of each noun.

13. Buddy

MODEL > Buddy's

14. Boris
15. teacher
16. Elena
17. Mavis
18. dog

19. town
20. Mr. Morris
21. Anne
22. grass

**D. Revising Sentences**  Write each sentence. Change the underlined words to include a singular possessive noun.

23. The art contest of the city was open to everyone.

MODEL > The city's art contest was open to everyone.

24. The judge of the contest was a famous artist.
25. The judge especially liked the watercolor belonging to Ari.
26. Everybody enjoyed the toothpick statue belonging to Jerry.
27. The sketches belonging to Susan took third place.
28. The self-portrait of Barry came in second.
29. The brother of Bethany won first place with an oil painting.
30. The decision of the judge surprised everyone.
31. The parents of Bess attended the exhibit.
32. The hours of the museum were extended for the contest.
33. The results of the contest were reported in the local newspaper.
34. The contest of next year will be just as exciting.

**E. 35. – 44. Writing Original Sentences**  Use each singular possessive noun you wrote for **C** in a sentence.

35. Buddy's

MODEL > Buddy's sister helped him with his painting.

## Application — Writing

**Contest Rules**  Imagine that you are organizing an art contest at your school. Decide who will judge the contest, who may enter, and what prizes will be presented to the winners. Write several basic rules for participating in the contest. Use singular possessive nouns.

# 8 Plural Possessive Nouns

◆ **FOCUS** A **plural possessive noun** shows ownership by more than one person or thing.

Remember that a singular possessive noun shows what one person or thing owns or has. A plural possessive noun shows what more than one person or thing owns or has.

To form the possessive of a plural noun that ends with *s*, add an apostrophe. The words in color in these sentences are plural possessive nouns.

1. The questions of tourists were good ones. The guide answered all the tourists' questions.
2. The appetites of the whales are impressive. The whales' appetites are enormous.

To form the possessive of a plural noun that does not end with *s*, add an apostrophe and *s*.

3. The eyes of the children never left the glass. The children's eyes stared at the large fish.
4. The curiosity of people was interesting. The people's curiosity was unending.

## Guided Practice

**A.** Identify which of the endings should be used to form the plural possessive form of each of the following.

1. dolphins
2. tides
3. fishermen
4. mammals
5. sailors
6. people
7. geese
8. women
9. guides

---

**THINK AND REMEMBER**

◆ Use a **plural possessive noun** to show ownership by more than one person or thing.
◆ To form the possessive of a plural noun ending in *s*, add only an apostrophe.
◆ To form the possessive of a plural noun not ending in *s*, add an apostrophe and *s*.

---

## Independent Practice

**B. Making Plural Nouns Possessive**  Write the plural possessive form of each of these nouns.

10. clouds

MODEL > clouds'

11. buoys
12. men
13. shops
14. beaches
15. artists
16. observers

17. fishing nets
18. women
19. lobsters
20. children
21. lighthouses
22. craftspeople

**C. Revising Sentences**  Rewrite each sentence. Change the underlined words to include a plural possessive noun.

23. Photographs show the <u>faces of the manatees</u>.

MODEL > Photographs show the manatees' faces.

24. Florida is the <u>home of manatees</u>.
25. <u>The studies of scientists</u> show that manatees are intelligent animals.
26. Manatees live in the <u>shallows of the lagoons</u>.
27. <u>The propellers of motorboats</u> can hurt manatees.
28. <u>The seriousness of the injuries</u> has caused much concern among animal lovers.
29. <u>The efforts of many people</u> help pass laws to save the manatees.
30. <u>The purpose of the new laws</u> is to keep motorboats out of the lagoons so the manatees will be safe.
31. <u>The carelessness of some boaters</u> is still a problem.

**D. 32.–44. Writing Original Sentences**  Use each plural possessive noun you wrote for **B** in a sentence.

32. clouds'

MODEL > We saw animals in the clouds' shapes.

## Application — Writing and Speaking

**Nature Notebook Entry**  Think about a group of animals you have observed at a zoo, in the wild, or on television. Imagine that you are a naturalist studying the creatures. Write a nature notebook entry about the animals' appearance and habits. Use plural possessive nouns. Read your entry to the class.

# Building Vocabulary
## Compound Words

The girl in the picture is having a daydream about being elected class president by her classmates. The words *classmates* and *daydream* are compound words. A compound word is made by putting together two or more words.

class + mates = classmates
day + dream = daydream

There are three kinds of compound words. **Closed compounds** are written as one word.

football   someone   seashell
weekend

**Open compounds** are written as separate words.

savings account   picnic table
swimming pool

**Hyphenated compounds** are written with hyphens (-).

merry-go-round   father-in-law
nose-dive

When you come across a compound word, try to figure out the meaning by looking at the separate words that compose it.

# Reading Practice

Read each sentence. Look for closed compounds, open compounds, and hyphenated compounds. Write each compound word and its definition. Use a dictionary if necessary.

1. In Kim's favorite daydream, she is elected president of the fifth grade, and her friend is elected vice president.
2. In her fantasy, she is riding on a fire engine across the playground, and all her classmates are cheering.
3. Flower girls throw forget-me-nots, and a reporter writes in his notebook.
4. Newspapers carry the headline "KIM ELECTED PRESIDENT IN A LANDSLIDE."
5. Kim invites all to a victory party at the seashore, where a lifeguard is on duty.

# Writing Practice

Rewrite each sentence. Replace the underlined words with a closed compound.

6. In my daydream, I am taking a flight in space.
7. My craft rises far above the tops of the trees.
8. The light of the moon looks beautiful.
9. I wear special glasses for the sun.
10. There are no storms with thunder.
11. I leave a print of my foot on the moon.

# Project

Work in a group to make a mural of an imaginary place. Create a path that leads through the place. Along the path, illustrate and label things that are named with compound words. For example, you might draw and label a strawberry or a skyscraper.

Skyscraper

Then write a story about someone who follows the path. Use the compound words on the mural in your story. Share your story and mural with the class.

# Language Enrichment
## Nouns

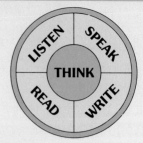

Use what you know about nouns to do these activities.

 **Zany Zoo**

Use nouns to put together a strange new animal. Work with a partner. Each of you should write the names of ten different body parts of animals on small pieces of paper. If you wish, add words that describe the parts. Here are some examples: *trunk, webbed feet, furry tail, horns like a cow's.*

Ask your partner to choose five pieces of paper from a box and read the nouns aloud. Then both of you draw a picture of an animal using those body parts. Compare drawings. Work together to think of names for your animals.

Put the pieces of paper back in the box and start over. This time you choose five pieces of paper. Soon you'll have a zoo of strange creatures.

 **Far-out Playground**

Imagine the most exciting playground in the world or in space. Write a description, telling about the playground's rides and equipment. Draw the playground, labeling the different parts. Share your work with your class.

 **Name Game**

Imagine that one day you have your own house, car, children, and pets. What names will you choose for them? Write names for eight places, people, animals, or things. Here's a sample list by Robin Webb.

| | |
|---|---|
| **house:** | Robin's Nest |
| **car:** | Mr. Wings |
| **child:** | Wendy |
| **pets:** | cat named Sunny, two goldfish named Atlantic and Pacific |

# CONNECTING

## LANGUAGE ◆➤ WRITING

In this unit you learned that nouns name people, places, things, and ideas. Nouns tell whom or what a sentence is about. Common nouns name any person, place, thing, or idea. Proper nouns name particular persons, places, or things.

◆ **Using Nouns in Your Writing** Knowing how to choose just the right noun to name something or someone is an important writing skill. When you use precise nouns, your readers get a clear picture of whom or what you are naming.

Pay special attention to the nouns you use as you do these activities.

### Compound Word Search

You learned about compound words on the **Building Vocabulary** pages. Use what you learned as you try this activity.

Take a page from a newspaper or an old magazine. Give yourself three minutes to see how many compound words you can find and circle. Put a check next to each compound word that is a noun.

Choose five of the most interesting compound words you have found and use them in sentences.

### People and Things on Parade

Here comes the parade! Imagine that you are the television announcer who must describe the parade for people watching at home. Write what you will say about the people and the things in the parade. Use precise nouns. Include the names of marchers, their hometowns, and other facts about them that your viewers may find interesting. Read what you have written to your classmates.

# Unit Checkup

| Think Back | Think Ahead |
|---|---|
| ◆ What did you learn about expository paragraphs in this unit? What did you do to write one? | ◆ How will what you learned help you when you read factual information? <br><br> ◆ How will knowing how to connect a main idea and details help you write an expository paragraph? A research report? |
| ◆ How did nouns help you name people, places, things, or ideas? How has that helped your writing? | ◆ What is one way you can use nouns to improve your writing? |

## Expository Paragraphs   *pages 70–71*

Read the expository paragraph. Then follow the directions.

> With kirigami, people of varying ages and skills can create lots of different objects for various purposes. Kirigami began in Japan. The word means "cutting paper." Whether you are young or old, Japanese or American, you can learn kirigami because it only involves using scissors and paper. You can use kirigami to create a gift for a child, like a jumping jack or a paper doll. Or if you are having a party, kirigami can be used to form invitations, party hats, or prizes for games. Kirigami excites everyone!

**1.** Write the topic sentence.        **2.** List key words in the topic sentence.

**3.** State one of the details in the paragraph.

## Connecting a Main Idea and Details   *page 72*

Read the following sentences. List all the words that describe the topic.

**4.** It is a good idea to spend time studying different kinds of art.

**5.** You might take a painting class at a museum.

**6.** The class would give you a chance to create some paintings.

**7.** You might discover artists who paint as you do.

## Using Examples   *page 73*

Read the following topic sentences. Write an example to support the main point of each topic sentence.

8. On any given day, your imagination sends you on a journey to faraway places.
9. Paintings are created through the use of imagination.
10. The works of many famous artists are found in art museums.
11. Some works of art are practical as well as beautiful.
12. If you study art long enough, you might uncover a hidden talent.

## The Writing Process   *pages 74−84*

13. If you were selecting a topic for an expository paragraph, which of the following topics would you cross off your list?
    **a.** imaginary plants          **b.** ones that interest you
    **c.** ones that you can find information about
14. Once you gather the information, what is the best way to organize it?
    **a.** Organize the information according to your interests.
    **b.** Present the main idea first, then arrange the related facts.
    **c.** Organize the information according to when it was found.
15. What is the purpose of an expository paragraph?
    **a.** to entertain          **b.** to inform          **c.** to persuade
16. Suppose a friend tells you that one of your examples is hard to understand. What should you do?
    **a.** Replace it with a simpler one.    **b.** Move the example.
    **c.** Check the spelling of the words in the example.
17. Which idea would be most appropriate for publishing?
    **a.** Put it in your writing log.    **b.** Keep it in your desk.
    **c.** Display the paragraph in your school library.

## Nouns   *pages 88−89*

Read each sentence. Write the nouns.

18. The teacher showed her students how to make a collage.
19. One student cut construction paper into different shapes.
20. Another student cut pictures from old magazines.
21. Each person glued the paper pieces or pictures on a poster.
22. The collages gave them artistic satisfaction.
23. One student even thought about becoming an artist.
24. He decided to make some more collages to give as gifts to family members.

## Singular and Plural Nouns   *pages 90–91*

Write each underlined noun. Then write *singular* or *plural* after it.

25. Andrew liked to ride on <u>bicycles</u>.
26. His brother Matthew preferred using his <u>tools</u>.
27. Matthew built imaginative <u>inventions</u>.
28. Andrew took bicycle trips to a secret <u>place</u>.
29. The two brothers enjoyed each other's <u>company</u>.
30. Their <u>friendship</u> is a nice thing to see.

## More Plural Nouns   *pages 92–93*

Write the plural form of each noun.

31. reindeer
32. calf
33. mosquito
34. belief
35. hero
36. fisherman
37. tooth
38. poncho
39. mouse
40. studio

## Common and Proper Nouns   *pages 94–95*

In each sentence the nouns are underlined. Write each noun. Then write *common* or *proper*.

41. <u>Manuel</u> visited the <u>National Air and Space Museum</u>.
42. He was very interested in outer-space <u>travel</u>.
43. Some <u>exhibits</u> showed <u>Manuel</u> older <u>forms</u> of air <u>travel</u>.
44. He liked the <u>exhibits</u> on space <u>travel</u> better.
45. He dreamed of working at the <u>Johnson Space Center</u>.

## Capitalization of Proper Nouns   *pages 96–97*

Write the proper nouns in each sentence correctly. Be sure to capitalize each important word.

46. We went on a wonderful vacation to florida.
47. Our family visited disney world and sea world.
48. Everyone enjoyed the sponge docks at tarpon springs.
49. Our favorite stops were miami beach and key west.
50. The cool breeze of the gulf of mexico was refreshing.

## Abbreviations   *pages 98–99*

Write each item. Abbreviate the underlined words.

51. (man) Thomas <u>Warren</u> Johnson, <u>Junior</u>
    Johnson Printing <u>Company</u>
    965 Maple <u>Street</u>

52. (doctor) Julio Ricardo Cardenas
    2201 Heartland Drive
53. (woman) Susan Tracy Anderson
    38 Pinewood Avenue
54. (reverend) James Bernard O'Malley
    4553 Beech Road
55. Creative Photographers, Incorporated
    6237 Jackson Boulevard

## Singular Possessive Nouns    *pages 100–101*

Write each sentence. Change the underlined words to include a singular possessive noun.

56. The visitors were fascinated by the shape of the sculpture.
57. The explanation of the museum guide only made them more curious about the sculpture.
58. One visitor liked the imagination of the sculptor.
59. Another person wanted to read about the life of the sculptor.
60. The guide wished the sculptor were present to answer the questions of the visitor.

## Plural Possessive Nouns    *pages 102–103*

Rewrite each sentence. Change the underlined words to include a plural possessive noun.

61. The audience watched the movements of the square dancers.
62. Some thought the steps of the dancers looked difficult.
63. The dancers increased the knowledge of the fans by telling them about the history of square dancing.
64. A few people wanted to take some classes and learn the dances of the performers.
65. They were glad to get the invitation of the square dancers.

## Compound Words    *pages 104–105*

Read each sentence. Write each compound word and its definition. Use a dictionary if necessary.

66. Bernard's great-great-grandfather was somewhat unusual.
67. His name was Patrick Forrest, and he worked as a bookkeeper.
68. Patrick Forrest dreamed of a different life, so he said farewell to his job and traveled west to homestead.
69. When he reached Colorado, he made money baking cupcakes and drawing lifelike pictures of people.

## 1-2 Cumulative Review

### Four Kinds of Sentences    *pages 36–37*

Read each sentence. Then write *declarative, interrogative, imperative,* or *exclamatory.*

1. Barry finally found the time to write a letter to his older sister, Beth.
2. When would she return home for a visit?
3. How pleased she was to receive Barry's letter!
4. Please write back soon.
5. I miss you so much!
6. Beth wrote Barry a letter and told him about her studies at college.
7. Tell me more about your latest hobby.
8. Barry and Beth have written many letters to each other over the years.
9. How many letters do you write per month?
10. I try to write to someone every week.

### Subjects and Predicates    *pages 38–39*

Add a simple subject or a simple predicate to each word group. Write the new sentence.

11. My family's broken _____ was fixed by someone from the telephone company.
12. My father _____ the telephone and talked for several minutes.
13. _____ told us that he could hardly hear what the speaker said.
14. My younger _____ watched the telephone worker as she used her tools.
15. Her metal _____ was filled with tools of all shapes and sizes.
16. The _____ rang more often than usual.
17. My best friend, Jill, _____ twice and asked me about our homework assignment.
18. _____ did well on her homework after she understood it.
19. The spelling lesson _____ Jill, but I helped her overcome her confusion.
20. Jill _____ her paper to her teacher with pride.

## Compound Subjects   *pages 46–47*

Write each sentence. Underline the simple subjects in each compound subject.

21. Flags, lights, and horns are three kinds of signals.
22. Smoke, drums, and fires are older types of signals.
23. Take-offs, landings, and course changes are controlled by signals to airplane pilots.
24. Boats, airplanes, and satellites help pass messages along in wartime.
25. Code books, flags, and messages are among the tools of people who send signals.

## Compound Predicates   *pages 48–49*

Write each sentence. Underline the simple predicates in each compound predicate.

26. Every summer, Pedro and his friends meet at a campsite and spend the night there.
27. Pedro packed his lunch and placed it in his knapsack.
28. He arrived at the campsite, saw his friends, and waved to them.
29. They hiked in the woods and stopped for lunch.
30. Pedro saw a bear and screamed.
31. He and his friends ran through the woods and left the campsite.
32. Pedro's scream warned and frightened them.

## Compound Sentences   *pages 50–51*

Write the compound sentences. If a sentence is not a compound sentence, write *simple sentence.*

33. She wants to communicate with her deaf brother, but she doesn't know sign language.
34. She plans to take a class and learn sign language.
35. Her brother is happy about her plan, and he has decided to help her practice.
36. She used to write him notes or wait for their mother to communicate for her.
37. Learning sign language will help her now, and she may use what she has learned in a future career.
38. She has learned enough sign language to express herself simply, but she still needs lots of practice.

## Nouns  *pages 88–89*

Write the nouns in each sentence.

39. Some people think museums mainly show the products of the imaginations of artists.
40. However, there are museums that teach people about real life.
41. The Arizona-Sonora Desert Museum seems more like a zoo or a garden than a museum.
42. The special museum is home to hundreds of plants and animals from the desert.
43. Visitors to this museum will find a garden full of cactus, as well as snakes, jaguars, and small deer.
44. At the museum, you won't have to imagine what the desert is like because you can see it for yourself.
45. The Sonora Desert is a region of the southwestern United States where water is hard to find.
46. The desert is often very hot during the day.
47. Sometimes, the temperature at noon can reach 120 degrees in the Sonora Desert.
48. In spite of the heat, many animals live in the desert.
49. Bats, snakes, tarantulas, lions, hawks, small rats, and mice can be found in regions where people live.
50. Cactuses come in various shapes and sizes.
51. The seeds of the cactus are scattered by animals and birds.
52. Some people think deserts are areas that have no life.
53. The Arizona-Sonora Desert is full of animals, birds, and plants.
54. The desert can be very beautiful at night when the sky is full of clear, bright stars.

## Singular and Plural Nouns  *pages 90–93*

Write each noun. Write *singular, plural,* or *both* after it. Write the plural form of each singular noun.

| | | |
|---|---|---|
| 55. trout | 62. ox | 69. press |
| 56. marches | 63. stereo | 70. thieves |
| 57. dancer | 64. paintbrush | 71. taxes |
| 58. rodeos | 65. cattle | 72. idea |
| 59. mystery | 66. author | 73. mass |
| 60. mosquitoes | 67. reef | 74. dye |
| 61. alley | 68. rhinoceros | 75. stories |

## Common and Proper Nouns  *pages 94–95*

Write each sentence. Underline the common nouns once.
Underline the proper nouns twice.

76. Bernard showed his friend Luis his latest drawing.

77. The picture looked wonderful to Luis.

78. Luis wondered how his friend got the ideas for his drawings.

79. They always showed unusual colors and shapes, and his latest drawing was an excellent example.

80. Luis told Bernard that he should take the artwork to school.

81. He could show the drawings to their teacher, Ms. Walker, and maybe she would exhibit the pictures.

82. Bernard was too shy to let Ms. Walker know about his drawings.

83. Luis thought Bernard should be proud of his skill.

84. Luis wanted to show the pictures to the entire class.

85. Ms. Walker asked the students for ideas for decorating the classroom.

86. Luis raised his hand, and Ms. Walker called on him.

87. Luis suggested that students who had drawings should bring them to display on the walls.

88. Ms. Walker said his idea was wonderful and asked students to volunteer to bring their artwork.

89. Bernard looked at Luis, smiled, and raised his hand.

## Singular Possessive Nouns and Plural Possessive Nouns  *pages 100–103*

Rewrite each sentence. Replace the underlined words with a
singular possessive noun or a plural possessive noun.

90. Sheila wanted a journal like the journal belonging to Elizabeth.

91. The mother of Sheila bought Sheila a journal with a blue leather cover.

92. Soon the stories of Sheila filled the blue journal.

93. The bookcases of many children contain journals.

94. The journals written by Sheila have stories about her daily life and her dreams for the future.

95. Journals are a great place for the ideas of Sheila.

96. Sheila enjoys writing about the activities of her friends.

# UNIT

# 3

# Giving Directions

◆ **COMPOSITION FOCUS:** How-to Paragraph
◆ **LANGUAGE FOCUS:** Verbs

The next time you go to the library or to a bookstore, ask for the "how-to" section. You'll be amazed at the number of how-to books you'll find and at the great variety of subjects. You'll discover books with directions and instructions for everything—from how to choose the best dog to how to hike in the Rocky Mountains.

Reading a how-to book is only one way in which people might follow directions. In fact, giving and following directions at school, at work, and at home are frequent and important daily activities.

For some of these activities, you *give* directions. For others, you *follow* them. In each case, directions provide important information.

Sometimes directions are given for fun activities. On the following pages you'll read how-to paragraphs written by fifth-graders in Oregon. The paragraphs tell how to make some simple and enjoyable arts-and-crafts items.

In this unit you will learn to write how-to paragraphs. You will also have opportunities to improve your skills in giving and following written and oral directions.

Sally Elizabeth Deck     Andy Sullivan     Kenna Elise Conklin     Cassidy Braverman

These fifth-graders wrote how-to paragraphs *to inform* others.

# Reading with a Writer's Eye
## How-to Paragraphs

Do you enjoy a hobby or an art activity that you would like others to know more about? The students in Mrs. Loveland's fifth-grade class at Eastside Alternative School in Eugene, Oregon, were asked to share their favorite arts-and-crafts activities with other fifth-graders. Here are four how-to paragraphs written by these student writers. Decide which one gives instructions that would be easiest for you to follow.

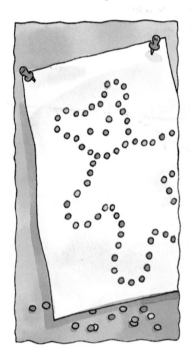

## How to Make Animal Dot Art
by Sally Elizabeth Deck

It is very easy to make animal dot art. It is also fun. First, you need one sheet (8½″ x 11″) of any color construction paper, a pencil, five to ten different colored scraps of paper, a hole punch, and a bottle of glue. With the pencil, draw an animal on the sheet of construction paper. Next, take the hole punch and punch out 75 little dots from the scraps of colored paper. Glue the dots on the lines of the animal. You can fill in the animal with dots if you want. As a final step, let it dry. You may hang it on a wall or make it into a card.

## How to Make a Tongue-Depressor Puppet
by Andy Sullivan

To make a tongue-depressor puppet, you need a tongue depressor, some paper, crayons, scissors, and glue. You start by cutting a shape out of paper with your scissors. Then, color the shape and, last but not least, glue it onto the tongue depressor. After you make some puppets, you can have a puppet show.

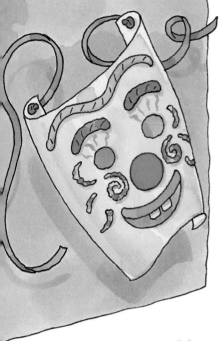

# How to Make a Mask
## by Kenna Elise Conklin

Masks are fun to make and wear. You need colored paper, scissors, a hole punch, elastic, glue, sparkles, and anything else you would like on your mask. First, you cut a piece of paper to fit the size of your head. Then, you cut out eye holes and cut the mask to be the shape you want. Next, glue sparkles or anything you want on your mask. Last, punch holes on either side of the mask with a hole punch and tie elastic in the holes so the mask will stay on your head. Then put it on!!!

# How to Make a Glue Picture
## by Cassidy Braverman

Here's how to make a glue picture. First, you need a piece of paper, glue in a plastic squeeze bottle, and any color tempera paint. Put the tempera paint into the glue bottle. Shake well. Then, squeeze the colored glue onto the paper. Make any design. Write your name or make a sentence. When you're done, let it dry for at least one hour.

## Respond

1. Which of the arts-and-crafts activities would you most like to try? Why? Would more information be helpful? If so, what questions would you like to ask the writer?

## Discuss

2. Which of these paragraphs is easiest for you to follow? What makes it easy to read and understand?
3. Without looking back, choose the paragraph you can remember best. Give the instructions in your own words. Then look back at the paragraph. Did you leave out anything?

# Thinking As a Writer
## Analyzing a How-to Paragraph

A how-to paragraph gives instructions for making or doing something. Kenna's directions for making the mask show what a good how-to paragraph should have: a topic sentence, a list of materials, and step-by-step instructions with time-order words.

Masks are fun to make and wear. You need colored paper, scissors, a hole punch, elastic, glue, sparkles, and anything else you would like on your mask. First, you cut a piece of paper to fit the size of your head. Then, you cut out eye holes and cut the mask to be the shape you want. Next, glue sparkles or anything you want on your mask. Last, punch holes on either side of the mask with a hole punch and tie elastic in the holes so the mask will stay on your head. Then put it on!!!

The **topic sentence** catches the reader's interest and indicates what kind of instructions will follow.

**Step-by-step instructions** tell how to make or do something. Time-order words make the instructions easier to follow. These may be single words such as *first, next, then,* and *finally,* or phrases such as *after you have finished* or *when the paper is dry.*

## Discuss

1. What is the topic sentence of the how-to paragraph? Does it tell clearly what the paragraph will be about? Explain your answer.
2. Where in the paragraph can you find the list of materials required to make a mask? Do you think this is a good place for the list? Explain your answer.
3. How many steps are described for making a mask? Are the steps in an order that seems to make sense? Why or why not? Which time-order words help explain the instructions step by step?

# Try Your Hand

**A. Analyze Topic Sentences**  Read the following how-to paragraphs. Each one has a topic sentence. Do you think the topic sentence of each paragraph catches the reader's interest? Why or why not?

1. This is how to make a peanut butter and banana sandwich. Make sure you have two slices of bread, peanut butter, a banana, a plate, and a knife. Place the two slices of bread on the plate. Spread peanut butter on one slice. Peel the banana and cut it in half the long way. Arrange the banana pieces on the peanut butter slice. Put the slices of bread together so that the banana slices are in the center.

2. This is how to make a miniature rock garden. Gather together the following materials: a shoe-box top, sand or dirt, small rocks, twigs, and leaves. Find a quiet place. Put a layer of sand or dirt in the top of a shoe box. Place the rocks in an interesting arrangement. Add small twigs or leaves for variety. Display your tiny rock garden, and look at it when you are in a quiet, thinking mood.

**B. Write Topic Sentences**  Reread each of the paragraphs in **A**. Replace each topic sentence with one that appeals more directly to the reader's interest.

**C. Add Time-Order Words**  Rewrite the body of each paragraph in **A**, adding a time-order word or phrase to each sentence.

**D. Read and Follow Instructions**  Choose one of the how-to paragraphs on pages 118 and 119, or find another how-to paragraph. Then gather materials and follow the directions. Display what you have made for your classmates.

## Writer's Notebook

**Collecting Time-Order Words**  Read the how-to paragraphs on pages 118 and 119 again. Also, look again at any other how-to paragraphs you found. Record sentences in your *Writer's Notebook* that have time-order words. Also, listen to the time-order words or phrases people use in their everyday conversations. Record some of these words and phrases in your *Writer's Notebook*. Try to use time-order words when you write or give directions.

# Thinking As a Writer
## Visualizing Steps in a Process

Before writing a how-to paragraph, a good writer makes a movie in his or her mind. The writer pictures the steps that need to be followed.

These are three of the steps for making a glue picture. Before writing them down, the writer visualized each step in the process. Visualizing each step helped the writer to remember that the glue bottle must be shaken before squeezing out the glue.

1. Put the tempera paint into the glue bottle.

2. Shake well.

3. Then, squeeze the colored glue onto the paper.

Before you write a how-to paragraph, be sure to make a movie in your mind of the process you want to describe. When you write your paragraph, describe the steps in the order in which they should be performed. Remember to use time-order words to help your readers follow the correct sequence.

## Discuss

1. In what ways can visualizing a process before writing anything down help a writer to give better how-to instructions?
2. Look again at the how-to paragraphs on pages 118 and 119. Do you think each writer visualized the instructions before writing his or her paragraph? Explain your answer.

## Try Your Hand

**Write Time-Order Words and Phrases** Picture an activity that you know how to do. Write three instruction steps, each in a separate sentence that begins with a single time-order word. On another sheet of paper, rewrite the sentences so that each begins with a time-order phrase such as *after shaking it* or *at the end*. Compare your time-order phrases with a partner's. Discuss which words and phrases work best to help a reader picture your activity.

# Developing the Writer's Craft
## Writing for an Audience and a Purpose

Good writers write instructions for the same task or project differently for different audiences. For example, instructions for planning a party would be short and simple for eight-year-olds but longer and more detailed for adults.

The writer's purpose is to make it possible for readers to understand and carry out instructions successfully.

Read these sentences from a student's how-to paragraph.

Next, take the hole punch and punch out 75 little dots from the scraps of colored paper. Glue the dots on the lines of the animal. You can fill in the animal with dots if you want. As a final step, let it dry.

The writer was giving directions to fifth-grade students. To make the directions clear, the writer told how to punch out and glue paper dots in four steps. Each step tells one task.

When you write your how-to paragraph, keep your audience and your purpose in mind. Remember to use language that will allow your audience to carry out your instructions successfully.

## Discuss

1. Look at the how-to paragraph on page 119 about making a mask. What are two details the writer might not have included for an adult audience?
2. If the writer were writing her instructions for first-grade students, she would have had to explain more. What are three more details the writer might have decided to include?

## Try Your Hand

**Adjust Instructions for Another Audience and Purpose**  Rewrite one of the how-to paragraphs on pages 118 and 119. Imagine that the directions will be used by first-grade students to make gifts for their families.

# 1 Prewriting
## How-to Paragraph

Susan, a student at Springhill Elementary School, needed to write a paragraph to accompany her project for the school crafts fair. She used the checklist in the **Writer's Guide** to plan her paragraph. Look at what she did.

**Writer's Guide**

**Prewriting Checklist**
- ☑ Brainstorm topics.
- ☑ Select a topic.
- ☑ Think about your audience and your purpose.
- ☑ Gather information.
- ☑ Put information in step-by-step order.

## ◆ Brainstorming and Selecting a Topic

First, Susan listed all the arts-and-crafts activities she could think of. Look at Susan's list.

Next, Susan looked over her list and crossed out activities that most students at her school might already know how to do. She also crossed out activities that might be difficult for students and topics that might take more than one paragraph to explain.

Finally, Susan circled the topic that would appeal to students, that would not be too difficult to do, and that she could explain most clearly.

> building a model railroad
> making snow sculptures
> *a theme collage*
> face painting
> underwater photography
> tracing cartoon characters

## Discuss

1. Look at the topics Susan crossed off her list. Which ones might students already know how to do? Which might be hard for students at her school to try by themselves? Which might need more than a short paragraph to explain?

**2.** Suppose that Susan were choosing a craft activity for a party instead of for a crafts exhibit. Which activity might she have chosen? Why? Describe how the audience and the purpose are different.

## ◆ Gathering Information

After Susan chose her topic, she decided to list all the materials and the steps she would need to cover in her paragraph. She made a list with two headings: *materials* and *steps*. Then she imagined herself going through the process of making a theme collage. As she pictured herself making the collage, she filled in her list of *materials* and *steps*.

Here is Susan's list.

> Materials
> old magazines
> construction paper
> glue
>
>
> Steps
> Select pictures in magazines.
> Pick a theme.
> Cut out pictures.
> Arrange pictures on construction paper.
> Glue pictures to paper.

## Discuss

1. Look at Susan's list of materials and steps. Why is it a good idea to picture yourself doing an activity when you are making such a list?
2. Susan has left out at least one item from her materials list. What is it? (The list of steps will give you a hint.)

# ◆ Organizing Information

After Susan had listed all the materials and the steps for her project, she was ready to organize them. She knew that the best way to explain a process to someone is to tell about one step at a time. She therefore decided to put the materials and the steps in time order.

Susan decided to list all the materials together near the beginning of her paragraph so that readers could have them ready before starting the collage. She then numbered the steps in time order.

*Materials*
*old magazines*
*construction paper*
*glue*

*Steps*
*2 Select pictures in magazines.*
*1 Pick a theme.*
*3 Cut out pictures.*
*4 Arrange pictures on construction paper.*
*5 Glue pictures down.*

To make sure that the sequence in her list was complete and clear, Susan showed it to her friend Robert. Robert asked her why choosing a theme came before selecting pictures in magazines. Also, he pointed out that Susan had not included scissors in her list of materials. Susan made notes of Robert's questions and comments to use when she wrote her how-to paragraph.

## Discuss

1. Susan first thought she would list "select pictures" before "pick a theme." Then, she changed her mind. Do you agree or disagree with her numbered revision?
2. Why is it important for both the listener and the direction-giver to picture themselves following the instructions?

# Try Your Hand

Now plan a how-to paragraph of your own.

**A. Brainstorm and Select Possible Topics** Brainstorm a list of possible topics for a how-to paragraph explaining an arts-and-crafts activity. Think about each topic. Think about the audience for whom you will write.

- ◆ Cross out activities that your audience would probably already know how to do.
- ◆ Cross out topics that might be hard for students to try on their own.
- ◆ Cross out topics that might be hard to explain in a short paragraph.

**B. List Materials and Steps** Imagine yourself doing the activity you have chosen. Make a list of materials and a list of steps for your activity. You may find it helpful to use one of these charts.

| Materials | Steps |
|-----------|-------|
|           |       |

**C. Check the Sequence** Look over your list of materials and steps.

- ◆ Read carefully to be sure you have included all the necessary steps.
- ◆ Add any missing materials or steps (for example, add *scissors* to Susan's list).
- ◆ Number the list of steps according to time order so that you can easily see the sequence of steps.

 **Save your list of materials and your numbered list of steps in your *Writer's Notebook*. You will use them when you draft your how-to paragraph.**

# Listening and Speaking
## Tips for Listening to and Giving Directions

## Listening to Directions

1. Give all your attention to the directions.
2. Think about the order of the steps in the directions. Picture yourself following the steps as you hear them.
3. Ask questions.
4. Make notes if necessary. Even points that seem clear while you are listening may not seem clear later unless you have taken notes.
5. If possible, try the activity to make sure you understand the directions.

## Giving Directions

1. Plan what you will say. Make notes ahead of time.
2. Give the steps in sequence. Use time-order words and phrases to help your listener.
3. Give complete details. Picture yourself going through the steps as you explain them.
4. Pause and check to make sure your listener understands. Ask if he or she has any questions.
5. If the listener is confused, try explaining in a new way.
6. If possible, demonstrate to the listener what steps to follow.

# 2 Drafting
## How-to Paragraph

Susan thought about her audience and the best way to make her explanation easy to follow. She followed the checklist in the **Writer's Guide** to draft her how-to paragraph. Look at what Susan did.

> **Writer's Guide**
>
> **Drafting Checklist**
> - ☑ Use your list of materials and your numbered list of steps for ideas.
> - ☑ Write a topic sentence first.
> - ☑ Explain the steps in time order.
> - ☑ Use one sentence for each step.

*A theme collage is a colorful way to express an idea. When I first heard the word collage, it reminded me of college! To make your collage, you will need to have a large table, scissors, old magazines, construction paper, and glue. Pick a theme. Then, select magazine pictures.*

## Discuss

1. Look at the first sentences of Susan's paragraph. What time-order words has she used?
2. What additional steps could you add to Susan's paragraph?

## Try Your Hand

Now you are ready to write a how-to paragraph.

**A. Review Your Information**   Look at the list you made in the last lesson. Does the time order still make sense? If not, renumber your list.

**B. Think About Your TAP**   Remember that your task is to write a how-to paragraph. Your purpose is to tell your audience how to do something.

**Task:** What?
**Audience:** Who?
**Purpose:** Why?

**C. Write Your First Draft**   Follow the steps in the **Drafting Checklist** to write your how-to paragraph.

When you write your draft, just put all your ideas on paper. Do not worry about spelling, punctuation, or grammar. You can correct the draft later.

**Save your first draft in your *Writer's Notebook*. You will use it when you revise your how-to paragraph.**

# 3 Responding and Revising
## How-to Paragraph

Susan used the checklist in the **Writer's Guide** to revise her how-to paragraph. To make sure that someone could follow the instructions in her paragraph, she read it to a classmate.

### ◆ Checking Information

When Susan read her first draft to Kim, Kim asked Susan if it was really necessary to have a table to make a collage. Susan realized that it was not. She used this mark ✄ to cut that information.

### ◆ Checking Organization

Kim also expressed some confusion about the order of the steps in the how-to paragraph. Susan agreed to add more time-order words by using this mark ∧ .

### ◆ Checking Language

When Susan checked the sentences in her paragraph, she realized that her audience needed to know the definition of *collage* at the beginning. She used this mark ◡ to move the definition. She also decided that the sentence about *collage* and *college* did not suit her purpose. She used this mark ✄ to cut it.

**Writer's Guide**

**Revising Checklist**
- ☑ Read your how-to paragraph to yourself or to a partner.
- ☑ Think about your audience and your purpose. Add missing steps or materials. Take out unnecessary steps, materials, or information.
- ☑ Check that the steps in your paragraph are given in time order.
- ☑ Check that your language is appropriate for your purpose and audience.

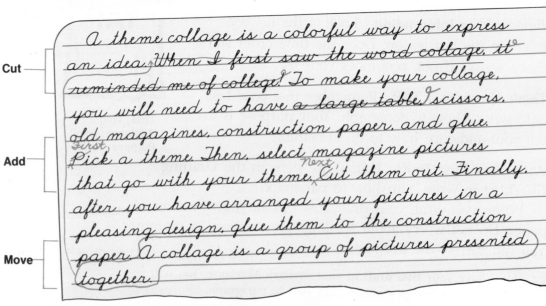

Cut —

Add —

Move —

A theme collage is a colorful way to express an idea. When I first saw the word collage, it reminded me of college! To make your collage, you will need to have a large table, scissors, old magazines, construction paper, and glue. First, Pick a theme. Then, select magazine pictures that go with your theme. Next, Cut them out. Finally, after you have arranged your pictures in a pleasing design, glue them to the construction paper. A collage is a group of pictures presented together.

## Discuss

1. Is the explanation of *collage* that Susan added helpful? Why or why not?
2. Should any other steps or materials be included in Susan's paragraph? Should any other sentences be moved? Explain your answer.

## Try Your Hand

Now revise your first draft.

**A. Read Your First Draft** As you read your how-to paragraph, think about your audience and your purpose. Read your paragraph silently or to a partner to see if it is complete and well organized. Ask yourself or your partner the questions in the box.

| Responding and Revising Strategies | |
|---|---|
| ✔ **Respond**<br>**Ask yourself or a partner:** | ✔ **Revise**<br>**Try these solutions:** |
| ◆ Have I included all the steps? | ◆ **Add** any missing steps. |
| ◆ Have I listed all necessary materials? | ◆ **Add** any missing materials to your list. |
| ◆ Are the steps easy to follow? | ◆ **Use** time-order words or phrases to indicate the step-by-step order. |
| ◆ Have I written sentences that are correct and concise? | ◆ **Rewrite** run-on sentences. See the **Revising Workshop** on page 132. |
| ◆ Have I used language that is appropriate for my audience and my purpose? | ◆ **Reword** what may be unclear to your audience or what may not suit your purpose. |

**B. Make Your Changes** If the answer to any question in the box is *no,* try the solution. Use the **Editor's Marks** to show your changes.

**C. Review Your Paragraph Again** Decide whether there is anything else you want to revise. Keep revising your how-to paragraph until you feel it is well organized and complete.

> **EDITOR'S MARKS**
> ∧ Add something.
> ✒ Cut something.
> ⤵ Move something.
> ⌃ Replace something.

 **Save your revised how-to paragraph in your *Writer's Notebook*. You will use it when you proofread your paragraph.**

# Revising Workshop
## Correcting Run-on Sentences

Good writers avoid run-on sentences. Look at these two pairs of sentences.

1. Henry picked up the glue he spread it on the poster.
2. Henry picked up the glue. He spread it on the poster.
3. The pictures were beautiful the captions were funny.
4. The pictures were beautiful, and the captions were funny.

The first sentence is a run-on sentence. The writer has combined two simple sentences without separating them with correct punctuation or connecting words. In the second item, the writer has corrected the run-on sentence by rewriting it as two simple sentences. The third item is also a run-on sentence. In the fourth item, the writer has corrected this run-on sentence by rewriting it as one compound sentence.

Run-on sentences may be rewritten as simple sentences or as compound sentences. Remember that the simple sentences must contain related ideas if you want to rewrite them as a compound sentence.

## Practice

Rewrite each run-on sentence to make either two simple sentences or one compound sentence. If you make a compound sentence, remember to add a comma plus *and, or,* or *but.*

1. Jackie wanted to make a collage she needed paper, scissors, and glue.
2. She picked up her mother's scissors her mother said they were too sharp.
3. Jackie's mother took them away she gave Jackie scissors with blunt points.
4. Jackie emptied a bag of colorful paper she found many lovely colors.
5. Jackie cut out all kinds of shapes she arranged them on a large sheet of paper.
6. Jackie decided to make her collage from the most interesting shapes the result was beautiful.

# 4 Proofreading
## How-to Paragraph

### Writer's Guide

**Proofreading Checklist**

☑ Check for errors in capitalization.

☑ Check for errors in punctuation. Be sure that you have used commas after time-order words.

☑ Check to see that your paragraph is indented.

☑ Check your grammar.

☑ Circle any words you think are misspelled. Find out how to spell them correctly.

⇨ For proofreading help, use the **Writer's Handbook.**

After Susan revised her how-to paragraph, she used the checklist in the **Writer's Guide** and the **Editor's Marks** to proofread it. Look at what she did.

> ¶ This collage can be an excellent
> ~~deceration~~ *decoration* for your room. ~~you~~
> can also make a special
> holiday greeting by putting
> your collage on the outside of a
> card. At first, I ~~planed~~ *planned* just to
> show my collage in the crafts
> ~~fare,~~ *fair* but I ended up ~~giveing~~ *giving* it
> to my aunt for her birthday.

## Discuss

1. Look at Susan's proofread paragraph. What kinds of mistakes did she make?
2. Which mark did Susan use to place commas after time-order words?

## Try Your Hand

**Proofread Your How-to Paragraph**  Now use the **Writer's Guide** and the **Editor's Marks** to proofread your paragraph.

Save your corrected how-to paragraph in your *Writer's Notebook.* You will use it when you publish your how-to paragraph.

### EDITOR'S MARKS

≡ Capitalize.

⊙ Add a period.

∧ Add something.

⋏ Add a comma.

ᵛⱽ Add quotation marks.

✂ Cut something.

⋀ Replace something.

∾ Transpose.

◯ Spell correctly.

⊬ Indent paragraph.

/ Make a lowercase letter.

# 5 Publishing
## How-to Paragraph

**Writer's Guide**

**Publishing Checklist**

☑ Make a clean copy of your how-to paragraph.

☑ Check to see that nothing has been left out.

☑ Check that there are no mistakes.

☑ Share your how-to paragraph in a special way.

Susan made a clean copy of her how-to paragraph and checked it to make sure she had not left anything out. Then she and her classmates posted their paragraphs next to their projects for the crafts fair. You can find Susan's paragraph on page 25 of the **Writer's Handbook.**

Here's how Susan and her classmates published their how-to paragraphs.

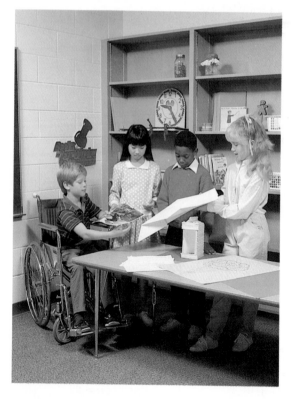

1. First, they set up a crafts fair. Susan and her classmates brought in their crafts projects. If the projects could not be carried to school, they brought photographs or drawings instead.

2. Next, the students arranged the crafts exhibits in the classroom, and posted their how-to paragraphs next to them. They made copies of each how-to paragraph and set a stack of copies next to each exhibit.

WRITING PROCESS

3. Susan and her classmates then enjoyed each other's crafts and explanations. They invited other classes to visit their crafts fair. They also gave copies of the how-to paragraphs to others who wished to try the projects themselves.

## Discuss

1. Why is it a good idea to have each how-to paragraph posted next to the craft it tells how to make?
2. Would observers be encouraged by the how-to paragraphs to try the crafts themselves? Why or why not?

## Try Your Hand

**Publish Your How-to Paragraph**   Follow the checklist in the **Writer's Guide.** If possible, have a class crafts fair, or try one of these ideas for sharing your how-to paragraph.

◆ Post your how-to paragraph on a bulletin board. Create an eye-catching bulletin board title like *How-to Hot Line.*
◆ Take copies of each other's paragraphs home, and try the projects.
◆ Make a class book, using a copy of each paragraph. Present the book to the school library, the local library, or your principal.

# Writing in the Content Areas

Writer's Guide

When you write, remember the stages of the Writing Process.
- Prewriting
- Drafting
- Responding and Revising
- Proofreading
- Publishing

Use what you learned to write about daily activities at your school. You could write a how-to paragraph for a new student. One way to publish your writing is to put together a booklet called "A Guide to Our School." Use one of these ideas or an idea of your own.

## Physical Education

When it comes to climbing a rope, shooting a basket, or swinging a baseball bat, you may be an expert. Look at one physical activity closely. Then write a paragraph in which you list each step and movement. Make sure that someone who has never tried the activity could learn how to do it from reading your paragraph.

## Social Studies

Make a map of your school. Include information that would be important to a new student. Then write a paragraph telling the new student how to follow your map in order to take a tour of your school. If you wish, use numbers on your map to show important places. Refer to the numbers as you guide the new student through your school.

## Health

Your stomach is growling. It's time for lunch! So what do you do? You head for your school cafeteria, of course. Once you get there, what steps do you take to get your meal? Write a guide to using your cafeteria for someone who has never been there before.

## Literature

Write clues for a library treasure hunt in which the treasure is a book, a film, or a magazine. In your first clue, tell a hunter how to find a listing for the item in the card catalogue. In the second clue, tell how to use the card to learn where in the library the item is located. Exchange clues with a classmate.

# CONNECTING
## WRITING ⬌ LANGUAGE

Writers of how-to articles take information they know and share it with their readers. A well-written how-to paragraph shows a reader exactly how to do or make something. It lets the reader see the steps in his or her mind before beginning. What do you see in your mind's eye as you read these instructions?

### How to Create a Perfect Baseball Glove

Do you want a perfect baseball glove this season? If so, start last fall. You heard me correctly! Shop for your glove at the end of the baseball season, when prices drop. This gives you all the time you need. Buy some linseed oil and a baseball. First, rub linseed oil into your glove. This protects it and makes it more flexible. Then, pour one tablespoon of linseed oil into the palm of the glove and rub it in with a rag. Push your hand into the glove until it feels comfortable. Find the place where the ball fits best, hold the ball in the glove, and remove your hand. Tie string tightly around the glove to keep the ball in place. Then, put your glove away and forget about it until the grass sprouts on the ball field.

◆ **Verbs in a How-to Paragraph**   The words in color are action verbs. They do the job of telling what action takes place. Verbs also help you know how many people or things perform an action. The verb *makes* ends in s so you know that *one* thing does the action.

◆ **Language Focus: Verbs**   The following lessons will help you use different kinds of verbs in your own writing.

# 1 Action Verbs

◆ **FOCUS** An **action verb** is a word that tells what the subject of a sentence does or did.

Remember that the predicate of a sentence tells what the subject does or did. The main word in the predicate is a verb. Most verbs are action verbs. The words in color are action verbs.

1. Ships carry people and cargo.
2. The passenger boards the airplane.
3. Buses travel along the highway.

> ### Link to Speaking and Writing
> You can paint a clear and vivid picture if you use strong action verbs. Why is *zooms* more vivid than *moves*? What other strong action verbs could you use?

*The plane moves down the runway.* (with "zooms" written above "moves")

## Guided Practice

**A.** Identify the action verb in each sentence.
1. Long ago people walked everywhere.
2. They wore sandals on their feet.
3. A five-mile trip took two hours.

**B.** Name a more vivid action verb for each sentence. Use your **Writer's Thesaurus** if you need help.
4. Boats move across the surface of the water.
5. The speeding boats hit some waves.
6. The bumps scare the passengers.

> **THINK AND REMEMBER**
> ◆ Use an action verb to tell what the subject of a sentence does or did.
> ◆ Use strong action verbs to paint a vivid picture.

# Independent Practice

**C. Identifying Action Verbs**  Read each sentence. Write the action verb.

7. Horses eat oats and hay.

MODEL > eat

8. People used horses for transportation.
9. Early Spanish settlers brought horses here.
10. American Indians called horses "big dogs."
11. Horses plowed fields for farmers.
12. Soldiers rode horses in the Revolutionary War.
13. A horse moves more quickly than a person.
14. Racehorses gallop at almost 50 miles per hour.

**D. Using Action Verbs in Sentences**  Read each sentence. Write an action verb from the box to fill in the blank.

15. The first plane _____ in 1903.

MODEL > flew

16. The Wright brothers _____ the first airplane.
17. They _____ the plane from Kitty Hawk, North Carolina.
18. Orville Wright _____ into the plane.
19. The plane _____ 120 feet in 12 seconds.
20. Wilbur Wright _____ from the ground.
21. Wilbur _____ a ride in the plane later that day.

| built |
| stepped |
| waved |
| flew |
| enjoyed |
| traveled |
| launched |

**E. Revising Sentences**  Rewrite each sentence. Replace the verb with a more vivid action verb. Use the **Writer's Thesaurus** for help.

22. The car moves along the road.

MODEL > The car bounces along the road.

23. The driver runs his car into a wall.
24. People come to his aid.
25. An ambulance takes him to the hospital.
26. The doctor looks at the patient.

## Application — Writing

**Journal Entry**  Imagine that the date is 100 years from today. A new mode of transportation has just been invented, and you try it. Write a journal entry describing your experience. Use action verbs to tell how the invention works and how you feel as you use it. If you need help writing a journal entry, see page 31 of the **Writer's Handbook.**

# 2 Linking Verbs

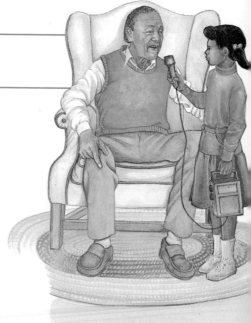

◆ **FOCUS**  A **linking verb** connects the subject to a word or words in the predicate.

Remember that an action verb tells what the subject of a sentence does or did. Not all verbs are action verbs. Notice the words in color in these sentences. They are linking verbs.

**1.** Ginnie is curious.

**2.** Grandpa was a teacher.

A linking verb is followed by a word or words in the predicate that name or describe the subject. In sentence 1, the verb *is* connects the subject *Ginnie* with the describing word *curious.* In sentence 2, the verb *was* connects the subject *Grandpa* with the noun *teacher.* Both *is* and *was* are forms of *be,* the most common linking verb. The chart shows the forms of *be.*

| Using the Forms of *Be* | | |
|---|---|---|
| Use *am* or *was* | with *I* | I am a surfer.<br>I was angry. |
| Use *is* or *was* | with *he, she, it,*<br>and singular nouns | She is a judge.<br>The cup was empty. |
| Use *are* or *were* | with *we, you, they,*<br>and plural nouns | We are students.<br>The pens were dry. |

The verbs *look, seem, feel, become, appear, taste, smell,* and *grow* are linking verbs when they connect the subject with a noun or a describing word.

**3.** Grandpa became the principal.     **4.** Ginnie felt happy.

## Guided Practice

**A.** Identify the linking verb in each sentence. Name the words that the linking verb connects.

**1.** Ginnie is a reporter for the school paper.

**2.** Grandpa appeared happy about the interview.

**3.** Grandpa was a child in 1935.

**4.** Life seemed different then.

## Independent Practice

**B. Identifying Linking Verbs**   Write each sentence. Underline each linking verb. Draw an arrow between the words each verb links.

5. The school was far from my house.

MODEL⟩ The school <u>was</u> far from my house.

6. The schoolroom felt cold.

7. The only heater was a wood stove.

8. The first snowflakes looked enormous.

9. The knocks on the door were noisy.

10. It was my father with his sleigh.

11. Soon, we were safe at home.

**C. Using the Linking Verb Be**   Write the form of *be* in parentheses ( ) that correctly completes each sentence.

12. Laura Ingalls Wilder (was, were) a teacher.

MODEL⟩ was

13. Her students (was, were) the children of farmers.
14. The school (was, were) a small house on the prairie.
15. This book (is, are) the story of Laura's experiences.
16. The title (is, am) *These Happy Golden Years*.
17. Jenny (is, am) eager to read the book.
18. I (was, were) lucky to find it at the library.
19. I (is, am) going to return it today.

## Application — Writing

**History Article**   Imagine that you are writing a paragraph for an article. This article will appear in an American history magazine for students. Describe how a normal daily activity was done a hundred years ago and how it is done today. Use linking verbs in your writing.

# 3 Main Verbs and Helping Verbs

♦ The **main verb** is the most important verb in the predicate.
♦ A **helping verb** works with the main verb to show action.

I was walking
at one year.

Remember that the simple predicate of a sentence is a verb. Sometimes the simple predicate is more than one word. It is made up of a main verb and a helping verb.

1. I was walking at eleven months old.
2. Now I have climbed a mountain.
3. My sister will come with me next time.

In sentences 1, 2, and 3, *was, have,* and *will* are helping verbs. They work with the main verbs *walking, climbed,* and *come.* The main verb is the most important verb in the simple predicate.

I have hiked up
Mount Baldy.

| Using Helping Verbs | |
|---|---|
| When the helping verb is *am, is, are, was,* or *were,* the main verb often ends in *ing.* | I *am* helping. <br> You *are* helping. <br> They *were* helping. |
| When the helping verb is *has, have,* or *had,* the main verb often ends in *ed.* | He *has* laughed. <br> We *have* laughed. <br> They *had* laughed. |
| When the helping verb is *will,* the main verb does not change. | You *will* become a citizen. |

## Guided Practice

**A.** Identify each underlined verb as a *helping verb* or a *main verb.*

1. I <u>was</u> <u>laughing</u> at my baby pictures.
2. My teacher <u>had</u> <u>asked</u> for a picture.
3. The class <u>will</u> <u>hang</u> the pictures on a bulletin board.
4. We <u>are</u> <u>matching</u> pictures with people's names.
5. In my picture I <u>am</u> <u>eating</u> baby cereal.
6. I <u>have</u> <u>changed</u> my eating habits since then.

## Independent Practice

**B. Identifying Main Verbs and Helping Verbs**   Make a chart with two columns. Head them *Helping Verbs* and *Main Verbs*. Write each underlined verb in the correct column.

7. Scientists <u>have</u> <u>studied</u> babies.

| Helping Verbs | Main Verbs |
|---|---|
| have | studied |

MODEL

8. Most children <u>will</u> <u>walk</u> at one year.
9. My other brother <u>had</u> <u>crawled</u> at eight months.
10. Now Barney <u>is</u> <u>pulling</u> himself up.
11. Soon the baby <u>will</u> <u>stand</u> alone.
12. Now I <u>am</u> <u>watching</u> him.
13. Barney <u>is</u> <u>holding</u> onto the bookshelf.
14. Suddenly he <u>has</u> <u>stepped</u> across the room!

**C. Using Helping Verbs**   Write a helping verb that will complete each sentence. Use *am, is, are, have, has,* or *will.*

15. I _____ developing good mountain-climbing skills.

MODEL  am

16. My family _____ hike up the mountain next Saturday.
17. People _____ building a hiking trail on the mountain.
18. They _____ chopped down some trees.
19. My friend _____ use the trail.
20. She _____ joining a mountaineering club.
21. The club _____ raised money for the new trail.
22. They _____ planned a hike for next month.

## Application — Writing

**Personal Narrative**   Recall something that you have learned to do. Write a narrative paragraph about this skill. Explain how you have used your skill and how you will use it in the future. Use main verbs and helping verbs in your writing. If you need help writing a personal narrative, see page 32 of the **Writer's Handbook.**

# 4 Present Tense

◆ **FOCUS** A **present-tense verb** shows action that happens now.

Gardeners plant peas in March.

A pea plant grows quickly.

The tense of a verb shows when an action happens. The words in color are present-tense verbs.

1. The gardener plants the peas carefully.

2. Peas grow rapidly.

There are two forms of present-tense verbs. In sentence 1, *plants* is a singular verb. A **singular verb** follows a singular subject. In sentence 2, *grow* is a plural verb. A **plural verb** follows a plural subject. When the correct present-tense verb is used, the subject and verb agree.

This chart shows how to spell the present-tense forms of many verbs.

| How to Spell Present-Tense Verbs |
|---|
| **Add s to most verbs.**<br>dig—digs          plant—plants |
| **For verbs ending in s, ss, ch, sh, x, and zz, add es.**<br>guess—guesses     watch—watches     fix—fixes |
| **For verbs ending with a consonant plus y, change the y to i and add es.**<br>try—tries          fly—flies |

## Guided Practice

**A.** Identify the form of the verb in parentheses ( ) that correctly completes each sentence.

1. Many people _____ gardens. (enjoy, enjoys)
2. First, you _____ away the grass. (take, takes)
3. I _____ a rake and a hoe. (find, finds)
4. The hoe _____ into the ground. (dig, digs)
5. Jeri _____ dirt from her hoe. (wash, washes)
6. A gardener _____ soil with fertilizer. (mix, mixes)
7. He _____ the weather carefully. (watch, watches)

## Independent Practice

**B. Identifying the Correct Verb Form**   Write the form of the verb in parentheses ( ) that correctly completes each sentence.

   **8.** Peas _____ well in cool weather. (grow, grows)

MODEL▷ grow

   **9.** The pea vine _____ up to my window. (reach, reaches)
  **10.** A bee _____ in through the window. (fly, flies)
  **11.** My sister _____ it for me in a jar. (catch, catches)
  **12.** We _____ the bee out the window. (toss, tosses)
  **13.** The bee _____ around the blossoms. (buzz, buzzes)
  **14.** It _____ nectar back to its hive. (carry, carries)

**C. Spelling Verbs Correctly**   Write the present-tense form of the verb in parentheses ( ) that correctly completes each sentence.

  **15.** The farmer _____ seeds into the soil. (press)

MODEL▷ presses

  **16.** Tiny corn plants _____ through the soil. (push)
  **17.** The farmer _____ about the hot weather. (worry)
  **18.** A hose _____ water over the corn plants. (spray)
  **19.** The water _____ my bare feet. (splash)
  **20.** The field _____ in the hot sun. (dry)
  **21.** Soon the plants _____ higher than my head. (rise)

**D. Writing Original Sentences**   Write two sentences using each verb. Write one sentence using the plural form. Then write one sentence using the singular form.

  **22.** sell

MODEL▷ Farmers sell the peas. The crop sells well.
  **23.** pass    **24.** empty    **25.** buy    **26.** watch    **27.** give

## Application — Writing and Speaking

**Riddle**   Choose a fruit or a vegetable. Write sentences that give information about the fruit or vegetable. Do not give its name. Use present-tense verbs in your sentences. Then read your riddle to a partner. Ask your partner to try to guess your fruit or vegetable.

# 5 Past Tense

◆ **FOCUS**  A **past-tense verb** shows action that already happened.

Remember that a verb in the present tense shows action that is happening now. A verb in the past tense shows action that already happened. The past tense of most verbs is formed by adding *ed*. The words in color are past-tense verbs.

1. Stoves and fireplaces warmed people in 1900.
2. They heated small areas at a time.

This chart shows how to spell the past-tense form of many verbs.

| How to Spell Past-Tense Verbs |
| --- |
| **For most verbs, add *ed*.** <br> stay—stayed      watch—watched |
| **For verbs ending in e, drop the e and add *ed*.** <br> live—lived      hope—hoped |
| **For verbs ending with a consonant plus *y*, change the *y* to *i* and add *ed*.** <br> study—studied      worry—worried |
| **For verbs ending with a consonant-vowel-consonant, double the last consonant and add *ed*.** <br> pop—popped      plan—planned |

## Guided Practice

**A.** Spell the past-tense form of the verb in parentheses ( ) to correctly complete each sentence.

1. My brothers _____ firewood into the house. (carry)
2. They _____ the wood into the stove. (stuff)
3. The dry wood _____ in the fire. (crackle)
4. We _____ bread over the fire. (toast)
5. It _____ delicious. (taste)
6. I _____ a brick on top of the stove. (warm)
7. Dad _____ the brick in a thick towel. (wrap)
8. He _____ the brick at the foot of my bed. (place)

## Independent Practice

**B. Using Past-Tense Verbs**   Write the past-tense form of each verb in parentheses ( ).

9. Early Americans _____ fireplaces for heat. (use)

MODEL ▷ used

10. They _____ their meals in the fireplace. (cook)
11. Settlers _____ down trees for firewood. (chop)
12. The dark cabins _____ light and warmth. (need)
13. The settlers _____ ashes in their fields. (bury)
14. The ashes _____ the soil. (improve)
15. Colonists _____ young trees in the forest. (plant)
16. The new trees _____ the old ones. (replace)

**C. Classifying Verbs**   Write the verb from each sentence. Then write *present* or *past.*

17. We open our history books.

MODEL ▷ open—present

18. We study early American food.
19. American Indians introduced popcorn to the settlers.
20. The little kernels pop in the hot air.
21. Settlers shipped popcorn to their friends in Europe.
22. The noisy snack amazed Europeans.
23. Americans like popcorn.
24. We all enjoy a healthful, delicious snack.

**D. 25. – 29. Revising Sentences**   Rewrite each sentence in C that has a present-tense verb. Change the verb to the past tense.

25. We open our history books.

MODEL ▷ We opened our history books.

## Application — Writing

**Museum Description**   Imagine that you are writing notes for a guided tour in a history museum. Describe the old-fashioned stove in the picture. Tell how you think it worked and how people used it. Use past-tense verbs in your description.

# 6 Future Tense

◆ **FOCUS**   A **future-tense verb** shows action that will happen.

Remember that a present-tense verb shows action that happens now.

**1.** The class closes the time capsule.
present tense

Remember that a past-tense verb shows action that already happened.

**2.** They filled the time capsule yesterday.
past tense

A verb in the future tense shows action that will happen.

**3.** They will bury it behind the school.
future tense

To form the future tense of a verb, use the helping verb *will* with the main verb.

**4.** Mr. Sanchez will dig the hole.

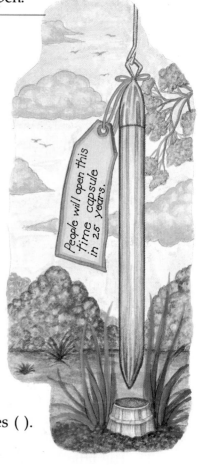

## Guided Practice

**A.** Name the future-tense form of the verb in parentheses ( ).

1. Mia (read) her letter aloud.
2. Jay (paint) a picture of the school.
3. Mr. Sanchez (buy) today's newspaper.
4. We (choose) important news articles.
5. Children (unlock) our time capsule years from now.
6. They (wonder) about our class.
7. Maybe my children (go) to this school.
8. They (search) for my letter in the time capsule.
9. I (be) an adult by then.
10. We (laugh) about my letter.

---

**THINK AND REMEMBER**

◆ Use a future-tense verb to show action that will happen.
◆ To form a future-tense verb, use the helping verb *will* with the main verb.

---

## Independent Practice

**B. Using Future-Tense Verbs**   Read each sentence. Write the future-tense form of the verb in parentheses ( ).

11. Someday people (drive) solar cars.

> MODEL  will drive

12. Solar cars (use) energy from the sun.
13. Some cars (look) like insects.
14. Solar collectors (turn) sunshine into electricity.
15. No one (need) gas stations.
16. Cars (create) less noise and pollution.
17. I (buy) a red solar car.
18. My dog (ride) in the back seat.
19. We (travel) across the United States.

**C. Classifying Verbs**   Write the verb from each sentence. Then write *present, past,* or *future* to identify the tense.

20. Satellites help people in many ways.

> MODEL  help—present

21. Satellites gather information about the weather.
22. A meteorite slammed into the satellite.
23. Astronauts will fix it.
24. Space shuttles carry equipment into space.
25. The shuttle stopped beside the satellite.
26. Scientists will build a new satellite.
27. They wanted a different kind of satellite.
28. It will reflect solar energy to Earth.
29. The new satellite saves time and energy.
30. They planned the project for years.

**D. 31. – 38. Revising Sentences**   Rewrite each sentence in C that has a present-tense or past-tense verb. Change the verb to the future tense.

31. Satellites help people in many ways.

> MODEL  Satellites will help people in many ways.

## Application — Writing

**Time Capsule Note**   Imagine that the students at your school are burying a time capsule. Write a note that could be read by students who attend your school 25 years from now. Predict how the world will change in the next 25 years. Use future-tense verbs.

# 7 Be and Have

◆ **FOCUS** The verbs *be* and *have* can be used as main verbs or as helping verbs.

A form of the verb *be* or *have* can be a main verb or a helping verb in the predicate of a sentence. The verb in a sentence must agree with the subject. The words in color are the simple predicates.

1. Science is my favorite subject.
2. We have three science lessons every week.
3. Bradley is writing in his science log.
4. Many of the experiments have surprised us.

In sentences 1 and 2, *is* and *have* are main verbs. In sentences 3 and 4, *is* and *have* are helping verbs. The form of *be* or *have* in each sentence agrees with the subject.

The chart shows the present-tense and past-tense forms of *be* and *have*. It also shows which verb forms are singular and which are plural.

**is frozen**

**has melted**

| | be | | have | |
|---|---|---|---|---|
| **Singular** | | | | |
| I | am | was | have | had |
| **you** | are | were | have | had |
| **he, she, it** | is | was | has | had |
| or **singular noun** | | | | |
| **Plural** | | | | |
| **we, you, they,** | are | were | have | had |
| or **plural noun** | | | | |

## Guided Practice

**A.** Identify the form of *be* or *have* in parentheses ( ) that correctly completes each sentence.

1. Jim (has, have) boiled water in a kettle.
2. The water (was, were) turning into steam.
3. Mr. Jones (am, is) explaining this process to us.
4. I (is, am) careful with the hot water.
5. The students (has, have) taken notes.

## Independent Practice

**B. Identifying Forms of *Be* and *Have***   Write the form of *be* or *have* in parentheses ( ) that correctly completes each sentence.

**6.** I (has, have) learned what causes freckles.

MODEL ▷ have

**7.** I (am, are) protecting my skin with lotion.

**8.** Freckles (is, are) all over my face anyway.

**9.** Melanin in my skin (has, have) gathered in spots.

**10.** My friend (is, are) silly.

**11.** He (has, have) suggested a freckle cure.

**12.** I (has, have) decided that I like them.

**13.** I (am, are) not looking for a cure!

**C. Writing Sentences with Forms of *Be* and *Have***   Write each sentence. Complete each one with the form of *be* or *have* that makes sense in the sentence.

**14.** The sun _____ gone down now.

MODEL ▷ The sun has gone down now.

**15.** The moon _____ rising in the east.

**16.** Artists _____ painted pictures of the moon.

**17.** The moon _____ orbited the Earth for countless years.

**18.** I _____ dreamed of traveling to the moon.

**19.** I _____ written a story about the moon.

**20.** The story _____ a funny title.

**21.** The title _____ "Moon Freckles."

**22.** We _____ hoping to perform it as a play.

## Application — Writing and Speaking

**Scientific Article**   Think of a natural event that you have observed. Write one paragraph describing the event for your classmates. Tell what happened and why you think it happened. If you wish, check an encyclopedia or another book for more information. Use verbs with forms of *be* and *have*. When you have finished, read your report aloud to your classmates.

# Building Vocabulary
## Synonyms and Antonyms

Look at what Ellen wrote in her scrapbook. Under the first photograph, she used the word *ran*. Above the second, she avoided using the word *ran* a second time by writing the word *sprinted*. The verbs *run* and *sprint* are synonyms. **Synonyms** are words that have almost the same meaning.

> sleep—doze     start—begin
> finish—end

You can use synonyms to avoid repeating the same word and to give your writing more variety. That is what Ellen did in her scrapbook.

Many words have several synonyms. For example, *jog, sprint,* and *dart* are all synonyms for *run*.

Many people *jog* in the park after work.
The runners *sprint* down the track.
The deer *dart* between the trees.

If you are not sure which synonym to use, check the exact meanings in a dictionary.

**Antonyms** are words that have opposite meanings.

> sleep—wake     start—finish
> laugh—cry

The careful use of antonyms can also help make your writing more lively and enjoyable to read.

Ellen *started* the race with little confidence, but she *finished* it with complete assurance.

## Reading Practice

Read each sentence. Write the underlined words.
Then write whether the words are *synonyms* or *antonyms*.

1. Ellen <u>runs</u> and <u>sprints</u> every day before a race.
2. As the race <u>starts</u>, Ellen <u>begins</u> to sweat.
3. The other runners <u>move</u> near her, but she <u>zooms</u>
   out ahead of them.
4. Parents <u>watch</u> the race to <u>see</u> how well their
   children run.
5. Ellen sometimes <u>agrees</u> and sometimes <u>disagrees</u>
   with her coach.
6. She is always a good sport whether she <u>wins</u> or <u>loses</u>.

## Writing Practice

Rewrite each sentence. In place of the blank,
write an antonym for the underlined word. Use the
**Writer's Thesaurus** if you need help.

7. Sometimes Ellen <u>laughs</u> and sometimes she
   _____ when she looks at her scrapbooks.
8. Happy memories <u>please</u> her, and unhappy
   memories _____ her.
9. Her first scrapbook <u>begins</u> with her birth and
   _____ with her fourth birthday.
10. Ellen <u>selects</u> what she wants in her scrapbook
    and _____ what she doesn't want.

## Project

Play "The Synonym-Antonym Game." One
person begins by saying a word that has both
synonyms and antonyms—for example, the word
*hate*. The other players write a synonym for *hate* (for
example, *dislike*) and an antonym (for example, *love*).
A player receives one point for each correct word if
no other player has written the same word. Use a
dictionary to check answers.

Keep a list of the synonyms and antonyms that
you used in the game. Write sentences that contain
pairs of synonyms and pairs of antonyms.

synonym—tidy

antonym—sloppy

# Language Enrichment
## Verbs

Use what you know about verbs to do these activities.

 **Eyewitness**

Become an eyewitness to this accident. Make a few notes to describe what happened. Use past-tense verbs in your notes. Make sure that all verbs agree with their subjects. Then, give your eyewitness report as part of a TV newscast for your classmates. Have them decide whether your eyewitness account is correct.

 **Verb Hangers**

Make a verb hanger using the linking verbs *tastes, feels, looks, smells,* and *sounds.* First, cut sheets of construction paper into strips about one inch wide. Then, write a linking verb such as *tastes* down the middle of the strip.

On a separate sheet of paper, write all the words you can think of that describe how something tastes. When you've finished, make a horizontal slit at the top of the list. Pull the strip through the slit. Glue or staple the ends of the strip together to form a loop.

Now work with your classmates to come up with complete sentences. Use the linking verbs to join the descriptive words to subjects they describe. Afterward, decorate your classroom with your verb hangers. Look up at them from time to time to help you as you write.

**Doing the Verb – – –Hop!**

List at least 10 verbs that describe dance movements, such as *spin* and *twist.* Then choose a record or tape of dance music, and use your list of verbs to create a dance to go with the music. Teach your dance to the class.

# CONNECTING
## LANGUAGE ⟷ WRITING

In this unit you learned that verbs do more than show action. In some sentences verbs provide the link that joins the subject with the predicate. Verbs tell when the action in a sentence takes place: present, past, or future.

◆ **Using Verbs in Your Writing** Knowing how to use verbs, especially colorful action verbs, is an important writing skill. Lively verbs add excitement. They help your reader see and feel what you are writing about.

Pay special attention to verbs as you do these activities.

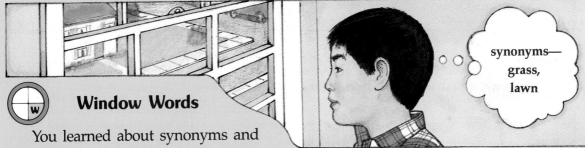

### Window Words

You learned about synonyms and antonyms on the **Building Vocabulary** pages. Try this synonym-antonym writing idea by using your powers of observation!

Look out a nearby window. How many synonyms and antonyms come to mind? Start with synonyms. For example, you might see *tires* and *wheels, concrete* and *pavement,* and colors of *red* and *scarlet.* Then go on to antonyms. You might spy *old* people and *young* children and *short* and *tall* trees or buildings. Make as long a list as you can. Use two of the most interesting pairs of synonyms and antonyms in sentences.

### What Does It Do?

Invent two objects that no one has ever seen. Make up a name and a purpose for each one. To help you think creatively, imagine each object to be as big as a building or as small as a pin.

Draw each object in action and write a brief paragraph explaining how each works. Use present-tense verbs in your paragraphs. Assemble your pictures and paragraphs into a booklet. Share your booklet with classmates.

# Unit Checkup

**3**

|  |  |
|---|---|
| **Think Back** | **Think Ahead** |
| ◆ What did you learn about how-to paragraphs? What did you do to write one? | ◆ How will your study of how-to paragraphs help you with oral or written instructions? |
| | ◆ How will knowing how to visualize the steps in a process help you write a how-to paragraph? A recipe? Directions? |
| ◆ What did you learn about verbs? How did that help you express being and action in writing? | ◆ What is one way you can use different kinds of verbs to improve your writing? |

## How-to Paragraphs  *pages 120–121*

Read the how-to paragraph. Then follow the directions.

> This is how you can begin an indoor garden. You will need several plant bulbs such as daffodils, a bowl-shaped dish, water, and soft dirt. First, fill the dish with water and some dirt. Next, place two or three bulbs in the dish. Then, pour water on the bulbs. Finally, place the dish where it will receive very little light. In about 10 days, the plants should have blossoming flowers.

1. Write the topic sentence.
2. Create a new topic sentence that is more interesting.
3. List the words that tell the materials needed.
4. Write any time-order words or phrases in the paragraph.

## Visualizing Steps in a Process  *page 122*

Use time-order words or phrases to complete each sentence.

5. To begin a sweet-potato vine, _____ stick two toothpicks into the fatter part of a sweet potato to form a ledge.
6. _____ , place the thinner end of the sweet-potato half in a glass.
7. _____ , pour water into the glass until it is half full.
8. _____ , place the glass on a windowsill where the potato can get sunlight.

## Writing for an Audience and a Purpose   *page 123*

Read the following sentences. Write a phrase that tells the writer's intended audience. Identify the sentences that would change if the audience were different. Rewrite those sentences.

9. To feed hungry birds in winter, find a windowsill.
10. Then save some bits of bread to feed the birds.
11. Open the window so you can place the bread on the sill.
12. Close the window and watch the birds gather to eat.
13. Be prepared to keep feeding them!

## The Writing Process   *pages 124−135*

14. When a writer selects the topic of a how-to paragraph, what is the most important consideration?
    a. The audience might get bored.        b. Pictures should be drawn.
    c. The activity might be too difficult.
15. After selecting a topic, what is the next step to consider?
    a. the audience and purpose        b. correct spelling of words
    c. how the paragraph will be published
16. When a writer drafts a how-to paragraph, why are time-order words important?
    a. They sound interesting.        b. They hold a reader's attention.
    c. They make the directions easy to follow.
17. Suppose you were revising your how-to paragraph. You find that you have placed three steps in one sentence. What should you do?
    a. Delete all three steps.        b. Write a sentence for each step.
    c. Shorten the sentence as much as possible.
18. Why is proofreading helpful before publishing a how-to paragraph?
    a. It makes the paragraph unusual.
    b. The paragraph will sound more boring.
    c. It will make the directions easy to understand.

## Action Verbs   *pages 138−139*

Read each sentence. Write the action verb.

19. People buy almost all their food and clothing.
20. Long ago most people ate food they grew themselves.
21. They planted crops of wheat, corn, and vegetables.
22. They raised cows, goats, and sheep for their meats.
23. Nowadays most people drive their cars to a grocery store.

## Linking Verbs   *pages 140–141*

Write each sentence. Underline each linking verb. Draw an arrow between the words each verb links.

24. Timothy is a new fifth-grade student at our school.

25. He and his family were happy to move to our neighborhood.

26. He became the newest student at our elementary school.

27. He seems very shy to us.

28. Our neighborhood looks strange to him.

## Main Verbs and Helping Verbs   *pages 142–143*

Write a helping verb that will complete each sentence. Use *am, is, are, have, has,* or *will.*

29. The Southwest _____ thirsting for water because of the drought.
30. In their search for water, Southwesterners _____ dammed rivers and drilled underground wells.
31. The water they have found _____ been supplied to farms, factories, and homes.
32. With more water available, the Southwest's cities _____ growing rapidly.
33. The warm, dry climate _____ always attracted many people.

## Present Tense   *pages 144–145*

Read each sentence. Write the present-tense form of the verb in parentheses ( ) that correctly completes each sentence.

34. Every day Juanita _____ her mother prepare tortillas. (watch)
35. Her mother _____ the dough, presses it into tortillas, and places each one on a hot griddle. (mix)
36. Then her mother _____ each tortilla over when bubbles form on its surface. (flip)
37. When a tortilla is ready, it _____ like a thin pancake. (look)
38. Juanita _____ to remember all the steps in making tortillas. (try)

## Past Tense   *pages 146–147*

Write the verb in each sentence. Then write *present* or *past* to identify the tense.
39. Last spring a female frog laid some eggs in the pond.
40. Several days later the frog eggs hatched in their underwater nursery.

41. Now the young frogs hop along the shore next to the pond.
42. They stayed near the pond by my house.
43. They catch flies and other bugs.

## Future Tense  *pages 148–149*

Write the verb in each sentence. Then write *present*, *past*, or *future* to identify the tense.

44. According to our teacher, a thunderstorm will come soon.
45. Then we will need our raincoats and umbrellas.
46. We glance at the gray, cloudy sky outside the window.
47. He gives us a homework assignment about the changes in clothing styles over the last 100 years.
48. Yesterday we watched a film about the history of clothing.

## Be and Have  *pages 150–151*

Write each sentence. Complete each one with the form of *be* or *have* that makes sense in the sentence.

49. Janet _____ visiting her grandparents.
50. They _____ lived in their house for a long time.
51. Janet's grandmother _____ watching out the window for her granddaughter's arrival.
52. Janet _____ noticed a lot of changes in her grandparents' neighborhood.
53. Builders _____ tearing down the old buildings and replacing them with new stores.
54. The old buildings _____ going to be missed.

## Synonyms and Antonyms  *pages 152–153*

Read each sentence. Write the underlined words. Then write *synonyms* or *antonyms*.

55. The desert amazed Juan, and he was so astounded by the growth of desert plants that he began reading about them.
56. Juan decided not to depend on books or rely on others' descriptions as the only ways to learn about the desert.
57. He wanted to know how such beautiful plants could grow in a rough place like a desert.
58. Juan's effort was rewarded when he made an attempt to convince his teacher to take his class to the desert.
59. In the desert, Juan looked at a mountain and wondered if it would ever become a valley.

# UNIT

# Comparing and Contrasting

◆ **COMPOSITION FOCUS:** **Paragraphs of Comparison and Contrast**
◆ **LANGUAGE FOCUS:** **Verbs**

You've been comparing and contrasting things all your life. For example, when you were little, you might have compared two foods and found that you "liked" one and "disliked" another. As you got older, you might have contrasted your favorite television programs with those of your parents. Comparing and contrasting like this has helped you to judge the value of things. This process is called **evaluating.**

To write the story on the following pages, Omar S. Castañeda (cas·tän·yā′da) had to evaluate the facts that were known about the ancient Mayan (mä′yən) civilization. Mr. Castañeda used his knowledge to imagine the things that could not be known, such as what Mayan people might have thought and said. The comparisons and contrasts in his story, therefore, are based on a mixture of facts and evaluations. In this unit, you will learn how to write paragraphs of comparison and contrast.

Omar S. Castañeda
created "When a Jaguar
Dreams" *to entertain* and
*inform* readers.

# Reading with a Writer's Eye
## Comparison and Contrast

Sky Jaguar, a Mayan boy living in the eighth century, is a product of Omar S. Castañeda's imagination. As you read "When a Jaguar Dreams," notice how skillfully the writer combines real facts about eighth-century Mayan life with details supplied by his imagination to create a story that both informs and entertains.

## When a Jaguar Dreams
### by Omar S. Castañeda

"Back to work," the teacher ordered.

Sky Jaguar was dreaming again about playing in the ball court. They had been studying on the Temple of the Masks overlooking the Great Plaza, with the Temple of the Giant Jaguar looming 180 feet into the air and the ball court extending invitingly out from the side. There, in one of the most important Mayan cities of the 8th century, it was difficult not to day-dream no matter how much a teacher scolded.

"But writing is boring," he complained. As the king's oldest son, Sky Jaguar was required to learn how to play ball, to read and write, to distinguish the planets Venus, Mars, and Jupiter, to be a soldier and politician, and to do mathematics using base twenty. But ball-playing was far and away the most enjoyable. That and maybe day-dreaming.

Sky Jaguar looked up at the roof of the Temple of the Giant Jaguar. There was a sculpture of an ancient king seated on a throne surrounded by scrolls painted white, red, and blue-green.

It felt like even the carving was telling him to get back to work. All the prince really wanted to do was go down, tie on the leather gloves, knee-pads, waist-guards, and shoulder-pads and knock a rubber ball around with other boys until one of them managed to hit it through a stone hoop set sideways high up on the wall. He was already one of the best players, and the only way he'd get better was by practicing.

But the teacher, a scribe named Alligator Parrot, knew he had to keep an eye on the prince. He was used to student tricks and knew that Sky Jaguar hated writing more than anything else. "Writing is kingly," he said, trying to convince the boy.

"Kings need to know how to rule and how to play ball," Sky Jaguar said. "Anyway, my scribes can write what I want written."

Alligator Parrot looked at the other boys and girls. They were all children of the most important families. Some were children of nobles from other cities such as Copan (kō·pän'), Uaxactun (wäsh·ak·tōōn'), and Naranjo (nä·räng'hō). The prince's own mother had come from Quirigua (kir·i·gwä'). The difference was that they were busy writing on bark paper while the prince was busy dreaming. They used reeds as pens and dipped them into different colored inks made of minerals, vegetables, and even insects. The writing was a complex system of shapes and symbols that looked a lot like drawing. The children had to learn different styles of writing. However, none of this interested the prince, who didn't care to write in any style.

"Just how will you know if the scribes wrote down what you wanted them to write?" Alligator Parrot asked.

But Sky Jaguar didn't answer. Again, he was dreaming about the game and how he would someday be dressed in jade, gold, and silver and stand before all the people of Tikal (ti·käl'). Someday soon, he would perform all the ceremonies as king. And one ceremony was to play a symbolic ballgame that showed time as working in cycles. But more importantly, the ballgame was also played for the fun of it. And fun was what Sky Jaguar really had in mind.

The teacher's voice cut into the prince's thoughts: "Well?"

"A king should know how to win at ball," Sky Jaguar replied. "You said that the games represent the cycles of life and of time, just like the changes in seasons and the cycle of day and night. Isn't it important for a king to understand that?"

"Now you remember yesterday's lessons."

"I promise I'll remember tomorrow's, too, especially if you let me play today."

Alligator Parrot looked suspiciously at Sky Jaguar. Finally he offered, "What if you day-dream first and then you play?"

Sky Jaguar didn't know how to answer. Why would the teacher ask if he wanted to do the two things he liked the most? He wondered if maybe Alligator Parrot was up to his own tricks.

But the old teacher led the prince down the steep stairs to the plaza and across to the ball court. "Look at the court," he said.

Sky Jaguar looked at the grass playing field, the two walls on either side, and the base of the Temple of the Giant Jaguar closing the far end of the rectangular court. He remembered the great ball court at Copan, the City of Artists, as it was sometimes called because of the spectacular artwork on all the buildings.

The courts were different in design, decoration, and location within the city. The court in Copan had walls that sloped steadily up to a platform that had rooms for the cheering spectators. The Tikal walls sloped a little bit, leveled off, then went straight up to roomless platforms for the spectators. The Copan court was also better decorated, with three markers set into each wall and three markers on the ball court floor. Tikal had no markers anywhere. The court in Copan was located at the head of the Great Plaza, while the court in Tikal was located off to the side of the Great Plaza.

Sky Jaguar looked up, as well, at the two stone hoops set into the walls on either side. It was through these vertical hoops that the rubber balls were elbowed, kneed, kicked, shouldered, or headed, since using hands wasn't allowed. During most days, like now, the court was quiet and empty.

It looked like Sky Jaguar had managed to trick the teacher again, when Alligator Parrot said, "I want you to pretend that this is the way the ball court always looks. Imagine that all the people are gone and that the court looks just as empty as this all the time."

Sky Jaguar nodded "okay." Thinking of the ball court was the easiest thing in the world. Usually people told him not to think about it and to think about more important things instead.

He was told to imagine that it was far into the future. It wasn't the year 765, but hundreds or thousands of years later.

"Imagine," Alligator Parrot said quietly, "that a boy your age walked through the woods and discovered this city. It would be like a lost city in the jungle. It would be like finding the buildings and sculptures left behind long, long ago by our ancestors."

Sky Jaguar closed his eyes and pictured the works of the long-forgotten artists, noting how similar they were to the works of his

own artists. Both did more than just create beauty; they told about life. The forgotten artists had left drawings just as lovely as the fabulous murals he had seen at Bonampak (bō·nam·päk′). The forgotten artists had also depicted the great events of their day, events as important to them as the events in the cave drawings at Nah Tunich (nah too·nēch′) were to him. The cave drawings told a story that Sky Jaguar knew by heart, the story of the game.

Alligator Parrot's voice echoed through the quiet ball court. "How would that boy know how to play this game? How would he know about you, a boy in Tikal?"

Suddenly, Sky Jaguar remembered the carving of the scrolls way atop the pyramid. He knew one answer, anyway: "By writing."

Alligator Parrot smiled and nodded.

Sky Jaguar immediately wondered what sorts of things a boy from the future would do. Would he dress the same? Eat the same? Would he play the same? Would he look the same? Would a boy from the future rather play ball than write a lesson? And would that boy from the future have a teacher like old Alligator Parrot?

The teacher smiled. "So, what are you going to write to that boy living a thousand years in the future?"

Sky Jaguar knew! "I'll tell him the rules of the game so at least someone can play ball."

And as they laughed together neither one knew which had tricked the other.

## Respond

1. Do you find it easy to understand Sky Jaguar's feelings as the story develops? Why or why not?

## Discuss

2. What kinds of facts about Mayan life does the writer include in his story to inform the reader and make the story sound realistic?

3. What parts of the story do you think the writer created simply as added entertainment for the reader?

# Thinking As a Writer

## Analyzing Paragraphs of Comparison and Contrast

Paragraphs of comparison and contrast tell how two or more things are alike and how they are different. When you show similarities, you are **comparing.** When you show differences, you are **contrasting.**

In these paragraphs, Omar S. Castañeda describes the ball courts mentioned in "When a Jaguar Dreams." Notice the examples he uses to support his topic sentences.

> **Writer's Guide**
>
> A paragraph of comparison
> ◆ compares things (shows their similarities).
> A paragraph of contrast
> ◆ contrasts things (shows their differences).

A **comparison paragraph** tells about the similarities of the things.

The ball courts at Copan and Tikal were similar in size and shape. Both were built for small audiences, unlike the massive spectator court at Chichen Itza (chē·chen' ēt·sä'). At both Copan and Tikal, spectators stood above the action, looking down onto sunken playing courts.

The **topic sentence** names the things that will be compared.

A **contrast paragraph** tells about the differences of the things.

The courts were different in design, decoration, and location within the city. The court in Copan had walls that sloped steadily up to a platform that had rooms for the cheering spectators. The Tikal walls sloped a little bit, leveled off, then went straight up to roomless platforms for the spectators. The Copan court was also better decorated, with three markers set into each wall and three markers on the ball court floor. Tikal had no markers anywhere. The court in Copan was located at the head of the Great Plaza, while the court in Tikal was located off to the side of the Great Plaza.

The **topic sentence** names the things that will be contrasted.

## Discuss

1. How can you tell that the first sentence of the first paragraph is the topic sentence?
2. What things does the writer compare in the first paragraph?
3. What things does the writer contrast in the second paragraph?

# Try Your Hand

**A. Identify Topics and Topic Sentences**  Read the following paragraphs. Identify the topic sentence of each paragraph. Then tell what two things are being compared.

> The redwood tree and the Monterey cypress tree are similar in some ways. Both the redwood and the Monterey cypress are needleleaf trees that grow on the Pacific Coast. The redwood may be found from southern Oregon to central California. The Monterey cypress is native to California's Monterey Peninsula. The two trees have striking appearances and thrive in the foggy, humid weather along the coast.
>
> Yet in some ways, the redwood and the Monterey cypress are quite different. The redwood can grow as tall as 275 feet, with a 12-foot diameter. The Monterey cypress reaches a height of only 80 feet, with a 20-inch diameter. The tall redwood stands straight in contrast to the twisted Monterey cypress, which is bent by ocean winds. Redwoods are forest giants, whereas Monterey cypresses are sometimes used as ornamental decoration by gardeners.

**B. Write a Title**  Write a title for the paragraphs of comparison and contrast about the two trees.

**C. Read Paragraphs of Comparison and Contrast**  Look again at the story "When a Jaguar Dreams" beginning on page 162, or find paragraphs of comparison and contrast in books and magazines. Work with a partner to discover as many comparisons and contrasts as possible. Notice how the writer compares and contrasts. Are all the similarities in one paragraph and all the differences in another? If not, how is the material organized? What comparisons and contrasts does the writer allow you to make for yourself?

*Writer's Notebook*

**Collecting Alike and Different Words**  Look at the story "When a Jaguar Dreams" beginning on page 162. Also, look again at any paragraphs of comparison and contrast you found in magazines or books. Record in your *Writer's Notebook* sentences with words that help compare or contrast. For example, the words *both, each, alike, different, similar, compare, contrast, also, too,* and *just as* are sometimes used when things are compared and contrasted.

# Thinking As a Writer
## Evaluating to Compare and Contrast

**Writer's Guide**

Before comparing or contrasting two things, good writers

♦ observe how they are alike and how they are different.

♦ evaluate them in terms of some of their important qualities.

Before a writer is ready to compare or contrast two things, he or she observes them carefully. The writer chooses a few important qualities that both things have and evaluates each thing in terms of these qualities. For example, a writer might evaluate two winter coats in terms of stylishness, warmth, and durability. The writer might evaluate two singers in terms of voice quality, range, and expression.

The writer might find it helpful to record similarities and differences on a chart or a diagram.

### Cats and Dogs as Pets

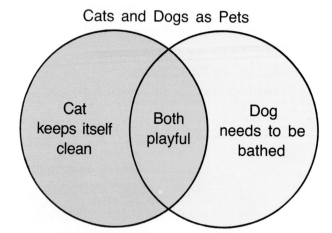

Cat keeps itself clean — Both playful — Dog needs to be bathed

Before you begin to write paragraphs of comparison and contrast, be sure to observe and evaluate important features.

## Discuss

1. What are some other benefits of having a cat?
2. What are some other benefits of having a dog?
3. What other benefits might both animals provide?

## Try Your Hand

**Make a Chart of Similarities and Differences**   Think about two hobbies or two sports that can be compared and contrasted. Choose four or five qualities to evaluate. Then make a chart in which you evaluate the two hobbies in terms of these qualities. Meet with a partner, and discuss the accuracy of each other's chart.

# Developing the Writer's Craft
## Using Formal and Informal Language

Good writers use the appropriate tone when they write. The tone the writer uses depends on his or her audience and purpose.

Read these sentences.

1. "My scribes can surely fill my writing needs," Sky Jaguar told his teacher.
2. "That was some game, guys," laughed Sky Jaguar.
3. The object of the game was to get the rubber ball through the hoop. Players were permitted to use various parts of their bodies.
4. This neat game is like basketball, rugby, and soccer rolled into one. When your team wins, you feel just great!

The tone of the first sentence is formal. In the second sentence, when Sky Jaguar speaks to his friends, his tone is informal. The formal language in the third set of sentences is appropriate for giving information in a report. The informal language in the fourth set of sentences is suitable for speaking or writing to a friend.

When you write your paragraphs of comparison and contrast, be sure to use a tone that suits your audience and your purpose.

## Discuss

1. Look again at the second complete paragraph on page 165. Is the tone formal or informal? Tell why you think so.
2. Reread the paragraph on page 165 that begins "Sky Jaguar immediately wondered." How is the tone of this paragraph different?
3. How could the writer change the tone in each paragraph?

## Try Your Hand

**Use Formal and Informal Tones**   Write some sentences inviting a good friend to come over to your house. Then write to the state representative from your district, inviting him or her to come speak to your class. Use the proper tone for each audience and purpose. Share your writing with a partner.

# 1 Prewriting
## Paragraphs of Comparison and Contrast

Diego, a student at Park Elementary School, wanted to write paragraphs comparing and contrasting plants or animals for a field guide his class was making. He used the checklist in the **Writer's Guide** to help him plan his paragraphs. Look at what he did.

## ◆ Brainstorming and Selecting a Topic

Diego had always enjoyed visiting the local zoo, which featured many animals that could be found in his state. He decided to visit there to find animals to write about. At the zoo, he listed the local animals he saw. Look at Diego's list.

Next, Diego looked over the list. He grouped animals that he might be able to write about in his paragraphs of comparison and contrast.

Finally, Diego circled the pair that would make the best topic for his paragraphs of comparison and contrast.

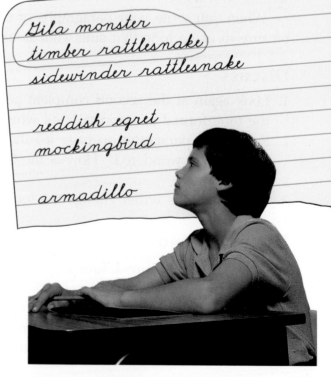

*armadillo*
*Gila monster*
*mockingbird*
*timber rattlesnake*
*reddish egret*
*sidewinder rattlesnake*

*Gila monster*
*timber rattlesnake*
*sidewinder rattlesnake*

*reddish egret*
*mockingbird*

*armadillo*

## Discuss

1. Look at the way Diego grouped the topics on his list. Why did he group *Gila monster, timber rattlesnake,* and *sidewinder rattlesnake* together? Why did he group *reddish egret* and *mockingbird* together?
2. Why do you think Diego decided to compare and contrast the Gila monster and the timber rattlesnake instead of the two kinds of rattlesnakes?

# ◆ Gathering Information

After Diego had chosen his topics, he decided to gather information for his paragraphs in two ways: by observing and by reading.

Diego went back to the zoo to observe the Gila monster and the timber rattlesnake more closely. He took notes on what he saw. He also asked the zookeeper some questions and took notes on the answers. Look at some of Diego's notes from his visit to the zoo.

*Gila monster*
black skin with yellow markings
short legs
long tail
*Timber rattlesnake*
dark skin with bands across back
rattles visible at end of tail
rattlesnakes have temperature
  sensor in head that helps
    them find prey

Diego also looked up information on timber rattlesnakes and Gila monsters in an encyclopedia. Here are some of his notes. Notice that his notes are in his own words and that they are not necessarily in complete sentences.

*Gila monster*
Poisonous lizard. Southwestern United States.
Some teeth have grooves for poison—it flows
into wounds the teeth make.

## Discuss

1. Look back at Diego's notes from his visit to the zoo. Which fact on the list did Diego probably learn from the zookeeper?
2. Why is it often a good idea to get information from other sources in addition to your own observation?
3. The encyclopedia entry contained many facts that Diego did not include in his notes such as information about how the Gila monster got its name. Why do you think he left that fact out?

# ◆ Organizing the Facts

After Diego had gathered all the facts he needed for his paragraphs of comparison and contrast, he was ready to organize his notes. He wanted his audience to be able to see clearly the similarities and differences he would be writing about. He decided to make a chart of the information from his notes. Here is part of Diego's chart.

| | Rattlesnake | Gila monster |
|---|---|---|
| Color: | dark brown/black ✓ light bands | ✓ black and yellow splotches |
| Type of animal: | ✓ reptile—snake | ✓ reptile—lizard |
| Food: | birds, small animals, eggs | rodents |

Diego then put check marks on the chart to show areas where the Gila monster and the timber rattlesnake are alike. From this information, he made two new charts that grouped similarities together and differences together. Here are parts of Diego's new charts.

| Compare (similarities) | Contrast (differences) | |
|---|---|---|
| Rattlesnake and Gila monster — poisonous active at night, at rest during day reptile | Rattlesnake — eats birds, small animals, eggs gives birth to live young | Gila monster — eats rodents lays eggs |

## Discuss

1. Why is a chart a good way to organize facts for paragraphs of comparison and contrast? Why is Diego's first chart probably more useful to him than his earlier lists for each animal?
2. Diego's chart labeled *Contrast* has fewer items than the chart labeled *Compare*. Why do you think this is so?
3. Look again at Diego's notes from the zoo on page 171. What facts about the rattlesnake and the Gila monster might he add to his *Compare* chart?

## Try Your Hand

Now plan paragraphs of comparison and contrast of your own.

A. **Brainstorm and Select a Topic**   Observe and think about animals or plants found where you live. Make a list of them. After you have your list, group together animals or plants that are alike in some way, as Diego did with his list of animals. (If Diego had made a list of plants, for instance, he might have grouped cholla cactus and saguaro cactus together.) Think about your topic and your audience.

   ◆ Remember that you will want to pick a pair of plants or animals that are alike in some ways and different in others.
   ◆ Cross out any plant or animal that is in a group by itself.
   ◆ If you have more than two plants or animals in a group, cross out ones that are too much alike.
   ◆ Circle the pair that would make the best topics for paragraphs of comparison and contrast.

B. **Observe and Make Notes**   Observe the animals or plants you will be comparing and contrasting. Take notes about their appearance and, for animals, their behavior. Use an encyclopedia or other reference book to find more facts about the subjects of your paragraphs. Take notes in your own words.

C. **Chart Your Facts**   Set up charts including all the facts from the notes you made when you were gathering information. Decide which facts are similar, and include them in your *Compare* chart. Put the facts that are different in your *Contrast* chart.

 **Save your notes and your charts in your *Writer's Notebook*. You will use them when you draft your paragraphs of comparison and contrast.**

# 2 Drafting
## Paragraphs of Comparison and Contrast

**Writer's Guide**

**Drafting Checklist**
- ☑ Use your notes and charts for ideas.
- ☑ Write the comparison paragraph. Begin with a topic sentence.
- ☑ Write the contrast paragraph. Begin with a topic sentence.

Diego followed the **Writer's Guide** to draft his paragraphs of comparison and contrast. Here is part of what he did.

> The timber rattlesnake and the Gila monster are interesting but dangerous reptiles. They can be found in Texas and other parts of the United States and Mexico.

## Discuss

1. Look at Diego's topic sentence. Do you think it would capture his audience's interest? Why or why not?
2. Should Diego have written a separate sentence to tell his audience that both animals are reptiles? Why or why not?

## Try Your Hand

Now you are ready to write paragraphs of comparison and contrast.

A. **Review Your Information**  Think about the facts you gathered and organized. Have you planned your paragraphs so that the similarities and differences are clear and separate?

B. **Think About Your TAP**  Remember that your task is to write paragraphs of comparison and contrast. Your purpose is to tell your audience about the similarities and the differences between two animals or two plants.

C. **Write Your First Draft**  Follow the steps in the **Drafting Checklist** to write your paragraphs of comparison and contrast.
   When you write your draft, just put all your ideas on paper. You can correct the draft later.

**Task:** What?
**Audience:** Who?
**Purpose:** Why?

 **Save your first draft in your *Writer's Notebook*. You will use it when you revise your paragraphs of comparison and contrast.**

# 3 Responding and Revising
## Paragraphs of Comparison and Contrast

Diego used the checklist in the **Writer's Guide** to revise his paragraphs of comparison and contrast. Look at what he did.

◆ **Checking Information**

Diego decided to take out the sentence about the way in which the animals give birth because it showed contrast rather than comparison. To show his change, Diego used this mark ✑ .

◆ **Checking Organization**

Diego decided to move the information about the venom to the end of the paragraph so that it would follow the information about attacking. To show that change he used this mark ∂ .

◆ **Checking Language**

Diego decided that he could join the two sentences about how venoms are transmitted. He used a comma and the conjunction *but* to do this. He also looked in a thesaurus to find a more formal way of saying *not quick*. To add a word he used this mark ∧ .

Cut

Move

Add

Add

> The timber rattlesnake and the Gila Monster are interesting but dangerous reptiles. They can be found in Texas and other parts of the United States and Mexico. The timber rattlesnake gives birth to live young, but the Gila monster lays eggs. The timber rattlesnake and the Gila monster both use venom to kill their prey. The timber rattlesnake's venom is forced through its hollow fangs. The Gila monster's venom flows down a groove in its sharp teeth. They both are active at night and rest during the day. Though they do not look sluggish quick, they are still quick to attack, even when they are resting.

## Discuss

1. Diego thought his paragraphs should have a more formal tone. Do you agree or disagree? Why?
2. Are there other changes that Diego should have made? Explain your answer.

## Try Your Hand

Now revise your first draft.

A. **Read Your First Draft** As you read your paragraphs, think about your audience and your purpose. Read your paragraphs silently or to a partner to see if they are complete and well organized. Use the questions in the box to help you.

| Responding and Revising Strategies | |
|---|---|
| ✔ **Respond**<br>**Ask yourself or a partner:** | ✔ **Revise**<br>**Try these solutions:** |
| ◆ Does my topic sentence tell my audience what I will be comparing or contrasting? | ◆ **Revise** your topic sentence to make it clearer. |
| ◆ Have I organized all the similarities into one paragraph and all the differences into another? | ◆ **Revise** the organization if necessary. |
| ◆ Have I joined sentences with conjunctions when this will help my audience understand? | ◆ **Use** conjunctions to help your reader see connections between ideas. See the **Revising Workshop** on page 177. |
| ◆ Have I chosen formal words to say what I mean? | ◆ **Use** the **Writer's Thesaurus** at the back of the book to help you find the right words. |

B. **Make Your Changes** If the answer to any question in the box is *no,* try the solution. Use the **Editor's Marks** to show your changes.

C. **Review Your Paragraphs Again** Decide if there is anything else you want to revise. Keep revising until you feel that your paragraphs are well organized and complete.

> **EDITOR'S MARKS**
> ∧ Add something.
> ✣ Cut something.
> ◯ Move something.
> ∧ Replace something.

Save your revised paragraphs of comparison and contrast in your *Writer's Notebook.* **You will use them when you proofread your paragraphs.**

# Revising Workshop
## Making Compound Sentences

Good writers show their audience the connection between ideas. By joining two related sentences with a conjunction and a comma, you can make your writing clearer and smoother.

Look at these examples.

1. The armadillo jumps into the river.
   The air that is trapped under its shell helps it float to the other side.
2. The armadillo jumps into the river, and the air that is trapped under its shell helps it float to the other side.

In the first example, the ideas in the two sentences are related. In the second example, the conjunction *and* is used to join the two sentences into one.

## Practice

Rewrite each pair of sentences, using *and* to join them. (Remember to replace the period with a comma. Remember to change the first word of the second sentence from uppercase to lowercase.)

1. The field mouse and the jack rabbit are both wild animals.
   They are very much alike.

2. Both are vegetarians.
   Almost any available plant can become part of their diet.

3. The field mouse is covered with grayish-brown fur.
   The jack rabbit's coloring is similar.

4. The jack rabbit is closely related to the domestic rabbits that people keep as pets.
   The field mouse is related to domestic gerbils, hamsters, and white mice.

5. Mice are numerous in the wild.
   They are pests in some regions.

6. Bats are also members of the rodent family.
   They have the ability to fly around trees and other obstacles at night.

# 4 Proofreading
## Paragraphs of Comparison and Contrast

After Diego revised his paragraphs of comparison and contrast, he used the **Writer's Guide** and the **Editor's Marks** to proofread them. Look at what he did.

### Writer's Guide

**Proofreading Checklist**

☑ Check for errors in capitalization.

☑ Check for errors in punctuation. Be sure that you have used apostrophes correctly in possessive nouns.

☑ Check to see that all your paragraphs are indented.

☑ Circle any words you think are misspelled.

⇨ For proofreading help, use the **Writer's Handbook.**

> ¶ The timber rattlesnake and the Gila monster are alike in some ways, but they have different hunting styles and habitats. The timber rattlesnake can grab its ~~pray~~ *prey* only with its mouth, but the Gila monster can use its strong claws. The timber rattlesnake's habitat is more likely to be in a cool area with trees. The Gila monster lives in the dry, barren ~~desserts~~ *deserts* of the southwestern United states and Mexico.

## Discuss

1. Look at Diego's proofread paragraph. What kinds of mistakes did he make?
2. Why did Diego transpose the apostrophe and the *s* in the word *rattlesnakes'* when he proofread?

## Try Your Hand

**Proofread Your Paragraphs of Comparison and Contrast**   Now use the **Writer's Guide** and the **Editor's Marks** to proofread your paragraphs.

Save your corrected paragraphs of comparison and contrast in your *Writer's Notebook.* You will use them when you publish your paragraphs.

### EDITOR'S MARKS

≡ Capitalize.

⊙ Add a period.

∧ Add something.

⋀ Add a comma.

✔✔ Add quotation marks.

✂ Cut something.

⌃ Replace something.

⇄ Transpose.

◯ Spell correctly.

⊤⊤ Indent paragraph.

/ Make a lowercase letter.

WRITING PROCESS

# Listening and Speaking
## Tips for Giving and Listening to an Oral Report

1. Speak clearly and loudly enough for your listeners to hear. Use expression in your voice.
2. Use notes to remind you of the order of your speech. Glance at the notes to refresh your memory, and then look up at the audience members when you speak.
3. Use your notes to read complicated facts, such as statistics, or to quote people directly.
4. Signal the difference between facts and your opinions with phrases such as *personally, I think, I believe,* and *in my opinion.*
5. Begin with an exciting introduction that will catch the audience's attention. (Don't begin with something like "My report compares and contrasts the bat and the owl." Instead, try something like "The bat and the owl are two eerie creatures that prowl through the air at night.")
6. Show your listeners how you feel. If you find something surprising, scary, or funny, let your audience know!
7. When you are in the audience, take note of important words or phrases that the speaker uses. Write enough to remind you of what the speaker said. Do not write so much that you miss other parts of the speech.

# 5 Publishing
## Paragraphs of Comparison and Contrast

Diego made a clean copy of his paragraphs of comparison and contrast and checked to make sure he had not left anything out. Then he presented his paragraphs in an oral report to his classmates. After all the students' oral reports had been given, Diego and his classmates collected the paragraphs into a field guide of plants and animals in their area. You can find Diego's paragraphs on pages 26 and 27 of the **Writer's Handbook.**

Here's how Diego and his classmates published their paragraphs of comparison and contrast.

1. First, they studied how published guides to wildlife and plant life are arranged to present information about similar but different species. Descriptions are often accompanied by pictures or drawings of the animals or the plants.

2. Next, using photos or drawings of the animals or the plants they selected, they drew or traced pictures of species and included them with their reports.

3. They mounted their paragraphs of comparison and contrast and their drawings on a large sheet of paper.

4. Diego and his classmates collected their finished paragraphs and drawings into a large folder. They put the label "Field Guide" on the folder.

5. They decided how they would share the field guide with another group who would appreciate the information.

## Discuss

1. Why does it help your audience if you use pictures or drawings as part of your field guide?
2. Do you think that the pictures and drawings alone would give as much information as is provided by the paragraphs plus the illustrations? Why or why not?

## Try Your Hand

**Publish Your Paragraphs of Comparison and Contrast** Follow the checklist in the **Writer's Guide.** If possible, give oral reports based on your paragraphs. Then work with your classmates to collect your paragraphs into a field guide for your area. You might also try one of these ideas for sharing your paragraphs of comparison and contrast.

◆ Post your paragraphs and pictures on a bulletin board in your classroom.
◆ Lend or give a copy of your field guide to a local zoo, library, or museum.
◆ Send a copy of your field guide to a class in another city or in another part of the United States. Ask the class to send you a field guide for their area.

# Writing in the Content Areas

Use what you learned to write about the area where you live. You could write paragraphs of comparison and contrast that show a new visitor what makes your area interesting. One way to publish your writing is to create a flier about your community. Donate your flier to the local library or chamber of commerce. Use one of these ideas or an idea of your own.

> **Writer's Guide**
>
> When you write, remember the stages of the Writing Process.
> - Prewriting
> - Drafting
> - Responding and Revising
> - Proofreading
> - Publishing

## Science

Think of birds and winged insects in your area. Choose two of the most interesting or most unusual ones. Give information telling where the animals live, how they behave, and what they eat. Show how the two creatures are alike and how they are different.

## Physical Education

Choose two sports. Describe them from the point of view of a player. Write about what you do when you play each sport. Include information about muscles you use, skills you need, and feelings you have while playing. Tell how the two sports are alike and how they are different.

## Social Studies

How does the place where you live compare with some other place in the world? Choose an area of the world that you know about. You may have visited it, read about it, or seen a program about it on television. Compare and contrast it with your community. Discuss the geography, climate, people, and daily life.

## Reading

Look at a local newspaper and a local magazine. Compare and contrast the special features they have that readers your age might enjoy. Conclude by recommending the periodical that you think has the most interesting features for your age group.

# CONNECTING
## WRITING ⬌ LANGUAGE

In good comparison-and-contrast writing, the writer focuses on interesting similarities and differences. According to the following paragraphs, how are New York and Los Angeles alike and different?

## New York and Los Angeles

Think about New York and Los Angeles, the two largest cities in the United States. You know that both are coastal cities. In each city, you'll find beautiful scenery and exciting tourist attractions. The people who make their homes in Los Angeles love sports. So do New Yorkers. People come to New York for theater, art, and music. They see Los Angeles, also, as a center for film, art, and music.

What's the difference? Some say black-and-white photographs give a true picture of New York's personality. Photographers almost always show Los Angeles in color. New Yorkers ride the subway. Los Angeleans drive. Palm trees and orange trees grow in L.A., where it's almost always warm. The seasons bring different weather to New York: hot and muggy in summer, cold and windy in winter, just lovely in spring and fall. A saxophone is the instrument that says the most about New York. If you sing about L.A., you'll need an electric guitar.

◆ **Irregular Verbs in Paragraphs of Comparison and Contrast**
The words highlighted in color are irregular action verbs. Irregular action verbs have special forms. Since irregular verbs are some of the most commonly used verbs, you will see them often as you read, and you will need them often as you write.

◆ **Language Focus: Verbs**  The following lessons will help you use different kinds of verbs and verb forms in your own writing.

# 1 Irregular Verbs

◆ **FOCUS**   An **irregular verb** does not end with *ed* in the past tense.

The past tense of most verbs is formed by adding *ed*. The past tense of some verbs is not formed by adding *ed*. These are called irregular verbs and have special past-tense forms. *Run* is an irregular verb. Its forms are in color in these sentences.

I  run . I  ran  Monday.

I  have run  all month.

This chart shows the forms of some irregular verbs.

| Irregular Verbs | | |
| --- | --- | --- |
| **Present** | **Past** | **Past with Helping Verb** |
| come | came | (has, have, had) come |
| eat | ate | (has, have, had) eaten |
| give | gave | (has, have, had) given |
| go | went | (has, have, had) gone |
| make | made | (has, have, had) made |
| ride | rode | (has, have, had) ridden |
| run | ran | (has, have, had) run |
| say | said | (has, have, had) said |
| see | saw | (has, have, had) seen |
| take | took | (has, have, had) taken |
| think | thought | (has, have, had) thought |
| write | wrote | (has, have, had) written |

## Guided Practice

**A.** Complete each sentence with the past-tense form of the verb in parentheses ( ).

1. Uncle Diego (take) us fishing last Monday.
2. Allison and I (ride) near the front of the boat.
3. My dog (run) all over the boat.

**B.** Complete each sentence with the form of the verb in parentheses used with a helping verb.

4. Our boat had (go) far out into the ocean.
5. Uncle Diego has (give) us water safety lessons.
6. We have (see) the sunset from the boat.

## Independent Practice

**C. Using Irregular Verbs in the Past Tense** Write the past-tense form of the verb in parentheses ( ).

7. My teacher (say) there was a writing contest.

MODEL ▷ said

8. I (write) a story about a shark.
9. Barney the shark (go) to the beach one day.
10. He (ride) the waves with the surfers.
11. The surfers (think) the shark was hungry.
12. They all (run) onto the beach.
13. Barney (see) someone's surfboard.
14. The shark (take) the surfboard out to sea.
15. He (come) home to his family at last.

**D. Using Irregular Verbs with Helping Verbs** Write the form of the verb in parentheses ( ) that correctly completes the sentence.

16. My father has (make) fish soup for tonight.

MODEL ▷ made

17. I have (eat) some strange foods from his kitchen.
18. Mom has (think) up some unusual meals also.
19. She has (give) us lobster pancakes for breakfast.
20. My brothers and I have (write) a letter of complaint.
21. Dad has (say) we should try everything once.
22. We have (come) across a new cookbook.
23. My brothers have (make) a very weird recipe.
24. I have (go) to the store for octopus and jelly.
25. My parents have (take) a taste of squid.
26. They have never (see) such a funny meal.

## Application — Writing

**Menu** Dream up a silly seafood dish. Use any ingredients found in the sea. Write a paragraph. Describe your dish for the menu of a seafood restaurant. Use the irregular verbs in this lesson in your writing. If you need help writing a descriptive paragraph, see page 29 of the **Writer's Handbook**.

# 2 More Irregular Verbs

◆ **FOCUS**   Some irregular verbs follow a pattern when they change form.

Remember that irregular verbs do not form the past tense by adding *ed*. Some irregular verbs follow patterns. The words in color follow a pattern in these sentences.

1. I always  lose  my beach towel.
2. I  lost  my towel last summer.
3. I  have lost  my beach towel every summer.

This chart shows more irregular verbs. Use the patterns to form the past tenses of these verbs.

| More Irregular Verbs | | |
|---|---|---|
| **Present** | **Past** | **Past with Helping Verb** |
| fly | flew | (has, have, had) flown |
| grow | grew | (has, have, had) grown |
| know | knew | (has, have, had) known |
| tear | tore | (has, have, had) torn |
| wear | wore | (has, have, had) worn |
| begin | began | (has, have, had) begun |
| swim | swam | (has, have, had) swum |
| break | broke | (has, have, had) broken |
| speak | spoke | (has, have, had) spoken |
| steal | stole | (has, have, had) stolen |
| freeze | froze | (has, have, had) frozen |
| choose | chose | (has, have, had) chosen |
| bring | brought | (has, have, had) brought |
| catch | caught | (has, have, had) caught |
| teach | taught | (has, have, had) taught |

## Guided Practice

**A.** Identify the past-tense form of each verb. Then, give the form of each verb when used with a helping verb.

1. fly
2. tear
3. steal
4. bring
5. grow
6. teach

## Independent Practice

**B. Using Irregular Verbs in the Past Tense**   Write the past-tense form of the verb in parentheses ( ).

7. The day (begin) early at the beach.

MODEL ▷ began

8. I (know) it would be a funny day.
9. A seagull (fly) through our kitchen.
10. It (steal) a piece of toast from the table.
11. My father (speak) firmly to the seagull.
12. It (know) it was in trouble.
13. Jane and Annie (wear) their new swimsuits to breakfast.
14. They (swim) every morning.
15. Annie nearly (freeze) in the chilly water.
16. Jane (catch) two fish.
17. The gull (choose) the biggest fish to snatch away.

**C. Using Irregular Verbs with Helping Verbs**   Write the form of the verb in parentheses ( ) that is used with a helping verb.

18. The town has (begin) a beachcombing contest.

MODEL ▷ begun

19. Mom has (speak) to us about the beachcombing contest.
20. Ace has (teach) us how to find sand dollars.
21. I have (break) Ace's sand dollar.
22. Bethany has (tear) her sandal at the beach.
23. Ace and Bethany have (swim) in the cool water.
24. They have (catch) enormous hermit crabs.
25. The committee has (chose) the contest winners.
26. The winners have (bring) their medals to the beach.

## Application — Writing

**Lost-and-Found Notice**   Imagine that you have found an unusual item on the beach. Write a lost-and-found notice to be posted on the community bulletin board. Tell about what you found and how you found it. Use irregular verbs from this lesson in your notice.

# 3 Direct Objects

◆ **FOCUS**   A **direct object** receives the action of the verb.

In some sentences the action verb is followed by a direct object. Read these sentences. The words in color are direct objects.

1. Abe likes caves .
2. Helmets protect heads .

A direct object answers the question *What?* or *Whom?*

3. A rock hit the helmet .   **Hit** *what?*
4. Caves shelter campers .   **Shelter** *whom?*

In sentence 3, the direct object *helmet* answers the question *Hit what?* In sentence 4, the direct object *campers* answers the question *Shelter whom?*

## Guided Practice

**A.** Identify the direct object in each sentence.

1. Bats inhabit the cave.
2. They like the dark.
3. Alana shines a flashlight at the bats.
4. She frightens the animals.
5. The bats blink their eyes.
6. Sudden movements startle Alana.
7. Randall Jarrell wrote a story about a group of bats.
8. The bats helped people in danger.
9. Alana read the story.
10. Now she likes bats.

---

**THINK AND REMEMBER**

◆ Remember that a **direct object** receives the action of the verb.

---

## Independent Practice

**B. Identifying Direct Objects**   Write the direct object in each sentence.

**11.** Our spelunking club enjoys caves.

<MODEL> caves

**12.** Spelunkers explore caves.

**13.** We visited Luray Caverns.

**14.** Everyone liked the tour.

**15.** We received advice about spelunking.

**16.** Always bring a friend along.

**17.** Never enter a cave without a guide.

**18.** I carry a flashlight in my backpack.

**19.** Once I lost a flashlight in an underground stream.

**20.** I told the guide about my experience.

**C. Classifying Direct Objects**   Write each sentence. Underline the action verb once. Underline the direct object twice. Then tell whether the direct object answers the question *whom?* or *what?*

**21.** Explorers found caves in 49 states.

<MODEL> Explorers found caves in 49 states. what

**22.** Indians made homes in New Mexico's cliffs.

**23.** Ladders connect the floors.

**24.** Next, I visited the Carlsbad Caverns.

**25.** They fascinate scientists.

**26.** Speleologists study caves.

**27.** My Uncle Pete teaches people about caves.

**28.** We met Pete near the cave entrance.

**29.** He knows everything about New Mexico's caves.

**D. Writing Original Sentences**   Use these verbs to write sentences that have direct objects.

**30.** see

<MODEL> I see stalactites in the caves.

**31.** climb          **32.** watch          **33.** write

## Application — Writing

**Instructions**   Write a paragraph for your classmates telling how to perform your favorite pastime. Use action verbs with direct objects in your paragraph. If you need help writing a how-to paragraph, see page 25 of the **Writer's Handbook.**

# 4 Easily Confused Verb Pairs

◆ **FOCUS**  Sometimes a verb is confused with another verb.

Some verbs have meanings that are similar but not quite the same. It is easy to confuse these verbs. The words in color in each sentence group are often confused. Notice the meaning of the verb provided after each sentence.

1. They sit in the treehouse. **rest**
   Set the binoculars here. **put**

2. She can spot birds well. **is able to**
   May Doreen help look? **is allowed to**

3. Doreen will teach me about forestry. **instruct**
   I will learn about the woods. **receive instruction**

4. Mina will let me borrow the binoculars. **permit**
   Leave the book on the shelf. **allow to stay**
   (or)
   I will leave now. **go**

## Guided Practice

**A.** Identify the word in parentheses ( ) that completes each sentence correctly.

1. We will (teach, learn) about trees in forestry class.
2. The ranger can (teach, learn) us to plant baby trees.
3. He will (let, leave) each of us plant three trees.
4. You should (let, leave) your dog at home.
5. I (can, may) tell an oak tree from a maple tree.
6. (Let, Leave) plenty of space around each tree.
7. Jon and Xiao (sit, set) each tree gently in its hole.
8. (Can, May) we have a tree party later?
9. We will (sit, set) the food under the big tree.
10. Amy will (teach, learn) us about a tree's life.

---

**THINK AND REMEMBER**
◆ Avoid confusing one verb with another.

---

# Independent Practice

**B. Identifying Verb Forms**   Write the verb in parentheses ( ) that correctly completes each sentence.

**11.** (Sit, Set) quietly and watch for birds.

> MODEL  Sit

**12.** (Can, May) you build your own treehouse?

**13.** This tape will (teach, learn) us woodpecker calls.

**14.** We will (teach, learn) to tell woodpeckers apart.

**15.** Where did you (sit, set) the bird book?

**16.** Don't (leave, let) your bird book in the woods.

**17.** I want to (teach, learn) what woodpeckers eat.

**18.** (Let, Leave) me see the nest in the tree.

**19.** Did you (let, leave) your binoculars at home?

**20.** Owls like to (sit, set) in pine trees.

**21.** (Teach, Learn) us more about nests.

**22.** Some people (sit, set) out birdseed in their yards.

**23.** (Can, May) Amy bring her little brother on the hike?

**24.** He (can, may) come with us any time.

**25.** You should (let, leave) your sister come, too.

**26.** She (can, may) do bird calls beautifully.

**C. Revising Sentences**   Read each sentence. If the underlined verb form is incorrect, write the correct verb. If the underlined verb form is correct, write *correct*.

**27.** Where <u>may</u> we find a book on birdcalls and bird songs?

> MODEL  can

**28.** <u>May</u> I bring father's tape recorder?

**29.** <u>Leave</u> George try his birdcall.

**30.** Mrs. Yamamoto can <u>learn</u> us about bird songs.

**31.** We can <u>set</u> here near the edge of the woods.

**32.** Where did she <u>learn</u> so much about birds?

**33.** Let's <u>sit</u> our nature notebooks on the ground.

**34.** Where did you <u>leave</u> your tapes of bird songs?

**35.** I <u>sit</u> them on the ground.

**36.** Any animal <u>may</u> take them away.

**37.** That will <u>learn</u> you not to do that again.

## Application — Writing and Speaking

**Tree Poem**   Imagine that you are a tree. Write a poem about something that happens to you. Use some of the verbs in this lesson in your poem. Read your poem to your classmates.

# 5 Contractions

◆ **FOCUS** A **contraction** is a shortened form of two words.

You can sometimes combine two words into a contraction. The words in color are contractions.

**1.** I haven't seen the rockets. **haven't = have + not**

**2.** They're on display now. **They're = They + are**

Some contractions are formed by joining a verb and *not*. Other contractions are formed by joining the words *I, you, he, she, it, we,* or *they* and a verb. An apostrophe takes the place of the letter or letters that have been dropped.

| Contractions Made from Verbs and *not* | | | |
|---|---|---|---|
| do not | = don't | have not | = haven't |
| does not | = doesn't | has not | = hasn't |
| did not | = didn't | had not | = hadn't |
| is not | = isn't | could not | = couldn't |
| are not | = aren't | would not | = wouldn't |
| was not | = wasn't | should not | = shouldn't |
| were not | = weren't | cannot | = can't |
| will not | = won't | must not | = mustn't |

| Contractions Made from *I, you, he, she, it, we,* or *they* and Verbs | |
|---|---|
| I + am | = I'm |
| you, we, they + are | = you're, we're, they're |
| he, she, it + is *or* has | = he's, she's, it's |
| I, you, we, they + have | = I've, you've, we've, they've |
| I, you, he, she, it, we, they, + had *or* would | = I'd, you'd, he'd, she'd, it'd we'd, they'd |
| I, we + will | = I'll, we'll |
| you, he, she, it, they + will | = you'll, he'll, she'll, it'll, they'll |

## Guided Practice

**A.** Identify the contraction for each pair of words.

1. do not    3. should not    5. would not    7. he had
2. she will    4. it has    6. have not    8. they are

## THINK AND REMEMBER

◆ Remember that a **contraction** is a shortened form of two words.

## Independent Practice

**B. Writing Contractions**  Write the contraction for each pair of words.

9. I will

MODEL ▷ I'll

10. they will
11. does not
12. he has
13. is not
14. he is
15. they have

16. you have
17. had not
18. she has
19. was not
20. I will
21. are not

22. you are
23. you will
24. we had
25. it had
26. she had
27. you had

**C. Revising Sentences**  Rewrite each sentence. Replace the underlined words with a contraction.

28. <u>You would</u> be surprised to hear about Dr. Franz.

MODEL ▷ You'd be surprised to hear about Dr. Franz.

29. Dr. Franz <u>has not</u> finished his project yet.
30. <u>I have</u> asked him many questions about it.
31. <u>He will</u> listen to my questions.
32. He <u>will not</u> answer any of them.
33. Dr. Franz wishes <u>he had</u> started earlier.
34. Then he <u>would not</u> be in such a rush.
35. <u>I am</u> the most curious reporter <u>he has</u> ever met.
36. You <u>must not</u> tell anyone what <u>I will</u> tell you.
37. <u>It is</u> the world's most advanced telescope.
38. Dr. Franz <u>does not</u> expect to finish it this year.
39. <u>He is</u> going to try to complete it in two years.
40. <u>You will</u> be able to see distant galaxies with it.
41. <u>I would</u> like to travel to outer space.
42. Someday, <u>we will</u> be able to visit other planets.

## Application — Writing

**Magazine Advertisement**  Imagine that you are working for a travel agency that sells vacations to outer space. Choose a place in space to visit. Possibilities include the moon, a planet, or a star. Write a magazine advertisement to encourage people to travel there. Use contractions in your advertisement.

# Building Vocabulary
## Prefixes

It's a mystery why these butterflies disappear and then suddenly reappear.

The scientist in the cartoon uses two interesting words: *disappear* and *reappear*. Each of these words is made up of two parts: a prefix and a base word.

A **prefix** is a word part added to the beginning of a base word to give it a new meaning. A **base word** is the simplest form of a word. In *reappear*, the prefix is *re* (meaning "again") and the base word is *appear*. The new word, *reappear*, means "to appear again."

This chart shows some common prefixes. By learning what they mean, you can guess the meanings of many new words.

| Prefix | Meaning | Example |
|--------|---------|---------|
| dis | opposite of | disapprove |
| mis | incorrectly | misspell |
| pre | before | pretest |
| re | again; back | repaint |
| un | not; opposite of | unpack |
| non | not; lack of | nonsense |
| in | not | inactive |
| im | not | impolite |

Notice that the prefixes *un, non, in,* and *im* all mean "not." If you are not sure which of these to use with a base word, check a dictionary.

## Reading Practice

Read each sentence. Write the word that begins with a prefix. Draw a line under the prefix. Then write a definition of the word based on the meanings of the prefix and the base word.

1. The scientist wanted to uncover a mystery.
2. He set out to find the disappearing butterflies.
3. He had preplanned every step of his expedition.
4. Somehow he misread his map.
5. He retraced his steps in the jungle.
6. He worked nonstop all day long.
7. He began to feel incapable of continuing.
8. Suddenly he saw what seemed impossible.
9. Hundreds of butterflies reappeared before him.

## Writing Practice

Rewrite each sentence. Replace the words in parentheses with a word that begins with one of these prefixes: *dis, mis, pre, re, un, non, in,* or *im.* Use the underlined word as the base word. If necessary, check the words in a dictionary.

10. The scientist (<u>wrote</u> again) his butterfly report.
11. He was (not <u>satisfied</u>) with the first draft.
12. He thought the last paragraph was (not <u>effective</u>).
13. He did not want to (<u>state</u> incorrectly) the facts.
14. He became (not <u>patient</u>) with himself.
15. He took a break and drank a glass of (not <u>fat</u>) milk.
16. He worked (not <u>disturbed</u>) all afternoon.
17. He asked a friend to (<u>view</u> before) his writing, and his friend thought the butterfly report was great.

## Project

Write a skit in which each of the characters is one of the prefixes in this lesson. Have the prefixes debate which one is the most important. Each prefix should introduce itself, say what its meaning is, and give examples of base words to which it can be added. Work with classmates to present your skit to the class.

# Language Enrichment
## Verbs

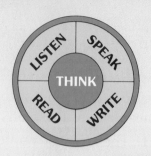

Use what you know about verbs to do these activities.

 **Weather Report**

Imagine that you are the woman in this picture. You are about to send a weather report on your computer to a news station. Write a paragraph telling about the changes in the weather and how they have affected your house and neighborhood. Use irregular verbs in the past tense. Read your report to a classmate. Find out if he or she has any suggestions for adding information to the report.

 **Fishing for Contractions**

Divide index cards into pairs. On one card write a contraction, for example, *won't*. On the other card write the two words that form that contraction: *will not*. Use a different contraction for each pair of cards. Deal seven cards to each player. Place the remaining cards in a stack facedown. One player begins by choosing a card in his or her hand and asking the other player for the match. For example, for *it is,* he or she should ask for *it's*. If the opponent does not have the card, he or she says, "Go Fish." Then the first player draws a card from the pile. When a player has a pair, he or she places the cards faceup on the table. Play ends when one player has no cards left.

 **Beastly Etiquette**

Write five silly directions for animals to follow in order to be polite. Correctly use as many easily confused verb pairs as you can. For example: *A well-mannered giraffe may sit while eating but should never set its front legs on the table.* Draw cartoons that show the animals in these situations. Share your cartoons with other students.

# CONNECTING
## LANGUAGE ↔ WRITING

In this unit you learned that a direct object is the noun or pronoun that receives the action of a verb. A direct object answers the questions *Whom?* or *What?* after an action verb.

◆ **Using Direct Objects in Your Writing** Knowing how to identify direct objects helps you better understand what you read. Knowing how to use direct objects in your own writing helps you clearly express your ideas to your readers.

Pay attention to direct objects as you do these activities.

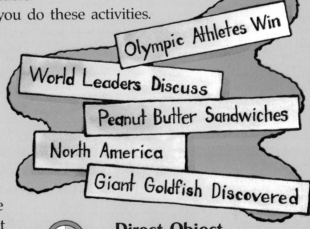

Olympic Athletes Win
World Leaders Discuss
Peanut Butter Sandwiches
North America
Giant Goldfish Discovered

### Vocabulary Woman Meets Mr. Un

You learned about prefixes on the **Building Vocabulary** pages. Use what you learned to try this activity.

Vocabulary Woman is a superhero who likes to supply needy people with happy words such as *possible, capable, sense, understand,* and *able.* Mr. Un is a prefix villain who likes to make people miserable by adding negative prefixes to form words such as *impossible, incapable, nonsense, misunderstand,* and *disable.*

Write a conversation between Vocabulary Woman and Mr. Un. Have them tell why they like their jobs and give examples of their work.

### Direct Object Scramble

Scan the headlines of a newspaper for action verbs with direct objects. Clip the headlines or copy them onto strips of paper. Then cut the direct objects away from the action verbs, make two piles, and scramble the cards in each pile. Close your eyes and randomly pick an action verb and a direct object from your two piles. Then write a short, silly news bulletin based on your scrambled headline. Read the bulletin to your class.

# 4 Unit Checkup

| Think Back | Think Ahead |
|---|---|
| ◆ What did you learn about paragraphs of comparison and contrast? What did you do to write one? | ◆ How will what you learned about paragraphs of comparison and contrast help you when you read factual information?<br><br>◆ How will knowing how to evaluate and to compare and contrast two things help you write paragraphs? A story? A research report? |
| ◆ What did you learn about verbs, direct objects, and contractions? How will that help you express action? | ◆ How can using what you learned about verbs, direct objects, and contractions help improve your writing? |

## Paragraphs of Comparison and Contrast  *pages 166–167*

Read the paragraphs. Then follow the directions.

The two more well-known seals, harbor seals and elephant seals, are alike in some important ways. Both kinds of seals are warm-blooded animals that live in or near the sea. Both have flippers which help them to swim, and these two types of animals have layers of blubber that help them keep their body heat.

However, the harbor seal and the elephant seal are quite different. Elephant seals have big heads and long, curved noses. Harbor seals are small and have short snouts. Harbor seals often shed a few hairs from their fur, while elephant seals lose large pieces of skin and hair and look shaggy. Another difference is in the sounds both animals make. Harbor seals will snort and growl at a high pitch, but elephant seals make loud, deep growls.

1. Write a sentence that tells what is being compared and contrasted.
2. List the similarities noted by the writer.
3. Write the topic sentence of the second paragraph.
4. List the differences noted by the writer.
5. Identify any comparison-and-contrast words used.

## Evaluating to Compare and Contrast   *page 168*

Read the following sentences. Make a chart of the comparisons
and contrasts used in the sentences.

6. The cowrie shell and the oyster shell belong to a family of
   animals called mollusks.
7. The oyster is valued for its meat and shell, but the cowrie's
   shell is its only valuable part.
8. In Africa and India, cowrie shells are used as money, while
   oyster shells are used for building roads in Caribbean islands.
9. The animal in a cowrie shell lives in warm seas, but the oyster
   makes its home in either warm or cold seas.
10. Both shells are hard coverings that have three layers.

## Using Formal and Informal Language   *page 169*

Read each sentence. Write *formal* if the sentence tone is formal.
Write *informal* if the sentence tone is informal. Rewrite each
sentence, changing its tone.

11. "Someday, I will become an astronaut," Jorge told his teacher.
12. He wrote to the Johnson Space Center and politely asked for
    suggestions on books about astronauts.
13. "How about this kid? He wants to go up in space!" a man
    exclaimed as he read Jorge's letter.
14. The man replied with suggestions for Jorge.

## The Writing Process   *pages 170–181*

15. When planning to write paragraphs of comparison and
    contrast, what is the first thing you should do?
    **a.** brainstorm possible topics    **b.** find facts in a book
    **c.** organize notes made from books read
16. Why should you use a chart to organize facts?
    **a.** A chart looks impressive.    **b.** A chart is easy to make.
    **c.** A chart helps group similarities and differences.
17. Suppose you were revising your paragraphs about two kinds
    of plants. The first paragraph has a sentence about a
    difference between the plants. What should you do with the
    sentence?
    **a.** leave sentence alone    **b.** cut the sentence
    **c.** move sentence to second paragraph
18. What is important to check when proofreading?
    **a.** how long the paragraphs are **b.** how interesting they are
    **c.** errors in capitalization, punctuation, and spelling

## Irregular Verbs    *pages 184–185*

Write the form of the verb in parentheses ( ) that correctly completes the sentence.

19. Scientists have (make) it possible to drink seawater safely.
20. With their method they have (take) the danger out of drinking it.
21. If a ship captain has (write) a warning sign about drinking seawater, then you should obey it.
22. No matter what you have (eat), a drink of seawater will make you very ill.
23. Many shipwrecked sailors have (go) to great lengths to obtain fresh water to drink.
24. Seawater turned into fresh water has (give) some factories the water they need.
25. Scientists have (think) the method might also help people living in desert areas.

## More Irregular Verbs    *pages 186–187*

Write the past-tense form of the verb in parentheses ( ).

26. Patrick (know) about the sand-sculpting contest for weeks.
27. He and his friends (begin) practicing for the contest.
28. Every Saturday for the last month, they (bring) their shovels to the beach at Galveston.
29. Patrick (teach) his friends the best method to use.
30. He and his friends (choose) a penguin as the subject of their sculpture.
31. Some sculptors (lose) the contest because they failed to construct their sand sculptures in time to be judged.
32. The dunes near Patrick's spot (break) the force of the wind.
33. He and his friends (grow) confident of their victory in the contest.

## Direct Objects    *pages 188–189*

Write the direct object in each sentence.

34. Gwendolyn enjoys science fiction books.
35. Her science fiction books give her lots of interesting ideas.
36. A space shuttle carries astronauts into outer space and back.
37. Gwendolyn owns a model of a space shuttle.
38. She reads many books about futuristic possibilities.
39. Gwendolyn once saw the actual space shuttle.
40. She visited a NASA installation on her vacation.
41. Gwendolyn plans a journey into outer space some day.

## Easily Confused Verb Pairs   *pages 190–191*

Write the verb in parentheses that correctly completes each sentence.

42. Felipe and Darryl (teach, learn) me about rocks.
43. Felipe (can, may) polish rocks so well that they gleam like gems when he is finished.
44. Darryl wants me to (teach, learn) him what I know.
45. Their parents (let, leave) them alone to hike along the seashore and look for interesting rocks to keep.
46. When they search for rocks, sometimes the two boys get tired, and they (sit, set) for a while.
47. If a rock has too much seaweed attached, they (let, leave) it alone.
48. Darryl and Felipe (can, may) invite their friends along when they hunt for rocks tomorrow.
49. They will (sit, set) their rocks on a bench to dry them.

## Contractions   *pages 192–193*

Rewrite each sentence. Replace the underlined words with a contraction.

50. We are standing on the northern edge of the Grand Canyon.
51. It has been the most incredible view we have seen so far.
52. Our guide told us that the Colorado River does not flow slowly.
53. If there is enough time, we would like to hike to the southern edge of the canyon.
54. Our guide says he cannot see how we will have enough energy to hike that far.
55. We could not have dreamed of a better vacation than this one!
56. When we return home, you will have to see the photographs we have taken of the canyon.

## Prefixes   *pages 194–195*

Read each sentence. Write the word that begins with a prefix.
Draw a line under the prefix. Then write a definition of the word
based on the meanings of the prefix and the base word.

57. Tracy's father hated to see anyone break rules and misbehave while on his fishing boat.
58. Because he wanted to be fair, Tracy's father was as impersonal as possible when she interviewed for a job on his boat.
59. His boat was not a place for disorder, and he kept every part neat and clean.
60. Before he left his home, he predetermined which part of the ocean he would visit.

# 1-4 Cumulative Review

## Compound Subjects   *pages 46–47*

Write each compound subject. Underline the simple subjects in each compound subject.

1. Martha and I live near San Antonio, Texas.
2. Martha and her parents sent a postcard from their visit to the River Walk in San Antonio.
3. My cousins and I went to the River Walk yesterday.
4. Flowers, boats, and shops were among the sights.
5. Postcards, photographs, and letters are three ways we can let others know about our trip.
6. Martha and I told our class about our visit to San Antonio.
7. A speech or a slide show would be a way to inform people.
8. Questions, answers, and comments ended our presentation to the class.

## Compound Predicates   *pages 48–49*

Write each compound predicate. Underline the simple predicates in each compound predicate.

9. A newspaper editor called and sent the photographer to the fire.
10. The photographer bought some film and took it with him.
11. He got into his car and drove toward the fire.
12. He jumped out of the car, locked the door, and ran down the street.
13. A firefighter grabbed the photographer and stopped him.
14. The photographer was too close and needed a safer spot.
15. He ran across the street and aimed his camera at the blazing building.
16. His photos arrived on time and satisfied the newspaper editor.

## Plural Nouns   *pages 90–93*

Write the plural form of each noun.

17. piano
18. burro
19. dictionary
20. halo
21. sheep
22. tale
23. cafeteria
24. trophy
25. bookshelf
26. mix
27. hunch
28. moss
29. display
30. punch
31. foot
32. fantasy
33. image
34. gas

## Singular and Plural Possessive Nouns   *pages 100–103*

Replace the underlined words with a singular possessive noun or a plural possessive noun.

35. The work of a cowboy can be difficult.
36. Horses are part of the equipment of a cowboy.
37. A day in the life of a cowboy might include riding his own horse and taming wild ones.
38. More experienced cowboys might work farther away from the stables belonging to ranchers.
39. The image of a person of the lonesome cowboy is a truthful one.
40. After the work of a hard day, cowboys like to share tall tales about brave deeds.
41. The best friends of cowboys are strong horses, ropes, boots, and saddles.

## Action Verbs ✓ *pages 138–139*

Write the action verb in each sentence.

42. Oliver hugged his puppy, Ranger.
43. He giggled at Ranger's clumsy movements.
44. Ranger stumbled over to his dish of water.
45. Oliver carried his puppy to the bedroom.
46. The dog slipped out of his owner's arms.
47. Ranger yelped at the sight of the bathtub.
48. The puppy splashed water all over the floor.
49. Oliver rubbed Ranger's fur with a clean towel.

## Linking Verbs ✓ *pages 140–141*

Write the verb in each sentence. Then write *action verb* or *linking verb*.

50. Yolanda seemed nervous about the volleyball game.
51. Her friend Terry approached her.
52. Terry appeared concerned about her.
53. Yolanda frowned at the volleyball on the floor.
54. Terry patted her friend on the shoulder.
55. Yolanda became very quiet.
56. Terry joked about her own mistakes in the last game.
57. Yolanda felt better after that.
58. Together they raced onto the volleyball court.
59. Yolanda smacked the ball for the first score.

## Main Verbs and Helping Verbs *pages 142−143*

Write each sentence. Underline the main verb once. Underline the helping verb twice.

60. Snakes will grow completely new skins several times a year.
61. People have found nearly perfect snakeskins in the rocky or the bushy homes of snakes.
62. We are planning a visit to a snake exhibit at the museum.
63. We will listen to a lecture from a snake expert.
64. He has studied snakes for many years.
65. As a child, the expert had feared snakes.
66. He is bringing snakes from his own collection.
67. We are hoping to see some of them at the exhibit.

## Present Tense *pages 144−145*

Write the present-tense form of the verb in parentheses ( ).

68. Evita _____ the stars every night. (watch)
69. She _____ the lens of her father's telescope. (adjust)
70. Sometimes her father _____ about his daughter's interest in astronomy. (joke)
71. She _____ to the telescope as soon as it gets dark. (rush)
72. Evita gladly _____ up watching television in order to watch the stars. (pass)
73. Her father _____ the stars too. (enjoy)
74. He _____ charts of the stars for his weather-reporting job. (design)
75. Together they _____ their eyes on the night sky. (fix)

## Past Tense and Future Tense *pages 146−149*

Write the verb in each sentence. Then write *present, past,* or *future.*

76. Bridget wants a cat of her own.
77. Last year her mother promised her a cat.
78. They walked to a nearby pet shop, but the shop had no more cats that day.
79. Bridget begs her mother for a cat.
80. Bridget's mother will bring home a kitten for her daughter.
81. Bridget will read a book so she will know how to care for her new kitten.

## ✓ Irregular Verbs    *pages 184–185*

Write the correct past-tense form of the verb in parentheses ( ).

82. Donald's father _____ a book about geysers. (write)
83. He _____ Donald would like to visit Yellowstone National Park. (think)
84. They _____ to the park because of its famous geyser, "Old Faithful." (go)
85. "Old Faithful" _____ them lots of information about geysers and volcanoes. (give)
86. While at the park the scientists _____ "Old Faithful" at work about once an hour. (see)
87. The powerful geyser _____ them think of a volcano. (make)
88. The water _____ from areas of great heat, deep within the earth. (come)

## ✓ More Irregular Verbs    *pages 186–187*

Write each sentence. Use the correct form of the verb in parentheses with the helping verb.

89. The seagulls have _____ on the water all morning. (swim)
90. The brisk morning wind has _____ my parents' patio chair onto its side. (blow)
91. They have _____ some other patio furniture because of the wind. (lose)
92. In a way, the wind has _____ my parents' patio furniture. (steal)
93. During a storm, the wind had _____ a big hole in the sail of our boat. (tear)

## Direct Objects    *pages 188–189*

Write each sentence. Underline each action verb once. Underline each direct object twice. If there is no direct object, write *no direct object.*

94. They launched the rocket.
95. The astronaut examined his equipment.
96. The view from the rocket was awesome.
97. Another astronaut flipped some switches inside the rocket.
98. She was excited about the journey.
99. They answered the radio.
100. The President congratulated them.

# UNIT

5

# Reporting Events

◆ **COMPOSITION FOCUS:** News Story
◆ **LANGUAGE FOCUS:** Pronouns

Robots Defy Gravity. Mysterious Disease Threatens Crops. Local Student Catches Monstrous Fish. Which of these events would you want to know about? Most people learn about unusual or important events through reports in radio programs, television news broadcasts, or newspapers.

Newspaper reporters and news broadcasters make their living by informing others about world, national, and local events. Jon Engellenner, for example, works as a newspaper reporter for the *Sacramento Bee* in Sacramento, California.

Jon Engellenner's job is to go where an event is taking place and to gather firsthand information about it. He makes notes about his observations and interviews people who may have witnessed the event or who took part in it. Back in the newsroom, he uses his notes to write a report about the event. Such reports, called **news stories,** form the backbone of any newspaper. In this unit you will learn how to report events through a news story.

Jon Engellenner writes *to inform* the public about important events.

# Reading with a Writer's Eye
## News Story

When a seagoing whale takes a wrong turn and swims up a river in California, that's news! Jon Engellenner and a flock of other reporters followed the lost whale, who became known as "Humphrey." As you read these news stories by Jon Engellenner and by another reporter, notice that the writers give facts that answer the questions *who, what, where,* and *when.*

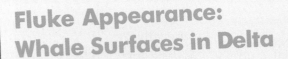

## Fluke Appearance: Whale Surfaces in Delta

By Jon Engellenner

RIO VISTA—Monday afternoon a humpback whale, estimated to be 35 or 40 feet long, evidently took a wrong turn at the Golden Gate and swam through San Francisco Bay and into the Sacramento-San Joaquin Delta.

At Rio Vista, 58 miles from the Golden Gate, the whale either realized its mistake or ran out of salt water.

The Coast Guard spent much of the late afternoon trying to turn the big mammal around, but it seemed content to circle in the semi-salty water just downstream from the Rio Vista bridge.

The Coast Guard had several 21-foot out-board boats tailing the whale, which showed a little of its back but no tail fin when it rose to spout.

Observers saw the whale run into light-marker posts in the river on two occasions, leading to speculation that it was disoriented and in poor health.

"It's been zigzagging below the bridge for several hours. I suppose it's quite confused," suggested Rio Vistan Junior Chapman. "I suppose if it were in the ocean, it would be going north."

"Too bad they don't have a recording of a whale that they could use to lead him back down the river," she said.

## Delta Whale Taking a Doomed Course

By Jon Engellenner

RIO VISTA—A 40-foot humpback whale, ignoring guide boats and recorded whale-talk, made a move toward the Pacific then swam upstream Tuesday.

It made a left turn into the Sacramento River Deep Water Ship Channel, taking what one marine biologist called a doomed course away from the sea.

Nobody can recall a whale moving so far inland—so far from the Pacific Ocean.

"At present course and speed, he'll be in Sacramento for breakfast," quipped Coast Guard spokesman John Reis as the whale passed from Solano County to Yolo County in the deep-water channel.

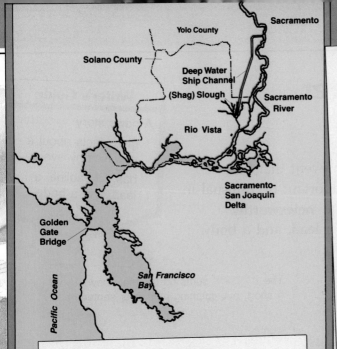

## Slough to Get Noisy for Whale

By Jon Engellenner

RIO VISTA—The government's quiet whale-watchers will become noisemaking whale-herders this week in an attempt to drive a 40-foot humpback whale out of a small Solano County slough.

The public will be kept half a mile away as federal scientists try a Japanese pipe-banging method used to herd dolphins, it was announced Wednesday in Rio Vista by Jim Lecky of the National Marine Fisheries Service.

"We've decided that the whale's been on its own long enough," he said.

"Leaving the 40-foot whale alone has been the strategy for the past week," he said, "but nothing has happened. The whale has decided to stay in the slough.

"He has not solved the problem himself. If he stays where he is, he's in a lot of trouble."

The experiment is expected to begin today or Friday. Other experiments with whale sounds and soft music haven't worked. Because whales use their own sonar for navigation and are extremely sensitive to sounds, the scientists will be backed up by patrols to keep people and airplanes away during the experiment.

## Humphrey Lured Back to Ocean by Whale Calls

SAN FRANCISCO (AP)—Humphrey the wayward whale, lured by the flute-like sounds of feeding humpbacks, splashed through the Golden Gate into the Pacific Ocean on Monday after a 3½-week fresh-water cruise that made him a celebrity.

Racing at three knots against a rising tide, the 40-foot, 45-ton leviathan cleared the fog-shrouded Golden Gate Bridge at 4:36 p.m. as crewmen aboard a flotilla of military and civilian boats cheered and waved goodbye.

After leaping spectacularly, almost vertically, early in the day and swimming playfully in circles, the endangered humpback sped two miles, then paused several hours to frolic beneath the San Rafael-Richmond Bridge, six miles from the Golden Gate.

He started moving again with flood tide in midafternoon, nosing in and out of San Francisco Bay and spouting water as 10 Navy boats chased him and clanged pipes to keep him going.

Busloads of tourists and local whale-watchers gathered along the shore near the chilly, fog-shrouded Golden Gate Bridge to catch a glimpse of Humphrey's exit.

## Respond

1. Which news story interests you the most? What information is included that makes you care about what is happening to the whale?

## Discuss

2. What facts do the writers give to answer *who, what, where,* and *when*? Where in each news story are these important facts presented?

3. People read about Humphrey almost every day for 24 days. What interesting details do the writers include to keep people reading about Humphrey?

# Thinking As a Writer
## Analyzing a News Story

**Writer's Guide**

A news story
- gives facts about a newsworthy event.
- has a headline, a lead, and a body.

A news story gives facts about an event that has just happened. The event must be important or unusual in some way. Such an event is said to be **newsworthy.**

Every news story has a **headline,** a **lead,** and a **body.**

## A Whale of a Monument Unveiled in Rio Vista

RIO VISTA—Today along the banks of the Sacramento River, Rio Vistans uncovered a polished granite monument erected to honor Humphrey, the wrong-way whale.

Humphrey's image decorates both sides of the monument. Viewed from the river, Humphrey is headed back to sea. Viewed from Rio Vista, Humphrey is headed upstream, where he frolicked for 3½ weeks in the fresh water of the Delta.

Also on the city side is a poem written by 12-year-old Richard Fonbuena to honor the whale.

Humphrey the humpback whale, a
mighty whale was he.
He swam into the Delta to see
what he could see.
The people stood and stared, the
fish were scared.
He was famous across the nation
until they ended his vacation.

Richard's poem was selected as the best of 15 entries in a poem-writing competition. Richard also won $50 and a Humphrey T-shirt.

The headline sums up the main news event using a short, eye-catching phrase or sentence.

The lead is the first paragraph of a news story. The lead tells *who* was involved, *what* happened, *where* it happened, and *when* it happened.

The body is everything that comes after the lead. The body gives details and background information about the event. The most important details come first, followed by those of less importance. The least important details come last.

## Discuss

1. Look at the headline, the lead, and the body of the news story about Humphrey. How is the information in each part different?
2. What information in the lead answers the questions *who, what, where,* and *when?*
3. What is the main news event in the story? What makes this event newsworthy?

# Try Your Hand

**A. Analyze Leads**  Read the following leads from news stories about other amazing animals. For each sentence, write *who* was involved, *what* happened, *where* it happened, and *when* it happened.

1.
> LONDON—George, the tallest giraffe on record, arrived from Kenya yesterday to take up residence in his new home at the Chester Zoo.

3.
> SAN DIEGO—Two 15-year-old cats are $415,000 richer today, following the reading in San Diego of their deceased owner's will, in which he left all his wealth and possessions to his feline friends.

2.
> LONDON—Last night at a national talking bird contest held here, an African gray parrot named Prudle won for the twelfth year in a row.

4.
> SILVERTON—Bobbie, a collie dog lost by his owners while they were on vacation in Indiana, walked 2000 miles and finally turned up at his owner's home in Oregon early last week.

**B. Add Information for the Body**
Look back at the leads for the news stories on this page. Write one sentence that might appear in the body of each story.

**C. Write Headlines**  Reread each lead, and look over the sentence you wrote for the body. Write a headline for each news story.

**D. Read News Stories**  Choose one of the news stories on pages 208–209, or find another news story in a current newspaper. Read the story aloud to a partner, identifying the headline, the lead, and the body.

## Writer's Notebook

**Collecting Social Studies Words**  Did you notice the social studies words such as *slough* and *delta* in the news stories about Humphrey? Read the stories again, and record in your *Writer's Notebook* any sentences that include social studies words you don't know. Look up the words in a dictionary, and record their meanings in your *Writer's Notebook*. Try to use your new social studies words when you write and when you speak.

# Thinking As a Writer
## Classifying Fact and Opinion

To write a news story, good writers present only facts. They do not include their personal opinions. A **fact** is a statement that someone can prove to be true or false.

**1.** Humphrey is a humpback whale.

The writer considered this statement a fact because its truth can be proved. Humphrey's features can be checked against information in a book about whales or in an encyclopedia.

The writer was careful to avoid any statements like these.

**2.** I think Humphrey knew that people were trying to help him.

**3.** Whales are always friendly.

These statements are opinions and cannot be proved true or false. They express the writer's personal attitudes and feelings about whales. When writers give their opinions, they often use words such as *I think, I believe, silly, awful,* and *best.*

As you write a news story, be sure to present only facts, not opinions.

## Discuss

**1.** Look back at the news story on page 210. Does the writer include only statements of fact? How can you tell?

**2.** "I believe more people should be involved in saving our valuable wildlife." Should a writer include this statement in a news story? Why or why not?

## Try Your Hand

**Write Facts and Opinions** Write three facts and three opinions about a subject that interests you. Trade sentences with a partner. Identify which of your partner's statements are facts and which are opinions. Then discuss with your partner how each of you could prove the facts.

# Developing the Writer's Craft
## Using Precise Words

Because reporters serve as the eyes and ears of their readers, their news stories must tell exactly what happened. To give an exact picture of an event, a good reporter uses precise words.

Read these sentences from the news stories about Humphrey.

1. It seemed content to <u>circle</u> in the semi-salty water.
2. It's been <u>zigzagging</u> below the bridge for several hours.

The writer carefully chose the underlined verbs to tell about Humphrey's movement. Each verb gives the reader a different and precise mental picture of the way Humphrey swam.

When you write your news story, try to capture on paper exactly what happened. Use precise words to help your readers picture the event.

## Discuss

1. Look at the last news story on page 209. Which verbs does the writer use to tell about Humphrey's movement? What mental picture do you have when you read each verb?
2. Which of the five senses does the reporter appeal to when he reports that the Navy boats "clanged pipes"? How does the use of the precise verb *clanged* help you understand what the reporter experienced firsthand?

## Try Your Hand

**Use Precise Words**  Look at the pictures of the three runners. Write a sentence for a story in your school newspaper that tells how each runner crossed the finish line. Use precise words like the ones in the box.

leaped
limped
raced
floated
sped
stumbled
tripped
zoomed

# 1 Prewriting
## News Story

**Writer's Guide**

**Prewriting Checklist**
- ☑ Brainstorm topics.
- ☑ Select a topic.
- ☑ Think about your audience and your purpose.
- ☑ Gather information.
- ☑ Organize the facts.

Joan, a student at Jackson Elementary School, wanted to write a news story for her classmates. She used the checklist in the **Writer's Guide** to help her plan her story. Look at what she did.

## ◆ Brainstorming and Selecting a Topic

First, Joan brainstormed a list of possible topics for her news story. Joan included as many recent events as she could think of. Look at Joan's list.

Next, Joan looked down her list and crossed out topics that were not newsworthy or that would not interest her audience. She also crossed off topics for which she would have trouble finding information.

Finally, Joan circled the most important topic left on her list. She decided to write about the spelling bee because the winner, Grover Lewis, was in her own class. Joan's audience would therefore be very interested in the story. Joan also knew that she could get enough information for her story by talking to Grover himself.

Jane fell off swing
Grover won citywide spelling bee
new mayor elected
skate sale
national bicycle race
author spoke at library

## Discuss

1. Look at each topic Joan crossed off her list. Why do you think she didn't choose it?
2. If Joan were writing a news story for her book club, which topic do you think she might have chosen? Why?

## ◆ Gathering Information

After Joan selected her topic, she gathered information for her news story. Joan used an announcement from the school office about the spelling bee to get facts to answer the questions *who, what, where,* and *when.*

Then, she decided to interview Grover Lewis to gather firsthand information about the event. An **interview** is a conversation between a reporter and a person involved in an event. Using a list of questions she had prepared, Joan interviewed Grover to get the main facts, some interesting details, and Grover's impressions.

During the interview, Joan took notes. After the interview, she looked over her notes to make sure they were clear and easy to read.

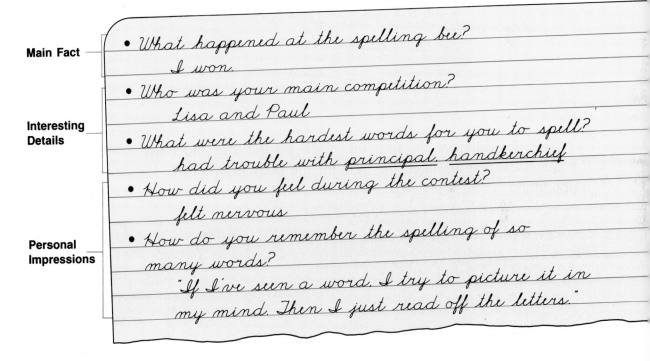

**Main Fact**
- What happened at the spelling bee?
  I won.
- Who was your main competition?
  Lisa and Paul

**Interesting Details**
- What were the hardest words for you to spell?
  had trouble with principal, handkerchief
- How did you feel during the contest?
  felt nervous

**Personal Impressions**
- How do you remember the spelling of so many words?
  "If I've seen a word, I try to picture it in my mind. Then I just read off the letters."

## Discuss

1. Look at the list of questions Joan prepared for her interview with Grover. Which questions ask for information that would be best in the body?
2. Why did Joan include in her notes some of Grover's exact words? What did he say? How will Joan remember that they are Grover's exact words?
3. What other questions could Joan have asked?

# ◆ Organizing the Facts

After Joan had gathered all the information she needed for her news story, she was ready to organize her notes. Joan knew that a news story should contain only facts. She selected from her notes the facts she wanted to include in her story. She chose those facts that she thought would interest her audience the most.

What happened at the spelling bee?
✓ Grover and two students
  are in final round.
✓ Grover won with accommodate.
  Grover is really smart.
✓ Lisa used one c, Paul used one m.
  Lisa won last year's bee.

Then, Joan divided the facts into those for the lead and those for the body. She arranged the facts for the body in order of importance.

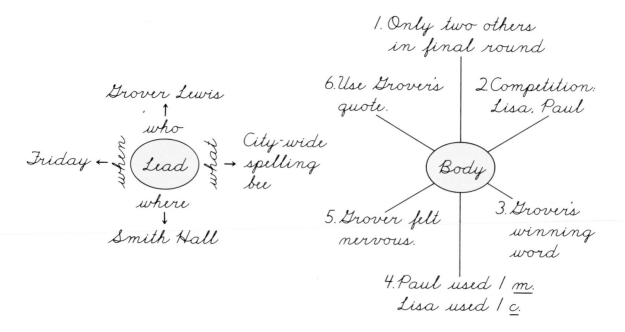

WRITING PROCESS

## Discuss

1. In which part of her news story did Joan plan to include the detail about Smith Hall? Why did she include it in that part?
2. Why did Joan leave out the part about Grover being smart?
3. During the interview, Joan asked Grover how his family felt when he won the spelling bee. If she had decided to add his answer to the body, where should she have placed it? Explain your answer.

## Try Your Hand

Now plan a news story of your own.

A. **Brainstorm and Select a Topic**  Brainstorm a list of possible topics. Include all the recent events that you can remember. Think about each topic and about your audience.

- Cross out topics that are not important or unusual enough for a news story.
- Cross out topics that won't interest your audience.
- Cross out topics for which you might have trouble finding information.
- Circle the most important topic left on your list. This will be the topic of your news story.

B. **Gather Information**  When you are satisfied with your topic, plan ways to gather information about the event. If you choose to interview someone, prepare questions that ask for the main facts, a few interesting details, and some personal impressions. If you need help, follow the **Tips on How to Interview** on page 218.

C. **Organize the Facts**  Look over your notes.

- A news story should contain only facts, so cross out any of your own opinions.
- Think about your audience. Choose the facts that would most interest your audience.
- Choose facts for the lead and the body. Arrange facts for the body in order from most important to least important. You may want to make a diagram like Joan's.

 **Save your notes and diagram in your *Writer's Notebook*. You will use them when you draft your news story.**

# Listening and Speaking
## Tips on How to Interview

1. Begin by introducing yourself and explaining why you want to do the interview.
2. Be friendly. Use polite language, such as "Excuse me" and "Would you please repeat that?"
3. During your interview, listen closely for the answers to your questions about *who, what, where,* and *when.* If you don't understand the answer to a question, ask the person to explain the answer further.
4. After you ask a question, listen carefully to the answer. The answer may cause you to think of a question that is not on your list.
5. Take notes. You may also want to use a tape recorder, but first ask the person you are interviewing whether you may use it.
6. Get the full name of the person you interview. Be sure to spell it correctly.
7. Ask the person you interview whether you can quote him or her. Also, ask for a telephone number. You may need to call to check facts or to ask for more details.
8. Thank the person for the information and the interview.

# 2 Drafting
## News Story

### Writer's Guide

**Drafting Checklist**

☑ Use your notes and diagram for ideas.

☑ Write the lead first.

☑ Write the body next.

☑ Write the headline that tells the main idea last.

Using her notes and her diagram, Joan followed the checklist in the **Writer's Guide** to draft her news story. Look at what she did.

> *Jackson Boy Wins Spelling Bee*
>
> *Grover Lewis won the citywide spelling bee at Smith Hall last Friday. I think Grover could spell any word.*
>
> *Only two other students were good enough to last into the final round. They were Lisa Rud and Paul Updike from Oakview School.*

## Discuss

1. Look at Joan's lead. What facts does she give to answer *who, what, where,* and *when*?
2. What additional details might you expect to see in the body of Joan's news story? Where would you add them? Why?
3. Did Joan write a good headline for her news story? Explain your answer.

## Try Your Hand

Now you are ready to write a news story.

A. **Review Your Information** Think about the information you gathered and organized in the last lesson. Decide whether you need more information. If so, gather it.

B. **Think About Your TAP** Remember that your task is to write a news story. Your purpose is to inform your audience about the topic you have selected.

C. **Write Your First Draft** Follow the steps in the **Drafting Checklist** to write your news story.

   When you write your draft, just put all your ideas on paper. Do not worry about spelling, punctuation, or grammar. You can correct the draft later.

**TAP**

**Task:** What?
**Audience:** Who?
**Purpose:** Why?

**Save your first draft in your *Writer's Notebook*. You will use it when you revise your news story.**

COMPOSITION: DRAFTING  News Story  **219**

# 3 Responding and Revising
## News Story

Joan used the checklist in the **Writer's Guide** to revise her news story. Look at what she did.

### ◆ Checking Information

Joan decided to take away the second sentence because it gives her opinion. To show her change, Joan used this mark ✐ . In the second paragraph, Joan added an interesting detail. To show the addition, she used this mark ∧ .

### ◆ Checking Organization

Joan decided to move the last sentence to the lead, because it tells who Grover is. To show that the sentence should be moved, she used this mark ↻ .

### ◆ Checking Language

In the third paragraph, Joan replaced several words with one word. She used this mark ⊼ to make her change.

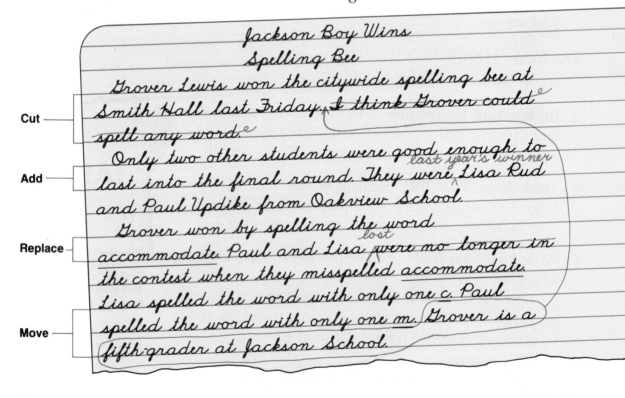

Cut — Add — Replace — Move

Jackson Boy Wins
Spelling Bee
Grover Lewis won the citywide spelling bee at Smith Hall last Friday. I think Grover could spell any word.
Only two other students were good enough to last into the final round. They were last year's winner Lisa Rud and Paul Updike from Oakview School.
Grover won by spelling the word accommodate. Paul and Lisa were no longer in the contest when they misspelled accommodate. Lisa spelled the word with only one c. Paul spelled the word with only one m. Grover is a fifth-grader at Jackson School.

## Discuss

1. Joan thought her audience would be interested in the detail she added about Lisa. Do you agree or disagree? Why?
2. Is Joan's news story better than her draft? In what ways?
3. Are there other changes Joan could have made? Explain your answer.

## Try Your Hand

Now revise your first draft.

A. **Read Your First Draft** As you read your news story, think about your audience and your purpose. Read your story silently or to a partner to see whether it is complete and well organized. Ask yourself or your partner the questions in the box.

| Responding and Revising Strategies | |
|---|---|
| ✔ **Respond**<br>**Ask yourself or a partner:** | ✔ **Revise**<br>**Try these solutions:** |
| ◆ Have I answered the questions *who, what, where,* and *when* in the lead? | ◆ Find the answers in your notes and **add** them to your lead. |
| ◆ Have I given only facts, not opinions? | ◆ **Cut** opinions or **replace** them with facts. |
| ◆ Have I given all information in order of importance? | ◆ **Move** any sentences that seem to be out of place. |
| ◆ Does each word in my news story add something to its meaning? Have I checked for wordy language? | ◆ **Cut** unnecessary words, or **replace** them with fewer words that mean the same thing. See the **Revising Workshop** on page 222. |
| ◆ Have I summed up the news event clearly in my headline? | ◆ **Replace** any words that give a wrong impression about the event. See the **Writer's Thesaurus** at the back of the book. |

B. **Make Your Changes** If the answer to any question in the box is *no,* try the solution. Use the **Editor's Marks** to show your changes.

C. **Review Your News Story Again** Keep revising your story until you feel it is well organized and complete.

**EDITOR'S MARKS**

∧ Add something.
⟋ Cut something.
◌ Move something.
⌄ Replace something.

Save your revised news story in your *Writer's Notebook.*
You will use it when you proofread your story.

# Revising Workshop
## Avoiding Wordy Language

Good writers use as few words as possible to get their message across. They avoid using wordy language. Look at the underlined words and phrases in these sentences.

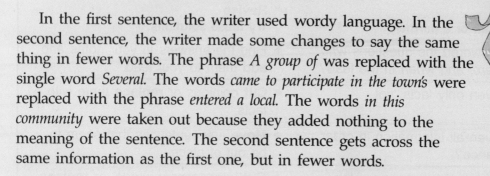

1. A group of children from Downers Grove, Illinois, came to participate in the town's kite-flying contest in this community today.
2. Several children from Downers Grove, Illinois, entered a local kite-flying contest today.

In the first sentence, the writer used wordy language. In the second sentence, the writer made some changes to say the same thing in fewer words. The phrase *A group of* was replaced with the single word *Several*. The words *came to participate in the town's* were replaced with the phrase *entered a local*. The words *in this community* were taken out because they added nothing to the meaning of the sentence. The second sentence gets across the same information as the first one, but in fewer words.

## Practice

Rewrite each sentence. Take out the words in parentheses ( ), or replace them with fewer words that mean the same thing.

1. Twelve children (put together) their own kites.
2. (The homemade kites that the children brought to the contest) were of all shapes and sizes.
3. Soon after the judge's signal, all 12 kites (took only a few seconds to get up) into the sky.
4. Everything (seemed to be going pretty well) until a strong gust of wind came along.
5. The sudden gust caught the kites and pushed them (higher into the clouds).
6. Some kite strings snapped, and many kites (could no longer be seen).
7. The judges (came to the conclusion) to postpone the contest until another day.

# 4 Proofreading
## News Story

After revising her news story, Joan used the **Writer's Guide** and the **Editor's Marks** to proofread it. Look at what she did.

### Writer's Guide

**Proofreading Checklist**

☑ Check for errors in capitalization.

☑ Check for errors in punctuation. Be sure that you have used quotation marks to show people's exact words.

☑ Check to see that all your paragraphs are indented.

☑ Check your grammar.

☑ Circle any words you think are misspelled. Find out how to spell them correctly. For proofreading help, use the **Writer's Handbook.**

> After the spelling bee was over, grover relaxed with his family in the park. He explained his *strategy* (strategie) for spelling. "If I've seen a word, I try to picture it in my mind. Then I just read off the letters, he said.

### EDITOR'S MARKS

≡ Capitalize.

⊙ Add a period.

∧ Add something.

⩚ Add a comma.

⩔⩔ Add quotation marks.

✐ Cut something.

⋀ Replace something.

⤮ Transpose.

◯ Spell correctly.

⊓ Indent paragraph.

/ Make a lowercase letter.

## Discuss

1. Look at Joan's proofread story ending. What kinds of mistakes did she make?
2. Why did Joan use quotation marks in the last two sentences of her story?

## Try Your Hand

**Proofread Your News Story** Now use the **Writer's Guide** and the **Editor's Marks** to proofread your story.

 **Save your corrected news story in your** *Writer's Notebook.* **You will use it when you publish your story.**

COMPOSITION: PROOFREADING  News Story  **223**

# 5 Publishing
## News Story

Joan made a clean copy of her news story and checked it to be sure she had not left anything out. Then she and her classmates published their news stories in a class newsletter. You can find Joan's story on page 39 of the **Writer's Handbook.**

Here's how Joan and her classmates published their newsletter.

1. First, the students decided on a name for the newsletter and designed the front page. Then, for each page, they made a layout to show the columns where the stories will be placed.

2. Next, they typed the stories to a width that fit the columns on the page layout.

3. They pasted the stories onto the layout, added illustrations, and numbered each page.

4. Once the stories were in place, they duplicated the pages and stapled them together.

5. Then, they spread the news far and wide—or at least to the class next door!

## Discuss

1. What might happen if the class forgot to plan a layout for each page?
2. Why is it important to number the pages of your newsletter in step 3?

## Try Your Hand

**Publish Your News Story** Follow the checklist in the **Writer's Guide.** If possible, create a class newsletter, or try one of these ideas for sharing your news story.

◆ Cut a large, fat zigzag pattern from yellow construction paper. Print *NEWS FLASH!* in large letters at the top of the paper, and copy your news story underneath. With your teacher's permission, tape your "news flash" to the classroom wall.

◆ Form a news team with three or more classmates. Present your stories to your class as a TV newscast.

# Writing in the Content Areas

### Writer's Guide

When you write, remember the stages of the Writing Process.

◆ Prewriting
◆ Drafting
◆ Responding and Revising
◆ Proofreading
◆ Publishing

Use what you learned to write about something that is happening at your school. You could write a news story or a paragraph. One way to publish your news story is by posting it with the work of other students on a bulletin board display titled *What's New at Our School*. Use one of these ideas or an idea of your own.

## Literature

What's new in the school library? Ask the librarian what books have recently been added to the library collection. Find out what books your librarian would recommend for students who don't enjoy reading. What are the most popular books? What programs has your librarian planned for the coming weeks?

## Physical Education

Support your athletic team. Write a sports story about the team's last game. Find out whom they played as well as when and where the game took place. Give the final score and tell who won. Include information about the team's best plays, how they got ready for the game, and the most exciting moment in the game.

## Science/Social Studies

Has a class in your school recently taken a science or social studies field trip? Find out when and where the class went. Ask students what they enjoyed most about the trip and if anything unexpected happened. Find out how the trip helped the students in science or social studies.

## Health

Cooking lunch for a crowd of hungry students is not an easy job. Ask the cafeteria manager how the daily menu is planned and how the basic food groups are included in each menu. Find out which foods are school favorites. You may want to include next week's menu in your report.

# CONNECTING
## WRITING ⬌ LANGUAGE

Reporters keep readers informed about big and little news events. A well-written news story can make readers feel as if they were at the scene of an event. It also gives readers the most important facts about what happened and who was involved. Whom and what is this news story about?

## A Winning Hitter From His Wheelchair

WEST HARTFORD, CONNECTICUT—When 11-year-old Jonathan Slifka hit a three-run home run to lead his team to its ninth straight victory in the West Hartford Youth Baseball League, he never left home plate.

Jonathan never runs the bases; he has spina bifida, and uses a wheelchair. But that has not prevented him from being an important contributor to his team, the Red Sox, which recently finished the season with a 10−2 record.

Jonathan had 22 hits for the season, batting well over .300, said his coach, Mark Wertheim. He also held his own while playing second base along with a teammate.

◆ **Pronouns in a News Story** The words highlighted in color are pronouns. They work together with nouns to help you know who or what a story is about. The pronoun *he* in the first paragraph takes the place of the noun *Jonathan Slifka*. The reporter used a pronoun to avoid writing Jonathan's name twice in the same sentence. Since news stories always tell *who* or *what*, you will find many pronouns as you read the newspaper.

◆ **Language Focus: Pronouns** The following lessons will help you use different kinds of pronouns in your own writing.

# 1 Pronouns

◆ **FOCUS** A **pronoun** is a word that takes the place of a noun or nouns.

Read these sentences. The words in color are pronouns.

1. The editor expects a man.
2. He will be surprised.
3. Nellie Bly waits for him .
4. She enters the office.

In sentences 2 and 3, the pronouns *he* and *him* replace the word *editor.* In sentence 4, the pronoun *she* replaces *Nellie Bly.*

This chart shows the singular and plural pronouns.

*The new reporter is here.*

| Singular Pronouns | Plural Pronouns |
|---|---|
| I, me | we, us |
| you | you |
| she, he, it, her, him | they, them |

*Show him in.*

> ### Link to Speaking and Writing
> Use a pronoun to avoid repeating a noun. Why did the writer replace words in the second sentence?

*Nellie traveled the world for*
*~~her~~ editor.   ^the ^she Nellie wrote many*
*stories for ~~her~~ editor.   ^him*

## Guided Practice

**A.** Identify the pronoun in each sentence.

1. You may know this person as Elizabeth Cochrane.
2. She read a newspaper article.
3. It said that a woman's place is in the home.
4. The editor found an angry letter waiting for him.

**B.** 5.—7. Identify the noun that each pronoun replaces in sentences 2—4 in **A.**

## Independent Practice

**C. Identifying Pronouns**  Read each sentence. Write the pronoun or pronouns.

8. Have you heard the song "Nellie Bly"?

MODEL ▷ you

9. In 1885, most women stayed at home, where they raised children.
10. Elizabeth Cochrane was different from them.
11. The editor nicknamed her "Nellie Bly."
12. She read *Around the World in Eighty Days.*
13. Jules Verne wrote it.
14. He wrote about a man named Fogg.
15. He went around the world in two months and two days.
16. Nellie tried to beat him by traveling faster.
17. Some people laughed at her.
18. She astonished them with that trip.

**D. Recognizing Nouns Replaced by Pronouns**  Find the pronoun in the second sentence of each pair. Write the pronoun and the noun it replaces.

19. **a.** Robin Lee Graham sailed around the world.
    **b.** He was the youngest person to make the trip alone.

MODEL ▷     he—Robin Lee Graham

20. **a.** Robin's boat was 24 feet long.
    **b.** It was called *Dove.*
21. **a.** Two cats kept Robin company.
    **b.** They were named Kili and Fili.
22. **a.** Robin met Patti on the island of Fiji.
    **b.** Later, she became Robin's wife.
23. **a.** Patti went home alone to California.
    **b.** Robin wrote letters to her.

## Application — Writing

**Travel Itinerary**  Plan your own trip around the world. Decide in which direction you will travel. Write a paragraph about your plan. Tell what parts of the world you will visit and what sights you hope to see. Use pronouns.

# 2 Subject Pronouns

◆ **FOCUS** A **subject pronoun** takes the place of a noun or nouns in the subject of a sentence.

Remember that a pronoun takes the place of a noun or nouns. The words in color are subject pronouns.

1. **a.** Sequoya was a Cherokee Indian.
   **b.** He was a Cherokee Indian.
2. **a.** The Cherokee people honor Sequoya.
   **b.** They honor Sequoya.

In sentence 1.b. the pronoun *he* replaces the noun *Sequoya*. In sentence 2.b. the pronoun *they* replaces *the Cherokee people*.

Subject pronouns also take the place of nouns that follow forms of the linking verb *be*.

3. **a.** The chief was Sequoya.
   **b.** The chief was he .

The subject pronouns are *I, you, he, she, it, we,* and *they.* The subject pronoun *I* is always capitalized. When you use *I* with another noun or pronoun as a compound subject, you should put *I* last.

4. She and I wrote a skit about Sequoya.

## Guided Practice

**A.** Identify the subject pronoun in each sentence.

1. Have you read about Sequoya's alphabet?
2. He invented an alphabet for the Cherokee.
3. They did not have a written language before Sequoya developed one.
4. We taught my sister to read Cherokee.
5. She learned very quickly.
6. I also like learning languages.
7. We enjoy speaking Cherokee more than any other language.

## Independent Practice

**B. Identifying Subject Pronouns**   Read each sentence. Write the subject pronoun.

 8. You read Braille with your fingertips.

 MODEL ▷ You

 9. It was invented by Louis Braille.

 10. He created the writing system at age 15.

 11. We make letters with raised dots.

 12. They are formed by a machine called a Braille stylus.

 13. She reads Braille better than Mary does.

 14. I would like to learn Braille.

 15. The teachers are Phyllis and she.

 16. Kara and I are learning fast.

 17. We can communicate in Braille now.

**C. Revising Sentences**   Write each sentence. Replace the underlined word or words with a subject pronoun.

 18. Helen Keller could not hear or see.

 MODEL ▷ She could not hear or see.

 19. Helen's parents found a teacher named Anne Sullivan.

 20. At first Helen's father did not like Miss Sullivan.

 21. Anne Sullivan was a very strict teacher.

 22. Then Miss Sullivan taught Helen to communicate through touch.

 23. My mother and I read Keller's autobiography, *The Story of My Life.*

 24. The book was inspiring.

 25. My brother and his friend plan to read it soon.

## Application — Writing

**Award Certificate**   Think of someone who has helped you learn something important. The person might be a teacher, a classmate, or a family member. Create an award certificate to give to him or her. On the certificate write a paragraph telling how the person has helped you. Use subject pronouns.

# 3 Object Pronouns

◆ **FOCUS**  An **object pronoun** follows an action verb or a word such as *at, for, to,* or *with*.

Remember that in some sentences the action verb is followed by a direct object. Object pronouns replace nouns used as direct objects. The words in color are object pronouns.

1. **a.** Coach Watson congratulated the boys and girls.
   **b.** Coach Watson congratulated them .

2. **a.** Jenny gave Coach Watson the trophy.
   **b.** Jenny gave him the trophy.

In sentence 1.b. the pronoun *them* replaces the nouns *boys* and *girls.* In sentence 2.b. the pronoun *him* replaces the noun *Coach Watson.*

Object pronouns can also follow words such as *at, for, to,* and *with.*

3. This trophy is for you .

4. Coach showed the trophy to me .

The object pronouns are *me, you, him, her, it, us,* and *them.*

## Guided Practice

**A.** Identify the object pronoun in each sentence.

1. The Bolton Bats beat them last year.
2. Coach Watson gave advice to us.
3. Jenny stood with me in the outfield.
4. The ball hit me on the wrist.
5. The crowd cheered for me.
6. Mort threw the ball to them.
7. Jenny batted it over the fence.
8. The newspaper reporter interviewed her.

---

**THINK AND REMEMBER**

◆ Use *me, you, him, her, it, us,* and *them* as object pronouns.

---

# Independent Practice

**B. Identifying Object Pronouns**  Read each sentence. Write the object pronoun.

    **9.** The coach put Jean and me on the team.

MODEL ⟩ me

    **10.** The other team members watched us.
    **11.** Then, Jean told them about an important law.
    **12.** U.S. Representative Patsy Mink wrote it for Congress.
    **13.** The coach asked her about the law.
    **14.** Patsy Mink sent an explanation of the law to him.
    **15.** The law tells you about boys' and girls' teams.
    **16.** A school must give equal opportunities to them.

**C. Revising Sentences**  Rewrite each sentence. Replace each underlined word or words with an object pronoun.

    **17.** Jackie Robinson joined the Brooklyn Dodgers.

MODEL ⟩ Jackie Robinson joined them.

    **18.** Branch Rickey persuaded Robinson to join.
    **19.** Rickey wanted black men to participate in major league baseball.
    **20.** Soon, other blacks played major league baseball.
    **21.** Robinson encouraged the new players.
    **22.** The star wrote autographs for fans.

**D. Choosing the Correct Pronoun**  Write each sentence. Use the correct pronoun in parentheses ( ).

    **23.** (We, Us) read a biography about Jackie Robinson.

MODEL ⟩ We read a biography about Jackie Robinson.

    **24.** (I, Me) enjoyed learning about his boyhood.
    **25.** Jackie Robinson is a hero to (we, us).
    **26.** This great man is an inspiration to (I, me).
    **27.** The sport of baseball owes much to (he, him).
    **28.** (He, Him) will always be remembered.

# Application — Writing

**Personality Profile**  Imagine that you are a sportswriter for your school newspaper. Write a paragraph of information about a sports hero. Tell what this person has done, and show why he or she is considered to be a hero. Use object pronouns in your report. If you need help writing a paragraph of information, see page 24 of the **Writer's Handbook.**

# 4 Subject or Object Pronoun?

◆ **FOCUS**   Pronouns can be subjects or objects in sentences.

Remember that a pronoun takes the place of a noun or nouns in a sentence. It is important to know when to use subject pronouns and when to use object pronouns.

1.  a. Jeb won three gold medals.
    b. He won three gold medals.   **subject pronoun**

2.  a. The judges gave the medals to Jeb.
    b. The judges awarded him the medals.   **object pronoun**

Use this chart to review the subject pronouns and the object pronouns.

| Subject Pronouns | | Object Pronouns | |
|---|---|---|---|
| I | we | me | us |
| you | you | you | you |
| he, she, it | they | him, her, it | them |

Notice that *you* and *it* can be subject pronouns or object pronouns.

3. You can come to the race too.   **subject pronoun**
4. Martha will drive you to the track.   **object pronoun**
5. It was an exciting race.   **subject pronoun**
6. Jim won it .   **object pronoun**

## Guided Practice

**A.** Identify the pronoun in parentheses ( ) that correctly completes each sentence.

1. (I, Me) read about the athletes in ancient Greece.
2. (They, Them) came from far away to compete.
3. (He, Him) won't believe the story of Theogenes.
4. Please tell (I, me) the story.
5. Theogenes surprised (they, them) all.
6. (He, Him) was only nine years old.
7. A statue towered above (he, him) in the town square.
8. (They, Them) say Theogenes carried it home.

## Independent Practice

**B. Identifying Subject and Object Pronouns**   Write each sentence
using the correct pronoun in parentheses ( ). Then write *subject
pronoun* or *object pronoun*.

9. Jesse and (he, him) raced.

MODEL > he, subject pronoun

10. Jesse asked (I, me) for help.
11. I held the stopwatch for (they, them).
12. (They, Them) ran around the track.
13. (I, Me) enjoyed helping the runners.
14. Sue Ann met (he, him) after the race.
15. (She, Her) congratulated Jesse.
16. Jesse smiled at (she, her).
17. Jesse thanked (we, us) for our help.
18. Tomorrow (we, us) will race again.

**C. Using Pronouns Correctly**   Read each pair of sentences. Write
the pronoun that correctly completes the second sentence in
each pair.

19. Rick ran the marathon. _____ finished in third place.

MODEL > He

20. The road winds through the hills. _____ is sandy.
21. The photographers followed Rick. _____ filmed Rick.
22. Rick was thirsty. A spectator gave _____ water.
23. Rick felt tired. _____ wanted to stop.
24. Rick's knee ached. _____ was red and swollen.
25. Ellen watched for Rick. _____ saw Rick on the hill.
26. Rick saw Ellen. He waved to _____ .
27. The race was long and hard. Finally, _____ was over.

## Application — Writing and Speaking

**Silly Olympics Rules**   Create an event in the Silly Olympics. For
example, participants might win a medal for opening a jar of
peanut butter, drying their hair, or dialing a telephone. Write a
paragraph describing the event's rules. Use subject pronouns and
object pronouns. Read your paragraph to a classmate.

# 5 Possessive Pronouns

◆ **FOCUS**   A **possessive pronoun** shows ownership.

Remember that possessive nouns show who or what has something. A possessive pronoun replaces a possessive noun.

There are two kinds of possessive pronouns. One kind is used before a noun.

1. Midori's violin string broke.
2. Her violin string broke.

The other kind of possessive pronoun stands alone.

3. This violin is Midori's.
4. This violin is hers.

This chart shows the two kinds of possessive pronouns.

| Possessive Pronouns Used Before Nouns | | Possessive Pronouns That Stand Alone | |
|---|---|---|---|
| **Singular** | **Plural** | **Singular** | **Plural** |
| my | our | mine | ours |
| your | your | yours | yours |
| his, her, its | their | his, hers, its | theirs |

## Guided Practice

**A.** Identify the possessive pronoun in each sentence. Tell whether the pronoun comes before a noun or stands alone.

1. Midori's violin lost one of its strings.
2. Another performer gave Midori his.
3. She showed her courage by finishing the solo.
4. I brought my autograph book.
5. Did you bring yours?
6. Maybe Midori will sign both of ours.

---

**THINK AND REMEMBER**
◆ Remember that a **possessive pronoun** shows ownership.

---

## Independent Practice

**B. Identifying Possessive Pronouns**   Read each sentence. Write the possessive pronoun. Then write *before a noun* or *stands alone.*

   7. Itzhak Perlman gave a concert in your city.

MODEL > your; before a noun

   8. As a performer, Perlman is a favorite of mine.
   9. His home is in Israel.
   10. A talent scout brought Perlman to our country.
   11. Perlman walks on stage with his crutches.
   12. That violin is the same type as yours!

**C. Using Possessive Pronouns**   Write the pronoun in parentheses ( ) that correctly completes each sentence.

   13. (Our, Ours) will be the best concert ever.

MODEL > Ours

   14. (Their, Theirs) practice starts at 4 o'clock.
   15. I will play (my, mine) guitar.
   16. We carry (our, ours) instruments to the hall.
   17. Which seats are (our, ours)?
   18. Do the other musicians know (their, theirs) parts?
   19. Are you sure you know (your, yours)?
   20. The last solo is (my, mine).

**D. Revising Sentences**   Rewrite each sentence. Replace the possessive pronoun with the correct form.

   21. Mother calls Perlman hers hero.

MODEL > Mother calls Perlman her hero.

   22. Who is your?
   23. Ours record of Perlman's music is broken.
   24. Will you borrow our?
   25. I bought concert tickets for yours birthday.
   26. Then you can hear this hero of my.
   27. Mine friends bought tickets too.
   28. Their are for the last performance.

## Application — Writing

**Record-Jacket Description**   Think of your favorite song. Write three or four sentences for the jacket of the record on which the song might appear. Describe what the song is about and why you think it was written. Use possessive pronouns.

# 6 Reflexive Pronouns

◆ **FOCUS**    A **reflexive pronoun** refers to the subject.

A reflexive pronoun reflects the action of the verb back to the subject. The words in color are reflexive pronouns.

1. Joe taught himself to play guitar.
2. The girls built themselves a treehouse.

In sentence 1 the reflexive pronoun *himself* reflects the action of the verb *taught* back to the subject *Joe.* In sentence 2 the reflexive pronoun *themselves* points the action of the verb *built* back to the subject *girls.*

| Reflexive Pronouns | |
|---|---|
| **Singular** | **Plural** |
| myself | ourselves |
| yourself | yourselves |
| himself, herself, itself | themselves |

## Guided Practice

**A.** Identify the reflexive pronoun in each sentence.

1. Many heroes have set high goals for themselves.
2. You should set yourself a goal.
3. Tell yourself that you are smart, strong, and talented.
4. I set myself a goal.
5. I will buy myself a present if and when I finally reach my goal.
6. My brother bought a book and taught himself the rules of soccer.
7. We play great games just between ourselves.

> **THINK AND REMEMBER**
> ◆ Remember that a **reflexive pronoun** refers to the subject.

# Independent Practice

**B. Identifying Reflexive Pronouns**   Read each sentence. Write the reflexive pronoun.

   **8.** We brought ourselves to the game on bikes.

[MODEL] ourselves

   **9.** The goal posts practically set themselves up.
   **10.** You found yourselves seats near the trees.
   **11.** The captain introduced himself to the players.
   **12.** The ball seemed to lift itself over my head.
   **13.** We found ourselves behind the other team by four touchdowns.
   **14.** I couldn't see myself in a game like that.
   **15.** My mother shouted herself hoarse.
   **16.** You pushed yourself to the limit.
   **17.** Each team conducted itself well after the game.

**C. Writing Sentences with Reflexive Pronouns**   Write each sentence. Use a reflexive pronoun in the blank.

   **18.** Some athletes push _____ to great accomplishments.

[MODEL] Some athletes push themselves to great accomplishments.

   **19.** Jim Thorpe worked hard to prepare _____ for the 1912 Olympic Games.
   **20.** The judges surprised _____ by their total agreement.
   **21.** Sonja Henie of Norway won four figure-skating championships _____ between 1928 and 1932.
   **22.** Johnny Weissmuller earned five gold medals _____ for swimming in 1924 and 1928.
   **23.** My friends and I train _____ on the track.
   **24.** Are you and Sue teaching _____ a new sport?
   **25.** Jerry, are you entering _____ in next week's race?
   **26.** Good runners stay in control and pace _____ in a competition.
   **27.** The course winds around _____ .
   **28.** I give _____ the challenge to do my best.

## Application — Writing

**Do-It-Yourself Guide**   Think of something that you know how to do. Write a one-paragraph guide for doing this activity. Write clear directions for someone who knows nothing about the activity. Use reflexive pronouns in your paragraph. If you need help writing a how-to paragraph, see page 25 of the **Writer's Handbook.**

# 7 Agreement of Pronouns

◆ **FOCUS**   A pronoun should agree with its antecedent.

Remember that pronouns refer to nouns. When you use a pronoun, make clear whom or what you are talking about.

**1.** Bo and Jo waited for their hero.

In sentence 1 *Bo and Jo* is the antecedent of *their.* An **antecedent** is a word or group of words to which a pronoun refers. A pronoun must agree with its antecedent.

When you use a pronoun, make sure you know who or what the antecedent is. Decide whether the antecedent is male, female, or neuter (neither male nor female). Then, decide whether the antecedent is singular or plural.

**2.** Superduck wears a cape . Jo touched it .

**3.** Superduck put on her cape.

---

**Link to Speaking and Writing**

Be sure that your verb agrees with your subject pronoun. Why did the writer change *flex* to *flexes?*

*She flex~~flexes~~ her muscles.*

## Guided Practice

**A.** Give a pronoun to fill in each blank. Tell the pronoun's antecedent.

**1.** Everyone likes Superduck. _____ is very popular.

**2.** Superduck cannot fly without _____ red cape.

**3.** Superduck and I are friends. _____ help each other.

**B.** Choose the verb in parentheses ( ) that is correct.

**4.** He (wants, want) Superduck's autograph.

**5.** She (uses, use) a blue pen.

**6.** I (wants, want) an autograph, too.

## Independent Practice

**C. Identifying Pronouns and Their Antecedents**   Write the pronoun that correctly completes each sentence. Then, write the pronoun's antecedent.

7. Robin Hood lived in Sherwood Forest. _____ is located in England.

MODEL ▷ It—Sherwood Forest

8. Robin Hood rested the bow on _____ shoulder.
9. Robin loved Maid Marian. He asked for _____ hand.
10. Little John was in trouble. Robin Hood saved _____ .
11. The sheriff and Prince John looked for Robin. _____ couldn't find him.
12. Robin Hood and his men wore green. Nobody could see _____ among the trees.

**D. Making Verbs Agree with Pronouns**   Write the second sentence in each pair. Use the correct present-tense form of the verb in parentheses ( ).

13. People enjoy reading about superheroes. They (wish) they could do unusual things themselves.

MODEL ▷ They wish they could do unusual things themselves.

14. Paul Bunyan is a lumberjack. He (chop) down trees.
15. Ole cooks for Paul. He (mix) batter for pancakes.
16. Babe is Paul's ox. She (catch) pancakes in her mouth.
17. Slewfoot Sue is a cowgirl. She (live) in the West.
18. Pecos Bill and Slewfoot Sue are friends. They (ride) the range together.

## Application — Writing

**Character Description**   Dream up a superhero. Write a description of the superhero for your classmates. Use pronouns. Make sure your pronouns agree with their antecedents. Make sure the verb in each sentence agrees with the subject pronoun. If you need help writing a descriptive paragraph, see page 29 of the **Writer's Handbook.**

# Building Vocabulary
## Multiple-Meaning Words: Newspaper Jargon

To catch the humor of this cartoon, you have to know that the word *scoop* has more than one meaning. In its common use, a *scoop* is a small tool. To newspaper reporters, however, it means a news story that one newspaper prints first.

Every field or occupation has a specialized vocabulary, or *jargon*. Study the chart to see how the common meaning of a word changes when it is part of newspaper jargon.

*This is the only scoop I could get all week.*

| Word | Common Meaning | Newspaper Meaning |
|---|---|---|
| copy | a reproduction of something; a duplicate: *Jorge made one copy of his story.* | words to be printed in the newspaper: *The reporter wrote one page of copy.* |
| ears | the parts of the body with which we hear: *Mary covered her ears to muffle the sound of the jackhammer.* | small boxes that appear in the upper corners of the front page of a newspaper. Ears often contain a quotation, an advertisement, or weather information: *The ears in Saturday's paper always give advice for the day.* |
| grapevine | a vine on which grapes grow: *Workers carefully picked ripened grapes off the grapevine.* | an informal source of information: *Nina heard through the grapevine that the mayor was about to resign.* |
| scoop | a small tool that is shaped like a shovel and has a short handle: *The baker used a scoop to get some flour from the bin.* | an important news story that appears first in only one newspaper: *The* City Daily *printed a scoop on the large warehouse fire.* |
| type | a group of persons or things that are alike in certain ways: *A cardigan is a type of sweater.* | printed letters: *Printers use large type for headlines.* |

## Reading Practice

Read each sentence. To tell which meaning of the underlined word is used, write *common meaning* or *jargon*. Then, write the definition of the word as it is used in the sentence.

1. The famous writer is the <u>type</u> of celebrity who keeps all her plans secret.
2. Robert heard through the <u>grapevine</u>, however, that she would be at Babbit's Bookshop tomorrow after her new book is released.
3. Many people plan to be there to get a <u>copy</u> of her book.
4. Robert plans to be there to get the <u>scoop</u> for his newspaper.

## Writing Practice

Rewrite the following paragraph. Replace the underlined words with newspaper jargon.

Allison heard through the <u>secret source of newsworthy information</u> about the President's visit to a local factory. Allison rushed to the factory to get the <u>exclusive story</u> for the *City Daily*. After interviewing the President, she quickly prepared her <u>words to be printed in the newspaper</u> for the city editor. That evening, the headlines for Allison's story appeared on the front page in large <u>letters</u>, under the left <u>box</u> containing the daily quotation.

## Project

Look in your library for books about newspapers and newspaper reporting to find more examples of newspaper jargon. Look up the meanings of the words in the dictionary. Next, work with your classmates to make a long list of the words and their meanings. Check your list to find words that describe parts of a newspaper. Then, glue pages of a newspaper to a poster and label as many parts as you can.

# Language Enrichment
## Pronouns

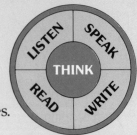

Use what you know about pronouns to do these activities.

 ### Looking for "It"

Choose an object in the classroom. Write clues that would lead someone to locate the object. Use pronouns. For example, here are clues that might lead to a yellow marker under the windows: (1) To find "it," start at the door. (2) Turn to your right. (3) Walk past my desk to the windows. (4) Look under them. (5) "It" is small and yellow and in your sight.

Exchange clues with a classmate. See if you can find each other's object.

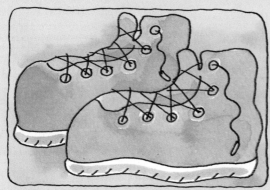

 ### Clothes Make You

What is your favorite article of clothing? Make an outline drawing of it. Then, inside the drawing, write a description of it, telling what it looks like, how it feels, and why you love it. Show your reader why this article of clothing is YOU. Use pronouns in your writing. Have a class "fashion show" and share your descriptions and drawings with each other.

 ### Mystery Guest

Stand in front of your classroom and silently choose a person in your class. Ask everyone to stand. Do not look directly at the person you have chosen. Begin giving one-sentence descriptions of the person you chose. Use pronouns in your sentences. Start generally. For example: *He is a boy.* Then all the girls must sit down. Make your descriptions more specific. For example: *His hair is brown.* Then the boys who do not have brown hair must sit down. Continue giving descriptions, being more specific each time. For example: *He has blue pants. He writes with his left hand. He wears red sneakers.* Your descriptions should continue until only one person is left—your mystery guest!

# CONNECTING
## LANGUAGE ◄► WRITING

In this unit you learned that pronouns are words that take the place of nouns. A subject pronoun takes the place of a noun as the subject of a sentence. An object pronoun takes the place of a noun as the object of a verb. A possessive pronoun indicates ownership and replaces a possessive noun.

◆ **Using Pronouns in Your Writing**  Knowing how and when to use different pronouns helps you avoid repetition. Careful use of pronouns also helps you communicate more clearly.

Pay attention to pronouns as you do these activities.

 **Really Cooking!**

You learned about newspaper jargon on the **Building Vocabulary** page. Here are some other special vocabularies for you to have fun with.

Create a list of words based on cooking, construction, or gardening. Then use the words on your list to write five sentences that describe people in everyday situations.

**Example:** cooking: *steam, boil* Hearing lies makes my blood boil.

 **Hall of Fame**

Choose someone you think should receive a special achievement award. It might be a national or community leader. It could be a family member or friend. Write a short speech telling what the award is for and why the person deserves it. Use pronouns in your writing. Read your speech to the class. If you wish, create a special achievement certificate and send or present it to the person.

# 5 Unit Checkup

| Think Back | Think Ahead |
|---|---|
| ◆ What did you learn about news stories? What did you do to write one? | ◆ How will your study of a news story help you when you read a newspaper? |
| | ◆ How will knowing how to classify facts and opinions help you write a news story? A persuasive letter? A speech? |
| ◆ What did you learn about pronouns? How did pronouns help you vary your writing? | ◆ What is one way you can use pronouns to improve your writing? |

## News Stories  *pages 210–211*

Read the news story. Then follow the directions.

> MILWAUKEE—Yesterday, 10-year-old Stephanie Crane became the heroine of her school when she outspelled everyone at the city's annual spelling bee. She will go to the National Spelling Bee later this year.

1. Write a headline for the news story.
2. Give the words that tell *what* happened.
3. Write the word that tells the reader *when* the event happened.
4. List the words that tell *where* the event happened.
5. Write the words that tell *who* was involved.

## Classifying Fact and Opinion  *page 212*

Write whether each sentence is *fact* or *opinion*.

6. Fort Larned was an Army post in western Kansas.
7. The soldiers at Fort Larned were the bravest men around.
8. The Plains Indians called them "Buffalo Soldiers" because their thick, curly hair reminded them of the buffalo.
9. Fort Larned is now a national historic site.
10. You will love visiting Fort Larned.

## Using Precise Words  *page 213*

Write the following sentences. Choose the more precise word in parentheses ( ).

11. Donna _____ to the store before it closed. (went, raced)
12. She _____ needed glue to finish her project. (desperately, really)
13. Donna _____ some glue from the shelf. (took, grabbed)
14. The clerk _____ Donna speeding toward him. (spied, saw)
15. She _____ the money on the counter. (dumped, put)

## The Writing Process  *pages 214–225*

16. Suppose you were selecting a topic for a news story. Which of the following topics should you cross out?
    a. ones that you cannot find information about
    b. ones about recent events      c. ones that will interest your audience
17. Why does a writer interview someone involved in an event?
    a. to have a good time writing
    b. to tell the person what he or she knows
    c. to get facts, interesting details, and the person's impressions
18. When writing a news story, how do you select your facts?
    a. choose what the audience would be most interested in
    b. choose what the writer agrees with   c. include everything
19. Suppose you were revising your news story. You find that the lead tells *what, where,* and *who.* What should you do?
    a. Leave the lead alone.         b. Add *when* to the lead.
    c. Move the lead to the middle of the news story.

## Pronouns  *pages 228–229*

Find the pronoun in the second sentence of each pair. Write the pronoun and the noun or nouns it replaces.

20. a. Juneteenth is a holiday in Texas.
    b. It celebrates the end of slavery in Texas.
21. a. On June 19, 1865, General Gordon Granger came to Galveston, Texas, with the official news.
    b. He was a general in the Union Army.
22. a. The war ended in April 1865.
    b. However, it was fought in Texas until June 1865.
23. a. On Juneteenth, Texans attend parades and picnics.
    b. They remember those who fought for freedom.
24. a. A holiday is set aside for workers and students.
    b. They are able to have time off from work or school.

## Subject Pronouns  *pages 230–231*

Write each sentence. Replace the underlined word or words with a subject pronoun.

25. Warren wanted to make a map of his neighborhood.
26. The neighborhood has a lot of interesting buildings.
27. Warren and his parents made a list of places.
28. The list contained more than 20 places.
29. Warren's sister helped him draw the map.

## Object Pronouns  *pages 232–233*

Rewrite each sentence. Replace the underlined word or words with an object pronoun.

30. Father gave Josephina a book about Miguel Hidalgo.
31. The book described Miguel Hidalgo and his part in Mexico's independence from Spain.
32. The priest Hidalgo worked with the Indians.
33. The priest encouraged the Indians to declare independence from Spanish rule.
34. Hidalgo is a hero to Josephina.

## Subject or Object Pronoun?  *pages 234–235*

Write each sentence using the correct pronoun in parentheses ( ). Then write *subject pronoun* or *object pronoun*.

35. Andy and (I, me) walked our dog, Flash.
36. I held the leash for (he, him) while he mailed a letter.
37. Flash barked at (he, him) when he stepped into the street.
38. Flash warned (he, him) of the approaching car.
39. Flash and (I, me) stayed on the curb and waited.

## Possessive Pronouns  *pages 236–237*

Write the pronoun in parentheses ( ) that correctly completes each sentence.

40. Annette wants the main part in (her, hers) dance class's annual performance.
41. She hopes the part will be (her, hers).
42. The dance instructors have watched (their, theirs) students carefully.
43. I want (my, mine) part to be in the chorus.
44. Finally the instructors made (their, theirs) announcement of the parts for the program.

## Reflexive Pronouns   *pages 238–239*

Write each sentence. Use a reflexive pronoun in the blank.

**45.** Imagine _____ in Amelia Earhart's airplane.

**46.** What might she have told _____ as she flew alone?

**47.** She might have reminded _____ that she made many preparations for the flight.

**48.** Pilots cannot teach _____ but must take flying lessons.

**49.** In _____ , flying is difficult, but Amelia Earhart also chose to fly distances no woman had ever tried before.

**50.** She encouraged _____ to have goals and to reach them.

## Agreement of Pronouns   *pages 240–241*

Write the pronoun that correctly completes each sentence. Then write the pronoun's antecedent.

**51.** Scientists often do important work. _____ search for solutions to problems and ways to make life better for people.

**52.** Students who want to become scientists might study a subject such as chemurgy. _____ involves the use of farm and forest products for manufacturing.

**53.** George Washington Carver studied chemurgy. Because of _____ work, we know that peanuts can be used to manufacture more than 300 different products.

**54.** If you are mainly interested in planets and stars, _____ studies might focus on astronomy.

**55.** As an astronomer, you might work for the space program. _____ helps astronauts travel to the moon.

**56.** We all need scientists. Without _____ efforts, we would not have the kind of lives we lead today.

## Multiple-Meaning Words   *pages 242–243*

Read each sentence. To tell which meaning of the underlined word is used, write *common meaning* or *jargon*. Then use a dictionary to write the definition of the word as it is used in the  sentence.

**57.** In the Old West, cowboys cooked <u>chuck</u> that was sometimes the result of an exciting hunt.

**58.** When a new barn was built, <u>paint</u> was rarely added.

**59.** Cowboys worked hard and were hungry for the <u>grub</u> served at mealtime.

**60.** The <u>cookie</u> at the ranch prepared all the meals.

# UNIT

6

# Painting Pictures with Words

◆ **COMPOSITION FOCUS:  Descriptive Paragraph**
◆ **LANGUAGE FOCUS:  Adjectives**

Awaken your senses to the world around you! Look! The skies are sometimes inky black, sometimes pink and red. Listen! The rivers gurgle and splash. Smell! Roses, jasmine, and lilacs scent the air. Touch! A grassy river bank welcomes you with its pillowy softness. Taste! Eat spicy tacos. Drink tart lemonade.

It's fun to describe to others what you have seen, heard, smelled, touched, and tasted. You will find description in all kinds of writing. Notice as you read how writers try to make their descriptions vivid and exciting.

In the next few pages, you will read a selection by writer Laura Ingalls Wilder. The selection is filled with her vivid descriptions of a place called Silver Lake. In this unit you will study the descriptive paragraph. You will also learn more about using the senses to describe.

Laura Ingalls Wilder wrote about memories of her childhood on the prairie *to entertain* readers the world over.

# Reading with a Writer's Eye
## Description

Laura Ingalls Wilder's pioneer childhood made a very strong impression on her. She later described her early life so vividly in her fiction that her readers knew what it felt like to be there. As you read this excerpt from *By the Shores of Silver Lake,* notice that the writer uses sensory details to recreate the life she once knew.

## *from* By the Shores of Silver Lake
### by Laura Ingalls Wilder

The lake lay at their left shimmering in the sunshine. Little silvery waves rose and fell and lapped upon the shore as the wind ruffled the blue water. The shore was low, but firm and dry, with little grasses growing to the water's edge. Across the glittering lake, Laura could see the east bank and the south bank, rising up as tall as she was. A little slough came into the lake from the northeast, and Big Slough went on toward the southwest in a long curve of tall wild grasses.

Laura and Mary and Carrie walked slowly along on the green shore by the rippling silver-blue water, toward the wild Big Slough. The grasses were warm and soft to their feet. The wind blew their flapping skirts tight against their bare legs and ruffled Laura's hair. Mary's sunbonnet and Carrie's were tied firmly under their chins, but Laura swung hers by its strings. Millions of rustling grass-blades made one murmuring sound, and thousands of wild ducks and geese and herons and cranes and pelicans were talking sharply and brassily in the wind.

All those birds were feeding among the grasses of the sloughs. They rose on flapping wings and settled again, crying news to each other and talking among themselves among the grasses, and eating busily of grass roots and tender water plants and little fishes.

The lake shore went lower and lower toward Big Slough, until really there was no shore. The lake melted into the slough, making small ponds surrounded by the harsh, rank slough grass that stood five and six feet tall. Little ponds glimmered between the grasses and on the water the wild birds were thick.

As Laura and Carrie pushed into the slough grasses, suddenly harsh wings ripped upward and round eyes glittered; the whole air exploded in a noise of squawking, quacking, quonking. Flattening their webbed feet under their tails, ducks and geese sped over the grass-tops and curved down to the next pond.

Laura and Carrie stood still. The coarse-stemmed slough grass rose above their heads and made a rough sound in the wind. Their bare feet sank slowly into ooze.

"Oo, the ground is all soft," Mary said, turning back quickly. She did not like mud on her feet.

"Go back, Carrie!" Laura cried. "You'll mire down! The lake is in here among the grasses!"

The soft, cool mud sucked around her ankles as she stood, and before her the little ponds glimmered among the tall grasses. She wanted to go on and on, into the slough among the wild birds, but she could not leave Mary and Carrie. So she turned back with them to the hard, higher prairie where waist-high grasses were nodding and bending in the wind, and the short, curly buffalo grass grew in patches.

Along the edge of the slough they picked flaming red tiger lilies, and on higher ground they gathered long branching stems of purple buffalo bean pods. Grasshoppers flew up like spray before their feet in the grasses. All kinds of little birds fluttered and flew and twittered balancing in the wind on the tall, bending grass stems, and prairie hens scuttled everywhere.

"Oh, what a wild, beautiful prairie!" Mary sighed with happiness. "Laura, have you got your sunbonnet on?"

Guiltily Laura pulled up her sunbonnet from where it hung by its strings down her neck. "Yes, Mary," she said.

Mary laughed. "You just now put it on. I heard you!"

It was late afternoon when they turned back. The little shanty, with its roof slanting all one way, stood all by itself and small at the edge of Silver Lake. Tiny in the doorway, Ma shaded her eyes with her hand to look for them, and they waved to her.

They could see the whole camp, scattered along the lake shore north of the shanty. First was the store where Pa was working with the big feed store behind it. Then the stable for the work teams. The stable was built into a swell of the prairie, and its roof was thatched with slough grass. Beyond it was the long, low bunkhouse where the men slept, and still farther away was Cousin Louisa's long boardinghouse shanty, with supper smoke already rising from its stovepipe.

Then for the first time Laura saw a house, a real house, standing all by itself on the lake's northern shore.

"I wonder what that house can be and who lives there," she said. "It isn't a homestead because there's no stable and no land plowed."

She had told Mary all that she saw, and Mary said, "What a pretty place it is with the clean, new shanties and the grass and the water. There's no use wondering about that house; we can ask Pa about it. Here comes another flock of wild ducks."

Flock after flock of ducks and long lines of wild geese were coming down from the sky and settling to stay all night on the lake. And the men were making a racket of voices as they came from their work. In the shanty's doorway again, Ma waited till they reached her, windblown and full of the fresh air and sunshine, bringing her their armfuls of tiger lilies and purple bean pods.

Then Carrie put the big bouquet in a pitcher of water while Laura set the table for supper. Mary sat in her rocking chair with Grace in her lap and told her about the ducks quacking in the Big Slough and the great flocks of wild geese going to sleep on the lake.

## Respond

1. Which passages seem most vivid to you?

## Discuss

2. What details does the writer include to create such a powerful impression?
3. Why do you think the writer put so many descriptive passages into her writing?

# Thinking As a Writer
## Analyzing a Descriptive Paragraph

A descriptive paragraph gives a picture of a person, a place, an object, or an event. The paragraph should help the reader to see what is being described by giving a variety of sensory details.

Notice how Laura Ingalls Wilder uses details in this excerpt from *By the Shores of Silver Lake.*

Laura and Mary and Carrie walked slowly along on the green shore by the rippling silver-blue water, toward the wild Big Slough. The grasses were warm and soft to their feet. The wind blew their flapping skirts tight against their bare legs and ruffled Laura's hair. Mary's sunbonnet and Carrie's were tied firmly under their chins, but Laura swung hers by its strings. Millions of rustling grass-blades made one murmuring sound, and thousands of wild ducks and geese and herons and cranes and pelicans were talking sharply and brassily in the wind.

The **topic sentence** tells what is being described.

**Detail sentences** give particular details about the subject. The details should enable the reader to see, hear, smell, feel, or taste what is being described. Details should contribute to the mood or feeling the writer wants to create.

## Discuss

1. Look first at the topic sentence, and then at the details in the descriptive paragraph about the Ingalls sisters. What is being described?
2. Which of the details appeal to the reader's senses? To which senses do these details appeal?
3. Think of the feeling you had when you read the excerpt from *By the Shores of Silver Lake* on pages 252–255. How would you describe the mood or feeling that Laura Ingalls Wilder has created in this paragraph?

# Try Your Hand

**A. Analyze Topic Sentences** Read the following topic sentences from other descriptive paragraphs. For each sentence, write the subject that is being described.

1. No one in the world had eyes as blue or hair as red as my Uncle George.

3. Laramie Street was only one block long, but everything a cowboy needed was there.

2. Ted would never forget the look of the old chicken coop before they fixed it up and turned it into a fancy day camp.

4. Many trees in our neighborhood are bigger and more impressive than our apple tree, but none are more important to me.

**B. Identify Descriptive Words** Look back at the topic sentences in **A.** Write the descriptive words that appear in items 1–4.

**C. Add Details** Look back at the topic sentences in **A.** Write one sentence that might appear as a descriptive detail for each paragraph.

**D. Read Descriptions** Choose a passage from the selection on pages 252–255, or find another descriptive passage in a book or a magazine. Read the passage aloud to a partner, and discuss with your partner both the subject of your passage and some of the details that created a picture in your mind.

*Writer's Notebook*

**Collecting Words with Sensory Appeal** In *By the Shores of Silver Lake*, phrases such as *shimmering in the sunshine* and *the wind ruffled the blue water* help you picture the scenes the writer is describing. Read the selection again, and record in your *Writer's Notebook* any words or phrases that seem particularly vivid and that appeal to your senses. Try to use some of these when you write descriptively.

# Thinking As a Writer
## Observing Details in Spatial Order

In a description, a writer may organize details by arranging them in spatial order. For example, a writer can describe something from left to right, back to front, or top to bottom.

Reread the last paragraph on page 254. In this paragraph the writer describes the camp by beginning with details seen up close and moving farther away. Since the scene is described from across the lake, this way of arranging details in a spatial order makes sense. The writer may have mapped the details this way.

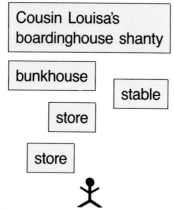

As you write a descriptive paragraph, be sure to present your details in some kind of spatial order. Choose the arrangement that works best for you.

## Discuss

1. Look again at the first paragraph of the story, on page 252. In what spatial order has the writer organized the details?
2. How might her descriptions have been different if she had not used spatial order?

## Try Your Hand

**Map Details in Spatial Order** Draw two diagrams of spatial order that you might use to describe a bridge that joins two parts of a city. Tell which arrangement would make the most sense. Trade work with a partner, and consider each other's ideas.

# Developing the Writer's Craft
## Using Sensory Images

The writer of a good descriptive passage makes the reader feel as if he or she were seeing, hearing, smelling, touching, or tasting the thing being described. The writer does this by using sensory words. Sensory words are words that appeal to your five senses: sight, hearing, smell, touch, and taste.

Look back at the story passage on pages 252–255. Notice which details almost make it possible for you to see, hear, feel, smell, or taste what is being described. Observe which details might appeal to more than one sense.

| SIGHT | HEARING | SMELL | TOUCH | TASTE |
|---|---|---|---|---|
| green shore silver-blue water wild birds | flapping skirts rustling blades of grass sharp and brassy bird sounds | grasses wind | soft grasses wind ruffling hair tight strings under chins | wind |

When you write your descriptive paragraph, use sensory words to help your readers picture what you are describing.

## Discuss

1. How many of the five senses does the writer appeal to when she writes, "The soft, cool mud sucked around her ankles as she stood, and before her the little ponds glimmered among the tall grasses"? Draw a chart like the one above, and fill it in with the writer's sensory details.
2. Do you agree that when you read this description carefully, more of your senses become involved? Why or why not?

## Try Your Hand

**Use Sensory Language**  Imagine that you are writing about a trip with your family. Use sentences to answer these questions about your trip: How do the flowers in the hotel garden smell? What does the fruit served at breakfast taste like? What does the evening sky look like? How does the breeze feel on your face?

# 1 Prewriting
## Descriptive Paragraph

**Writer's Guide**

**Prewriting Checklist**

☑ Brainstorm and select a topic.

☑ Think about your audience and your purpose.

☑ Gather information that includes sensory words and descriptions.

☑ Organize the information using spatial order.

Mark, a student at Biscayne Elementary School, wanted to write a paragraph describing a recent trip for a class presentation. Mark used the checklist in the **Writer's Guide** to help him plan his description. Look at what he did.

## ◆ Brainstorming and Selecting a Topic

First, Mark brainstormed a list of possible topics for his descriptive paragraph. Because Mark wanted to describe a *place* in his paragraph, he wrote down information about all recent trips that he had taken to specific places. Look at Mark's list.

Next, Mark reviewed his list and crossed out topics that might not interest his audience or that might be too difficult to describe in the space of one paragraph.

Finally, Mark circled the most interesting topic that was left on his list. He decided he wanted to describe the Everglades to encourage other students to go there.

*a visit to the art museum*
*a trip to the shopping mall*
*a trip to the Everglades*
*a visit to the state capital*
*a trip to the movies*
*a visit to a hospital*

### Discuss

1. Look at the topics that Mark crossed off his list. Why do you think he decided to eliminate each one?

2. If Mark were writing a paragraph about forms of entertainment, which topics might he have chosen? Why do you think so?

# ◆ Gathering Information

After Mark selected his topic, he gathered information for his descriptive paragraph. Mark decided that sensory words and descriptions would help his readers feel as if they were seeing, hearing, smelling, touching, and tasting what he was describing. Mark brainstormed clusters of sensory impressions from his trip. Look at Mark's clusters.

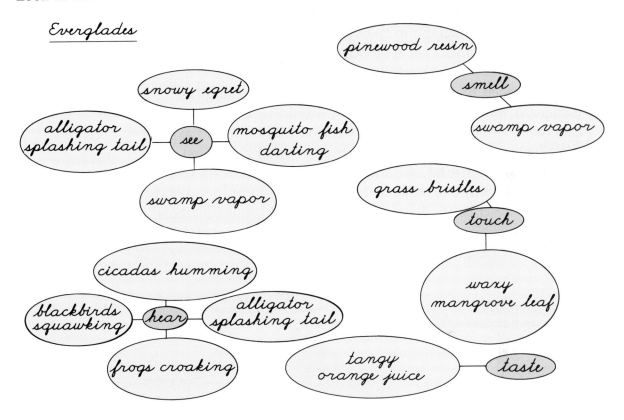

## Discuss

1. Look at Mark's clusters. Which items appear in more than one cluster? Why do you think these items appear more than once?
2. How is the entry in the *taste* cluster different from all the entries in the other clusters? Why would you expect the *taste* cluster to have the fewest entries for Mark's trip? If Mark were describing Thanksgiving dinner instead of his trip to the Everglades, would the *taste* cluster have more entries? Why?
3. Some activities or experiences do not involve all the senses. Can you think of any activities or experiences that leave one or two senses uninvolved? (Example: Feeling your way through a dark room does not involve sight.)

## ◆ Organizing Information

After Mark had clustered the sensory ideas for his descriptive paragraph, he was ready to organize the information. He thought about how he might best describe his trip for his classmates.

He considered organizing his paragraph in time order. He decided not to do that because he had gone back to see some areas more than once and felt that a paragraph organized in time order might be confusing and repetitive. He thought about organizing his paragraph in the way he had made his clusters—one sense at a time. This approach would also be repetitive, he decided. He saw *and* heard the alligator, for example.

He decided that the best order to use in organizing his paragraph was spatial order. Since he would be describing the experience of being in a boat, he decided that he would explain what he saw and heard in a circle from where he sat. First, he would explain what he saw and heard on the left shore; then, he would explain the sights and sounds in front of him. Finally, he would describe the things to his right and behind the boat.

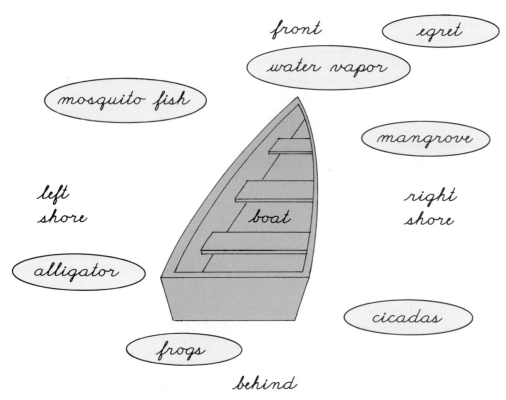

Now Mark had a clear plan for writing his descriptive paragraph.

## Discuss

1. Assume that vapor was coming off all parts of the water. Why do you think Mark would put the circle for the vapor right in front of the boat?
2. Mark could present information from top to bottom, from left to right, or in a clockwise circle. Which of these three choices do you think would work best? Why?

## Try Your Hand

Now plan a descriptive paragraph of your own.

A. **Brainstorm and Select a Topic**   Think about a place you would like to describe. Think about including your description in a class travel book.

   ◆ Cross out topics that are not interesting enough for a descriptive paragraph.
   ◆ Cross out topics for which you would have trouble finding sensory descriptions.
   ◆ Circle the most interesting topic left on your list. This will be the topic of your descriptive paragraph.

B. **Gather Information**   When you are satisfied with your topic, plan to gather sensory details about the place you wish to describe.

   ◆ To think of sensory details, imagine yourself in the scene you will describe.
   ◆ Make clusters for the five senses. Include as many sensory details as you can think of.
   ◆ When making your clusters, do not worry about putting items in any particular order. Just add entries as you think of them.

C. **Organize Information**   When you have completed your clusters, decide which details would most interest the audience for whom you are writing. Decide on the order in which you plan to present these details. If you decide to use spatial order, make a diagram or a chart to help you arrange the details in a clear sequence.

   **Save your clusters and your diagram or chart in your *Writer's Notebook*. You will use them when you draft your descriptive paragraph.**

# Listening and Speaking
## Tips for Listening to Poetic Techniques

Poets use special ways of writing to help the audience understand and feel their poetry. These special ways of writing are called **poetic techniques.** Good writers often borrow these techniques to describe people, places, and things more vividly. You can borrow some of them too! Here are some poetic techniques to listen for when writers read their work aloud.

1. When you listen to language that has a beat to it, you are listening to **rhythm.** When a poem, a song, or a rap is read aloud, you can hear a repeated pattern of beats in the words or syllables.

   I hear the rhythm of the rain.
   It taps upon my windowpane.

2. When you hear the same sound at the end of two or more lines, you are listening to **rhyme.** Rhyme can also occur within a line.

   Words can rhyme anytime.

3. When you hear the same sound at the beginning of two or more words, you are listening to **alliteration.** Alliteration can create an interesting, musical effect in language.

   The quails flew quickly through the quarry.

4. When you hear a word or a phrase and its sound imitates or suggests its meaning, you are listening to **onomatopoeia.** Some words that illustrate onomatopoeia are *crunch, whoop, pop,* and *giggle.*

# 2 Drafting
## Descriptive Paragraph

Using his notes and his diagram, Mark followed the checklist in the **Writer's Guide** to draft his descriptive paragraph. Look at what he did.

*I am going to describe just one spot we stopped at on our boat trip into the Everglades. It was a very warm and humid day, so vapor was rising off the water everywhere we looked.*

### Writer's Guide

**Drafting Checklist**

☑ Use your cluster and your diagram or chart for ideas.

☑ Write the topic sentence first.

☑ Write the body of the descriptive paragraph next.

☑ Write your paragraph in spatial order or in whatever order you decided on when doing your clusters and your diagram.

## Discuss

1. Look back at Mark's diagram for organizing his details on page 262. Where in the diagram is he starting his descriptive paragraph? Why do you think he might be starting there?
2. What are some additional details you might expect to see in the rest of Mark's descriptive paragraph?

## Try Your Hand

Now you are ready to write a descriptive paragraph.

**A. Review Your Information** Think about the details you gathered and organized. Decide whether you need more information or whether you need to rearrange any information.

**B. Think About Your TAP** Remember that your task is to write a descriptive paragraph. Your purpose is to describe something to your audience as vividly as you can.

**C. Write Your First Draft** Follow the steps in the **Drafting Checklist** to write your descriptive paragraph.

When you write your draft, just put all your ideas on paper. Do not worry about spelling, punctuation, or grammar. You can correct the draft later.

**TAP**

**Task:** What?
**Audience:** Who?
**Purpose:** Why?

**Save your first draft in your *Writer's Notebook.* You will use it when you revise your descriptive paragraph.**

# 3 Responding and Revising
## Descriptive Paragraph

Mark used the checklist in the **Writer's Guide** to revise his descriptive paragraph. Look at what he did.

### ◆ Checking Information

When Mark read over his draft, he decided to replace a sensory detail about the alligator. To show his change, Mark used this mark ⌃. In the same sentence, Mark decided to take out another detail. To show that change, he used this mark ✐.

### ◆ Checking Organization

To make his spatial order easier to follow, Mark decided to move the sentence about the mosquito fish. To show that the sentence should be moved, he used this mark ⌒.

### ◆ Checking Language

Mark noticed that he could make one sentence out of two by adding a comma and the word *and*. He also changed some of the wording to make his writing more vivid and special.

**Writer's Guide**

**Revising Checklist**

☑ Read your descriptive paragraph to yourself or to a partner.

☑ Think about your audience and purpose. Add or cut information. If necessary, add sensory details.

☑ Check to see that your descriptive paragraph is organized in spatial order.

☑ Check to see if you can make your writing more concise by combining subjects and predicates.

Replace — Cut — Move —

> I am going to describe just one spot we stopped at on our boat trip into the Everglades. It was a very ~~warm~~ (hot) and humid day, so vapor was rising off the water everywhere we looked. We could see mosquito fish darting in front of the boat. A ~~big~~ (monstrous) old alligator sat sunning itself on the left bank, and Then it suddenly splashed into the water. A snowy egret soared ahead of us into the distance. Behind the mangroves on our right we heard cicadas humming like a radio that hasn't been tuned in right. On the banks behind the boat, frogs were croaking to each other. We ate our lunch on the boat and enjoyed this wonderful nature show.

# Discuss

1. Why did Mark move the sentence about the mosquito fish?
2. Mark changed *very warm* to *hot*. Why?
3. How did Mark combine the two sentences about the alligator? Was it a good idea to combine the sentences? Why or why not?

# Try Your Hand

Now revise your first draft.

**A. Read Your First Draft** As you read your descriptive paragraph, think about your audience and purpose. Read the paragraph silently or to a partner. Ask yourself or your partner the questions in the box.

| Responding and Revising Strategies | |
|---|---|
| ✔ **Respond**<br>**Ask yourself or a partner:** | ✔ **Revise**<br>**Try these solutions:** |
| ◆ Have I written a topic sentence that clearly sets the stage for my description? | ◆ Write or **revise** your topic sentence to let your audience know what you are describing. |
| ◆ Have I organized my information in an order that is easy for my audience to follow? | ◆ **Revise** the organization as necessary to make it clearer for your audience. |
| ◆ Have I combined subjects and predicates when I can to make my writing smoother and more unified? | ◆ **Combine** subjects and predicates to make your writing clearer and more concise. See the **Revising Workshop** on page 268. |
| ◆ Have I used the most vivid language to help my audience picture what I am writing about? | ◆ Use your **Writer's Thesaurus** to help you choose the best word. |

**B. Make Your Changes** If the answer to any question in the box is *no,* try the solution. Use the **Editor's Marks** to show your changes.

**C. Review Your Descriptive Paragraph Again** Keep revising your descriptive paragraph until you feel it is well organized and complete.

> **EDITOR'S MARKS**
> ∧ Add something.
> ✗ Cut something.
> ○ Move something.
> ⌒ Replace something.

Save your revised descriptive paragraph in your *Writer's Notebook.* You will use it when you proofread your paragraph.

# Revising Workshop
## Combining Subjects and Predicates

Good writers write concisely, avoiding unnecessary repetition. When they can, they combine subjects and predicates to make their writing smoother and more direct. Look at these sentences.

1. After passing under the bridge, the sailboat slowly turned. It headed back toward the harbor.
2. After passing under the bridge, the sailboat slowly turned and headed back toward the harbor.

In the first example, one subject (the sailboat) performs two actions. Notice how the writer combined the two predicates to make a smoother, more concise statement. Look at these sentences.

3. I had never seen a sailboat race, and my brother had never seen a sailboat race either.
4. My brother and I had never seen a sailboat race.

In the third example, two subjects perform the same action. Notice how the writer combined the two subjects to make a statement that is less wordy and more direct.

## Practice

Rewrite each of the following sentence pairs. Combine subjects or predicates to make sentences that are more concise.

1. Just before the hailstorm, the animals in the barnyard suddenly grew very still. The birds suddenly grew very still.
2. Soon the hail fell. It bounced off our living room window.
3. The drumming sound of the hail scared our dog, Speckles. Our loud laughter and yelling scared him too.
4. After the storm, I took a walk in the park. My brother took a walk in the park too.
5. Before long, the sun came out from behind a cloud. It quickly warmed the air.
6. The barnyard animals basked in the sunlight. Speckles basked in the sunlight too.

# 4 Proofreading
## Descriptive Paragraph

Mark used the **Writer's Guide** and the **Editor's Marks** to proofread what he had written. Look at what he did.

### Writer's Guide

**Proofreading Checklist**

☑ Check for errors in capitalization. Be sure that you have capitalized place names correctly.

☑ Check for errors in punctuaton.

☑ Check to see that your paragraph is indented.

☑ Check your grammar.

☑ Circle any words you think are misspelled. Find out how to spell them correctly.

⇨ For proofreading help, use the **Writer's Handbook.**

*In the boat were my dad, my cousin Fred, and me. He is from homestead, Florida. We turned off the enjin so we wouldn't frightn the animals away.*

### EDITOR'S MARKS

≡ Capitalize.

⊙ Add a period.

∧ Add something.

⋏ Add a comma.

∨∨ Add quotation marks.

✄ Cut something.

⋀ Replace something.

∼ Transpose.

◯ Spell correctly.

⊓ Indent paragraph.

∕ Make a lowercase letter.

## Discuss

1. Look at Mark's proofread paragraph. What kinds of corrections did he make?
2. Where did Mark need to add a comma? Why?

## Try Your Hand

**Proofread Your Descriptive Paragraph**   Now use the checklist in the **Writer's Guide** and the **Editor's Marks** to proofread your descriptive paragraph.

Save your corrected descriptive paragraph in your *Writer's Notebook.* **You will use it when you publish your paragraph.**

# 5 Publishing
## Descriptive Paragraph

**Writer's Guide**

**Publishing Checklist**

☑ Make a clean copy of your descriptive paragraph.

☑ Check to see that nothing has been left out.

☑ Check to see that there are no mistakes.

☑ Share your descriptive paragraph in a special way.

Mark made a clean copy of his descriptive paragraph and checked it to make sure he had not left out anything. Then he and his classmates made oral presentations of their paragraphs to the class. These oral presentations were recorded on videotape and on audiotape. You can find Mark's descriptive paragraph on page 29 of the **Writer's Handbook.**

Here is how Mark and his classmates recorded their oral presentations on videotape and audiotape.

1. First, the students made sure they had the necessary video and audio equipment and people who knew how to operate the equipment correctly. Then, they planned how to begin and how to end the taping of the presentation.

2. Next, they gave oral presentations of their descriptive paragraphs to the class. They spoke clearly and directly into the microphone.

**3.** They looked at their classmates and at the camera.

**4.** Then, Mark and his classmates labeled their audiocassettes and videocassettes. They put them in the school's audiovisual collection for listening or viewing by others.

## Discuss

1. Why is it important to discuss the taping of the performance with the equipment operator beforehand?
2. Why might a performance be improved by taping it before a live audience?

## Try Your Hand

**Publish Your Descriptive Paragraph** Follow the checklist in the **Writer's Guide.** If possible, create a videotape or an audiotape, or try one of these ideas for sharing your descriptive paragraph.

◆ Put the descriptive paragraphs on the bulletin board in your classroom. Decorate the bulletin board display with photographs or drawings of the subjects being described.
◆ Organize the descriptive paragraphs in a class booklet called *See! Hear! Smell! Touch! Taste!*

# Writing in the Content Areas

Use what you learned to write about your experiences, feelings, and thoughts. You could write a descriptive paragraph or a journal entry. One way to publish a descriptive paragraph would be to send it in a friendly letter to one of your teachers. Use one of these ideas or an idea of your own.

**Writer's Guide**

When you write, remember the stages of the Writing Process.
- Prewriting
- Drafting
- Responding and Revising
- Proofreading
- Publishing

## Science

Find an interesting leaf or fern. Trace its outline onto a sheet of paper. Inside the outline, describe how and where you found the leaf or the fern. Describe the shape and the length of the stem. Does it grow in a group? How high above the ground does it grow? What made it catch your eye?

## Physical Education

Think of a game that you have never played in your physical education class. Describe the game. Tell how many players are required, what equipment is needed, and how the game is played. Suggest ways that the game could be worked into the physical education program at your school.

## Literature

Recall a story or a book that you read recently. Describe the setting (the place where it happened) or one of the characters. Tell why the setting or the character interested you.

## Health

Remember a time that you had a cold, the flu, a broken leg, or another illness or injury. Describe what happened to you. Tell what you did and how you felt. Include adjectives that clearly and vividly describe the experience.

# CONNECTING

Writers appeal to the five senses—seeing, hearing, smelling, touching, and tasting—when they write a descriptive paragraph. Often they describe things they have seen or experienced. A well-written descriptive paragraph helps the reader imagine what the writer saw, heard, smelled, touched, and tasted. What do you "see" as you read this paragraph?

## Uuugh! A Bug!

Yesterday, I found one of the most interesting insects I have ever seen. I was walking home from school when I saw something on the ground. At first, I thought it was a stone. When I looked closer, I saw skinny legs. Whew! It gave me a shock. It was a black beetle, about two inches long. Its back was hard and shiny, and its side was brown-and-black-striped. It had six thin legs and very small antennae. It made a faint buzzing sound with its wings. I picked it up. Its fuzzy legs tickled my arm as it walked up to my shoulder. I tried to show it to my friend, but all she said was, "Uuugh! Get that bug away from me!" I guess people don't always have the same idea of what is interesting.

◆ **Adjectives in a Descriptive Paragraph** The words highlighted in color are descriptive adjectives. Some tell you how the beetle looked. Adjectives can also tell *how many* or can be used to compare. You will probably use many adjectives when you write descriptive paragraphs.

◆ **Language Focus: Adjectives** The following lessons will help you use adjectives in your own writing.

# 1 Adjectives

◆ **FOCUS**   An **adjective** is a word that describes a noun or a pronoun.

Read these sentences. The words in color are adjectives.

1. Hot air fuels bright balloons.
2. Few people are standing in line.

An adjective tells *what kind* or *how many*. The adjectives *hot* and *bright* describe *what kind*. The adjective *few* tells *how many*.

Two or more adjectives can be used to describe one noun.

3. Huge, colorful stripes cover the balloon.
4. One small tank of gas fuels the balloon.

Notice that in sentence 3, a comma is used to separate the adjectives. When both adjectives describe *what kind*, a comma is usually used. When one of the adjectives tells *how many*, a comma is not used, as in sentence 4.

beautiful
exciting
cheap

FOR SALE

---

**Link to Speaking and Writing**
Use vivid adjectives to paint clear word pictures. Why is the revised sentence better?

*The balloon floats through the cool air.*
*frigid*

---

## Guided Practice

**A.** Identify the adjective or adjectives that describe each underlined noun. Tell whether each adjective tells *what kind* or *how many*. (Do not include *a, an,* or *the*.)

1. We bought a nice, new <u>balloon</u>.
2. Let's go for a short <u>trip</u>.
3. Up we go into the blue <u>sky</u>.
4. Wave at the tiny <u>people</u>.
5. Here are two <u>maps</u> of the pretty <u>countryside</u>.

**B.** **6.–10.** Replace each adjective that tells *what kind* in **A** with a more vivid adjective. Use the **Writer's Thesaurus.**

## Independent Practice

**C. Identifying Adjectives** Write the adjective that describes each underlined noun. Also write whether the adjective tells *what kind* or *how many.* (Do not include *a, an,* or *the.*)

11. The balloon is made of 50 yards of fine silk.

`MODEL` 50—how many; fine—what kind

12. Balloons come in bright colors.
13. A big machine is used to sew them.
14. The bottom of the balloon is a brown basket.
15. Each balloon carries a small tank.
16. A balloonist needs a roomy van for the equipment.

**D. 17.–22. Revising Sentences** Replace each adjective that tells *what kind* in **C** with a vivid adjective. Use the **Writer's Thesaurus.** Write the new sentence.

17. The balloon is made of 50 yards of fine silk.

`MODEL` The balloon is made of 50 yards of delicate silk.

**E. Proofreading Sentences** Each sentence contains two underlined adjectives. Some tell *how many* and some tell *what kind.* Write each sentence. Add commas between two adjectives that tell *what kind.*

23. Big colorful balloons are filled with helium.

`MODEL` Big, colorful balloons are filled with helium.

24. People guide the light airy giants in parades.
25. One small factory makes all the balloons.
26. The designers work on funny unusual ideas.
27. They sew together huge thick sheets of material.
28. Five talented artists will paint the balloon.
29. The big bumpy nose will be green.

## Application — Writing

**Advertisement** Write an advertisement for your local newspaper about a hot-air balloon festival. Describe the festival for the newspaper's readers. Use vivid adjectives.

# 2 Articles and Demonstrative Adjectives

### FOCUS
◆ The adjectives *a, an,* and *the* are **articles.**
◆ *This, that, these,* and *those* are special adjectives that point out nouns.

The words *a, an,* and *the* are adjectives called **articles.** *A* and *an* refer to any person, place, thing, or idea. *The* refers to a specific person, place, thing, or idea. Articles always tell *which one* about a noun.

1. I tripped on a rock.   **any**
2. I landed on the rock next to it.   **specific**

The words *this, that, these,* and *those* are **demonstrative adjectives.** They also tell *which one. This* and *these* describe things close by. *That* and *those* describe things farther away.

3. Look at this rock by these trees.   **near**
4. I'll meet you at that rock by those bushes.   **far**

| Articles and Demonstrative Adjectives | | |
|---|---|---|
| **a** | Use before singular words. Use when a noun or the word before a noun begins with a consonant sound. | a mountain a high cliff |
| **an** | Use before singular words. Use when a noun or the word before a noun begins with a vowel sound. | an eagle an odd hour |
| **the** | Use before singular and plural words. | the map the trails |
| **this, that** | Use before singular words. | that bird |
| **these, those** | Use before plural words. | those lakes |

## Guided Practice

**A.** Identify the adjective that completes each sentence.

1. Look at (a, the) mountains.
2. Today we'll climb (this, that) mountain.
3. I hope (this, these) boots fit.
4. (The, A) sky is very clear.
5. I hope we see (an, a) eagle.
6. (This, These) is a thrilling sight!

## Independent Practice

**B. Identifying Articles and Demonstrative Adjectives**   Write the adjective in parentheses ( ) that completes each sentence.

7. I looked down into (an, a) eagle's nest.

MODEL ⟩ an

8. (This, These) nest had two eggs inside.
9. One egg had (a, the) tiny crack.
10. As I watched, (a, the) eaglet hatched.
11. Look at (this, that) photograph in my hand.
12. Are (that, those) photographs on the wall yours?

**C. Identifying Adjectives and the Nouns They Describe**   Write each sentence. Underline the adjectives. Draw an arrow from each adjective to the noun it describes.

13. Orienteering is a new sport in this country.

MODEL ⟩ Orienteering is a new sport in this country.

14. This sport takes place in the woods or the mountains.

15. You need an accurate compass and a good map.

16. Use this map to plan a careful route.

17. That marker is hidden behind those big rocks.

18. These bright flags have numbers on them.

19. There are ten markers on this trail.

20. Try to find the markers before I do.

## Application — Writing and Speaking

**Object Clues**   Choose an object in your classroom. Write a clue that will help someone guess the object. Do not mention the object by name. Instead, describe the objects near it. Use articles and demonstrative adjectives. Then read your clue aloud. See whether your classmates can guess the object.

# 3 Proper Adjectives

◆ FOCUS   A **proper adjective** is formed from a proper noun.

Remember that a proper noun names a particular person, place, or thing. The words in color in these sentences are proper adjectives.

1. The Italian food in Italy is delicious.
2. This Chinese vase comes from China.
3. Do Arctic winds begin in the Arctic?

A proper adjective begins with a capital letter. When a proper noun is changed into a proper adjective, the proper noun usually changes. Notice that in sentences 1 and 2, the proper nouns *Italy* and *China* changed. In sentence 3, *Arctic* did not change.

When a proper adjective is made up of two or more words, each important word is capitalized.

4. The South American people live on the continent of South America.

## Guided Practice

**A.** Identify the proper adjective in each sentence. If it is formed from a proper noun, identify the noun. Use a dictionary if you need help.

1. We traveled the Pacific coastline.
2. We ate tacos in a Mexican restaurant.
3. Some California beaches are rocky.
4. Many of the towns had Spanish names.
5. We feasted on delicious Chinese food in a San Francisco restaurant.
6. We bought some South American jewelry.
7. Some Japanese tourists talked with us.

> **THINK AND REMEMBER**
> ◆ Remember that a **proper adjective** is formed from a proper noun.
> ◆ Capitalize each important word in a proper adjective.

# Independent Practice

**B. Identifying Proper Adjectives**  Write each proper adjective. Then, write the proper noun from which it is formed. Use a dictionary if you need help.

  8. Last year I sunbathed on a European beach.

  MODEL  European—Europe

  9. There I met a French swimmer.
  10. The man beside her was her German swimming coach.
  11. He was wearing a Hawaiian shirt.
  12. The coach timed the swimmer with a Swiss watch.
  13. She dove in and did the Australian crawl.
  14. Next year she will compete in an American competition.

**C. Proofreading Sentences**  Write each sentence. Capitalize the proper adjectives.

  15. Magellan was a portuguese sailor.

  MODEL  Magellan was Portuguese sailor.

  16. He sailed around the south american continent.
  17. The spanish language is spoken in Argentina.
  18. Santiago is the chilean capital.
  19. The panamanian people helped to build and operate an important canal.
  20. The caribbean countries are islands.
  21. The haitian people speak the french language.

**D. Writing Proper Adjectives**  Write the proper adjective that is formed from each proper noun in parentheses ( ). Use a dictionary for help.

  22. New York is a center for _____ foods. (Asia)

  MODEL  Asian

  23. Yellow rice is common in _____ dishes. (India)
  24. Raw fish is a _____ specialty. (Japan)
  25. _____ restaurants serve rice. (Vietnam)
  26. Have you ever eaten _____ food? (Korea)
  27. People worldwide drink _____ orange juice. (Brazil)

## Application — Writing

**Food Review**  Imagine that you are a writer for your local newspaper. Write a review of the food served at a street fair. Describe the foods you tried. Tell how they tasted and from which countries they came. Use proper adjectives.

# 4 Adjectives That Follow Linking Verbs

◆ FOCUS   An adjective that follows a linking verb describes the subject.

The most common linking verbs are forms of *be*. Some other linking verbs are *look, seem, feel, become, appear, taste, smell,* and *grow*. Notice the adjectives in color in these sentences. They follow linking verbs and describe the noun or pronoun in the subject.

1. Mysteries **are** clever .

2. They also **seem** scary .

In some sentences different adjectives in different positions can describe the same noun or pronoun.

3. The eager reader **was** curious about the book.

The night was dark and stormy.

### Link to Speaking and Writing

Three or more adjectives can be used to describe a noun or pronoun. A comma is placed between the adjectives and before the word *and*.

*The night was dark, dreary, and stormy.*

## Guided Practice

**A.** Identify the adjective in each sentence. Then, name the noun or the pronoun it describes.

1. Tom's castle was famous for its attic.
2. The attic smelled musty.
3. I was uncertain about climbing the stairs.
4. My footsteps seemed loud on the steps.
5. The cobwebs felt sticky.

### THINK AND REMEMBER

◆ Remember that an adjective that follows a linking verb describes the subject of a sentence.
◆ In some sentences different adjectives in different positions describe the same noun or pronoun.

# Independent Practice

**B. Identifying Adjectives That Follow Linking Verbs**  Write the adjective in each sentence. (Do not include *a, an,* or *the.*) Then, write the noun or pronoun it describes.

   6. Arthur's typewriter is ancient.

   MODEL ▷ ancient, typewriter

   7. At times it seems alive.
   8. The typewriter's keys grow dusty.
   9. The keys are sticky.
   10. Arthur's idea is fabulous.
   11. An editor appears enthusiastic about the story.

**C. Identifying Adjectives in Different Positions in a Sentence**
Write each sentence. Underline the adjectives. (Do not include *a, an,* or *the.*) Draw an arrow from each adjective to the noun it describes.

   12. Arthur's new story is incomplete.

   MODEL ▷ Arthur's new story is incomplete.

   13. Poor Arthur seems fearful of his new computer.

   14. The bright screen appears strange to Arthur.

   15. The rickety typewriter looks lonely.

   16. A fresh piece of paper tastes wonderful to the typewriter.

   17. Now, Arthur seems comfortable.

**D. Proofreading Sentences**  Write these sentences. Add commas between the adjectives and before the word *and.*

   18. This book is old dusty and moldy.

   MODEL ▷ This book is old, dusty, and moldy.

   19. Mysteries are fun clever and eerie.
   20. The clues are creative imaginative and unusual.
   21. Houses look desolate dark and creepy.
   22. Detectives often appear silly stupid and dull.
   23. The hero seems smart forceful and honest.

## Application — Writing

**Setting for a Scary Story**  Write a paragraph that describes a setting for a scary story. Use adjectives to describe the setting. Place the adjectives in different positions in your sentences. Be sure to use adjectives that follow linking verbs.

# 5 Comparison with Adjectives: *er, est*

◆ **FOCUS**    Adjectives can be used to compare nouns.

Remember that an adjective is a word that describes a noun or a pronoun. Adjectives can also be used to compare two people, places, things, or ideas.

1. The red monster is taller than the green one.
2. The blue monster is tallest of all.

When adjectives are used to compare two nouns or pronouns, *er* is usually added to the adjective. When three or more are compared, *est* is often added to the adjective. The spelling of some adjectives changes when *er* or *est* is added. This chart shows how an adjective can change.

---

1. When an adjective ends with e, drop the e and add *er* or *est*.

    large          larger          largest

2. When an adjective ends with a consonant plus *y*, change the *y* to *i* and add *er* or *est*.

    ugly           uglier          ugliest

3. When a one-syllable adjective ends with a vowel plus a consonant, double the consonant and add *er* or *est*.

    big            bigger          biggest

---

## Guided Practice

**A.** Identify the form of the adjective that completes each sentence.

1. It was the (long) night of my life.
2. The kitchen is (dark) than my room.
3. My flashlight shines (bright) than Mom's.
4. I saw eyes (red) than a rabbit's.
5. Mom shouted the (loud) yell I ever heard.

---

**THINK AND REMEMBER**
◆ Add *er* to most adjectives to compare two things.
◆ Add *est* to most adjectives to compare more than two.
◆ Follow the rules in the chart to spell adjectives that compare.

---

# Independent Practice

**B. Identifying Adjective Forms**   Write the correct form of the adjective in parentheses ( ) to complete each sentence.

6. The (odd) creature I know is the Loch Ness Monster.

MODEL oddest

7. Nessie's story seems (true) than the story of Bigfoot.
8. Some say that Nessie is the world's (old) dinosaur.
9. They say its body is (big) than a school bus.
10. Its head may be (small) than a horse's head.
11. Nessie is not the world's (friendly) monster.
12. The (early) sighting of Nessie took place more than 1,500 years ago.
13. Loch Ness is Scotland's (busy) tourist attraction because of this legendary creature.
14. Only the (lucky) people of all see Nessie.

**C. Revising Sentences**   Some of the sentences have incorrect adjective forms. If the adjective form is correct, write *correct*. If it is incorrect, write the sentence correctly.

15. The story of Icarus is one of the older myths of all.

MODEL The story of Icarus is one of the oldest myths of all.

16. Icarus, his father Daedalus, and the Minotaur were locked in the world's trickiest maze.
17. No monster was ugliest than the Minotaur.
18. Each day the Minotaur moved closest to Icarus and Daedalus.
19. Flying out of the maze was Daedalus' wiser idea.
20. Daedalus was heavier than Icarus.
21. Icarus flew nearest to the sun than Daedalus.
22. As Icarus flew higher, his wax wings melted.
23. The boy's fall into the sea was the unhappier moment of his father's life.
24. This story is the sadder of all the Greek myths.

## Application — Writing

**Monster Contest**   Imagine that you are the judge of a monster contest. Choose one of the pictured monsters or select another monster that you have seen illustrated. Describe the monster. Explain to the other judges why it should win the contest. Use adjectives that end in *er* and *est*.

# 6 Comparison with Adjectives: More, Most

◆ **FOCUS** *More* or *most* is used with an adjective of two or more syllables to make comparisons.

Most adjectives with two or more syllables do not take the endings *er* and *est.* When two people, places, things, or ideas are compared, *more* is used with the adjective. When three or more people, places, things, or ideas are compared, *most* is used with the adjective.

1. Kwong is an athletic skier.
2. Kwong is more athletic than I am.
3. Kwong is the most athletic skier on the team.

Notice that when *most* is used, the word *the* often comes before it.

4. Skiing is the most dangerous sport I have ever tried.
5. Jeff does the most exciting jumps.

> **Link to Speaking and Writing**
> Do not use *more* or *most* before adjectives that have *er* or *est* added to them.

*This hill is more steeper than that one.*
*This hill is the most steepest of the three.*

## Guided Practice

**A.** Tell whether *more* or *most* belongs in each sentence.

1. Derek is a _____ graceful skier than Katy.
2. He took Katy to the _____ challenging trail of all.
3. I would be _____ nervous than Katy was.
4. This was not the _____ sensible decision Derek has made.
5. Katy fell on the _____ difficult part of the trail.
6. Her ankle was _____ painful than her elbow.
7. The ski patrol members are the _____ skillful skiers of all.

## Independent Practice

**B. Identifying Adjective Forms**   Read each sentence. Write *more* or *most* to complete each one.

8. Learning to ski is _____ complicated than it looks.

MODEL▷ more

9. The _____ important rule of all is to bend your knees.
10. The _____ dangerous trails are labeled "challenging."
11. Ice is _____ slippery than snow.
12. Icy snow is _____ risky than dry snow.
13. Falling is _____ painful than I thought it would be.
14. Even the _____ careful skiers fall sometimes.
15. Some skiers look for the _____ challenging trails in the world.

**C. Revising Sentences**   Some of the sentences have incorrect adjective forms. If the adjective form is correct, write *correct*. If it is incorrect, write the sentence correctly.

16. Colorado's snow is more finer than Vermont's.

MODEL▷ Colorado's snow is finer than Vermont's.

17. The Alps have some of the most famous ski resorts in the world.
18. Which of these two mountains has the more nicer view?
19. This view is the more spectacular I've ever seen.
20. This hill was more steeper than that one.
21. Skiing is most enjoyable than skating.
22. Skiing is my most favorite sport.
23. I want to ski down the most tallest mountain.

## Application — Writing and Speaking

**News Feature**   Write a paragraph in which you compare two sports or vacation places. Use adjectives with *more* and *most.* Deliver your news feature to a classmate or a family member. If you need help writing a paragraph of comparison, see page 26 of the **Writer's Handbook.**

# 7 Comparison with Adjectives: Special Forms

◆**FOCUS**   Some adjectives that compare have special forms.

Remember that you often use adjectives with the endings *er* or *est* to compare. At other times you use *more* or *most* before adjectives to compare. Notice how the adjective *bad* changes in these sentences.

1. The skies looked  bad  on Monday.
2. The winds became  worse  on Tuesday.
3. The hurricane on Wednesday was the  worst  of all.

Other adjectives that have special forms are *good, little, much,* and *many.* This chart shows the special forms. Notice that *many* and *much* have the same forms.

|  | good | bad | little | many, much |
|---|---|---|---|---|
| **When two nouns are compared, use** | better | worse | less | more |
| **When more than two are compared, use** | best | worst | least | most |

Read these sentences.

4. The chickens were  littler  than the ducks.
5. I had  less  time than Will to watch the ducks.

The adjective *little* sometimes takes the endings *er* or *est. Littler* and *littlest* refer to size. *Less* and *least* refer to amount.

## Guided Practice

**A.** Identify the adjective that correctly completes each sentence.

1. I had the (better, best) time ever at Lazy Days Farm.
2. (More, Most) people like the farm, but some don't.
3. The weather is (better, best) there than at home.
4. We only had one day of (bad, worst) weather.
5. It was the (worse, worst) thunderstorm ever.
6. The (littlest, least) trees were uprooted.
7. We have (littler, less) trouble with the weather at home.

## Independent Practice

**B. Identifying Special Forms of Adjectives**  Write the form of the adjective in parentheses ( ) that completes the sentence.

 8. My new piglet was the (better, best) of the litter.

MODEL  best

 9. I picked a (bad, worst) day to carry my pig home.
 10. As we walked, a (little, least) wind sprang up.
 11. (Many, More) times I wished I had my bike.
 12. I felt (better, best) jogging than walking.
 13. (Many, More) other pigs I know are fairly patient.
 14. The (worse, worst) time of all was when my pig jumped down.
 15. The (better, best) thing to do was to run home.
 16. It was (good, best) to see my pig in front of my home.
 17. I hope my pig will be the (better, best) at the fair.
 18. (Much, most) fuss will be made over my pig by the judges.

**C. Using the Adjective *Little***  Read each sentence. Write the form of the adjective *little* that makes sense.

 19. Out in the field I found a _____ hole.

MODEL  little

 20. From it peeked an even _____ head.
 21. It was the head of the _____ snake I'd ever seen.
 22. The snake spent _____ time in its hole than out of it.
 23. It ate _____ in the morning than in the evening.
 24. It was the _____ scary-looking snake I've ever seen.
 25. Then the _____ snake crawled away.

## Application — Writing

**Weather Report**  Imagine that you have been in a bad storm. Write a paragraph that describes the storm. Tell why it was the worst storm you have ever seen. Use the special forms of the adjectives in this lesson. If you need help writing a descriptive paragraph, see page 29 of the **Writer's Handbook.**

# Building Vocabulary
## Suffixes

In 1909, Admiral Robert Peary and Matthew Henson made a successful attempt to reach the North Pole.

Remember that you can change the meaning of a base word by adding a prefix to the beginning of it. Remember also that a base word is the simplest form of a word. A **suffix** is a word part added to the end of a base word.

For example, the word *successful* is made up of the base word *success* and the suffix *ful*. The suffix *ful* means "full of." The word *successful* means "full of success."

The following charts show how you can add suffixes to base words to form adjectives and nouns.

| Adjective-Forming Suffixes | | |
|---|---|---|
| **Suffix** | **Meaning** | **Example** |
| ful | full of | fearful |
| less | without | careless |
| able | able to be | understandable |
| y | having; like | worthy |
| ish | like; somewhat | childish |

| Noun-Forming Suffixes | | |
|---|---|---|
| **Suffix** | **Meaning** | **Example** |
| er | one who | player |
| or | one who | sailor |
| ness | quality of being | kindness |
| ship | state or condition of | friendship |
| ment | process of; state of | government |

## Reading Practice

Read each sentence. Write each underlined word. Underline the suffix. Then write a definition of the word based on the meanings of the suffix and the base word.

1. One moment of <u>greatness</u> in United States history was the <u>achievement</u> of Admiral Robert Peary and Matthew Henson.
2. This <u>fearless</u> <u>leader</u> and his talented assistant made several attempts to reach the North Pole.
3. Some people thought Peary and Henson were <u>foolish</u> to go on such dangerous and <u>uncomfortable</u> expeditions.
4. Peary's <u>careful</u> planning in 1909 proved to be <u>lucky</u>, and he was praised for his <u>leadership</u>.
5. I saw a movie about the life of Robert Peary, and the <u>actor</u> who played the admiral was excellent.

## Writing Practice

Add a suffix from the charts on the opposite page to each of these words. Use each new word in a sentence. If necessary, check the words in a dictionary.

6. dust
7. heart
8. invent
9. peace
10. citizen

11. boy
12. shy
13. announce
14. drink
15. sad

16. fix
17. farm
18. baby
19. laugh
20. harm

## Project

Work with a partner to create a list of adjectives with suffixes and a list of nouns with suffixes. Then match a word on the adjective list with a word on the noun list to make phrases. These phrases can be serious ("thoughtful teacher") or silly ("goofy government"). With your partner, illustrate five of your phrases. Write a sentence under each illustration, using the phrase that inspired it.

The tallish sailor hit his head on the boom.

# Language Enrichment
## Adjectives

Use what you know about adjectives to do these activities.

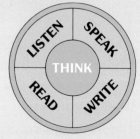

 **Good Lunch, Bad Lunch**

Make two outline drawings of a lunch bag or lunch box. In one, use adjectives to write a descriptive list of your favorite foods: *spicy chili, crunchy apples*. In the other, use adjectives to write a descriptive list of your least favorite foods: *soggy cornflakes, raw broccoli*. Compare your lists with a classmate's. Discuss the adjectives you used. Think about why some adjectives might show up on one person's "good" list and on another's "bad" list.

 **Rating Writing Instruments**

Work in groups of three or four students. All of you should put your writing instruments (pens or pencils) on one desk. Have each student carefully examine and write with each pen and pencil. Then, think of as many adjectives as you can that describe the color, the shape, and the size of each pen or pencil. Next, think of adjectives to compare the writing instruments. For example, pencils might be rated *sharp, sharper,* and *sharpest*; pens might be rated *dark, darker,* and *darkest*. Finally, rate the writing instruments *good, better,* and *best*. Make lists of your adjectives. Share your lists and rating system with your classmates.

 **Wave Your Flag**

Design a flag for yourself. Include your favorite colors, words, symbols, or anything else that is meaningful to you. Then, write a paragraph to describe your flag. Use adjectives to tell about the different parts and colors of your flag and to explain how you chose each. Share your flag and your paragraph with your class.

# CONNECTING

## LANGUAGE ⟷ WRITING

In this unit you learned that adjectives are words that show how something looks, feels, tastes, smells, or sounds. They are words that help you describe.

◆ **Using Adjectives in Your Writing** Knowing how to use adjectives that express exactly what you mean is an important writing skill. Precise, colorful adjectives create a vivid picture for your readers. They help them to see and feel what you are writing about.

Pay special attention to the adjectives you use as you do these activities.

### Hearing Things

Work with a partner. Close your eyes and listen to the sounds around you. Both of you should write about what you hear. Describe the sounds by using adjectives: for example, the *steady ticking of the clock*. Also, compare one sound to another by using adjectives that compare with *er, est, more,* and *most.* For example, *The constant dripping of water in the sink was louder than the distant splashing of rain on the roof.* Exchange descriptions with your partner. Talk about what you heard and about the different adjectives you chose to describe similar sounds.

### Pinning Down Suffixes

You learned about suffixes on the **Building Vocabulary** pages. Here's an enjoyable suffix game you can play.

Open any book. Close your eyes and place your finger anywhere on the page. Open your eyes and read the word by your finger. If the word has a suffix, give yourself one point. If it has no suffix, try to add a suffix to it. If you make a real word, give yourself two points. Write each word on a score sheet. See how many points you can get in three minutes. Then start over. See if you can top your first score.

| Think Back | Think Ahead |
|---|---|
| ◆ What did you learn about descriptive paragraphs? What did you do to write one? | ◆ How will what you learned about a descriptive paragraph help you when you read a story?<br><br>◆ How will knowing how to observe details in a spatial order help you write a descriptive paragraph? A story? |
| ◆ What did you learn about adjectives? How will that help you express *what kind* and *how many*? | ◆ What is one way you can use adjectives to improve your writing? |

## Descriptive Paragraphs   *pages 256–257*

Read the descriptive paragraph. Then follow the directions.

> Carla, Jill, and I decided to make some shakes, while we told each other lots of silly jokes. We ran downstairs, and while Jill and I placed the blender on the counter by the sink, Carla opened the refrigerator. Way in the back, behind jars of salad dressing, pickles, and other items, was the milk. Carla started pushing the jars out of the way, but I guess she was too eager to reach the milk. I turned toward her just in time to watch jar after jar tumble out and smash onto the red-and-white tile floor. Carla screamed, and Jill dropped the blender into the sink. Sharp vinegar and sweet pickle juice odors rose from the floor where red, orange, and green piles of spilled food now mixed. From upstairs, we heard my father yelling about all the noise we were making. My pajama party was now a mess!

1. Give the subject that is being described.
2. Write the topic sentence.
3. List any words that appeal to your sense of sight.
4. List any words that appeal to your sense of smell.
5. List any words that appeal to your sense of hearing.

## Observing Details in Spatial Order    *page 258*

Read the sentences. Write *left to right, back to front, top to bottom,* or *close to far* to show how each sentence's details are presented.

6. The woman's straw hat matched her dress and shoes.
7. We walked from the back door of the theater to the first row.
8. The bird on my hand was tiny, while the one in the tree was huge.
9. From the tall, narrow tower, the people below looked like bugs.
10. The boy glanced first to the left and then the other way.

## Using Sensory Images   *page 259*

Complete the following sentences. Use sensory words to describe the details. Then write *sight, hearing, smell, touch,* or *taste* to show what kind of sensory images are used.

11. The _____ mountains make good places to ski.
12. As we drove, we smelled the _____ mountain air.
13. Along the way we heard several _____ eagles.
14. There are always lots of skiers drinking _____ cocoa.
15. If you fall, the ground will feel _____ .

## The Writing Process   *pages 260–271*

16. When you plan to write a descriptive paragraph, what is a helpful way to gather information?
    a. reading a book about interesting places
    b. conducting an interview      c. clustering sensory details
17. What organization is most appropriate for a descriptive paragraph?
    a. time order      b. spatial order      c. cause and effect
18. Why do writers sometimes combine subjects and predicates?
    a. to save space on paper      b. to add more words
    c. to make the writing less wordy and more direct

## Adjectives   *pages 274–275*

Write the adjective that describes each underlined noun. Also write whether the adjective tells *what kind* or *how many.*

19. Dwayne's parents planned a surprise party for him.
20. His parents bought red streamers to decorate the house.
21. Dwayne's father took him to a basketball game.
22. Meanwhile, the six guests arrived for the party.
23. When Dwayne got home, his shocked expression told his parents that the surprise had worked.

## Articles and Demonstrative Adjectives   *pages 276–277*

Write each sentence. Underline the adjectives. Draw an arrow from each adjective to the noun it describes.

24. An adventure story can take readers to fascinating places.

25. A tropical island and that icy North Pole are among

    the many locations to be discovered.

26. Imagine yourself on the highest mountaintop in the world—

    that famous peak, Mount Everest.

27. What might happen if you could dive to a part of

    those oceans of more than 8,000 meters deep?

28. These experiences make an adventure tale worth reading.

## Proper Adjectives   *pages 278–279*

Write each sentence. Capitalize the proper adjectives.

29. Charles Wilkes was an american explorer who was the first to announce that Antarctica is a continent.

30. In 1899 a group of british explorers became the first humans to spend a winter on Antarctica.

31. There were other antarctic explorations.

32. The norwegian Roald Amundsen reached the South Pole in 1911.

33. Seventeen years later, a british pilot named Hubert Wilkins became the first to fly over Antarctica.

## Adjectives That Follow Linking Verbs   *pages 280–281*

Write each sentence. Underline the adjectives. (Do not include *a, an,* or *the.*) Draw an arrow from each adjective to the noun it describes.

34. The frontiersman was worried.

35. The chances of winning the battle seemed grim.

36. He and the others felt defeated.

37. Davy Crockett was wrong about the Americans winning.

38. Their battle became hopeless when the Mexicans attacked.

## Comparison with Adjectives: *er, est*   *pages 282–283*

Write the correct form of the adjective in parentheses ( ) to complete each sentence.

**39.** The Mississippi is the (long) river in the United States.

**40.** The Nile River is over 400 miles (long) than the Mississippi.

**41.** The cargo ship on the Mississippi today is a (heavy) craft than the raft that Huckleberry Finn used in Mark Twain's story.

**42.** To people who enjoy sailing, few sights are (lovely) than a group of brightly colored sailboats cruising along a lake.

**43.** The (speedy) sailboats can carry passengers more quickly, but some travelers would rather have a long-lasting trip.

## Comparison with Adjectives: *More, Most*   *pages 284–285*

Read each sentence. Write *more* or *most* to complete each one.

**44.** Dawn's summer was the _____ unusual one she had ever had.

**45.** She spent it with the _____ interesting relative in her family.

**46.** Her aunt is the _____ outstanding zookeeper in the state.

**47.** Dawn visited the zoo _____ often than other children.

**48.** Each visit held _____ adventures than the one before.

## Comparison with Adjectives: Special Forms   *pages 286–287*

Write the form of the adjective in parentheses ( ) that correctly completes each sentence.

**49.** Paul and Jorge often complained about their (bad, worse) neighborhood park.

**50.** They agreed that it was the (worse, worst) park in the city.

**51.** Jorge wondered if the truck was bringing (better, best) play equipment than the broken swings that were now there.

**52.** The truck held (less, least) equipment than Paul and Jorge had hoped it would contain.

**53.** They hoped the new play equipment would be as (good, better) as the equipment at their school.

## Suffixes   *pages 288–289*

Add the suffix *ful, less, able, y, ish, er, or, ness, ship,* or *ment* to each of these words. Use each new word in a sentence. If necessary, check the words in a dictionary.

**54.** yellow

**55.** decorate

**56.** settle

**57.** ill

**58.** scorn

**59.** produce

**60.** achieve

**61.** raw

**62.** observe

# UNIT

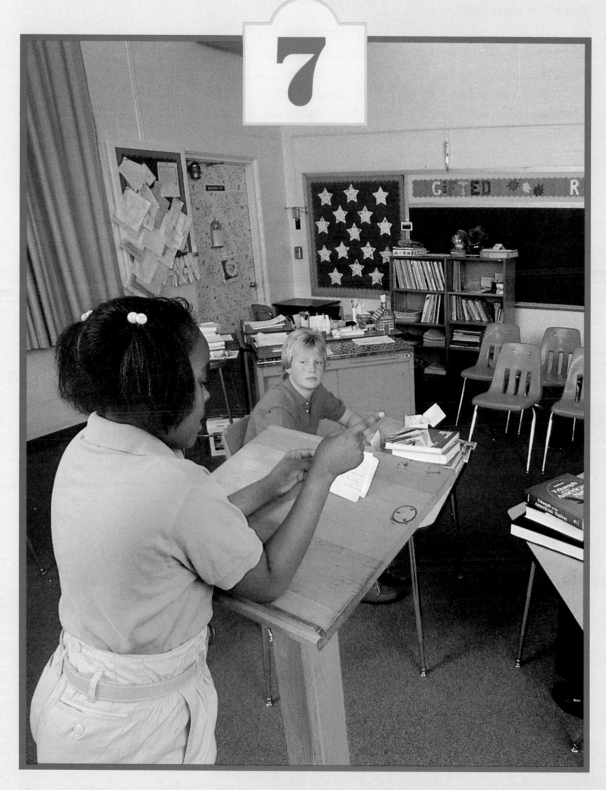

# Communicating Your Opinions

◆ **COMPOSITION FOCUS:** **Persuasive Paragraph in a Business Letter**

◆ **LANGUAGE FOCUS:** **Adverbs**

Imagine that you are persuading your family to take a vacation. Your suggestion is to go camping at Yosemite National Park in California. Here are reasons you might use to convince the others that your suggestion is the best.

◆ We've been to all the other places but never to Yosemite.
◆ Camping would be a lot cheaper than staying in motels, which we'd have to do at the other places.

When you try to get others to agree with you and to do as you suggest, you are practicing the art of persuasion.

In the following pages you'll read about Ramona Quimby. Ramona is the main character in a series of books by Beverly Cleary. As Ramona's fans know, she is a very lively and interesting character, and a very persuasive one too. In this unit you will learn more about persuasion in the form of the persuasive paragraph. You will also learn more about writing business letters.

Beverly Cleary creates characters, like Ramona, who try *to persuade* others.

# Reading with a Writer's Eye
## Persuasion

In this excerpt from *Ramona and Her Father*, the author Beverly Cleary has the determined Ramona try as hard as she can to persuade her father to stop smoking. As you read the selection, notice the various things Ramona does to convince her father that he should give up his habit.

### *from* Ramona and Her Father
by Beverly Cleary

The next day after school Ramona found the Scotch tape and disappeared into her room to continue work on her plan to save her father's life. While she was working, she heard the phone ring and waited, tense, as the whole family now waited whenever the telephone rang. She heard her father clear his throat before he answered. "Hello?" After a pause he said, "Just a minute, Howie. I'll call her." There was disappointment in his voice. No one was calling to offer him a job after all.

"Ramona, can you come over and play?" Howie asked, when Ramona went to the telephone.

Ramona considered. Of course they would have to put up with Howie's messy little sister, Willa Jean, but she and Howie would have fun building things if they could think of something to build. Yes, she would like to play with Howie, but saving her father's life was more important. "No, thank you. Not today," she said. "I have important work to do."

Just before dinner she taped to the refrigerator door a picture of a cigarette so long she had to fasten three pieces of paper together to draw it. After drawing the cigarette, she had crossed it out with a big black X and under it she had printed in big letters the word BAD. Beezus giggled when she saw it, and Mrs. Quimby smiled as if she were trying not to smile. Ramona was filled with fresh courage. She had allies. Her father had better watch out.

When Mr. Quimby saw the picture, he stopped and looked while Ramona waited. "Hmm," he said, backing away for a better view. "An excellent likeness. The artist shows talent." And that was all he said.

Ramona felt let down, although she was not sure what she had expected. Anger, perhaps? Punishment? A promise to give up smoking?

The next morning the sign was gone, and that afternoon Ramona had to wait until Beezus came home from school to ask, "How do you spell pollution?" When Beezus printed it out on a piece of paper, Ramona went to work making a sign that said Stop Air Pollution.

"Let me help," said Beezus, and the two girls, kneeling on the floor, printed a dozen signs. Smoking Stinks. Cigarettes Start Forest Fires. Smoking Is Hazardous to Your Health. Ramona learned new words that afternoon.

Fortunately Mr. Quimby went out to examine the car, which was still making the tappety-tappety noise. This gave the girls a chance to tape the signs to the mantel, the refrigerator, the dining-room curtains, the door of the hall closet, and every other conspicuous place they could think of.

This time Mr. Quimby simply ignored the signs. Ramona and Beezus might as well have saved themselves a lot of work for all he seemed to notice. But how could he miss so many signs? He must be pretending. He had to be pretending. Obviously the girls would have to step up their campaign. By now they were running out of big pieces of paper, and they knew better than to ask their parents to buy more, not when the family was so short of money.

"We can make little signs on scraps of paper," said Ramona, and that was what they did. Together they made tiny signs that said, No Smoking, Stop Air Pollution, Smoking Is Bad for Your Health, and Stamp Out Cigarettes. On some, Ramona drew stick figures of people stretched out flat and dead, and on one, a cat on his back with his feet in the air. These they hid wherever their father was sure to find them—in his bathrobe pocket, fastened around the handle of his toothbrush with a rubber band, inside his shoes, under his electric razor.

Then they waited. And waited. Mr. Quimby said nothing while he continued to smoke. Ramona held her nose whenever she saw her father with a cigarette. He appeared not to notice. The girls felt discouraged and let down.

Once more Ramona and Beezus devised a plan, the most daring plan of all because they had to get hold of their father's cigarettes just before dinner. Fortunately he had tinkered with the car, still trying to find the reason for the tappety-tappety-tap, and had to take a shower before dinner, which gave the girls barely enough time to carry out their plan.

All through dinner the girls exchanged excited glances, and by the time her father asked her to fetch an ashtray, Ramona could hardly sit still she was so excited.

As usual her father pulled his cigarettes out of his shirt pocket. As usual he tapped the package against his hand, and as usual a cigarette, or what appeared to be a cigarette, slid out. Mr. Quimby must have sensed that what he thought was a cigarette was lighter than it should be, because he paused to look at it. While Ramona held her breath, he frowned, looked more closely, unrolled the paper, and discovered it was a tiny sign that said, Smoking Is Bad! Without a word, he crumpled it and pulled out another—he thought— cigarette, which turned out to be a sign saying, Stamp Out Cigarettes! Mr. Quimby crumpled it and tossed it onto the table along with the first sign.

"Ramona." Mr. Quimby's voice was stern. "My grandmother used to say, 'First time is funny, second time is silly—'" Mr. Quimby's grandmother's wisdom was interrupted by a fit of coughing.

Ramona was frightened. Maybe her father's lungs already had begun to turn black.

Beezus looked triumphant. See, we told you smoking was bad for you, she was clearly thinking.

Mrs. Quimby looked both amused and concerned.

Mr. Quimby looked embarrassed, pounded himself on the chest with his fist, took a sip of coffee, and said, "Something must have caught in my throat." When his family remained silent, he said, "All right, Ramona. As I was saying, enough is enough."

Ramona scowled and slid down in her chair. Nothing was ever fair for second-graders. Beezus helped, but Ramona was getting all the blame. She also felt defeated. Nobody ever paid any attention to second-graders except to scold them. No matter how hard she tried to save her father's life, he was not going to let her save it.

## Respond

1. How do you feel about Ramona's campaign to get her father to stop smoking? Why do you think Ramona is willing to work so hard at it?

## Discuss

2. What arguments does Ramona use to persuade her father to stop smoking? Of these, which one is most likely to convince a smoker to stop? Why?

3. Do you think the author is in favor of Ramona's methods of persuasion? Give reasons for your answer.

# Thinking As a Writer

## Analyzing a Persuasive Paragraph in a Business Letter

Writers use persuasion to try to convince others. In a persuasive paragraph, the writer states an opinion on an issue. Then the writer gives facts and reasons to explain why he or she holds that opinion and why others ought to agree. The purpose of a persuasive paragraph is to change other people's opinions about an issue by influencing their thinking.

I am writing to ask the city council to ban smoking in public places. I feel this would be a good idea for three reasons. First, smoking bothers many nonsmokers. Second, smoking sets a bad example for young people. Third, the tars and nicotine in smoke can damage the lungs of nonsmokers as well as smokers. It is not right for children to be forced to inhale smoke in public, so it should be banned immediately.

The **topic sentence** states the writer's opinion on a specific issue.

**Supporting arguments** are reasons or facts that back up the writer's position.

The **concluding argument** is the final, strongest reason. It should include a call for action.

## Discuss

1. What is the purpose of this persuasive paragraph?
2. What would you expect to find in the first sentence of a persuasive paragraph?
3. Why is it a good idea to place the strongest argument last?

Often, you write a business letter to a person you do not know. This fact makes a business letter different from a friendly letter. The purpose of a business letter is to ask for information, to order something, or to express an opinion. A business letter should be clear and have a polite and formal tone.

319 Lilac Road
Hamilton, Vermont 05059
September 21, 19—

Mayor Elizabeth Phillips
1 Main Street
Hamilton, Vermont 05059

Dear Mayor Phillips:

    I am writing to ask the city council to ban smoking in public places. I feel this would be a good idea for three reasons. First, smoking bothers many nonsmokers. Second, smoking sets a bad example for young people. Third, the tars and nicotine in smoke can damage the lungs of nonsmokers as well as smokers. It is not right for children to be forced to inhale smoke in public, so it should be banned immediately.

        Sincerely yours,

        *Marta De Witt*

        Marta De Witt

The **heading** contains the address of the writer and the date.

The **inside address** gives the name and address of the person to whom the letter is written. The **greeting** gives the title and the name of the person addressed and ends with a colon.

The **body** contains facts listed in a logical order. The order in which the reasons are given is shown by the time-order words *first, second,* and *third.*

The **closing** is a polite way to end the letter.

The **signature** is hand-written and typed beneath. It gives the name of the writer.

## Discuss

1. What are the six parts of a business letter?
2. How is the body of the letter like a persuasive paragraph?

# Try Your Hand

**A. Add Letter Parts and Number Words**  Read these two persuasive paragraphs, which recommend removing the cement under the playground monkey bars. Choose the paragraph that expresses the opinion with which you agree. Write that paragraph as a business letter. Add a heading (with your address and today's date), an inside address (to the mayor of your city or town), a greeting (to the mayor), a closing, and your signature. In addition, begin each of the reasons with the number word *first, second,* or *third.*

> Our playground needs help! The cement under the monkey bars should be replaced with grass. Grass would soften any tumbles the climbers took. Grass is prettier than cement. Playing on grass would make children feel like they were playing in the country. Please consider making this important change soon.

> I am writing to ask you to replace the cement in the playground with sand. Sand makes a very soft landing place for someone who falls. Sand is cheaper to care for than grass. Sand is not damaged by the kind of use it would have in a playground. Please give serious consideration to my suggestion.

**B. Add Formal Words**  Words or phrases such as *I would like to suggest, Please consider,* and *Thank you* give a business letter a polite tone. Rewrite one of the sentences in your letter by adding words that contribute to this formal feeling. You may simply edit in the words, using this mark ∧ .

**C. Read a Persuasive Paragraph**  Find a persuasive paragraph in the *Letters to the Editor* section of a newspaper or magazine. Read your letter aloud to a partner, identifying the opinion and the supporting reasons.

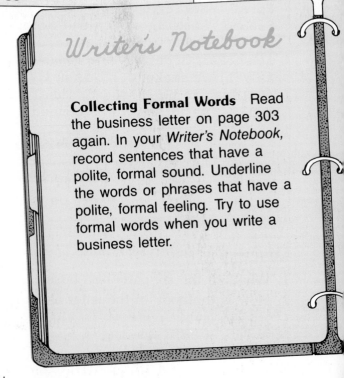

*Writer's Notebook*

**Collecting Formal Words**  Read the business letter on page 303 again. In your *Writer's Notebook,* record sentences that have a polite, formal sound. Underline the words or phrases that have a polite, formal feeling. Try to use formal words when you write a business letter.

# Thinking As a Writer
## Evaluating Reasons to Support an Opinion

In a persuasive paragraph, writers try to persuade readers to feel the same way they do about something. Before writing, writers list all the reasons that support their opinion. They then evaluate the reasons by deciding which ones would be the most convincing to their particular audience.

Before Marta wrote to Mayor Phillips, she listed all the reasons that supported her opinion and evaluated each reason.

| Reason | Evaluation |
| --- | --- |
| **1.** Smokers look dumb. | weak |
| **2.** Smoke makes nonsmokers' eyes tear and throats burn. | strong |
| **3.** Smokers set a bad example for children. | strong |
| **4.** Smoke smells funny. | weak |

First, in planning a persuasive paragraph, list all the reasons that support your opinion. Then, evaluate the reasons, and select the ones that are most likely to convince your audience.

## Discuss

1. Look again at the list of reasons in the box. Which reasons might Marta have eliminated or included if she had been writing to persuade a classmate never to begin to smoke?
2. Are there other reasons Marta might include? Explain your choice.

## Try Your Hand

**Write an Opinion and Evaluate Supporting Reasons** Write your opinion about some subject that interests you, and list at least four reasons to support your opinion. Then think of a particular audience you want to persuade, and evaluate each reason in terms of its effectiveness. Share your list with a partner. Evaluate each other's reasons.

# Developing the Writer's Craft
## Capturing the Reader's Interest

The writer of a business letter must capture the reader's interest quickly. Read this opening sentence from Marta's letter to Mayor Phillips.

> I am writing to ask the city council to ban smoking in public places.

The writer immediately states her reason for writing. She is clear and to the point. After this good beginning, the reader will probably be curious to find out Marta's recommendation. Now read Marta's ending sentence.

> It is not right for children to be forced to inhale smoke in public, so it should be banned immediately.

This last sentence will leave the mayor with something to think about.

When you write your persuasive business letter, make sure that your beginning sentence is clear and to the point. Give your letter an ending that your reader will remember.

## Discuss

1. Look once more at the letter on page 303. What is another way Marta might begin her letter that would both state her purpose for writing and capture the mayor's interest?
2. What is it about Marta's ending sentence that helps the reader remember it?

## Try Your Hand

**Write a Good Beginning and Ending**  Imagine a vacant lot filled with junk. What do you think should be done about it? Whom do you want to persuade? Write a beginning sentence stating your opinion in the clearest, strongest terms. Then  write an ending sentence that your reader will remember.

# 1 Prewriting
## Persuasive Paragraph in a Business Letter

**Writer's Guide**

**Prewriting Checklist**
- ☑ Brainstorm topics.
- ☑ Select a topic.
- ☑ Think about your audience and your purpose.
- ☑ Gather information that helps support your opinion.
- ☑ Organize your reasons in order of importance.

Ellen, a student at Hidden Canyon Elementary School, wanted to write a persuasive letter to be published in the local newspaper. She used the checklist in the **Writer's Guide** to help plan her persuasive letter. Look at what she did.

### ◆ Brainstorming and Selecting a Topic

First, Ellen brainstormed a list of issues in her community that she thought she might want to write about. She included as many issues as she could. Look at Ellen's list.

Next, Ellen looked over her list and crossed out topics that she felt would not work. She crossed out topics that were too broad for a short letter and topics that would probably not interest the readers of the newspaper.

Finally, Ellen circled the topic about which she felt she could write most persuasively. She decided to write about putting a stop sign at an intersection in her neighborhood because she had strong feelings on the subject and felt it would interest others in her audience.

*Protecting the natural environment*
*Putting stop signs at the intersection of River Street and E Street*
*The number of reruns on TV during the summer*
*Making recesses longer during rainy-day schedule at school*
*Further exploration of outer space*

### Discuss

1. Look at each topic Ellen crossed off her list. Why do you think she eliminated it?
2. If Ellen were writing a letter to her *school* newspaper instead of her town's newspaper, which topic might she have chosen?

## ◆ Gathering Information

After Ellen selected her topic, she gathered information for her persuasive paragraph. To get ideas about how she might best persuade her audience, she looked at the *Letters to the Editor* section of the newspaper. Ellen made a chart of the types of reasons letter writers gave to support their ideas. Look at Ellen's chart.

| Safety | Money | Convenience | Other |
|--------|-------|-------------|-------|
|        |       |             |       |

Then Ellen thought about reasons to support her proposal to put stop signs at the intersection of River Street and E Street. She listed her reasons in the categories on her chart. Look at what she did.

| Safety | Money | Convenience | Other |
|--------|-------|-------------|-------|
| Will protect all pedestrians, especially children | Won't need crossing guards during school hours<br><br>Won't need traffic police during special events | Drivers won't have to drive to closest intersection three blocks away to cross E Street during rush hour | Less high-speed traffic noise |

Ellen then shared the list of reasons with her mother and her older brother to get their reactions. Ellen's mother thought the reason under *Safety* on Ellen's chart was especially strong. However, Ellen's mother did not find the reason about school crossing guards under *Money* convincing, because she thought that crossing guards would still be needed even if there were stop signs. Ellen's brother liked Ellen's reasons but was not sure what she meant by "special events" under *Money*.

Ellen listened to their comments and made notes to use when organizing her information and writing her persuasive paragraph.

# Discuss

1. Look at Ellen's chart. She has more reasons than she will probably use in her paragraph. Is it a good idea to have more reasons at first than you will need? Why or why not?
2. Which of the reasons on Ellen's chart might interest a parent reading the newspaper? Which reason might interest a reader who drives near this intersection on the way to work?
3. Can you think of any additional reason to add stop signs at a busy intersection? Under which category would your reason fit?
4. Ellen asked her mother and brother to respond to her ideas. Why is this an especially good idea for a persuasive paragraph?

## ◆ Organizing Information

After Ellen had gathered all the reasons she needed for her persuasive paragraph, she was ready to organize her information. She wanted to make a strong impression on her audience, and she knew that the order in which she presented the reasons was important. She decided to organize her information according to its importance to her audience. She could do this in two ways. She could start with the reason they would consider most important and then give those they considered less important, or she could start with the least important reason and build to the most important. To leave the readers with the strongest point, Ellen decided to organize the points in her paragraph in order from least important to most important.

Ellen numbered the reasons in her chart according to how important she thought they were to her audience. She gave the most important reason a *1* and the least important a *5*. Look at what she did.

| Safety | Money | Convenience | Other |
|--------|-------|-------------|-------|
| *1* Will protect all pedestrians, especially children | *5* Won't need crossing guards during school hours  *3* Won't need traffic police during special events | *2* Drivers won't have to drive to closest intersection three blocks away to cross E Street during rush hour | *4* Less high-speed traffic noise |

Ellen decided she would not use the reason she had numbered 5 since she agreed with her mother that it was not a very strong argument. She decided to present the other reasons in order of increasing importance, starting with number 4 and ending with number 1.

## Discuss

1. Even though most of her readers will be adults, Ellen still chose protection of children as her most important argument. Was this a good choice? Why or why not?
2. Ellen might have organized her information from most important to least important. Do you agree with the organization Ellen chose? Why or why not?

## Try Your Hand

Now plan a persuasive paragraph of your own.

A. **Brainstorm and Select a Topic**  Brainstorm a list of local issues that interest you. Think about each topic and your audience. If you already know who your audience will be, you can pick the topic that will most interest them. If a particular topic really excites you, you can decide what audience would be most interested in it.

   ◆ Cross out topics that are too broad, would not interest your audience, or are things that people cannot do anything about.
   ◆ Circle the topic about which you feel you can write most persuasively.

B. **Gather Information**  Think about your topic. You might want to see how other people have approached your topic or your audience, as Ellen did in looking through the local newspaper. As you read these arguments, be on the lookout for propaganda techniques. If you need help, follow the **Tips on How to Recognize Propaganda Techniques** on page 311.

   ◆ Chart all the reasons you can think of to support the topic you have chosen.
   ◆ After you have listed all the reasons you can think of, share them with other people and note their reactions. Which reasons do they find persuasive? Which reasons are not?

C. **Organize the Facts**  Make sure you have all the reasons you can think of. Then organize your reasons in order of importance. Depending on your audience and your purpose, you may decide to move from least important to most important or from most important to least important.

 **Save your notes, lists, and charts in your *Writer's Notebook*. You will use them when you draft your persuasive paragraph.**

# Listening and Speaking
## Tips on How to Recognize Propaganda Techniques

Speakers sometimes try to persuade by using methods known as **propaganda techniques.** Listen to recognize the techniques used in the following statements.

1. When a speaker has not taken the time to form a worthwhile opinion, he or she has made a **Hasty Generalization.**

   > Don't bother listening to that new radio station, KAND. They never play any good songs. I listened for ten minutes, and they played two songs I really hate.

2. When you hear a famous person trying to convince you to use a product, you are listening to a **Testimonial.**

   > Hi! I'm Andy Lane, star of the hit movie *Flash.* When I want a refreshing, nutritious treat, I reach for a Reelfrute Frozen Juice Bar. You should too!

3. When you hear a speaker trying to convince you to do something because "everyone else is doing it," you are listening to a technique called the **Bandwagon.**

   > Join the voters of this county in supporting Stacey Frank for supervisor. On election day, you don't want to be the only one marking the wrong box on your ballot.

4. When you hear a speaker praising or attacking an individual instead of dealing directly with an issue, you are listening to the **Personality** technique.

You should donate at least $10 to the Good Deed Drive. My neighbor Mr. Anderson did, and he is one of the nicest people on our block. Don't give any money to the Good Deed Drive. My neighbor Ms. Hamilton supports it, and she's one of the meanest people on our block!

# 2 Drafting
## Persuasive Paragraph in a Business Letter

Using her notes, lists, and charts, Ellen followed the checklist in the **Writer's Guide** to draft her persuasive paragraph. Look at what she did.

> Our neighborhood needs stop signs at River Street and E Street. They would save money. They would help commuters and protect pedestrians. Cars speed through the intersection at all hours and sometimes wake me up.

**Writer's Guide**

**Drafting Checklist**

☑ Use your notes, lists, and charts for ideas.

☑ Write the topic sentence first.

☑ Write your arguments in order of importance.

☑ End by urging the action you want.

☑ Follow the correct form for a business letter.

## Discuss

1. Look at Ellen's topic sentence. Why is it important to have a topic sentence in a persuasive paragraph?
2. Is the first reason Ellen presents a strong one? Why or why not?

## Try Your Hand

Now you are ready to write a persuasive paragraph.

**A. Review Your Information** Think about the reasons you gathered and organized in the last lesson. Decide whether you need more information. If so, gather it.

**B. Think About Your TAP** Remember that your task is to write a persuasive paragraph. Your purpose is to persuade your audience to your point of view.

**C. Write Your First Draft** Follow the steps in the **Drafting Checklist** to write your persuasive paragraph.
   When you write your draft, just put all your ideas on paper. Do not worry about spelling, punctuation, or grammar. You can correct the draft later.

**Task:** What?
**Audience:** Who?
**Purpose:** Why?

**Save your first draft in your *Writer's Notebook*. You will use it when you revise your persuasive paragraph in a business letter.**

# 3 Responding and Revising

## Persuasive Paragraph in a Business Letter

### Writer's Guide

**Revising Checklist**

- ☑ Read your persuasive paragraph to yourself or to a partner.
- ☑ Think about your audience and your purpose. Add or cut information.
- ☑ Check to see that your reasons are organized in the most effective order.
- ☑ Check for ways to combine information, using *and*.

Ellen used the **Writer's Guide** to revise her persuasive paragraph. Look at what she did.

### ◆ Checking Information

When Ellen read over her draft, she decided to take out the argument about waking up because that was not important to others. To show her change, she used this mark ℒ .

### ◆ Checking Organization

Ellen decided to move the sentence about rush hours to a place where it would be more effective. To show this change, she used this mark ◌ .

### ◆ Checking Language

Ellen noticed that some of the language seemed too informal for a business letter. She crossed out this informal language. She also found a way to combine ideas from two sentences to make them more concise and more interesting to read.

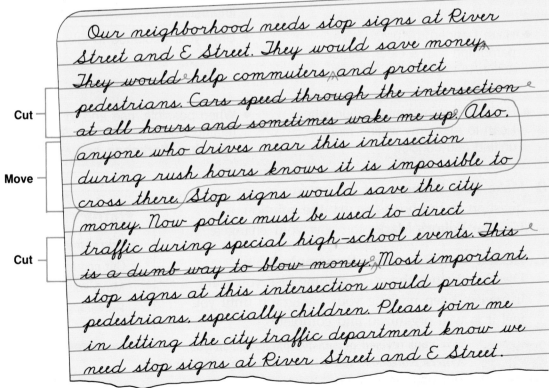

Cut

Move

Cut

Our neighborhood needs stop signs at River Street and E Street. They would save money. They would help commuters and protect pedestrians. Cars speed through the intersection at all hours and sometimes wake me up. Also, anyone who drives near this intersection during rush hours knows it is impossible to cross there. Stop signs would save the city money. Now police must be used to direct traffic during special high-school events. This is a dumb way to blow money. Most important, stop signs at this intersection would protect pedestrians, especially children. Please join me in letting the city traffic department know we need stop signs at River Street and E Street.

# Discuss

1. Why do you think Ellen made the deletions that you see?
2. Why did Ellen move the argument about rush-hour traffic?
3. Is the last sentence of Ellen's paragraph a good call for action?
4. Can you think of any other ways Ellen could have made her persuasive paragraph stronger? If so, what are they?

## Try Your Hand

Now revise your first draft.

**A. Read Your First Draft**  As you read your persuasive paragraph, think about your audience and your purpose. Read your paragraph silently or to a partner to see whether it is complete and well organized. Ask yourself or your partner the questions in the box.

---

### Responding and Revising Strategies

| ✔ **Respond** Ask yourself or a partner: | ✔ **Revise** Try these solutions: |
| --- | --- |
| ◆ Have I written a topic sentence that states my purpose clearly? | ◆ **Revise** your topic sentence to make your point clearer. |
| ◆ Have I arranged my ideas in order of importance? | ◆ **Rearrange** your points as necessary to make the strongest impression. |
| ◆ Have I ended my persuasive paragraph with a clear call for action to capture the reader's interest? | ◆ Urge your audience to take the action you want. |
| ◆ Have I combined information when I can to make my writing more unified and concise? | ◆ When possible, use *and* to connect related words in a series. See the **Revising Workshop** on page 315. |

---

**B. Make Your Changes**  If the answer to any question in the box is *no*, try the solution. Use the **Editor's Marks** to show your changes.

**C. Review Your Persuasive Paragraph Again**  Decide whether there is anything else you want to revise. Keep revising your paragraph until you feel it is well organized and complete.

> **EDITOR'S MARKS**
> ∧ Add something.
> ✐ Cut something.
> ◌ Move something.
> ∧ Replace something.

Save your revised persuasive paragraph in your *Writer's Notebook*. You will use it when you proofread your paragraph.

# Revising Workshop
## Combining Sentences

Good writers put related ideas and information together. Instead of spreading out one point over two or three sentences, they often use *and* to join a series of related words. Look at the underlined words in these sentences.

1. The museum should add an insect zoo. It would be <u>different</u>. It would also be <u>educational</u>. It would be <u>fun</u>, too.
2. The museum should add an insect zoo. It would be <u>different</u>, <u>educational</u>, and <u>fun</u>.

In the first example, the writer used three sentences to describe the benefits of the insect zoo. In the second example, the writer used *and* to join the words describing the benefits. Notice that a comma follows each item except the last in a series of three or more items.

Look at this pair of examples.

3. A monthly bus pass would let students travel <u>more easily</u>. It would also let them travel more <u>quickly</u>.
4. A monthly bus pass would let students travel <u>more easily</u> and <u>quickly</u>.

In the fourth example, the writer gets the information across more concisely and clearly by using *and* to combine related words.

## Practice

Rewrite each of the following series of sentences. Use *and* to combine related information into one sentence.

1. Bicyclists should be required to have driver's licenses, just like drivers of cars. Drivers of trucks also have licenses. So do drivers of motorcycles.
2. Licensing bicyclists would make the roads safer for everyone. Licensing would also make the roads more orderly.
3. The test for this license should include questions on safety. It also should include questions on traffic laws and bicycle care.
4. A bicyclist's license would help riders file reports on stolen bikes. It would also help them file reports on accidents.
5. A bicyclist who passes the test would be more careful and better informed. The bicyclist would also be more courteous.

# 4 Proofreading
## Business Letter

After Ellen revised her persuasive paragraph in her letter to the newspaper, she used the **Writer's Guide** and the **Editor's Marks** to proofread the letter. Look at what she did.

### Writer's Guide

**Proofreading Checklist**

☑ Be sure that words and abbreviations in the opening and closing parts of the business letter are capitalized correctly.

☑ Be sure that the opening and closing parts of the business letter are punctuated correctly.

☑ Check to see that your paragraph is indented.

⇨ For proofreading help, use the **Writer's Handbook.**

---

354 Eagle Street
Cody, Wyoming, 82414
october 1, 19--

Editor
The Cody Cronicle    *Chronicle*
756 Bison Drive
Cody, Wyoming 82414

Dear Editor:
    Our neighborhood needs stop signs at River Street and E Street. They would save money, help commuters, and protect pedestrians.

---

### EDITOR'S MARKS

≡ Capitalize.

⊙ Add a period.

∧ Add something.

⋀ Add a comma.

ⱽⱽ Add quotation marks.

✂ Cut something.

⋀ Replace something.

~ Transpose.

◯ Spell correctly.

⊬ Indent paragraph.

/ Make a lowercase letter.

## Discuss

1. Look at Ellen's proofread letter. What kinds of corrections did she make?
2. Why is it important to include your complete return address in the heading of a business letter?
3. What punctuation mark should follow *Sincerely*?

## Try Your Hand

**Proofread Your Business Letter** Now use the **Writer's Guide** and the **Editor's Marks** to proofread your business letter.

 **Save your corrected business letter in your** *Writer's Notebook.* **You will use it when you publish your letter.**

# 5 Publishing
## Business Letter

Writer's Guide
Publishing Checklist
☑ Make a clean copy of your business letter.
☑ Check to be sure that nothing has been left out.
☑ Check that there are no mistakes.
☑ Share your business letter in a special way.

Ellen made a clean copy of her letter to the newspaper and checked it to be sure she had not left out anything. Then she addressed the envelope and mailed the letter to the newspaper. You can read Ellen's business letter on page 44 of the **Writer's Handbook.**

Here's how Ellen published her letter.

Ellen checked her letter over carefully and then stamped and addressed the envelope. She made sure that the name, address, city, state, and ZIP code of the person she was sending the letter to were on the front of the envelope. She checked that her return address was in the upper left corner.

## Discuss

1. Should you ever expect a letter back from the audience you address in a letter to the editor? Why or why not?
2. What other kinds of responses might Ellen get instead of a letter?

## Try Your Hand

**Publish Your Business Letter** Follow the checklist in the **Writer's Guide.** If possible, mail your business letter, or try one of these ideas for sharing your persuasive paragraph.

◆ Post all students' persuasive paragraphs on the bulletin board in your classroom along with any newspaper or magazine articles on the same subjects.

◆ Read the persuasive paragraphs aloud in class. Discuss the pros and the cons for each of the issues raised.

# Writing in the Content Areas

**Writer's Guide**

When you write, remember the stages of the Writing Process.

◆ Prewriting

◆ Drafting

◆ Responding and Revising

◆ Proofreading

◆ Publishing

Use what you learned to write a persuasive paragraph about a local problem or situation that concerns you. One way to publish your writing is to send your persuasive paragraph in a business letter to someone who might help you make changes in your school or your community. Use one of these ideas or an idea of your own.

## Social Studies

Think about an improvement that could make your favorite playground a better or safer place. Explain what you want done. Give reasons for your idea. Suggest ways that your idea might be put into action. If you wish, write to the director of your community's recreation department.

## Fine Arts

Imagine that you want your school to have an art show that displays students' work. Write a paragraph giving strong reasons for why the art show would be a good idea for your school. If you wish, send your paragraph in a letter to the school principal.

## Literature

Write a letter to your teacher, suggesting that your class read your favorite book, magazine, newspaper, or other piece of literature as part of your language arts lessons. Give reasons to persuade your teacher that this literature would be good for your class to study.

## Science

Imagine that deer are eating the leaves from all the bushes in your local park. Some people say that deer repellent should be sprayed on the bushes. Others say this will deprive the deer of food they need. What do you think should be done? Think of a plan. Write a paragraph that describes your plan and gives reasons to support it.

Often, people express their opinions in business letters. A well-written business letter presents reasons for an opinion. What reasons does the writer of this letter give to persuade the reader to agree with her opinion?

630 Anderson Street
Trenton, New Jersey 08620
September 3, 19—

Thomas Episcopo
The Food Stop
2556 White Horse Road
Trenton, New Jersey 08619

Dear Mr. Episcopo:

I am writing to suggest politely that you immediately remove the plastic grocery bags from your store. I often use paper bags for garbage. The plastic bags don't work because they fall messily onto the floor. Also, plastic bags threaten the environment terribly. Please, sir, act quickly. Replace the plastic bags with good old paper ones!

Sincerely,

Anne C. Bell

Anne C. Bell

◆ **Adverbs in a Business Letter** The words highlighted in color are adverbs. They do the job of telling you *how, when,* or *where* an action happens. Adverbs such as *immediately* are often used for emphasis. You will frequently find them in business letters requesting action.

◆ **Language Focus: Adverbs** The following lessons will help you use adverbs in your own writing.

# 1 Adverbs

♦ **FOCUS**   An **adverb** is a word that describes a verb.

Many verbs show action. An adverb tells *where,* *when,* or *how* an action happens. The words in color are adverbs.

1. Stand there until the race starts.  **where**

2. The race begins soon .  **when**

3. The hare brags loudly .  **how**

Notice in sentence 3 that *loudly* ends in *ly.* Many adverbs that tell *how* end in *ly.* Some do not.

4. Together the tortoise and hare begin the race.  **how**

5. The hare runs fast .  **how**

> ### Link to Speaking and Writing
> Use vivid adverbs to make your writing clear. Why did the writer add an adverb to this sentence?

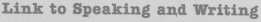

*The hare moved quickly along the trail.*

## Guided Practice

**A.** Identify the adverb that describes the underlined verb in each sentence. Tell whether the adverb tells *where, when,* or *how.*

1. The judge <u>shouts</u> suddenly.
2. The speedy hare <u>jumps</u> high.
3. The tortoise <u>shuffles</u> away.
4. The hare <u>arrives</u> first at the halfway mark.
5. The hare lazily <u>decides</u> to have a rest.

**B.** Add an adverb to make each sentence more vivid.

6. The tortoise <u>comes</u> down the road.
7. The tortoise <u>passes</u> the hare.
8. The amazed crowd <u>cheers</u>.
9. The hare <u>wakes</u> from its nap.
10. The slow and steady tortoise <u>wins</u> the race.

## Independent Practice

**C. Identifying Adverbs**   Write the adverb that describes each underlined verb. Then, write whether the adverb tells *how, when,* or *where.*

11. The sun <u>shines</u> hotly on Tom Sawyer's head.

> MODEL  hotly—how

12. Swiftly he <u>paints</u> whitewash on the fence.
13. He silently <u>wonders</u> how he can avoid his chores.
14. A smile <u>spreads</u> slowly across Tom's face.
15. His friend <u>arrives</u> then.
16. Slyly Tom <u>convinces</u> his friend to try painting.
17. More friends <u>come</u> along.
18. Tom <u>drops</u> his paintbrush quietly.
19. He <u>sneaks</u> away from the fence.
20. Tom joyfully <u>dives</u> into the swimming hole.

**D. Revising Sentences**   Add an adverb to each sentence to make it more vivid. Write the new sentence.

21. The snowstorm rages around Laura and Mary.

> MODEL  The snowstorm rages wildly around Laura and Mary.

22. Little Carrie follows.
23. The snow swirls around the girls.
24. Will they find their way?
25. Pa finds them.
26. Ma welcomes them.
27. The storm blows outside the cozy house.

## Application — Writing

**Fable**   "The Tortoise and the Hare" is a fable. A fable is a short story that teaches a lesson. It usually has animal characters. Write a one-paragraph fable. At the end of your fable, write a moral. The moral is the sentence that gives the lesson of the story. Use adverbs in your writing. If you need help writing a story, see page 33 of the **Writer's Handbook.**

# 2 Comparison with Adverbs

---

◆ **FOCUS**    Adverbs can be used to compare two or more actions.

---

Adjectives can be used to compare nouns. Adverbs can be used to compare actions. Like adjectives, adverbs have special forms for making comparisons.

Short adverbs add *er* to compare two actions and *est* to compare more than two actions.

1. The Ankylosaurus moved fast .
2. The Allosaurus moved faster .
3. The Tyrannosaurus Rex moved fastest .

Most adverbs that end in *ly* use *more* or *most* to compare actions.

4. The Ankylosaurus attacked fiercely .
5. The Allosaurus attacked more fiercely .
6. The Tyrannosaurus Rex attacked most fiercely .

The adverbs *well* and *badly* have special forms for comparison.

|  | To Compare Two | To Compare More Than Two |
|---|---|---|
| ate *well* played *badly* | ate *better* played *worse* | ate *best* played *worst* |

## Guided Practice

**A.** For each adverb, identify the form that is used to compare two actions. Then, identify the form that is used to compare more than two actions.

1. hard
2. well
3. quickly
4. easily
5. soon
6. late
7. fast
8. badly
9. nicely

---

**THINK AND REMEMBER**

◆ Remember that adverbs can be used to compare actions.
◆ Add *er* or *est* to short adverbs.
◆ Use *more* or *most* with adverbs that end in *ly*.
◆ Remember that *well* and *badly* have special forms.

---

# Independent Practice

**B. Identifying Adverbs** Write the form of the adverb in parentheses ( ) that correctly completes each sentence.

10. The scientists dug (deep) here than in the valley.

MODEL> deeper

11. They searched (long) than ever before.
12. Dr. Casey found a fossil the (soon) of them all.
13. Dr. Santiago dug the (skillfully) of all.
14. Dr. Mason identifies fossils (successfully) than her partner.
15. Each day she arrives the (early) of anyone on the team.
16. Baby fossils were found (recently) than adult ones.
17. Evidence shows that the Stegosaurus walked (heavily) than the Kritosaurus.
18. No evidence can show which dinosaur roared (loudly) of all.
19. Dr. Josef looked the (hard) of all for the tracks.
20. Ms. Alison built a dinosaur skeleton (neatly) than Mr. Yamamoto.
21. I saw the dinosaur skeleton (often) than you did.

**C. Completing Sentences with Forms of *Well* and *Badly*** Write each sentence. Complete it with a form of *well* or *badly* that makes sense.

22. You will organize our museum trip (well) than I.

MODEL> better

23. You give directions (well).
24. I even write directions (badly).
25. My little sister behaved (badly) than your brother.
26. Kim's little brother behaved the (badly) of all.
27. Our museum guide explained the history of dinosaurs the (well) of all the guides.
28. She used her voice (well).
29. I liked the dinosaur exhibit (well) than the energy exhibit.
30. The dinosaur models were designed (well).
31. Only one model appeared (badly) built.
32. It was formed (badly) than the one next to it.

## Application — Writing

**News Story** Imagine that you discover dinosaur fossils near your home. Write a story for your local newspaper to tell about your discovery. Use adverbs that compare. If you need help writing a news story, see page 39 of the **Writer's Handbook.**

# 3 Adverbs Before Adjectives and Other Adverbs

◆ **FOCUS**   Adverbs can describe adjectives and other adverbs.

Remember that an adverb describes a verb. Adverbs can also describe adjectives and other adverbs by telling *to what extent.*

**1.** Frozen yogurt melts  too  quickly in the heat.

**2.** Waffles are  very  tasty with frozen yogurt.

In sentence 1 the adverb *too* describes the adverb *quickly.* In sentence 2 the adverb *very* describes the adjective *tasty.*

The adverbs in this chart often are used to describe adjectives and other adverbs.

| | | | |
|---|---|---|---|
| quite | almost | certainly | very |
| rather | totally | unusually | so |
| terribly | slightly | incredibly | too |

## Guided Practice

**A.** Identify the adverb that describes each underlined adverb or adjective.

1. Abe Doumar's frozen concoction tastes extremely delicious.
2. The paper cups are almost always a litter problem.
3. Waffles fold quite easily into a cone shape.
4. People snatch up the cones very eagerly.
5. The cone is a wonderfully simple invention.
6. The Doumars sell them very successfully.
7. The line for cones is unusually long.
8. The wait is certainly worthwhile.
9. People in line are incredibly patient.
10. Most people eat their cones rather quickly.

---

**THINK AND REMEMBER**

◆ Remember that an adverb can be used to describe an adjective or another adverb.

---

# Independent Practice

**B. Identifying Adverbs That Describe Adjectives and Other Adverbs** Write the adverb that describes the underlined adjective or adverb.

11. Dr. J. L. Plimpton very <u>cleverly</u> invented roller skates.

MODEL ▷ very

12. He became quite <u>rich</u> from his invention.
13. The skates were made so <u>simply</u> from wood.
14. Today's skates seem rather <u>complex</u>.
15. Early skates sounded incredibly <u>loud</u>.
16. Everett Barney invented slightly <u>different</u> skates.
17. The metal skates were quite <u>modern</u>.

**C. Identifying Words That Adverbs Describe** Write each sentence. Draw an arrow from the underlined adverb to the adjective, other adverb, or verb it describes.

18. Families <u>very</u> often bought toothpaste in jars.

MODEL ▷ Families <u>very</u> often bought toothpaste in jars.

19. They dug the toothbrushes <u>quite</u> deeply into the jars.

20. This was <u>rather</u> inconvenient.

21. Shared jars were <u>terribly</u> unclean.

22. Dr. W. W. Sheffield was <u>extremely</u> unhappy about them.

23. He made a <u>slightly</u> flexible tube.

24. The toothpaste came out <u>almost</u> immediately.

**D. 25.–30. Writing Adverbs in Original Sentences** Choose five adverbs from the chart on page 324. Use each one in a sentence. Underline the adverb. Draw an arrow to the word it describes.

25. quite

MODEL ▷ Ice skating and roller-skating are <u>quite</u> different.

# Application — Writing

**Contest Entry** Imagine that you are entering a contest for new inventions. Write a paragraph telling about something that you would like to invent. Explain why your invention would be useful. Use adverbs that describe adjectives or other adverbs.

# 4 Negatives

◆ **FOCUS**  A word that means *no* or *not* is called a **negative.**

The words in color in these sentences are negatives.

1. The astronaut had never gone on such a long trip.
2. There was no oxygen on the moon.

Contractions made with *not* are also negatives.

3. The camera didn't work properly.
4. They weren't able to take many pictures.

This chart shows some common negatives.

| no | never | not | no one |
|----|-------|-----|--------|
| nowhere | nothing | nobody | none |

Only one negative should be used in a sentence. It is incorrect to use a double negative. A **double negative** is two negatives in one sentence.

**Incorrect:** The astronauts have not found no moon rocks.

**Correct:** The astronauts have found no moon rocks.

**Correct:** The astronauts have not found moon rocks.

## Guided Practice

**A.** Identify the word in parentheses ( ) that correctly completes each sentence. Avoid double negatives.

1. Haven't you (ever, never) wanted to go to the moon?
2. Hadn't (anybody, nobody) been there before 1969?
3. Not many people (have, haven't) been there even now.
4. The astronauts didn't find (any, no) plants.
5. Nothing (would, wouldn't) stop me from taking a trip to the moon.

---

**THINK AND REMEMBER**

◆ Remember that **negatives** are words that mean *no* or *not.*
◆ Avoid using a double negative in a sentence.

---

# Independent Practice

**B. Identifying Negatives in Sentences**  Write the word in parentheses ( ) that correctly completes each sentence. Avoid double negatives.

6. Not all space passengers (are, aren't) astronauts.

> MODEL  are

7. No spiders had (ever, never) been in space before.
8. There (is, isn't) no gravity in space.
9. (Were, Weren't) spiders not able to weave their webs?
10. Not (everyone, no one) was interested in the answer.
11. The spiders (had, hadn't) no problem making the webs.
12. They hoped for flies, but there (were, weren't) none.
13. There (was, wasn't) nothing in their webs.
14. Didn't (anybody, nobody) ask the space museum director about the spiders-in-space experiment?
15. Why (did, didn't) no one tell me about the trip to the space museum?
16. I didn't have (any, no) other plans for Saturday.
17. Didn't (anybody, nobody) talk to you about it?
18. I haven't (never, ever) been to the museum.

**C. Revising Sentences**  Cut or replace at least one of the negatives in each sentence. Write the sentence correctly.

19. There isn't nobody in space right now.

> MODEL  There is nobody in space right now.
>        There isn't anybody in space right now.

20. Aren't none of the astronauts planning a trip?
21. Couldn't no one decide where to go?
22. Don't you want to go nowhere?
23. Why didn't nobody ask me to plan a voyage?
24. I can't think of nothing I'd rather do.
25. My friend doesn't never want to go into space.
26. The life of an astronaut is not never for him.
27. Nobody can't change my friend's mind.

## Application — Writing

**Postcard**  Imagine that you have traveled to the moon. Write a postcard to a friend on Earth. Tell about what you see and do not see on the moon. Use negatives in your writing.

# 5 Adverb or Adjective?

**FOCUS**

◆ An **adverb** describes a verb, an adjective, or another adverb.

◆ An **adjective** describes a noun or a pronoun.

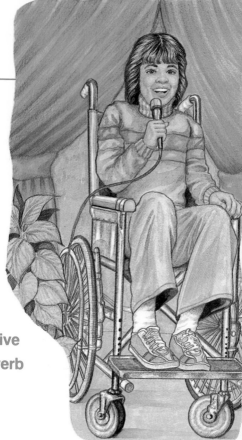

An adverb and an adjective sometimes may look similar. Be careful to use each correctly.

1. Maria gave a beautiful performance.
2. Maria performs beautifully .

In sentence 1 the adjective *beautiful* describes the noun *performance*. In sentence 2 the adverb *beautifully* describes the verb *performs*.

The words *good* and *well* are often used incorrectly. *Good* is always an adjective. *Well* may be used as an adverb to describe a verb or as an adjective to mean "healthy."

3. Emmy did not feel well before the race.   **adjective**
4. She ran well despite her nervous stomach.   **adverb**
5. Emmy did a good job in the race.   **adjective**

## Guided Practice

**A.** Identify the word in parentheses ( ) that correctly completes each sentence.

1. Jeff grabbed the rope (firm, firmly).
2. He put his (strong, strongly) hands around the rope.
3. He pulled himself (slow, slowly) higher.
4. His knees held (tight, tightly) to the rope.
5. The rope was tied (careful, carefully) to the ceiling.
6. The class gave a (loud, loudly) cheer for Jeff.

**B.** Identify whether *good* or *well* belongs in each sentence. Then, tell whether the word is an *adjective* or an *adverb.*

7. Our class did _____ in the sports contest.
8. Almost everyone is a _____ jumper.
9. Alice did not feel _____ before the long jump.
10. Mary jumps _____ too.
11. She has a _____ chance to win.
12. _____ jumpers don't always have long legs.

## Independent Practice

**C. Distinguishing Between Adjectives and Adverbs**   Write the word in parentheses ( ) that correctly completes each sentence.

**13.** Our class (fair, fairly) won the scavenger hunt.

MODEL ▷   fairly

**14.** Angela found a tennis ball (easy, easily).

**15.** Barney knew where a (pretty, prettily) flower was.

**16.** We got (terrible, terribly) stuck trying to find a file.

**17.** Everyone offered (creative, creatively) suggestions.

**18.** Carlos had a (bright, brightly) idea.

**19.** He (quick, quickly) handed a computer disk with many "files" on it to our teacher.

**20.** It was a (strange, strangely) way to win the hunt!

**D. Completing Sentences with *Good* and *Well***   Write each sentence, using *good* or *well* to complete it. Then write whether the word is an *adjective* or an *adverb*.

**21.** I had a _____ idea for the poster contest.

MODEL ▷   good—adjective

**22.** We must find someone who paints _____ .

**23.** Jamie is a _____ artist.

**24.** She spilled purple paint on her _____ shoes.

**25.** Clean them _____ , and they'll be like new again.

**26.** Jamie's shoes match the poster _____ .

**27.** It was a _____ entry for the poster contest.

**28.** Ed's poster was done _____ too.

**29.** It looks _____ enough to win.

## Application — Writing

**Paragraph of Information**   Think of a person who is considered a winner. Write a paragraph to tell your class how this person became a winner. Use adverbs and adjectives, including *good* and *well,* in your writing. If you need help writing a paragraph of information, see page 24 of the **Writer's Handbook.**

# Building Vocabulary
## Homophones and Homographs

*They're going over there to pick up their awards.*

The words *they're, there,* and *their* are homophones. **Homophones** are words that sound the same but have different spellings and meanings. In the following sentence, the homophones are highlighted.

You're the best speller in your class.

When you write, be sure to use the correct homophone so that your readers understand your ideas. This chart lists some homophones you use every day.

| Homophones | | | |
|---|---|---|---|
| your | belonging to you | its | belonging to it |
| you're | you are | it's | it is *or* it has |
| their | belonging to them | too | also |
| they're | they are | to | in the direction of |
| there | at that place | two | the number 2 |

**Homographs** are words that are spelled alike but have different meanings. In the following sentence, the highlighted words are homographs.

The bird in the shed began to shed its feathers.

The word *shed* can mean both "a small building" and "to throw off."

Sometimes homographs have different pronunciations, too.

Here is her birthday present. (prez'ənt)
We will present it to her tomorrow. (pri zent')

# Reading Practice

Read each sentence. Write the homophone in parentheses ( ) that correctly completes each sentence.

1. (Its, It's) time for the spelling bee.
2. Contestants should leave (they're, their, there) belongings backstage.
3. "Janice, it's (your, you're) turn to spell."
4. (They're, Their, There) announcing the winners now.
5. The winners should stand over (they're, their, there) to meet the mayor.

# Writing Practice

Write each sentence. Use one homograph from the box to complete each sentence. If necessary, use a dictionary.

| bow | close | row | watch | well |
|---|---|---|---|---|

6. One of the winning spellers took a _____ on stage, and the _____ in her hair fell out.
7. One contestant wasn't feeling _____ after taking a drink from an outside _____ .
8. A newspaper reporter at the spelling bee was late and started to _____ his _____ .
9. An angry _____ broke out in the last _____ of seats before the mayor spoke.
10. At the _____ of the spelling bee, the mayor said, "It was a _____ and exciting contest."

# Project

Each word in the box below is a homograph with different pronunciations. Choose five words. Write two definitions for each homograph. If necessary, use a dictionary. Then write a sentence for each definition.

Show your definitions and sentences to a partner. See if your partner can match each definition with the sentence you wrote for it.

conduct: to lead
conduct: behavior

| bass | desert | object | use |
|---|---|---|---|
| conduct | lead | record | wind |
| content | live | tear | wound |

# Language Enrichment
## Adverbs

Use what you know about adverbs to do these activities.

 **Ready, Set, Race!**

Think of three animals or three people who might have an unusual kind of race. For example, three spiders might have a web-spinning race, or three students might have a chalkboard-erasing race. Write a short news story about this race for the sports page of a wacky newspaper called the *Goofy Gazette*. Use adverbs that compare to make your story as exciting and action-packed as you can. Read your story to the class. Find out if the adverbs helped listeners picture the race.

 **I Took a Journey**

Play the "I Took a Journey" game. Sit in a circle with a small group or your whole class. The first person says, "I took a journey and traveled quickly on a jet plane." The second person repeats what the first has said and adds another adverb and form of transportation: "I took a journey and traveled quickly on a jet plane and lazily on a banana boat." When a player forgets something, he or she is out. Play then starts again. The last player remaining wins the game. Have a student keep a list of the adverbs used. Post the list and refer to it when you're looking for a lively adverb in your writing.

**Adverb Hunt**

Play this game with three or four classmates. Give each player a page from a newspaper or an old magazine. (Make sure each page has about the same number of words.) The players then circle as many adverbs as they can find on their page in 30 seconds. As a group, make sure each circled word on a player's page is an adverb. The player with the most adverbs wins.

# CONNECTING
## LANGUAGE ⬌ WRITING

In this unit you learned that adverbs are words that describe verbs. Adverbs tell *where, when,* and *how* an action is done.

◆ **Using Adverbs in Your Writing**  Knowing how to choose exactly the right adverb to describe an action is an important writing skill. Lively, colorful adverbs add excitement to your writing. They help your reader see the action as you see it.

Pay special attention to adverbs as you do these activities.

### Lend Me Your Ears

You learned about homophones and homographs on the **Building Vocabulary** pages. Use what you learned as you do this activity.

Make a large outline drawing of an ear. Label it *Homophones.* Write homophones and their definitions in the ear. Below the ear, write a short conversation in which someone confuses two homophones. Here's an example.

Person A: "I don't like the dog tale. Let's get rid of it."

Person B: "I don't like the dog tail either, but we can't just get rid of it."

Person A: "Why not? We have a whole collection of animal tales."

Person B: "You can't just stick a new tail on a dog!"

Person A: "No! No! Not a tail on a dog. A tale about a dog!"

### See How It Goes

A pantomime is a play in which the actors express their meaning without speaking.

Write a script for a short pantomime for one person. Think of an activity that could be expressed without speaking. You could, for example, have an actor with an armload of packages try to open a door. Give stage directions telling the actor exactly what to do. Use adverbs to describe how the actor should do each action. Next, ask a partner to perform the pantomime.

Then, ask your partner to rewrite your pantomime, changing every adverb. Finally, act out the pantomime yourself with the new adverb directions. How is it different? How is it the same? Discuss the similarities and differences with your partner.

# 7 Unit Checkup

| Think Back | Think Ahead |
|---|---|
| ◆ What did you learn about persuasive paragraphs? What did you do to write one? | ◆ How will what you learned about a persuasive paragraph help you when you read a letter published in the newspaper? <br><br> ◆ How will evaluating reasons help you write a persuasive paragraph in a business letter? A research report? A letter of complaint? |
| ◆ What did you learn about adverbs? How has that helped you express actions? | ◆ What is one way you can use different kinds of adverbs to improve your writing? |

**Persuasive Paragraphs in Business Letters**  *pages 302–304*
Read the business letter. Then follow the directions.

> 925 South Indiana Avenue
> Chicago, Illinois 60619
> August 19, 19—
>
> Whitney Young Library
> 7901 South King Drive
> Chicago, Illinois 60619
>
> Dear Librarian:
>
>    I am writing to recommend that you continue having the study periods at Young Library. I feel that the study periods should continue for two reasons. First, the study periods give me a chance to do my homework in a quiet place. Second, many young people may stop coming if the study periods don't continue. The study periods help young people progress in their educations. They should be continued.
>
>           Sincerely,
>           *Bernard Thompson*
>           Bernard Thompson

1. Write the opinion expressed in the letter.
2. Write the reasons given that support the opinion.
3. List the words or phrases that give the letter its formal tone.

## Evaluating Reasons to Support an Opinion   *page 305*

Read the following sentences. Write *strong* or *weak* to show your opinion of the effectiveness of the reasons stated.

4. Littering is terrible because it looks bad.
5. Littering is unsafe because of the germs in garbage.
6. Litterbugs are unkind to others who prefer neatness.
7. A bottle tossed in the road may cause a flat tire.

## Capturing the Reader's Interest   *page 306*

Read these opening and ending sentences. Revise each sentence so that the opening states a clear and strong opinion, and the ending is memorable and powerful.

8. You should vote for me as president of the school council. Your vote means a lot to me.
9. We should get awards for good grades. It isn't easy to achieve high grades.
10. All who enter the spelling contest should receive an award. An award for everyone would make us all happy.

## The Writing Process   *pages 307–317*

11. What is the major consideration when selecting the topic of a persuasive letter?
    a. publishing the letter
    b. the writer's opinion
    c. whether the subject involves friends

12. What is important to include when gathering information?
    a. reasons for your opinion     b. sensory details
    c. materials and directions for an activity

13. Why should an informal tone be avoided in a business letter?
    a. It is boring.     b. It is unfriendly.     c. It is unsuitable.

14. Why is a newspaper an appropriate place to publish a persuasive letter?
    a. Many people will read the letter and be persuaded by it.
    b. The writer of the letter might become famous.
    c. The writer gets to see his opinion in print.

## Adverbs  *pages 320–321*

*add numbers only!*

Add an adverb to each sentence to make it more vivid. Write the new sentence.

15. Bob Lemmons acted like a wild horse so he could catch and tame horses.
16. In the Old West, wild horses roamed in the rugged, mountainous area.
17. Wild horses were fast animals and could gallop.
18. Bob Lemmons gained the wild horses' trust so he could ride among them and catch a herd of them.
19. At first, he kept his distance from a herd; then, he guided his horse toward the herd until the horses got used to him.
20. Later, he drove the herd's stallion away and made the rest of the herd think he was the stallion.
21. By that time, he and the herd rode together.

## Comparison with Adverbs  *pages 322–323*

Write the form of the adverb in parentheses ( ) that correctly completes each sentence.

22. Shawn writes the words on the spelling test (quickly) than most of her classmates.
23. Of all her subjects, she studies spelling (often).
24. Shawn believes that she learns the spelling words (easily) than she did at the beginning of the school year.
25. She spells (correctly) than ever before, and her test scores show her improvement.
26. Shawn may start studying (early) each afternoon.
27. She may also study until (late) in the evening.

## Adverbs Before Adjectives and Other Adverbs  *pages 324–325*

Write the adverb that describes the underlined adjective or adverb.

28. Chris has been practicing extremely <u>hard</u> to master the violin.
29. He is trying for a very <u>desirable</u> position in the band, the violin soloist.
30. Chris has been playing the violin since he was a rather <u>young</u> child.
31. His parents give him an incredibly <u>large</u> amount of support.
32. Although Chris is quite <u>nervous</u>, he will do well.

## Negatives  *pages 326—327*

Cut or replace at least one of the negatives in each sentence. Write the sentence correctly.

33. There aren't no places to practice our songs.
34. We won't know none of the words unless we practice.
35. The choir director hasn't no space for us.
36. Couldn't none of our parents let us practice at home?
37. If nobody won't give us any space, we can rent some with the money from our ticket sales.

## Adverb or Adjective?  *pages 328—329*

Write the word in parentheses ( ) that correctly completes each sentence.

38. Maria walked up (proud, proudly) to receive her trophy.
39. The day before, she had spoken (clear, clearly) whenever one of the judges asked her a question.
40. Her science fair exhibit examined the (dead, deadly) effects of pollution in her neighborhood.
41. Maria's (confident, confidently) manner impressed the judges.
42. Her (thorough, thoroughly) understanding of the subject was what earned her a first-place award.
43. Her parents were (extreme, extremely) pleased.
44. (Soft, Softly) she thanked the judges.

## Homophones  *pages 330—331*

Read each sentence. Write the homophone in parentheses ( ) that correctly completes each sentence.

45. Jeremy waited impatiently by the curb for the (mail, male) to arrive.
46. (For, Four) two months he had waited to hear about the contest he entered.
47. He was sure his (tale, tail) of a family's trip to Texas had won the top prize.
48. Jeremy grabbed the (blew, blue) envelope and opened it immediately.
49. When he read the good news, he dashed up the (eight, ate) steps to his doorway.
50. He burst (threw, through) the door and shouted out the good news to everyone.

# Cumulative Review

## Four Kinds of Sentences    *pages 36–37*

Read each sentence. Then write *declarative, interrogative, imperative,* or *exclamatory.*

1. Businesses display signs to communicate with customers.
2. Have you ever noticed any of the signs in your neighborhood?
3. Some signs are meant to attract customers.
4. Look at that huge electric sign!
5. Signs can also tell customers about the days and hours that a business is open and closed.
6. Describe the most unusual business signs you have seen.
7. Do you ever think about making any business signs yourself?
8. What a great sign for a lemonade stand!
9. It is hard to resist a tall, cool glass of lemonade on a hot day.
10. Don't forget to throw your paper cup in the wastebasket.

## Singular and Plural Nouns    *pages 90–93*

Write each noun. Write *singular, plural,* or *both* after each noun. If the noun is singular, write the plural form.

11. galaxy
12. record
13. geese
14. area
15. series
16. volley
17. principal
18. fish
19. child
20. bus
21. knives
22. chief
23. company
24. women
25. dresses
26. match
27. patches
28. sandal
29. secretaries
30. moose
31. pleas
32. city
33. peaches
34. pens
35. life
36. armadillo
37. reindeer
38. cowboy
39. telegrams
40. motto
41. salesman
42. heroes

## Be and Have  *pages 150–151*

Write the correct form of *be* or *have* in parentheses ( ).

43. Jenny _____ collected postage stamps since she was eight years old. (has, have)
44. Her stamp album _____ filled with stamps from all over the world. (is, are)
45. She _____ decided to add some unusual stamps to her collection. (has, have)
46. The stamps _____ purchased from the catalogues her father gets from the post office. (is, are)
47. Jenny _____ planning a display of her large collection. (is, are)
48. Her collection _____ grown to 150 stamps. (has, have)
49. Her whole family _____ developed an interest in stamps. (has, have)
50. She _____ showing her sister how to select stamps from the stamp book. (is, are)

## Irregular Verbs  *pages 184–185*

Write the correct past-tense form of the verb in parentheses.

51. An Egyptian named Imhotep _____ an incredible pyramid. (make)
52. Imhotep's pyramid _____ travelers something remarkable to see when in Egypt. (give)
53. Some travelers _____ to Egypt just to see the pyramid. (come)
54. They _____ the pyramid was quite impressive. (say)
55. I _____ about visiting Egypt myself. (think)
56. I would like to say that I once _____ a camel. (ride)
57. Our class _____ slides of several pyramids. (see)

## More Irregular Verbs  *pages 186–187*

Write each sentence. Use the correct form of the verb in parentheses ( ) with the helping verb.

58. Felipe's father has _____ to South America. (fly)
59. He and other scientists have _____ a spot in Peru for their studies. (choose)
60. They have _____ about the ancient treasures beneath the surface. (know)
61. Felipe's father has _____ lots of tools along. (bring)
62. Felipe has _____ to his father about his travels and his work. (speak)

## Direct Objects  *pages 188–189*

Write each sentence. Underline the action verb once. Underline the direct object twice. If there is no direct object, write *no direct object*.

63. Karen and Christine followed the zoo guide.

64. Karen dropped her wrapper into a trash basket.

65. The zebras' area was very interesting.

66. Karen and Christine enjoyed the monkeys most of all.

67. They bought souvenirs in the gift shop.

68. They boarded a large bus from their school.

69. Christine felt excited about the trip.

70. She read the signs next to each cage.

71. Karen admired the zebras because of their beautiful stripes.

72. Karen and Christine liked their visit to the zoo.

## Subject or Object Pronoun?  *pages 234–235*

Write the correct pronoun in parentheses ( ). Then, write *subject pronoun* or *object pronoun*.

73. (They, Them) found the first object in the treasure hunt.

74. Philip and (I, me) hunted for the next object.

75. Others searched for the objects with (we, us).

76. (They, Them) followed the path marked on the map.

77. A sound in the bushes scared Philip and (I, me).

78. (We, Us) heard an eagle screeching.

79. (I, Me) ran toward the source of the sound.

80. Philip and (I, me) leaned against a pine tree.

81. The whistle told (we, us) that our time was almost gone.

82. Philip and (I, me) were surprised by the results.

83. (We, Us) had collected more treasure than all the others.

84. The prize was awarded to (we, us).

## Possessive Pronouns  *pages 236–237*

Write each sentence. Use the correct possessive pronoun in parentheses ( ).

85. Susan thought she smelled smoke outside _____ bedroom door. (her, hers)

86. We learned about fires from _____ teacher. (our, ours)

87. Homes like _____ can burn quickly. (their, theirs)

88. We were glad Susan's family had an escape plan, and the teacher reminded us about _____ . (our, ours)

89. Does _____ family have an escape plan in case of a fire? (your, yours)
90. If you live in a large apartment building like _____ , your escape plan will be different from one for a small home. (my, mine)
91. In a small home like _____, several escape routes can be planned. (our, ours)
92. Susan's father put a map showing fire-escape routes on the back of _____ bedroom door. (her, hers)

## Agreement of Pronouns   *pages 240–241*
Write each sentence, choosing a pronoun to fill in each blank. Underline the pronoun's antecedent.

93. Rosa Parks lived in Montgomery, Alabama. _____ became known as the "Mother of the Civil Rights Movement."
94. In 1955, she boarded a bus to go home. _____ was segregated by race.
95. Ms. Parks was supposed to sit in the back of the bus, but _____ sat in a seat near the front.
96. Rosa Parks's resistance led to new laws about segregation. _____ was no longer legal.
97. Rosa Parks was admired by many people for her courage. _____ was praised for doing what she felt was right.
98. Many people became aware of the unfairness of the segregation laws. _____ began to push for change.
99. The laws were finally changed. _____ made segregation against the law.

## Adjectives   *pages 274–275*
Read each sentence. Then, write the noun or pronoun that the underlined adjective describes.

100. Maria's mother gave her an exciting book.
101. Maria read the first chapter quickly.
102. She liked the interesting plot of the book.
103. She read two chapters after dinner last night.
104. She waited anxiously for another chance to read her book.
105. She was happy to come home and sit in her comfortable chair.
106. Maria wanted to finish the mystery book.
107. She still had six pages to read.

## Adjectives That Follow Linking Verbs   *pages 280–281*

Write each sentence. Underline the adjectives once. Draw an arrow from each adjective to the noun it describes. Underline the linking verbs twice.

108. Beatrice thought her uncle's story was fascinating.

109. His journey through the desert was tiring.

110. The lizards looked strange.

111. Her uncle's car became dusty from the trip.

112. She never grew tired of hearing about his travels.

113. He appeared pleased that Beatrice asked him for more stories.

## Comparison with Adjectives: *er, est*   *pages 282–283*

Write the correct form of the adjective in parentheses ( ).

114. As far as they knew, this was the _____ flood in the history of their town. (bad)
115. The water rose _____ until it rushed into their house. (high)
116. Using the canoe was a _____ way to escape than the plan their brother suggested. (good)
117. The boys rowed to the _____ emergency shelter. (near)
118. Their neighbors in the shelter looked _____ than the boys had ever seen them. (sad)
119. The _____ one of all was Mr. Peterson. (unhappy)
120. He lost the _____ number of possessions. (large)
121. All of us looked forward to _____ days. (dry)
122. We'll need the _____ mops in the world to clean up the mess. (big)

## Adverbs   *pages 320–321*

Write the sentences below. Underline the adverb in each sentence, and draw an arrow to the verb it describes.

123. Some people hunt tirelessly for objects from the past.

124. Thomas Jefferson searched hard for objects.

125. He dug carefully so he would not break anything he found.

126. He accurately recorded the objects for future reference.

127. When searches are done recklessly, people have a difficult time being accurate.

**128.** Jefferson's work greatly helped future researchers.

**129.** He neatly recorded all of his findings in his notebooks.

**130.** Jefferson wrote clearly about objects he found.

**131.** Historians sincerely appreciate Jefferson's dedication.

## Comparison with Adverbs   *pages 322–323*

Write the correct comparing form of the adverb in parentheses ( ).

**132.** At a rodeo, cowboys compete to see who can wrestle a bull to the ground _____ than anyone else. (quickly)

**133.** Audiences watch bulldogging events _____ than all the other rodeo contests. (enthusiastically)

**134.** Of all the bulldoggers of his time, Bill Pickett wrestled bulls _____ . (skillfully)

**135.** With each rodeo stunt, the audience cheered _____ . (wildly)

**136.** Bill Pickett's bulldogging was one of the _____ attended events in rodeo. (regularly)

**137.** Of all the bulldoggers, Bill Pickett entered the ring _____ . (confidently)

**138.** Bill Pickett's arms moved around the bull's head _____ than any other contestant's. (swiftly)

**139.** His style was _____ imitated than the style of any other bulldogger. (widely)

## Adverb or Adjective?   *pages 328–329*

Write the word in parentheses ( ) that correctly completes each sentence.

**140.** Beth was _____ to enter her recipe for brownies in the contest. (eager, eagerly)

**141.** Beth walked _____ to the mailbox. (slow, slowly)

**142.** She was _____ of her recipe for brownies, but she wasn't sure if it would win the contest. (proud, proudly)

**143.** Each day she waited _____ for the mail to arrive. (patient, patiently)

**144.** Her parents told her she should win because she was a _____ cook. (great, greatly)

**145.** When Beth learned that she had won second prize, she smiled _____ . (happy, happily)

# UNIT

# 8

# Informing Others

◆ **COMPOSITION FOCUS:** **Research Report**
◆ **LANGUAGE FOCUS:** **Prepositions, Conjunctions, Interjections**

Do you like mysteries? Do you enjoy discovering clues and adding them up to explain something that happened? If you do, then you might find that looking for facts in the library can be as enjoyable as solving a mystery.

Looking for information about a topic is called **research.** Having good research skills will help you throughout your life. Remember that it is not important for you to *know* every fact. It is important, however, for you to know *where to look* for any fact you need.

The research report you will read next was written by Matt Neapolitan of Cookeville, Tennessee. Matt offers this advice, "It is important to choose a topic that interests you because writing the research paper comes easier when you know what you are writing about. Also, ask the librarian for help if you have any questions."

In this unit you will learn more about how to write a research paper. You will also learn the important skills of taking notes and summarizing.

Matt Neapolitan wrote a research report *to inform* his classmates about Benjamin Franklin.

# Reading with a Writer's Eye
## Research Report

Matt Neapolitan entered a writing contest for students his age. Each contestant had to write about one of the signers of the United States Constitution. Matt was especially interested in Benjamin Franklin because, at an advanced age, he had made a tremendous contribution to the Constitutional Convention. As you read Matt's research report, notice how he includes information about Ben Franklin's age and health.

## Benjamin Franklin: Prominent Signer of the Constitution
### by Matt Neapolitan

Ben Franklin was many things, such as inventor, printer, publisher, author, scientist, diplomat, and signer of the Constitution of the United States. He was born in 1706 and was in his eighties by the time of the Constitutional Convention in 1787.

He couldn't attend the beginning of the convention because he was sick. So he asked Robert Morris to read his speech, which nominated George Washington as Chairman of the Constitutional Convention. When Ben arrived, he still had a weak voice, so he had written material for other people to read.

Being sick and having a weak voice were some of the bad points about being old, but having experience and wisdom made up for those bad points. There were many times that Ben used his experience and wisdom to help settle arguments about the Constitution.

At the Constitutional Convention, Ben Franklin, believing in the common man, said that not only landowners should be able to vote. Everyone, including common people, should vote, because "acres alone do not bring wisdom."

Other debates at the convention were about the president. Again, Ben Franklin's experience and knowledge gave him opinions. He believed that the president should have no salary, no absolute veto, and be able to be impeached. He had examples to support his opinions—he knew of other presidents who had too much power and became like kings.

The biggest problem of the Constitutional Convention was how many representatives each state should have. Some people wanted it to be by population—the more people in the state, the more representatives. Some wanted it to be equal—all states getting equal numbers of representatives.

Ben Franklin, who had been a negotiator in England, tried to cool tempers and offered a compromise. He said that in governing matters, representatives should be equal, but in money matters, they should be by population. Again, he had written material for this because of his weak voice. In the end, he headed the committee that worked out "The Great Compromise" based on his ideas.

On the last day of the convention, James Wilson read a speech that was written by Ben Franklin. It was supposed to calmly encourage everyone to sign the Constitution. He said that, in his experience, he had been wrong before, so he could be wrong about his doubts of the Constitution. He was signing because it might not be a perfect constitution, but it was the best that they could make. This convinced everyone to sign the Constitution.

Even though he was old and had a weak voice, Ben Franklin was still an important person at the Constitutional Convention. His experience and wisdom helped him make important contributions. Carved on the back of the chair that George Washington was sitting in was a sun on the horizon. Nobody could tell if the sun was rising or setting. As the last people were signing the Constitution, Ben Franklin said it was definitely a rising sun.

## Respond

1. Which of Ben Franklin's many jobs or careers would you like to write about? What questions about that part of Franklin's life would you want to find the answers to in your library research?

## Discuss

2. Which facts in this research report are you already familiar with? Which facts are new to you?

3. Which sentence in the research report seems to sum up all the facts that are given about Ben Franklin? Why do you think that sentence is the most important?

# Thinking As a Writer
## Analyzing a Research Report

A **research report** gives information about a topic. The information can be drawn from various sources such as books, magazines, or interviews. A research report usually has an introduction, a body, and a conclusion. Notice how the writer arranged the information in this excerpt from "Benjamin Franklin: Prominent Signer of the Constitution."

> Ben Franklin was many things, such as inventor, printer, publisher, author, scientist, diplomat, and signer of the Constitution of the United States.

> At the Constitutional Convention, Ben Franklin, believing in the common man, said that not only landowners should be able to vote. Everyone, including common people, should vote, because "acres alone do not bring wisdom."

> Even though he was old and had a weak voice, Ben Franklin was still an important person at the Constitutional Convention. His experience and wisdom helped him make important contributions. Carved on the back of the chair that George Washington was sitting in was a sun on the horizon. Nobody could tell if the sun was rising or setting. As the last people were signing the Constitution, Ben Franklin said it was definitely a rising sun.

**Writer's Guide**

A research report
- gives information about a topic.
- draws facts from various sources.
- has a title, an introduction, a body, and a conclusion.

The **introduction** identifies the topic and arouses interest in the subject of the report. Notice how the first sentence gives information that shows why this is an interesting subject.

The **body** gives specific information that the writer has gathered. Each paragraph in the body deals with a different main idea.

The **conclusion** signals the end of the report and gives a sense of completeness. It may sum up the information given and draw a conclusion about the subject. Often, it leaves the reader with a desire to find out more about the topic.

## Discuss

1. Why does a research report need an introduction?
2. How is the body of a research report organized?
3. What is the purpose of the conclusion?

# Try Your Hand

**A. Identify Parts of a Research Report**  All of the following paragraphs come from the same research report. For each paragraph, write whether it comes from the *introduction,* the *body,* or the *conclusion* of the report.

1. Sacajawea and her husband, Toussaint Charbonneau, had many adventures during their journey. Sacajawea blazed trails. She also helped keep peace with Indians living along the way.

2. Sacajawea earned the respect of the explorers for her hard work and bravery on the trip to and from the lands of the Pacific Northwest. Even today, her legend lives on in books and films about her adventure. Her story still serves to inspire new generations of explorers.

3. On May 14, 1804, Sacajawea set off on a long and famous journey. Sacajawea was the Indian woman who guided the explorers Lewis and Clark. Lewis and Clark had been hired by President Thomas Jefferson to explore the Louisiana Territory.

**B. Identify Details**  Make a list of specific facts and details included in the paragraphs in **A.**

**C. Write a Title**  Write a title for the research report that includes the paragraphs in **A.**

**D. Read a Research Report**  With a partner, read aloud another research report or article about a topic that interests you. Identify the introduction, the body, and the conclusion of the report. Discuss whether each part is well written and why you do or do not think so.

## Writer's Notebook

**Collecting Research Topics**
Read the parts of the research report on page 348 and the report on this page. Write a brief sentence in your *Writer's Notebook* telling what each research report is about. Also, listen and watch for interesting topics in your daily reading and conversations, in newspapers and magazines, and on the radio and the television. Record in your *Writer's Notebook* some of these topics.

# Thinking As a Writer
## Summarizing to Organize Notes

**Writer's Guide**

In organizing notes for a research report, good writers
- use note cards and keep them organized.
- summarize statements that have common ideas into one statement.

In gathering information for a research report, a good writer takes many notes. These notes usually contain more facts than can be used. How can you gather all the information you need and still remain organized? One good way is to summarize the facts.

When you **summarize,** you make one statement that tells what several statements have in common. Look at these note cards from different sources.

During the Civil War, Harriet Tubman worked as a nurse helping the wounded.

Harriet Tubman once served as a cook in the Union Army.

Harriet Tubman was sometimes sent out to spy on the Confederate Army.

Her experiences in the South with the Underground Railroad made her a valuable guide for the army.

These statements can be put onto one note card.

During the Civil War, Harriet Tubman worked for the Union Army as a nurse, spy, cook, and guide.

As you gather information for your research report, summarize statements that have common ideas. Summarizing is a good way to keep your notes organized.

## Discuss

1. Look at the four note cards. What ideas do they have in common?
2. What information was left out on the summary note card? Why?

## Try Your Hand

**Summarize** Work with a partner. Choose a subject that interests both of you. Work independently to list five statements about your subject. Then trade lists. Summarize the information on your partner's list. Discuss how you summarized the statements.

# Developing the Writer's Craft
## Using Quotations

The writer of a research report can make the report much more vivid by including direct quotations.

Read these sentences from the research report written by Matt Neapolitan.

> At the Constitutional Convention, Ben Franklin, believing in the common man, said that not only landowners should be able to vote. Everyone, including common people, should vote, because "acres alone do not bring wisdom."

In these sentences Matt not only reports what Ben Franklin said but gives Franklin's actual words. A direct quotation like this one adds weight and interest to what you write. It can also demonstrate how people spoke in a time and place that may not be familiar to your readers. Quotations may be from the subject of your report, from eyewitnesses to an event, from experts, or from other sources such as books and magazines.

Try to use at least one direct quotation when you write your own research report. Remember to put quotation marks before and after someone's exact words.

## Discuss

1. Look at the parts of the research report on Benjamin Franklin on page 348. What quotation did the writer include in the report? Do you think the quotation adds interest to the report? Explain your answer.
2. What kinds of quotations might the writer of the report about Sacajawea on page 349 have found and used?

## Try Your Hand

**Use Quotations** Write a one-paragraph report about an interesting experience that you and your classmates have had recently. Ask one of your classmates for his or her reaction to the experience, and include the quotation in your report.

# 1 Prewriting
## Research Report

Greg, a student at Great Lakes Elementary School, wanted to write a research report on some part of United States history. He used the checklist in the **Writer's Guide** to help him plan his research report. Look at what he did.

**Writer's Guide**

**Prewriting Checklist**

☑ Brainstorm and select a topic.

☑ Think about your audience and your purpose.

☑ Use your note cards to gather information.

☑ Organize information in an outline.

◆ **Brainstorming and Selecting a Topic**

Because his class had been studying American history, Greg could think of several topics that interested him. He listed those topics so that he could look them over and decide which would be best for his report. Look at Greg's list.

Next, Greg looked over his list and crossed out topics that he did not want to use. One topic, the American Revolution, had been covered so thoroughly in class that Greg was not sure he could find anything new on the subject. Since he wanted to do a report on something further in the past, he crossed out a couple of topics that seemed too recent. Greg also crossed out a topic that seemed a part of world history rather than just United States history.

Finally, Greg circled the remaining topic, the Civil War, in which he was particularly interested. He realized, however, that the Civil War was a very broad topic. He decided to make another list, this time of famous people from the Civil War era. After reading an encyclopedia article on the Civil War, he wrote down some important names.

> Revolutionary War
> Apollo moon
>   landing program
> The Great Depression
> Civil War
> Founding of
>   United Nations
> 1988 Presidential
>   election

> Abraham Lincoln
> Jefferson Davis
> John Brown
> Harriet Tubman
> Robert E. Lee
> Ulysses S. Grant

In the class discussion and in the reading he had done, Greg had been particularly fascinated by the Underground Railroad, which helped slaves escape to freedom. The encyclopedia article mentioned Harriet Tubman as one of the leaders of this movement. Greg decided to write his research report about her. He decided to title his research report "Harriet Tubman."

## Discuss

1. Greg decided that the Civil War was too broad a topic for his research report. Would any of the other topics also have been too broad? Explain your answer.
2. Suppose that Greg had decided to write on the 1988 Presidential election. How might he have narrowed that topic?
3. Greg used an encyclopedia article to get ideas for his Civil War research report. Why was an encyclopedia article probably a better source than a long book on the Civil War?

## ◆ Gathering Information

After Greg had selected his topic, he gathered information for his research report. The encyclopedia had a brief article on Harriet Tubman. In the card catalogue, Greg found more sources of information on her. The reference librarian suggested that Greg look at a collection of biographical sketches of famous black Americans.

Greg took notes from each of these sources. He did not copy down everything word for word. Instead, he summarized main ideas and copied every word only when he wanted to quote someone directly.

Look at Greg's notes from the book of biographies.

Harriet Tubman
Born around 1820
Abolitionist—called "Moses" of her people
Escaped from plantation. Went north by Underground
    Railroad—not really a railroad
Helped more than 300 slaves escape
Sometimes forced tired slaves to continue by threatening them
    with a revolver
John Brown said, "We call her 'General Tubman.'"
Served as spy during Civil War
Died in 1913

## Discuss

1. Why was it a good idea for Greg to use sources for his report other than the original encyclopedia article on the Civil War?
2. Greg used the card catalogue to find a book on the Civil War. You can usually find a book listed in a card catalogue under the title, the author's name, or the subject of the book. Which method do you think Greg used to find the book on the Civil War?
3. Look at Greg's notes from the book of biographies. Which part of his notes is a direct quote? Why do you think he quoted this part instead of putting it in his own words?
4. In his notes Greg does not explain what the Undergound Railroad was or who John Brown was. If he mentions them in his research report, will he have to add information about them? Explain your answer.

## ◆ Organizing Information

After Greg had gathered all the information he needed for his research report, he was ready to organize it. He decided to make an outline to help plan the organization of his report. Look at what he did.

I. Harriet Tubman before Civil War
   A. Escaped from plantation in 1849 and went north by Underground Railroad (a secret network of safe-houses)
   B. Helped more than 300 slaves escape
   C. Sometimes used loaded pistol to keep slaves going
   D. Slaves called her "Moses" and abolitionist John Brown called her "General Tubman"

II. Harriet Tubman during and after Civil War
   A. Served as nurse, cook, guide, and spy with Union Army
   B. During one military campaign helped free 750 slaves
   C. After war, helped raise money for black schools
   D. In 1908 established home for elderly and needy blacks
   E. Died in 1913, buried with full military honors

## Discuss

1. What are the two major headings in Greg's outline? Does this seem like a good way to organize his research report? Why or why not?
2. What information from Greg's notes on page 353 appears in his outline? What other information has he included?
3. What do you notice about the form of Greg's outline? How is information indented? What words are capitalized? Is everything in complete sentences?

## Try Your Hand

Now plan a research report of your own.

**A. Brainstorm and Select a Topic**  Brainstorm a list of American history topics that interest you. Think about each topic and your audience.

- ◆ Cross out topics that are too broad, that include subjects other than just United States history, or that might not be interesting to you and your audience.
- ◆ Once you have selected a topic from the list, decide whether the topic needs to be narrowed further. If it does, brainstorm narrower topics, as Greg did for his Civil War paper.
- ◆ Choose a topic about which you feel you can write a good report.

**B. Gather Information**  Use the library to find information about your topic. You can consult the card catalogue and the reference librarian to get ideas for sources of information. Make notes in your own words from these sources.

**C. Organize Information**  Review your notes to make sure that you have all the information you need.

- ◆ Outline your information. Use Greg's outline on page 354 as a model.
- ◆ Make sure that your outline shows all the information you want to include in your research report.
- ◆ Make sure the information is in the order in which you want to present it.

 **Save your notes and your outline in your *Writer's Notebook*. You will use them when you draft your research report.**

# 2 Drafting
## Research Report

**Writer's Guide**

**Drafting Checklist**
- ☑ Use your notes and outline for ideas.
- ☑ Write the title of your research paper.
- ☑ Use your outline as a guide to write the introduction, the body, and the conclusion.

Using his notes and his outline, Greg followed the checklist in the **Writer's Guide** to draft his research report. Look at what he did.

> *Harriet Tubman*
>
> *Harriet Tubman was very active in helping slaves escape before the Civil War. She escaped in 1849 from the plantation where she was a slave and went north by the Underground Railroad.*

## Discuss

1. Look at the topic sentence for Greg's first paragraph. Does it match up with Roman numeral I in his outline? What information would you expect next?
2. What would you expect the topic sentence for the second paragraph to be about?

## Try Your Hand

Now you are ready to write a research report.

A. **Review Your Information** Think about the information you gathered and outlined in the last lesson. Decide whether you need more information. If so, gather it.

B. **Think About Your TAP** Remember that your task is to write a research report. Your purpose is to inform your audience about a topic.

**TAP**

**Task:** What?
**Audience:** Who?
**Purpose:** Why?

C. **Write Your First Draft** Follow the steps in the **Drafting Checklist** to write your research report.
   When you write your draft, just put all your ideas on paper. Do not worry about spelling, punctuation, or grammar. You can correct the draft later.

**Save your first draft in your *Writer's Notebook*. You will need it when you revise your research report.**

# 3 Responding and Revising
## Research Report

Greg used the checklist in the **Writer's Guide** to revise his research report. Look at what he did.

### ◆ Checking Information

When Greg read over his draft, he decided to add information to identify John Brown. To show his change, he used this mark ∧ . He also added quotation marks to show John Brown's exact words. To do so, he used these marks ⱽⱽ .

### ◆ Checking Organization

Checking his research report against his outline, Greg noticed that he had accidentally switched the order of two points. To show that the information should be moved, he used this mark ↺ .

### ◆ Checking Language

As Greg checked the sentences in his research report, he noticed that they all seemed to start in the same way. He decided to change a sentence so that his writing would have more variety.

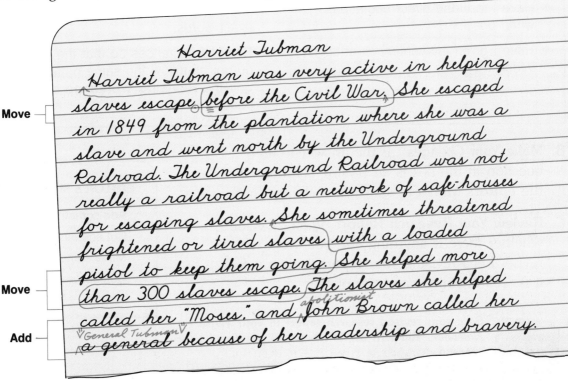

**Writer's Guide**

**Revising Checklist**

☑ Read your research report to yourself or to a partner.

☑ Think about your audience and your purpose. Add or cut information.

☑ Check that you have used quotation marks for people's exact words.

☑ Be sure that your research report is organized correctly.

☑ Look for ways to give your sentences more variety.

Harriet Tubman

Harriet Tubman was very active in helping slaves escape before the Civil War. She escaped in 1849 from the plantation where she was a slave and went north by the Underground Railroad. The Underground Railroad was not really a railroad but a network of safe-houses for escaping slaves. She sometimes threatened frightened or tired slaves with a loaded pistol to keep them going. She helped more than 300 slaves escape. The slaves she helped called her "Moses," and an abolitionist John Brown called her a general because of her leadership and bravery.

General Tubman

**Move**
**Move**
**Add**

## Discuss

1. How did Greg add variety to one of his sentences? How did he make this change?
2. Are there other changes that Greg should have made? Explain your answer.

## Try Your Hand

Now revise your first draft.

**A. Read Your First Draft** As you read your research report, think about your audience and your purpose. Read your report silently or to a partner to see whether it is complete and well organized. Ask yourself or your partner the questions in the box.

---

### Responding and Revising Strategies

✔ **Respond**
**Ask yourself or a partner:**

✔ **Revise**
**Try these solutions:**

| | |
|---|---|
| ◆ Have I followed the organization in my outline? | ◆ **Check** your outline and follow its organization. **Move** sentences that seem out of place. |
| ◆ Have I included all the important facts in my report? | ◆ **Add** any necessary information. |
| ◆ Have I included direct quotations when possible? | ◆ **Add** quotations to show people's exact words. |
| ◆ Have I given my sentences enough variety? | ◆ **Reword** sentences so that they do not all follow the same pattern. See the **Revising Workshop** on page 359. |

---

**B. Make Your Changes** If the answer to any question in the box is *no,* try the solution. Use the **Editor's Marks** to show your changes.

**C. Review Your Research Report Again** Decide whether there is anything else you want to revise. Keep revising your report until you feel it is well organized and complete.

> **EDITOR'S MARKS**
> ∧ Add something.
> ⌐ Cut something.
> ◯ Move something.
> ∧ Replace something.

 **Save your revised research report in your *Writer's Notebook.* You will use it when you proofread your report.**

WRITING PROCESS

# Revising Workshop
## Giving Your Sentences More Variety

Good writers avoid using the same sentence pattern all the time. For example, instead of starting every sentence with the subject, they use other kinds of words or phrases to begin. Sometimes these words or phrases can be moved from somewhere else in the sentence. Look at the underlined words in these sentences.

1. Thomas Jefferson wrote most of the Declaration of Independence <u>in 1776</u>.
2. <u>In 1776</u>, Thomas Jefferson wrote most of the Declaration of Independence.

There is, of course, nothing actually wrong with the first sentence. If it appeared in a paragraph where all the other sentences followed the same pattern, however, a writer might decide to revise some sentences to add variety.

Take a look at this example.

3. Jefferson <u>originally</u> supported the Embargo Act of 1807.
4. <u>Originally</u>, Jefferson supported the Embargo Act of 1807.

In the above example the second sentence not only varies the pattern but also changes the emphasis. The writer stresses the word *originally* by putting it first. This helps the reader anticipate the contrast to come in the second half of the sentence. Use a comma after an introductory word, such as *originally*, or after an introductory phrase, such as *In 1776*.

## Practice

Rewrite each sentence. Move a word or phrase to the beginning of the sentence so that it no longer starts with the sentence subject.

1. Almost all teachers before John Dewey believed that children should learn only by memorizing.
2. Dewey suggested in the early twentieth century that students should learn by doing rather than just by memorizing.
3. His ideas were originally very shocking to some people.
4. Many teachers came to accept some of his ideas after a while.
5. Dewey did not always agree with the way people applied his ideas later in his life.

# 4 Proofreading
## Research Report

After Greg revised his research report, he used the checklist in the **Writer's Guide** and the **Editor's Marks** to proofread it. Look at what he did in this paragraph.

### Writer's Guide

**Proofreading Checklist**

- ☑ Check for errors in capitalization. Be sure that you have capitalized every important word in the title.
- ☑ Check for errors in punctuation.
- ☑ Check to see that all your paragraphs are indented.
- ☑ Circle any words you think are misspelled. Find out how to spell them correctly.
- ⇨ For proofreading help, use the **Writer's Handbook.**

¶ Harriet Tubman continued to be very active both during and after the civil war. She served as a cook, guide, and spy with the Union army. During one military campaign she helped free 750 (black) slaves. Later she supported schools by raising (mony) *money* for them.

### EDITOR'S MARKS

- ☰ Capitalize.
- ⊙ Add a period.
- ∧ Add something.
- ⋏ Add a comma.
- ⱽ ⱽ Add quotation marks.
- ✄ Cut something.
- ⋀ Replace something.
- ∿ Transpose.
- ◯ Spell correctly.
- ¶ Indent paragraph.
- ╱ Make a lowercase letter.

### Discuss

1. Look at Greg's proofread report. What kinds of corrections did he make?
2. Why did Greg move the word *black*?

### Try Your Hand

**Proofread Your Research Report**   Now use the **Writer's Guide** and the **Editor's Marks** to proofread your research report.

**Save your corrected research report in your *Writer's Notebook.* You will use it when you publish your report.**

WRITING PROCESS

# Listening and Speaking
## Tips for Good Speakers and Good Listeners

**A good listener**

1. Pays complete attention to the speaker.
2. Takes brief notes on important facts while continuing to listen.
3. Responds to the speaker's presentation through eye contact, smiles, and other appropriate signals.
4. Asks questions at the end of the presentation.
5. Offers compliments and suggestions after the presentation.

**A good speaker**

1. Prepares well ahead of time, organizing information and ideas in outline form.
2. Writes important facts and quotations on note cards.
3. Speaks clearly and loudly, varying his or her tone of voice.
4. Checks note cards periodically, and then returns to making eye contact with the audience.
5. Uses appropriate gestures for emphasis.
6. Communicates enthusiasm.

# 5 Publishing
## Research Report

Greg made a clean copy of his research report and checked it to be sure he had not left out anything. He presented his report orally to his classmates, using the **Tips for Good Speakers and Good Listeners** on page 361. Then Greg and his classmates created a *Step Back into History* corner for their finished reports. You can read Greg's report on pages 40–41 of the **Writer's Handbook.**

1. Greg and his classmates selected a corner of the classroom and designed a banner to identify the area as a *Step Back into History* corner. They arranged bookcases and tables to create a separate area.

2. Next, the students looked in encyclopedias, biographies, and history books for pictures and portraits of famous Americans.

3. Greg and his classmates made copies of the pictures by drawing or tracing them.

4. They collected the reports and placed them on the bookshelves, grouping the reports by subject. They invited another class to visit their *Step Back into History* corner.

## Discuss

1. Why is it important to take notes when you are going to comment on someone's oral presentation?
2. How can a list like the one on page 361 help you prepare for an oral report? How can it help you give comments?
3. Almost everyone is a little nervous before speaking to a group. What are some of your tips for relaxing? What are some of your classmates' tips?

## Try Your Hand

**Publish Your Research Report**   Follow the checklist in the **Writer's Guide.** If possible, present your report orally to your classmates or try one of these ideas for sharing your report.

◆ As a class, collect your written reports into a class encyclopedia and present a copy to the school library or the local community library.

◆ Post your reports on the class or library bulletin board. Group together reports that have related topics, such as those on American Presidents or on women in United States history. Reports may also be grouped according to time periods.

# Writing in the Content Areas

**Writer's Guide**

When you write, remember the stages of the Writing Process.
- Prewriting
- Drafting
- Responding and Revising
- Proofreading
- Publishing

Use what you learned to write a paragraph that answers a question you have about the world. One way to publish your paragraph is to post it on a bulletin board titled *Questions and Answers*. Use one of these ideas or an idea of your own.

## Science

How does an animal grow up? Choose a mammal, a bird, an insect, a reptile, or a fish. Use reference books and other resources to learn how this animal is born, what it is like as a baby, and what stages it goes through as it grows to be an adult.

## Language Arts/History

Choose an interesting word that you found while doing research. Tell why the word is interesting to you. Also explain what language the word comes from and what its different meanings are. Use a dictionary to research this information. Include examples of ways your word might be used in sentences.

## Physical Education/Health

Choose a sport, game, or exercise that you enjoy in your physical education class. Use reference books and other resources to learn which parts of your body and which physical skills this activity helps to develop.

## Art

In an art book or an encyclopedia, find a painting that interests you. In a paragraph, tell why the painting caught your eye. Also tell the name of the painting, who painted it, and when it was painted. If possible, tell what kind of paint was used, and describe the place or person the artist used as a model.

# CONNECTING
## WRITING ⬌ LANGUAGE

Writers of research reports look in books and other resources to find information about their topic. A well-written research report helps the reader easily understand information about a topic that is new to him or her. What is the important information in this paragraph from a research paper?

## Flying Squirrels

When you list the animals that live near your house, you might not name flying squirrels. Many people don't know that they have flying squirrels in their neighborhoods, but they do! Flying squirrels are much like the red squirrels and gray squirrels that we see in the daytime, but they are nocturnal. They live in trees. They find nuts and hide them under the ground or high in the treetops. Like daytime squirrels, they climb quickly and jump far. When they jump, they seem to fly through the air!

◆ **Prepositions in a Research Report** The groups of words highlighted in color are prepositional phrases. The first word in the prepositional phrase is the preposition, which gives the direction of the action: *in, under, through,* and so on. The other words in the preposition give information such as *where, when,* or *what kind.* In this research report the prepositional phrases do the job of showing the reader the familiar places where an unfamiliar animal may appear. They help to make the report clearer and more understandable.

◆ **Language Focus: Prepositions, Conjunctions, Interjections** The following lessons will help you use prepositions, conjunctions, and interjections in your own writing.

# 1 Prepositions

◆ FOCUS   A **preposition** is a word that relates a
noun or a pronoun to another word in the sentence.

A preposition gives information about the
relationship between a noun or a pronoun and
another word in a sentence. The prepositions are in
color in these sentences.

**above**

**1.** My mother tells me stories  about  Norway.

**2.** She often skied  down  the mountains.

A preposition is always followed by a noun or a
pronoun. This noun or pronoun is called the **object
of the preposition.**

object of the preposition

**3.** Mother's cousins lived  near  Narvik.

object of the preposition   object of the preposition

**4.** She skied  with  them  during  family visits.

**below**

| Common Prepositions | | | | |
|---|---|---|---|---|
| about | before | except | off | to |
| above | behind | for | on | toward |
| across | below | from | onto | under |
| after | beside | in | out | until |
| along | between | inside | outside | up |
| among | by | into | over | with |
| around | down | near | past | without |
| at | during | of | through | |

## Guided Practice

**A.** Tell whether the underlined word in each sentence is a
*preposition* or the *object of a preposition*. If the underlined word
is the object of a preposition, name the preposition.

**1.** My father was born in <u>Switzerland</u>.
**2.** His home town was <u>between</u> two mountains.
**3.** He climbed many steep slopes with his <u>brother</u>.
**4.** Father once hiked across the <u>Alps</u> alone.
**5.** <u>After</u> all these years, he still loves the mountains.

## Independent Practice

**B. Identifying Prepositions**   The underlined word in each sentence is the object of a preposition. Write the preposition for each object.

  6. Finland is a country in Northern Europe.

  MODEL➤ in

  7. Russia is near Finland.
  8. Northern Finland is inside the Arctic Circle.
  9. Lapps are people of the north.
  10. They could not live without reindeer.
  11. Reindeer pull their sleds across the fields.
  12. Lapp children are chilly after the ride.
  13. Things are easier during summer.
  14. My grandfather brought his sled to America.
  15. A horse pulls the sled around the countryside.

**C. Writing Prepositions**   Read each sentence. Write a preposition that makes sense. Then, write the object of the preposition.

  16. In 1919 my grandparents sailed _____ the ocean.

  MODEL➤ across—ocean

  17. Grandma told me _____ the journey.
  18. Storms raged _____ the ship.
  19. Grandma and Grandpa stayed _____ deck.
  20. They reached New York _____ a month.
  21. The ship sailed _____ the Statue of Liberty.
  22. My grandparents passed _____ Ellis Island.
  23. Finally, they got _____ Manhattan.
  24. They took their baggage _____ the boat.
  25. Grandpa searched the dock _____ Uncle Hans.

## Application — Writing

**Interview Questions**   Imagine that you are meeting an exchange student. Think of five questions you would like to ask about his or her culture. Use prepositions in each question.

# 2 Prepositional Phrases

◆ **FOCUS** A **prepositional phrase** is made up of a preposition, the object of the preposition, and all the words in between.

A preposition is always the first word in a prepositional phrase. A prepositional phrase may be at the beginning, in the middle, or at the end of a sentence. In the following sentences, the prepositional phrases are in color.

1. At the market Lisa will buy fresh vegetables.
2. The recipe for the soup is a family secret.
3. Her cousin taught her the recipe in Mexico.
4. Lisa serves the soup to her family.

**Link to Speaking and Writing**
Use prepositional phrases to give additional information about a topic.

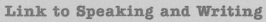

*The soup cooks* *for hours in a kettle*

## Guided Practice

**A.** Identify the prepositional phrase in each sentence. Name the preposition.

1. Lisa comes from Mexico.
2. She tells people about her Mexican heritage.
3. Europeans settled Mexico before settling the United States.
4. Lisa lived there until 1989.
5. She moved here after fifth grade.

**THINK AND REMEMBER**
◆ Remember that a **prepositional phrase** is made up of a preposition, the object of the preposition, and all the words in between.

# Independent Practice

**B. Identifying Prepositional Phrases**  Write the prepositional phrase from each sentence. Underline the preposition.

**6.** Let me tell you about my family.

MODEL> <u>about</u> my family

**7.** My mother was born in China.

**8.** My father comes from Brazil.

**9.** Mom and Dad visited New York at the same time.

**10.** They both went to the Empire State Building.

**11.** They talked during the elevator ride.

**12.** Together they walked around the city.

**13.** They were married in Central Park.

**14.** Now we live across the Hudson River.

**15.** We all speak Chinese except Dad.

**C. Revising: Adding Prepositional Phrases**  Write each sentence, adding a prepositional phrase.

**16.** My grandparents have an apartment.

MODEL> My grandparents have an apartment in the city.

**17.** We visited my mother's sister there.

**18.** My grandparents surprised us.

**19.** They met us.

**20.** My mother speaks English.

**21.** The weather was beautiful, and we walked.

**22.** We took the ferry.

**23.** The ferry sailed.

**24.** Crowded trains carried passengers.

**25.** My mother met a Chinese tourist.

**26.** They had a conversation.

**27.** I didn't understand what they said.

**28.** I asked them to speak more slowly.

**29.** I translated the conversation.

## Application — Writing and Speaking

**Recipe**  Imagine that you have a pen pal in another country. Think about where this pen pal might be. Then think about a recipe that you would like to share. Write sentences telling your pen pal how to prepare your favorite food. Use prepositional phrases.

# 3 Preposition or Adverb?

◆ **FOCUS** Some words can be used as prepositions or as adverbs.

You can tell whether a word is used as an adverb or as a preposition by identifying how it is used in a sentence.

**1.** The mailman passed by .  adverb
**2.** He stopped by the mailbox.  preposition

In sentence 1 *by* is used as an adverb to describe the verb *passed*. In sentence 2 *by* is used as a preposition. It begins the prepositional phrase *by the mailbox*.

The words in this chart can be used as adverbs or as prepositions.

| | | | | |
|---|---|---|---|---|
| about | before | down | off | over |
| above | behind | in | on | through |
| along | below | inside | out | under |
| around | by | near | outside | up |

## Guided Practice

**A.** Tell whether the underlined word is a *preposition* or an *adverb*.

1. I wrote <u>to</u> my cousin in Holland.
2. We have exchanged letters <u>before</u>.
3. I put my letter <u>by</u> the door.
4. Dad took a walk <u>down</u> the street.
5. He took my letter <u>along</u>.
6. Dad dropped my letter <u>inside</u> the mailbox.
7. The mail carrier will pick it <u>up</u>.
8. It must go <u>through</u> the post office.
9. A plane takes it <u>across</u> the ocean.
10. My cousin will go <u>out</u> and get the letter.

---

**THINK AND REMEMBER**
◆ Remember that some words can be used as prepositions or as adverbs.

---

# Independent Practice

**B. Identifying Prepositions and Adverbs**  Write whether the underlined word is a *preposition* or an *adverb.*

11. Last winter I traveled <u>to</u> Holland.

MODEL preposition

12. I stayed in Amsterdam <u>with</u> my cousins.
13. I got very excited when the plane touched <u>down</u>.
14. It was snowing <u>outside</u>!
15. My cousins live <u>between</u> two canals.
16. Dutch people skate on canals <u>during</u> the winter.
17. I looked <u>up</u> at the night sky.
18. Lights were strung all <u>along</u> the canals.
19. They twinkled <u>above</u> like a thousand stars.
20. The lights shone on the people <u>below</u>.
21. I could soon spin <u>around</u> and <u>around</u>!
22. Suddenly, the music came <u>on</u>.
23. We linked our arms and skated <u>off</u> toward the sound.
24. It was like skating <u>through</u> a wonderland.
25. I was so sorry when that trip was <u>over</u>.

**C. Revising Sentences: Adding Prepositional Phrases**  Write each sentence, adding a prepositional phrase.

26. I would love to travel _____ .

MODEL I would love to travel around the world.

27. If I am lucky, I will sail _____ .
28. We will visit exotic countries _____ .
29. _____ I plan to see the museums.
30. _____ I will visit the Swiss Alps.
31. The ancient ruins in Greece beckon _____ .
32. _____ the English countryside will be beautiful.
33. We might see the Queen of England _____ .
34. I long to see the Scottish heather _____ .
35. I would rest _____ in Spain.
36. The people _____ would be interesting to meet.
37. I would return home _____ .

# Application — Writing

**Thank-You Note**  Imagine that you have returned from a trip to the Netherlands. Write a thank-you note to your relatives. Thank them for showing their country to you. Use some of the words in this lesson both as prepositions and as adverbs in your writing.

# 4 Conjunctions

◆ **FOCUS**   A **conjunction** is a word that connects words or groups of words in a sentence.

Compound subjects have two or more nouns or pronouns. The conjunctions *and, but,* and *or* join compound subjects together. The conjunctions *and, but,* and *or* are also used in compound predicates and compound sentences. The conjunctions are in color in these sentences.

1. Palm trees  and  flowers decorate Puerto Rico.
2. I went by boat,  but  my father went by plane.
3. Would you rather sail  or  fly?

The conjunctions *and, but,* and *or* have different meanings. The word *and* is used to join words. The word *but* is used to show contrast. The word *or* is used to show choice. Notice how conjunctions join other word groups in these sentences.

4. San Juan was beautiful  and  exciting.   **adjectives**
5. A hurricane arrived slowly  but  powerfully.   **adverbs**
6. Did it cause any injuries  or  accidents?   **nouns**

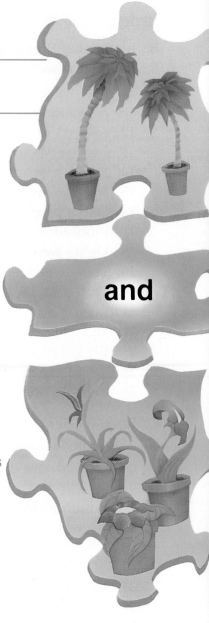

and

## Guided Practice

**A.** Name the conjunction in each sentence.

1. My mother and grandmother lived in Puerto Rico.
2. They took my brother and me to visit.
3. We could have flown, but we traveled by ship.
4. Puerto Rico is green and lovely.
5. We swam and sunbathed in the afternoon.

**B.** Complete each sentence with the conjunction that has the meaning shown in parentheses ( ).

6. Hurricanes bring wind _____ rain. (join)
7. People seek shelter in their homes _____ in big buildings. (choice)
8. Hurricanes can cause damage _____ loss of life. (join)
9. Stay inside, _____ listen to the radio. (contrast)
10. Board up the windows, _____ protect them with tape. (choice)

## Independent Practice

**C. Identifying Conjunctions**   Write the conjunction in each sentence.

11. Our cruise ship was big and roomy.

> MODEL  and

12. There were many contests and other activities.
13. You could join in the fun or just relax.
14. I tried fishing, but I did not catch anything.
15. One man caught a 9- or 10-pound grouper.
16. He offered it to me, but I said, "No, thanks."

**D. Understanding the Meanings of Conjunctions**   Write the
conjunction that best adds the meaning shown in parentheses ( ).

17. San Juan is old, _____ it has its modern parts. (contrast)

> MODEL  but

18. People shop at expensive stores, _____ they bargain with
street vendors. (choice)
19. Tourism _____ farming are two important businesses. (join)
20. Visitors like the sunny beaches _____ the clear water. (join)
21. Stay for a week, _____ visit longer. (choice)
22. Puerto Rico is far away, _____ it's worth the trip. (contrast)

**E. Writing Sentences with Conjunctions**   Write each sentence.
Use the conjunction that best fits the sentence.

23. Many young men _____ women came here.

> MODEL  and

24. They left friends, _____ soon they found new ones.
25. Did you settle in Florida _____ in New York?
26. People here are friendly _____ neighborly.
27. Is your house on the corner of Main _____ Elm?
28. I like Florida, _____ I miss Puerto Rico.

## Application — Writing and Speaking

**Storm Warning**   Imagine that a hurricane is approaching your
area. Write a storm warning to be read on a radio station. Include
conjunctions in your writing. Deliver your radio announcement to
the class.

# 5 Interjections

◆ **FOCUS** An **interjection** is a word or a group of words that expresses strong feeling.

Wow!

An exclamatory sentence shows strong feeling. An interjection also expresses strong feeling and can be used to make your writing more interesting. The interjections are in color in these sentences.

1. Hooray! I get to visit my grandparents in Japan.
2. Oh, my, look how far away Japan is.
3. My grandparents write in Japanese, of course.

When an interjection expresses strong feeling, use an exclamation point. When an interjection expresses a slightly milder feeling, separate it from the rest of the sentence with a comma.

Below is a list of common interjections. You may be able to think of others.

| | | | | | |
|---|---|---|---|---|---|
| Aha! | Good grief! | My! | Oh, dear! | Oops! | Wow! |
| Alas! | Great! | Never! | Oh, my! | Ouch! | Yikes! |
| Eek! | Hey! | Of course! | Oh, no! | Phew! | Yow! |
| Gee! | Hooray! | Oh! | Oh, oh! | Well, well! | Yuck! |

## Guided Practice

**A.** Tell which word or group of words is an interjection.

1. Alas! I can't read this Japanese name.
2. Here comes my grandfather. Great!
3. Gee, would you translate this word, Grandfather?
4. Of course! That is my name.
5. Aha! I knew it looked familiar.
6. Well, well! I see you need Japanese lessons.
7. Oh, I was hoping you would say that.

---

**THINK AND REMEMBER**
◆ Remember that an **interjection** is a word or a group of words that expresses strong feeling.

---

# Independent Practice

**B. Identifying Interjections**  Write the interjection from each sentence.

MODEL **8.** Aha! I finally found our family tree.

Aha!

**9.** Phew, the paper smells really old.

**10.** Of course, it has been in this attic for years.

**11.** Eek! There are mice in this attic, too.

**12.** Wow! Here is my mother's name.

**13.** Hey! My great-grandparents were born in Hungary.

**14.** My! I bet they had some exciting stories.

**C. Using Interjections**  Read each sentence. Write an interjection to express strong feeling.

**15.** _____! I decided to make a family tree for our dog.

MODEL Hey!

**16.** Her mother was a French poodle, _____ .

**17.** _____ , her father was a mutt.

**18.** _____ , your dog must have been a cute puppy.

**19.** _____ ! She is five different colors.

**20.** _____ ! She has four brothers.

**21.** She is licensed, _____ .

**D. Revising: Punctuating Interjections**  Rewrite each sentence, using the correct punctuation with the interjection.

**22.** Gee Americans come from every continent on earth.

MODEL Gee! Americans come from every continent on earth.

**23.** Hey There are none from Antarctica.

**24.** Good grief You are right.

**25.** Golly Half of America had families from Europe.

**26.** Oh, my is it difficult to become a citizen?

**27.** Wow people who want to become citizens study hard.

**28.** Phew They must get tired from all that studying.

**29.** Oh, no they think it is worth it.

**30.** Hooray You are now a citizen of the United States.

## Application — Writing and Speaking

**Skit**  Imagine that a new student has moved to your neighborhood from a foreign country. Write a skit. Tell the newcomer all about your neighborhood. Use interjections in your writing. Work with a partner to present your skit to the class.

# Building Vocabulary
## Word Origins

Words come into the English language in interesting ways. Here are three important origins of words in our language.

*I think I'll call it . . . a Ferris wheel!*

## Words from Names

Some words in the English language come from the names of people and places. For example, the Ferris wheel was named after its inventor— G. W. Ferris.

Here are some other examples of words from names.

| Word | Named for: |
|------|-----------|
| badminton | Badminton, an estate in England where the game became popular |
| leotard | nineteenth-century French gymnast Jules Leotard, who first made this tight-fitting suit popular |
| jeans | Genoa, Italy, where the fabric used in blue jeans was first woven |

## Sound Words

Some words in our language come from the sounds they name. For example, the word *purr* imitates the soothing sound made by a happy cat. Other sound words that imitate animal noises include *gobble, quack, moo, growl,* and *whinny.*

Sound words imitate other kinds of noises too. For example, the word *ticktock* imitates the sound some clocks make. Other sound words of this kind are *beep, clatter, crunch,* and *zip.*

## Borrowed Words

Many English words we use every day are borrowed from other languages. For example, the word *kindergarten* was originally a German word meaning "children's garden." The first kindergarten was started in Germany. When it was decided to have kindergartens in American schools, we borrowed the German word.

## Reading Practice

Read each sentence, and study the underlined word. Then read the definition sentences that tell the history of each word. Write the letter of the definition that goes with each underlined word.

1. My head started to <u>buzz</u> with confusion.
2. We ordered <u>spaghetti</u> for dinner.
3. Jolene is learning to play the <u>saxophone</u>.
4. We had a <u>hamburger</u> and a <u>salad</u> for lunch.
5. The <u>raccoon</u> ran into the woods.
6. The tree fell into the lake with a loud <u>splash</u>.

a. This word comes from the Italian word *spaghetto*, meaning "cord" or "string."
b. This word comes from the Algonquian word *arahkun*, which names an animal with a bushy, ringed tail.
c. This word imitates the sound a bee makes.
d. This word is named after the city of Hamburg, Germany.
e. This word names the musical instrument invented by Adolphe Sax.
f. This word imitates the sound of an object hitting water.

## Writing Practice

Choose five words from the list below. Look up each word in a dictionary. Write a sentence that tells about the origin of the word. Then, write a sentence using the word as we use it today.

| | | | |
|---|---|---|---|
| cardigan | frankfurter | madras | sandwich |
| canoe | guppy | magnolia | sequoia |
| cologne | kimono | parka | yogurt |
| coyote | luau | patio | |

## Project

Work in a small group to write a funny radio script about a trip to the city or to the country. To help your listeners feel as if they are right there with you, use as many sound words as you can. Tape-record your script, or read it to the class. Use your voices to emphasize the sound words.

*Here we are in New York City, with cars and taxis zipping by us!*

# Language Enrichment
## Prepositions, Conjunctions, and Interjections

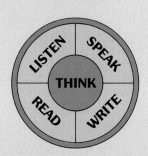

Use what you know about prepositions, conjunctions, and interjections to do these activities.

 **Eye Spy**

Use a picture of a large group of people or things. Choose one person or thing in the picture. Ask a partner to guess which person or thing you chose. Your partner should begin by pointing to one person or thing. You respond by using prepositions to explain the position of your choice. After your partner has identified your person or thing, switch roles.

 **Interjection Charades**

With your classmates, take turns acting out feelings. When your classmates identify the feeling you are expressing, they should name an interjection that fits. For example, if you show disappointment they might say "Oh, rats!" or "Oh, no!" Have a student write down the emotions and the interjections associated with them. Post the list in the classroom. Use the list when you are writing dialogue.

 **No *And's, But's,* or *Or's***

In a book, find a paragraph that has plenty of conjunctions. Then, read it aloud to a group of three or four classmates. Do not read the conjunctions *and, but,* and *or.* Instead, wave your hand each time you skip one of them. Then, read the paragraph aloud again sentence by sentence, still leaving out the conjunctions. Ask your listeners to guess which conjunction (*and, but,* or *or*) belongs in each sentence.

# CONNECTING

## LANGUAGE ↔ WRITING

In this unit you learned to use prepositions, conjunctions, and interjections. Remember that a preposition is a word that shows the relationship between words in a sentence. A conjunction connects words or groups of words. An interjection shows strong feeling.

◆ **Using Prepositions, Conjunctions, and Interjections in Your Writing** Using prepositions, conjunctions, and interjections will make your writing more complete, lively, and realistic.

Pay special attention to the prepositions, conjunctions, and interjections you use as you do these activities.

### Speaking of Names

You learned about the origins of words on the **Building Vocabulary** pages. Here is an entertaining activity that will put your imagination to work about word origins.

Each of the following terms comes from a person's name: *teddy bear, boycott, sousaphone.* Use a dictionary or other resource to find out whose name each word is based on and why. Choose the word origin that interests you the most. Then, imagine you are the person for whom the item is named. Write a paragraph that tells who you are, what the item is, and why it is named after you. Share your paragraph with the class.

*Oh, my! Oh, no! Oh, dear!*

### Dear Diary . . .

Imagine you are a character from your favorite book. You might choose to be Alice from *Alice in Wonderland* by Lewis Carroll or Wilbur from *Charlotte's Web* by E. B. White. Choose a moment in the story when something exciting happens. Write a diary entry. Use interjections. Read it to the class without telling them which character you are. See if they can guess the character.

# Unit Checkup

| Think Back | Think Ahead |
|---|---|
| ◆ What did you learn about research reports? What did you do to write one? | ◆ How will what you learned about a research report help you when you read an article in an encyclopedia? |
| | ◆ How will summarizing help you write a research report? A news story? An expository paragraph? |
| ◆ What did you learn about prepositions, conjunctions, and interjections? How did that help you express your ideas clearly and forcefully? | ◆ What is one way you can use prepositions, conjunctions, or interjections to improve your writing? |

**Research Reports**  *pages 348–349*

Read the research report. Then follow the directions.

Hundreds of years ago the Mayan people achieved a lifestyle that would make them famous for centuries. The Maya built huge cities such as Copan, Tikal, and Palenque at a time when there were no machines to help. Mayan priests developed a 365-day calendar by which they told the people when to plant crops or build huts. The Maya are the only Indians in America to create a complicated system of writing.

The Mayan achievements are well known, but much remains to be discovered. As yet, we do not know why this great culture changed for the worse. At some point during the 800's, the Mayan people abandoned the cities they had built. Some experts believe that the farmers became unhappy with their rulers and drove the rulers out of the cities. Other experts believe that the Maya were forced to leave by another warring group. As experts continue to study the buildings and writings that still exist, we will learn many more clues to the Mayan mystery.

1. Write a title for the research report.
2. Write the introductory sentence.
3. List the supporting details in the first paragraph.
4. Write the topic sentence for the second paragraph.
5. List the supporting facts in the second paragraph.

## Summarizing to Organize Notes   *page 350*

Read the following statements. Write a sentence that summarizes all of the statements.

6. In 1858 gold was discovered near what is now Denver, Colorado.
7. A band of gold miners settled along Cherry Creek because gold was first discovered there.
8. Colorado's "gold rush" began in 1859 when hundreds of people moved to the area.
9. Rough, lawless mining camps like Central City and Fairplay were developing.
10. Colorado was known as the "Jefferson Territory," and the area's first newspaper, the Rocky Mountain News, was established.

## Using Quotations   *page 351*

Read the following quotations. Write the quotations you think would add weight and interest to a research report.

11. "Pennsylvania borders Maryland on the north, and Delaware and the Atlantic Ocean form the eastern boundary."
12. When Francis Scott Key realized that Fort McHenry had survived a fierce battle, he became so excited that he wrote, "Oh! say, does that star-spangled banner yet wave O'er the land of the free and the home of the brave?"
13. William Penn was an "English Quaker leader and founder (1681) of Pennsylvania colony" where many Quakers were able to live in political and religious freedom.
14. John F. Kennedy called for a new vision of public service when he said in 1960, ". . . Ask not what your country can do for you—ask what you can do for your country."
15. "He was a Democratic congressman from Massachusetts (1947–1953) and in 1952 won a seat in the U.S. Senate."

## The Writing Process   *pages 352–363*

**16.** When you plan to write a research report, what is the first thing you should do?
  **a.** Go to the library.
  **b.** Make an outline.
  **c.** Brainstorm a list of topics.

**17.** What topic would be best for a research report?
  **a.** the history of Mexico
  **b.** great leaders in world history
  **c.** Barbara Jordan, a great Texan

**18.** What is the best way to gather and organize information?
  **a.** Take notes from books and make an outline.
  **b.** Conduct an interview and make a diagram.
  **c.** Make a cluster of sensory details.

## Prepositions   *pages 366–367*

The underlined word in each sentence is the object of a preposition. Write the preposition for each object.

**19.** Anna's German grandmother now lives in <u>Dallas, Texas</u>.
**20.** Her childhood home was in the Black Forest area of southwestern <u>Germany</u>.
**21.** The Black Forest is an area thickly wooded with dark fir <u>trees</u>.
**22.** Anna loves her grandmother's wonderful stories from the Black Forest <u>region</u>.
**23.** Anna hopes <u>she</u> will visit the Black Forest and learn more about the <u>area</u>.

## Prepositional Phrases   *pages 368–369*

Write the prepositional phrase or phrases in each sentence. Underline the preposition.

**24.** Jack is a Navajo Indian from northern Arizona.
**25.** When we had a family day at our school, Jack brought some jewelry and blankets.
**26.** One of the blankets Jack brought shows a white bird flying over three bands of color.
**27.** The jewelry is made of silver and turquoise.
**28.** His mother accompanied him and told us about her people's traditions.

## Preposition or Adverb? *pages 370–371*
Write whether the underlined word is a *preposition* or an *adverb*.

29. Guadalupe Day is celebrated <u>in</u> Mexico.
30. Mexicans <u>happily</u> begin the holiday by watching fireworks.
31. People stroll in the streets and buy treats <u>from</u> many vendors.
32. <u>In</u> the courtyards children play with fancy piñatas.
33. The children vigorously hit the piñata until it breaks and the treats shower <u>down</u>.
34. Many Mexican families remain <u>outside</u>, and musicians entertain them <u>with</u> traditional songs and guitar performances.

## Conjunctions *pages 372–373*
Write the conjunction from each sentence.

35. Nicaragua and Guatemala are part of Central America.
36. Spanish is the main language of these countries, but English is spoken too.
37. Central America is a mountainous land bridge connecting North America and South America.
38. Central Americans may live in rural areas or large cities.
39. Pottery making, fabric weaving, and jewelry crafting are among the skills passed down from the ancient Indians to those living in Central America today.

## Interjections *pages 374–375*
Read each sentence. Write an interjection to express strong feeling.

40. _____ ! We have to think of an idea for our social studies assignment.
41. _____ ! I think I've got a great idea!
42. _____ , let's describe the history of our neighborhood.
43. _____ ! We'd better get started.
44. _____ , I'm glad you like the idea.

## Word Origins *pages 376–377*
Choose five words from the list. Look up each word in a dictionary. Write a sentence that tells about the origin of the word. Then write a sentence using the word as we use it today.

45. boom
46. geyser
47. tangerine
48. roar
49. squash
50. cafeteria
51. braille
52. gumbo
53. zinnia
54. hiss
55. jersey
56. guy

# UNIT

## 9

# Entertaining Others

◆ **COMPOSITION FOCUS:** Tall Tale
◆ **LANGUAGE FOCUS:** Mechanics Wrap-up

People have always enjoyed the exaggerated plots and comical characters found in humorous stories. From the fables of Aesop to the novels of Mark Twain, humorous stories have made people feel happy. At the same time, humorous stories teach lessons about life. Humor has also been used to explain the origins of things in nature, such as how the elephant got its trunk. One kind of humorous story, the tall tale, has been used to explain such things as how the Grand Canyon was formed and why there are no trees in a desert.

In the following pages you will read a humorous story about honesty and trickery by Rolando Hinojosa-Smith (hē·nō·hō′sä smith′). In his writing, he uses exaggeration to create characters who are either very, very good or very, very bad.

In this unit you will study the humorous story. You will also learn different ways to use exaggeration to make readers laugh. Then you will write a humorous tall tale using exaggeration.

Rolando Hinojosa-Smith created the humorous characters in "Don Bueno and Don Malo" *to entertain* his readers.

# Reading with a Writer's Eye
## Humorous Story

A storyteller creates an imaginary world for his or her readers. The writer invents characters, places, and events, giving the story a particular shape that will capture and hold the reader's interest. As you read this humorous story by Rolando Hinojosa-Smith, notice how the writer uses a problem and its solution to help shape his story.

## Don Bueno and Don Malo
### by Rolando Hinojosa-Smith

Don Bueno (dön bōō·ay′nŏ) was a poor man who lived in a very poor village. There was little work to be found there. Don Bueno, as his name tells us, was a good man. He was a hardworking man and an honest one, too. It is said that once, while working on another man's land, he found a box full of silver, diamonds, and gold. The landowner swore he had never owned such valuables. However, don Bueno pointed out that the silver, diamonds, and gold were found on the man's property and were therefore his. Don Bueno insisted that the landowner keep them, and he would not even accept a reward.

His wife, doña Lista (dö'nyah lees'tă), was also hardworking and honest, and, as her name tells us, she was bright and sharp and clever. It is said that by looking at a field of corn, she could calculate not only the total number of ears to be harvested, but the total number of kernels. As doña Lista had once told her husband, "Since you work so hard for so little pay, I have to be bright and sharp and clever to spend our money wisely." Don Bueno had smiled and agreed with his wife.

Now don Malo (dön mah'lŏ), as his name tells us, was not a good man. He owned a lot of land, but he was never satisfied. He would try to cheat anyone who worked for him. He would call his workers together every morning and insist that they turn their watches over to him "for safekeeping." Then, while the workers were out in his fields, he would turn back the hands on their watches to cheat them out of many hours of labor. When the workers trudged in at sunset, don Malo would show them their watches and say that it was only noon. He would then send them back to the fields to "earn their day's pay."

One day, the good, hardworking, honest don Bueno went out looking for work. Sensing that he could easily trick such a man, don Malo hired him immediately. He promised don Bueno a bag of silver to rebuild the horse stables, to patch up part of the roof on the barn, to replace the broken rope on the water well, and to mend the broken fence. This was a lot of work, but the payment sounded fair to don Bueno. He took the job happily.

Don Bueno worked very hard and did everything that was asked of him. During his eight days at don Malo's, he noticed a great gray-colored bull. This was the biggest and the fiercest-looking bull that don Bueno had ever seen.

Don Malo called the great bull "El Rey Gris" (el ray'e grees) which means "The Silver King." This great bull was both a joy and a sadness to don Malo. He had once enjoyed showing the bull to

the other landowners. But the bull was also a sadness because it would go as wild as a lunatic once a month. It happened only at nine o'clock on the night when the moon was full. It was the great bull which had torn down the horse stables, had wrecked part of the roof on the barn, had broken the rope on the water well, and had smashed the fence into toothpicks. It is said that one time, in a rage, the bull jumped right at the full moon. The moon became so scared that it did not become full again for another three months.

Don Malo kept this wild side of the bull a secret. But doña Lista, who was bright and sharp and clever, had seen how the bull misbehaved on the nights the moon was full. She had calculated that it was the bull causing such damage to the stables, the barn, the rope, and the fence.

When don Bueno finished all of the repairs, he presented himself to don Malo and asked to be paid for his work. However, don Malo did not give the good, hardworking, honest don Bueno the bag of silver he had promised. With false tears in his eyes, don Malo told don Bueno that he had no bag of silver left to give. He told don Bueno to take away his pride and joy, The Silver King, instead.

Don Malo wept as he watched don Bueno lead the great bull away. He knew that that night, at nine o'clock, the moon would be full. When don Bueno and the bull were far enough away, don Malo laughed and laughed as hard as he could.

Don Malo then set to work. Today was his birthday, and he was hosting a great feast for himself. He had invited all the richest landowners to this feast, hoping they would shower him with expensive gifts. Gleefully he took out the fine crystal glasses, the very best dishes, and the expensive silverware. There was no danger that they would be broken tonight. The Silver King now belonged to don Bueno. Don Malo made a note to ride past what was left of don Bueno's house the next day.

Meanwhile, don Bueno and The Silver King arrived home. Don Bueno showed doña Lista his payment for eight days of work— for rebuilding the horse stables, for patching part of the roof on the barn, for replacing the broken rope on the water well, and for mending the broken fence. Doña Lista looked in horror at the great bull. She knew right away that her husband had been tricked out of his pay by don Malo.

"Don Bueno," she said, "this bull is as wild as a hurricane. It will destroy everything we own."

"But don Malo had no bag of silver," he replied. "And he wept to give up The Silver King!"

Doña Lista thought for a moment. "Don Malo might weep to give up a bag of silver, but never to give up The Silver King. But do not worry. All is not lost, my husband. I have a plan, and with this plan, we will recover the pay that is owed you."

Doña Lista and don Bueno tied The Silver King to a tree and entered the kitchen to eat their supper. Doña Lista, always bright and sharp and clever, looked at her old, old watch and said, "Tonight, at nine o'clock, the moon will be full. We will appear at don Malo's birthday party and give him The Silver King as a present."

Don Bueno was puzzled. He said, "But then don Malo will have his bag of silver and his bull. We will have nothing."

Doña Lista smiled and told him, "If we return The Silver King to him, the bull will break the fine crystal glasses, the very best dishes, and the expensive silverware. After that, The Silver King will wreck the horse stables, ruin the roof on the barn, chew up the rope on the water well, and destroy the fence again."

Don Bueno said, "But what if don Malo refuses to accept our gift?"

"He cannot do that," she replied. "That would be like admitting he had tricked you out of your pay. He cannot do that in front of the other landowners."

Don Bueno nodded. He went out and untied The Silver King. They all walked to don Malo's house, arriving just as the moon began to rise. When the couple entered the birthday feast, they bowed and addressed don Malo respectfully. They presented the bull to him in honor of his birthday. The Silver King began to snort and to paw at the ground. All the landowners smiled at such a display of affection, but don Malo turned as white as the fine linen tablecloth. He knew what the great bull would do to his fine crystal glasses, his very best dishes, and all of the expensive silverware.

Don Malo excused himself from the landowners and took the couple aside. He ordered them to leave with the snorting bull. Doña Lista refused. He then fell to his knees and begged them to go. But doña Lista, who was bright and sharp and clever, said, "First, you must pay my husband for eight days of hard work."

Don Malo assured her, "Come back tomorrow. I will find a small bag of silver for you somehow."

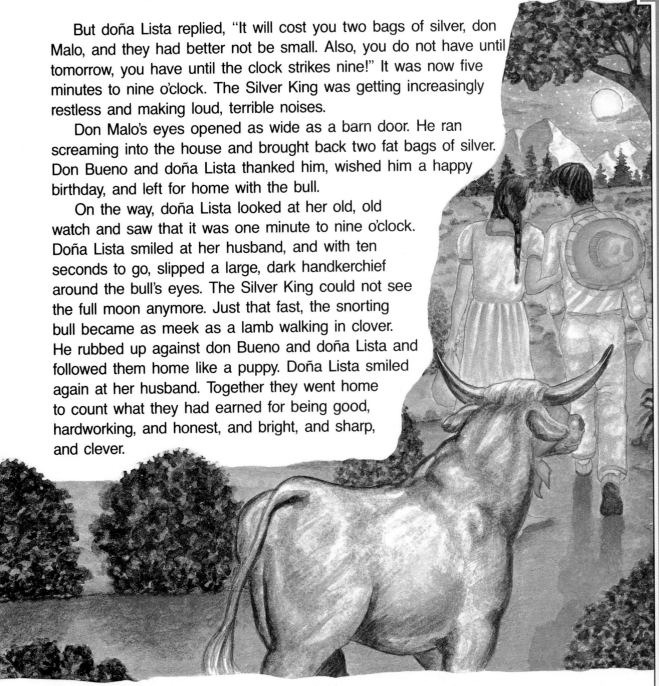

But doña Lista replied, "It will cost you two bags of silver, don Malo, and they had better not be small. Also, you do not have until tomorrow, you have until the clock strikes nine!" It was now five minutes to nine o'clock. The Silver King was getting increasingly restless and making loud, terrible noises.

Don Malo's eyes opened as wide as a barn door. He ran screaming into the house and brought back two fat bags of silver. Don Bueno and doña Lista thanked him, wished him a happy birthday, and left for home with the bull.

On the way, doña Lista looked at her old, old watch and saw that it was one minute to nine o'clock. Doña Lista smiled at her husband, and with ten seconds to go, slipped a large, dark handkerchief around the bull's eyes. The Silver King could not see the full moon anymore. Just that fast, the snorting bull became as meek as a lamb walking in clover. He rubbed up against don Bueno and doña Lista and followed them home like a puppy. Doña Lista smiled again at her husband. Together they went home to count what they had earned for being good, hardworking, and honest, and bright, and sharp, and clever.

## Respond

1. What parts of this story do you find funny? Why?

## Discuss

2. What problems do don Bueno and doña Lista face?
3. In what way are these problems a necessary part of the story? Could there be a story without problems? Explain your answer.

# Thinking As a Writer
## Analyzing a Humorous Story

A humorous story, like all stories, has characters, a setting, and a plot. Look at this story map.

**Don Bueno and Don Malo**

**Characters**
Don Bueno
Don Malo
Doña Lista
The Silver King

**Setting**
a poor village

The **title** tells what the story is all about.

The **characters** are the people or animals in the story. The main character usually is "larger than life" or has exaggerated qualities.

**Problem That Starts the Story**
Don Bueno is poor, and it is hard to find work.

The **setting** is the time and the place of the story.

**Additional Events**
1. Don Malo hires don Bueno to work for him for eight days.
2. Don Malo doesn't give don Bueno the silver he promised but instead gives him a bull that becomes wild when the moon is full.
3. Don Bueno takes the bull home, and doña Lista realizes that don Malo has cheated her husband.
4. She thinks of a plan to get the best of don Malo.

The **plot** is what happens in the story. The setting and characters are introduced in the beginning of the story. The plot begins with a problem the main character or characters have.

The plot develops with the addition of more events that continue the story.

**Turning Point**
Don Bueno and doña Lista take the bull to don Malo's fancy birthday party.

The action builds to a **turning point,** which is the most important or exciting event of the story.

**Conclusion**
Doña Lista's plan works, and she and don Bueno wind up with two bags of silver and a fine bull.

The **conclusion** closes the story and usually tells what happens to the characters.

A writer sometimes uses exaggeration to make a story humorous. Exaggeration can be used in any type of story. It is especially popular in tall tales, which are humorous stories that stretch the truth.

> It is said that one time, in a rage, the bull jumped right at the full moon. The moon became so scared that it did not become full again for another three months.

**Exaggeration** stretches the truth.

A writer can also use figures of speech such as similes and metaphors for a humorous effect.

> Don Malo's eyes opened *as wide as a barn door.*
> The bull was *as wild as a runaway bulldozer.*

A **simile** is a comparison that uses the word *like* or the word *as.* These similes compare don Malo's wide-open eyes to a barn door and the bull to a runaway bulldozer.

> Don Malo was a skunk.
> Doña Lista's *mind was a computer.*

A **metaphor** compares two things without using *like* or *as.* These metaphors compare don Malo to a skunk and doña Lista's mind to a computer.

## Discuss

1. If you were to add two or three important details to the story map, what would they be? In which part or parts of the map would you put them, and why?
2. Read this sentence from the story: "It is said that by looking at a field of corn, she could calculate not only the total number of ears to be harvested, but the total number of kernels." What main technique does the writer use to achieve humor? How is this sentence an example of that technique?
3. Read these two phrases describing the bull: *as wild as a lunatic; a dinosaur with a bee in its nose.* What two things are being compared in each figure of speech? Which figure of speech is a simile and which is a metaphor?

# Try Your Hand

**A. Identify Details** Find each simile, metaphor, and exaggeration in the following sentences, and write it.

1. Though as poor as a squirrel without nuts in winter, don Bueno was a true prince. He was so generous that he would gladly move to a cave if someone needed his bed.

2. Doña Lista was so gorgeous that people heard bells and fainted the first time they saw her. Doña Lista's hair was flowing silk. She had eyes like blue lakes.

**B. Add Similes and Metaphors** Reread the two examples. Write another simile and another metaphor to add to each humorous description of don Bueno and doña Lista.

**C. Add Exaggeration** Look over each example again. Then add a sentence that exaggerates don Bueno's goodness and generosity and one that exaggerates doña Lista's beauty.

**D. Write a Humorous Description** Write about some event that you see every day, such as a student doing homework, a driver trying to start a car, or a cook preparing a meal. Describe it by exaggerating the details and using similes and metaphors to make your description humorous.

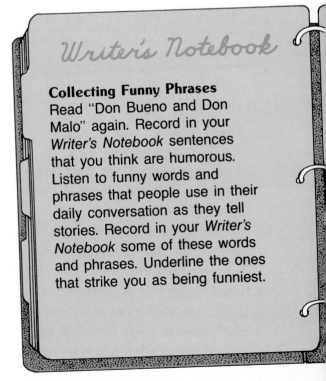

*Writer's Notebook*

**Collecting Funny Phrases** Read "Don Bueno and Don Malo" again. Record in your *Writer's Notebook* sentences that you think are humorous. Listen to funny words and phrases that people use in their daily conversation as they tell stories. Record in your *Writer's Notebook* some of these words and phrases. Underline the ones that strike you as being funniest.

# Developing the Writer's Craft
## Using Details and Dialogue to Create Good Characters

In stories, writers use various techniques to make their characters seem real. Read these sentences spoken by or about don Malo.

1. Don Malo said, "How can I give you silver when I have none? Do you think I am rich? I barely have enough to scrape by, don Bueno."
2. Don Malo wept as he watched don Bueno lead the great bull away. When don Bueno and the bull were far enough away, don Malo laughed and laughed as hard as he could.
3. Doña Lista told don Bueno, "That man has plenty of silver. He hangs on to it with every trick he can think of."

In the first example, don Malo's dialogue reveals how he sees himself. In the second example, the writer shows don Malo's actions so that the reader sees how he really is. In the third example, the writer uses another character to describe don Malo.

When you write your humorous story, use dialogue to reveal how your characters see themselves and others. Describe their actions to make them seem real.

## Discuss

1. Look at the selection on pages 386–391. Describe doña Lista. Find examples of two of the techniques explained above that are used to make the character seem real.
2. Read these sentences: "But don Malo had no bag of silver," replied don Bueno. "And he wept to give up The Silver King!" What method of revealing character is the writer using here? What do you learn about don Bueno from what he says?

## Try Your Hand

**Use Dialogue** Think of two characters and give each a definite personality trait. For example, one character could be shy and the other could be nosy. Write a few lines of dialogue that will show the reader what each character is like. Share your dialogue with a classmate.

# 1 Prewriting
## Tall Tale

Sabina, a student at Columbia Elementary School, wanted to write the kind of humorous story known as a tall tale for her class storytelling contest. She used the checklist in the **Writer's Guide** to help plan her tall tale. Look at what she did.

### Writer's Guide

**Prewriting Checklist**

☑ Brainstorm and select a topic.

☑ Think about your audience and your purpose.

☑ Gather information about the characters, the setting, and the plot.

☑ Organize information into a beginning, a middle, and an ending.

## ◆ Brainstorming and Selecting a Topic

Sabina knew that her story needed characters, a setting, and a plot. She also knew that all tall tales involve some sort of exaggeration. She decided to start by listing story ideas involving characters with exaggerated characteristics and problems.

Next, Sabina looked over each of her ideas. She did not know much about cowgirls, so she decided to cross that idea out. She could think of some funny ideas for the rest of the choices but was not always able to imagine a beginning, a middle, and an ending for her tall tale.

Finally, she chose to write about the clever farm boy. She circled that choice and began thinking about how to organize her tall tale.

> ~~strongest cowgirl in the world—is afraid of spiders~~
>
> *extremely clever boy, who knows nothing about farming, must take over a farm*
>
> ~~winter weather hot enough to fry an egg on the sidewalk~~
>
> a summer day so cold the ice in the stream was chattering

## Discuss

1. Each of Sabina's story ideas includes the element of exaggeration. For example, one emphasizes how strong someone is and another how hot a day could be. What other qualities might be included in tall-tale story ideas?

2. The first two ideas on Sabina's list include specific characters. Why are characters important to a tall tale?

WRITING PROCESS

# ◆ Gathering Information

After Sabina selected her character and story idea, she gathered information for her tall tale. She decided to name the clever character in her tall tale Clarence. She thought about farm chores and ways that Clarence might try to make them easier. To help herself come up with ideas, she made a chart. Look at what Sabina did.

| Chore | Clever Way to Do It |
|---|---|
| gathering firewood | teach the farm dog to fetch sticks and to pile them neatly beside the back door |
| gathering eggs | have hens lay eggs directly into the egg cartons |
| milking cows | train cows to press on foot-pedals to run the milking machines |
| feeding pigs | train pigs to come into the kitchen to clean up the mess and to eat the leftovers from the plates |
| grooming horses | put huge, car-wash sized brushes on the barn doors so that the horses get brushed every time they walk into the barn |

## Discuss

1. Do all of Sabina's ideas fit the requirements of a tall tale? Explain.
2. Are any of Sabina's ideas for doing chores on the farm practical? Does it matter? Why or why not?
3. Which of Sabina's solutions do you find the funniest? Why?
4. Can you think of any other chores for Sabina's tall tale? How might Clarence try to make them easier?

# ◆ Organizing Information

After Sabina had gathered all the information she needed for her tall tale, she was ready to organize it. She knew that a tall tale needed a title, a beginning, a middle, and an ending. She thought that the title "Clever Clarence" would be good for a humorous story. She decided to make a story map to show how the parts would fit together.

> **Title:** Clever Clarence

**Characters**
Clarence
Farmer McCoy
Chuck's wife

**Setting**
farm

**Problem That Starts the Story**
Farmer McCoy leaves the farm and must rely on Clarence to do the farm chores.

**Additional Events**
1. Clarence promises to take care of the farm.
2. Farmer McCoy leaves.
3. A neighbor named Chuck is supposed to help Clarence.
4. Chuck's wife says that Chuck can't help at all because he is sick.

**Turning Point**
Clarence gets the idea of having the animals act as his helpers.

**Conclusion**
Farmer McCoy comes home and is shocked and thrilled by what he sees. Clarence explains how he got the animals to do the chores. (Most of the exaggeration will come in here.)

# Discuss

1. What should the title of your tall tale tell your audience?
2. Why is it important to plan carefully the beginning, the middle, and the ending of your tall tale before you start writing it?
3. In her story map, Sabina does not say whether she plans to include dialogue. Would dialogue make her story better? Why or why not?
4. The ending of a tall tale should include some kind of exaggeration or surprise. Does the end of Sabina's tall tale fit that description? Explain.

# Try Your Hand

Now plan a tall tale of your own.

**A. Brainstorm and Select a Topic** Brainstorm a list of story ideas. Each idea should include a character with an exaggerated characteristic and a problem.

- ◆ Cross out the ideas that you feel are not funny.
- ◆ Cross out ideas for which you might not be able to think of details.
- ◆ Cross out ideas for which you might not be able to think of a beginning, a middle, and an ending.
- ◆ Circle the topic that would make the best tall tale.

**B. Gather Information** Think about your topic and decide whether you still want to write about it. If not, brainstorm more topics and select a new one.

- ◆ Imagine characters and problems that you could exaggerate in your tall tale.
- ◆ List as many as you can think of—the more outrageous, the better!

**C. Organize the Information** Review your notes.

- ◆ Make sure you have included every idea that might be useful to you in a humorous tall tale.
- ◆ Create a story map showing the beginning (characters, setting, and problem), the middle (events), and the ending (how things turn out) of your tall tale.

 **Save your notes and your story map in your *Writer's Notebook*. You will use them when you draft your tall tale.**

# 2 Drafting
## Tall Tale

Before Sabina started to draft her tall tale, she thought about how she could best entertain her audience with her story. Using her notes and her story map, she followed the checklist in the **Writer's Guide.** Look at what Sabina did.

> *Clever Clarence*
> *Once upon a time, Farmer McCoy had to leave his farm to go to the big city.*
> *His young friend Clarence had promised to take care of Farmer McCoy's chores, but Clarence had no experience with farming.*

## Discuss

1. How is the beginning of Sabina's tall tale like the beginning of her story map? How is it different?
2. Based on the story map, what might Sabina write about next? Explain why you think so.

## Try Your Hand

Now you are ready to write a tall tale.

**A. Review Your Information**   Think about the information you gathered and organized in the last lesson. Decide whether you need more. If so, gather it.

**B. Think About Your TAP**   Remember that your task is to write a tall tale. Your purpose is to entertain your audience.

**C. Write Your First Draft**   Follow the steps in the **Drafting Checklist** to write your tall tale.

When you write your draft, just put all your ideas on paper. Do not worry about spelling, punctuation, or grammar. You can correct the draft later.

**Task:** What?
**Audience:** Who?
**Purpose:** Why?

   **Save your first draft in your *Writer's Notebook*. You will need it when you revise your tall tale.**

# 3 Responding and Revising
## Tall Tale

Sabina used the checklist in the **Writer's Guide** to revise her tall tale. Look at what she did.

### ◆ Checking Information

Sabina noticed she had forgotten to tell how long Farmer McCoy would be away. She used this mark ∧ to add the information.

### ◆ Checking Organization

Sabina noticed that she had switched the order of some of the information in her story map. She moved the information by using this mark ⟳ .

### ◆ Checking Language

Sabina noticed a sentence that she could expand to make her writing more informative. She also added dialogue to make her writing more lively.

Clever Clarence

Once upon a time, Farmer McCoy had to
leave his farm to go to the big city. *for three days*

**Add**

His young friend Clarence had promised to
take care of Farmer McCoy's chores, but Clarence
had no experience with farming. Clarence was
depending on Farmer McCoy's neighbor Chuck
to help him with all the chores.

Farmer McCoy smiled and waved goodbye.
"You can depend on me," said Clarence.

**Move**

Clarence went to Chuck's house to get him to
help with the chores. Chuck's wife came to the door.
"I'm sorry, Clarence," she said. "Chuck has a
bad cold, and he won't be able to help you. *with any chores*

**Add**

Clarence worried and wondered how he could
do Farmer McCoy's chores all by himself.
Suddenly, he had an idea. *"That's it!" he shouted.*

**Add**

## Discuss

1. Was it a good idea for Sabina to move the information about Clarence's promise? Explain your answer.
2. Did Sabina add any important information when she expanded her sentences? Do you think she improved her story?

## Try Your Hand

Now revise your first draft.

**A. Read Your First Draft** As you read your tall tale, think about your audience and your purpose. Read your tall tale silently or to a partner to see whether it is complete and well organized. Ask yourself or your partner the questions in the box.

| Responding and Revising Strategies | |
| --- | --- |
| ✔ **Respond** <br> **Ask yourself or a partner:** | ✔ **Revise** <br> **Try these solutions:** |
| ◆ Have I followed my story plan and given my tall tale a solid beginning, middle, and ending? | ◆ **Revise** your tall tale so each part adds to the whole story. |
| ◆ Have I written dialogue that expresses my characters' ideas and moves the story along? | ◆ **Add** dialogue to make the tall tale seem more real. |
| ◆ Have I made my exaggerations funny and surprising? | ◆ **Stretch** your ideas to make your audience laugh. |
| ◆ Have I expanded sentences when I can? | ◆ **Add** information creatively to make your writing lively and concise. See the **Revising Workshop** on page 403. |

**B. Make Your Changes** If the answer to any question in the box is *no,* try the solution. Use the **Editor's Marks** to show your changes.

**C. Review Your Tall Tale Again** Decide whether there is anything else you want to revise. Keep revising your tall tale until you feel that it is well organized and complete.

**EDITOR'S MARKS**

∧ Add something.

⊱ Cut something.

◌ Move something.

⌃ Replace something.

Save your revised tall tale in your *Writer's Notebook.* You will use it when you proofread your tale.

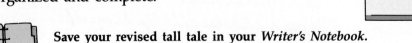

# Revising Workshop
## Expanding Sentences

Good writers sometimes use lots of details to make their writing interesting. To present details in a smooth and graceful way, writers sometimes expand sentences by adding prepositional phrases. Read these groups of sentences. Look at the underlined phrases.

1.  **a.** Clarence trained the pigs to clean the table.
    **b.** He also taught them to eat leftovers.
2.  **a.** Clarence trained the pigs to clean the table <u>after dinner</u>.
    **b.** He also taught them to eat leftovers <u>without making a mess</u>.
3.  **a.** Clarence trained the cows to milk themselves.
    **b.** They used foot pedals.
4.  **a.** <u>Through patience</u>, Clarence trained the cows to milk themselves.
    **b.** They used foot pedals <u>on their milking machines</u>.

In each pair of examples the writer has expanded the sentences by adding prepositional phrases that give more details. The added details make the writing more complete and more interesting.

## Practice

Expand each sentence by adding prepositional phrases. Begin your phrases with prepositions such as *above, after, before, between, during, from, on, over, through, under, up,* and *without.* Make your writing as interesting as you can.

1.  Dina woke up with the biggest appetite she had ever had.
2.  She raced downstairs to see what she could eat.
3.  Dina's mother filled a bowl with cereal.
4.  She added sliced banana and raisins.
5.  Dina was still starving.
6.  She wolfed down pancakes and French toast.
7.  She was still tempted by the yogurt and honey.
8.  She had eaten enough for three people.
9.  She continued to eat.
10. She was finally full.

# 4 Proofreading
## Tall Tale

Sabina used the **Writer's Guide** and the **Editor's Marks** to proofread her tall tale. Look at what she did.

### Writer's Guide

**Proofreading Checklist**

☑ Check for errors in capitalization and punctuation, especially in quotations.

☑ Be sure that all your paragraphs are indented, especially when a new quotation begins.

☑ Check your grammar.

☑ Circle any words you think are misspelled.

⇨ For proofreading help, use the **Writer's Handbook.**

> ¶ "How do you feed the pigs? Farmer McCoy asked.
>   "I lead them into the (dinning) _dining_ room after dinner." said Clarence. "The food is served on plates made of stale bread." he explained. "And the pigs eat the stale bread with all of the leftovers so that there's no mess.

### EDITOR'S MARKS

≡ Capitalize.

⊙ Add a period.

∧ Add something.

⋏ Add a comma.

ⱽⱽ Add quotation marks.

✂ Cut something.

⋀ Replace something.

↝ Transpose.

◯ Spell correctly.

¶ Indent paragraph.

／ Make a lowercase letter.

## Discuss

1. Look at Sabina's proofread tall tale. What kinds of mistakes did she make?
2. Why didn't Sabina capitalize *and* in Clarence's second quotation?

## Try Your Hand

**Proofread Your Tall Tale**   Now use the **Writer's Guide** and the **Editor's Marks** to proofread your tall tale.

Save your corrected tall tale in your *Writer's Notebook*. You will use it when you publish your tall tale.

WRITING PROCESS

# 5 Publishing
## Tall Tale

Sabina made a clean copy of her tall tale and checked it to make sure that she had not left anything out. Then she presented it in her class's tall-tale storytelling contest. You can read Sabina's finished tall tale on pages 34–35 of the **Writer's Handbook.**

Here's how Sabina and her classmates published their tall tales.

**Writer's Guide**

**Publishing Checklist**

☑ Make a clean copy of your tall tale.

☑ Check to see that nothing has been left out.

☑ Check that there are no mistakes.

☑ Share your tall tale in a special way.

1. First they planned a tall-tale storytelling contest for the class. They made arrangements to record each other's performances on tape.

2. When Sabina presented her tall tale to her classmates, she exaggerated her presentation to match the tale. See the **Tips for Performing in and Listening to Stories and Plays** on page 407 for some ideas on how to tell a tale.

**3.** The students awarded prizes for the presentations. They made up categories like Best Overall Tale, Funniest Tale, Most Outrageous Tale, Most Surprising Ending, and Most Energetic Performance.

**4.** They asked another class if they would enjoy a presentation of the prize-winning tall tales from the contest. Sabina and her classmates presented a live performance.

## Discuss

**1.** Why is hearing someone present a tall tale usually more fun than just reading it?

**2.** How is presenting a tall tale in a storytelling contest different from presenting an oral research report or a book report?

## Try Your Hand

**Publish Your Tall Tale**   Follow the checklist in the **Writer's Guide.** If possible, present your tall tale in a class storytelling contest or try one of these ideas for sharing your tale.

◆ Make a book of tall tales grouped by theme—biggest, smallest, strongest, hottest, fastest, and so on. Add illustrations and present the book to the library.

◆ Make an audiotape of your tall tales. Give or lend a copy of the tape to the community library, a senior citizens' center, or a children's hospital.

# Listening and Speaking
## Tips for Performing in and Listening to Stories and Plays

1. If you are going to perform, take time to plan thoroughly. Think about the characters in the story or play. How would they look? How would they sound? How would they move?
2. Work with the director. Decide on the look, voice, and manner for the character whom you will play. Then "stay in character." Do not suddenly become yourself again.
3. Exaggerate what you say and do. The more feeling you express with your voice and actions, the more your audience will be swept along by your presentation.
4. When you are in the audience, look at and listen to how the performers use their voices and bodies to tell their stories.
5. Let your appreciation show—applause and laughter are the two sweetest sounds for any entertainer.

# Writing in the Content Areas

Use what you learned to write a humorous paragraph that contains exaggerations. One way to publish your paragraph is to read it aloud to your class or to a group of younger children. Use one of these ideas or an idea of your own.

**Writer's Guide**

When you write, remember the stages of the Writing Process.
- Prewriting
- Drafting
- Responding and Revising
- Proofreading
- Publishing

## Mathematics

Invent an enormous pet. Tell how big your pet is by using similes and metaphors. Compare it to other things the same size, such as buildings, bridges, or mountains. Include descriptions of things such as your pet's food bowl, bed, and house.

## Physical Education

Imagine how a 3-inch-tall character and his or her friends would play basketball, baseball, or another popular sport or game. Write a tall tale about this game. Describe the equipment used and tell where and how the game is played.

## Social Studies

Look at some maps. Choose a lake or a mountain that has an interesting name, such as "Lost Lake" or "Bald Mountain." Make up a story that tells how the name came about.

## Literature and Art

What would happen if a giant statue came to life? Think of a big statue of a person, such as the statue of Abraham Lincoln in the Lincoln Memorial or the Statue of Liberty in New York Harbor. Write a story in which such a statue comes to life. Tell about one of its adventures.

# CONNECTING

## WRITING ↔ LANGUAGE

Story writers use special marks to show dialogue—people's exact words. As you read this beginning to a tall tale, can you identify the marks that are used to set off a character's words from the rest of the story?

## Aunt Gussie and Her Dog

The biggest dog I ever saw was my Aunt Gussie's Great Dane, Tiny. I'll never forget the day I first laid eyes on him.

"Here's Tiny," Aunt Gussie said, as if introducing him to me. "Of course, I don't think you'll find him the least bit tiny."

I didn't. Tiny was so big he had to stoop as he walked through the front door.

Uncle Jim laughed when he saw my reaction. "Tiny was quite a puppy," he explained. "Most puppies like to have a ticking clock nearby to remind them of their mother's heartbeat. Tiny was so big he snuggled up beside our grandfather clock!"

◆ **Punctuation Marks in a Tall Tale** The highlighted sections of this story show dialogue—people's exact words—and punctuation marks. Quotation marks and commas set dialogue apart from other words in a story.

◆ **Language Focus: Mechanics Wrap-up** The following lessons will help you use dialogue and punctuation marks in your own writing.

# 1 Capitalization and End Punctuation in Sentences

◆ **FOCUS**  Every sentence begins with a capital letter and ends with a punctuation mark.

Remember that there are four types of sentences.

1. Bonzo Bailey was a famous clown.   declarative
2. Begin juggling with your left hand.   imperative
3. What was Bailey's favorite trick?   interrogative
4. How he could juggle plates!   exclamatory

The first word of a sentence begins with a capital letter. A declarative and an imperative sentence both end with a **period.** An interrogative sentence ends with a **question mark.** An exclamatory sentence ends with an **exclamation point.**

## Guided Practice

**A.** Tell whether a period, a question mark, or an exclamation point should end each sentence.

1. Clown College is located in Sarasota, Florida
2. How I'd love to go there
3. Do you know any clown tricks
4. I know how to juggle rings
5. Learn to walk on stilts in your spare time
6. What a difficult feat that is
7. Keep trying
8. Will you try to walk on stilts
9. I would rather learn how to ride a unicycle
10. Did you know that clowning around required this much work

---

**THINK AND REMEMBER**

◆ Remember to begin each sentence with a capital letter.
◆ Remember to use the correct punctuation mark at the end of each sentence.

---

# Independent Practice

**B. Using Correct End Punctuation**   Write each sentence, using the correct end punctuation.

**11.** Stilts were first invented for practical reasons

MODEL ⟩ Stilts were first invented for practical reasons.

**12.** People used them to walk through swamps

**13.** How very tall that clown is

**14.** Do you think he's walking on stilts

**15.** How does he do it

**16.** Go over and ask him to show us

**17.** Oh no, he's falling down

**18.** That's how he gets off his stilts

**19.** Let's help him get back on

**20.** First, stand on one stilt

**21.** Would you hand me the other stilt

**22.** Now, he's ready to march in the parade

**C. Proofreading: Capitalizing and Punctuating Sentences**   Write each sentence. Capitalize the first word of each sentence, and add the correct end punctuation.

**23.** the best circuses have clowns, acrobats, and animals

MODEL ⟩ The best circuses have clowns, acrobats, and animals.

**24.** the most famous circus was Phineas T. Barnum's

**25.** his circus was called The Greatest Show on Earth

**26.** what was Barnum's motto

**27.** think big

**28.** tell me more about Barnum's circus

**29.** it had a large elephant called Jumbo

**30.** how impressive Jumbo was

**31.** didn't Jumbo belong to the London Zoo

**32.** mr. Barnum paid $10,000 for Jumbo and $20,000 to move him

**33.** what a wonderful thing a circus is

# Application — Writing

**Advertisement**   Imagine that you are a clown who entertains at children's parties. Write an advertisement for your services to post on community bulletin boards. The advertisement should convince parents to hire you for their children's parties. Use the four types of sentences in your writing. Begin each sentence with a capital letter. End each sentence with the correct punctuation mark.

# 2 Commas Within Sentences

◆ FOCUS   A comma is used to separate one part of a sentence from another to make the meaning clear.

A comma tells the reader to pause briefly. Commas also help make the meaning of sentences clear. This chart shows rules for comma usage.

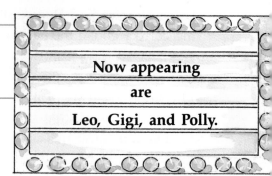

Now appearing
are
**Leo, Gigi, and Polly.**

| Rule | Example |
|---|---|
| Use a comma to separate words in a series of three or more items. | We saw a puppet show, mimes, and musicians in the park. |
| Use a comma to separate three or more simple subjects in a compound subject. | Leo, Gigi, and Polly are famous puppet characters. |
| Use a comma to separate three or more simple predicates in a compound predicate. | The children shout, laugh, and applaud at the puppet show. |
| Use a comma to separate simple sentences in a compound sentence. | Every culture has puppets, and people everywhere love them. |
| Use a comma to separate the name of the day from the date, the date from the year, and the year from words that follow. | We saw a wonderful puppet show on Saturday, June 25, 1988, in the park. |
| Use a comma to separate the name of a city from the name of a state. Use a comma after the state name to separate it from words that follow. | Will the theater company travel to Portland, Oregon, this summer? |
| Use a comma after words such as *yes, no,* and *well* when they begin a sentence. | Yes, the puppet show will travel through three states. |
| Use a comma to set off the name of a person who is spoken to directly in a sentence. | Susan, would you like to make your own puppets? |

## Guided Practice

**A.** Tell where you would add commas to these sentences.

1. There will be a puppet show on April 5 1991 at my house.
2. Shadow puppets are very old but they are still popular.
3. They are made in India from paper wood and paint.
4. Anna do you see how parts of the paper are cut out?
5. I found this puppet when I was in Tucson Arizona.

> **THINK AND REMEMBER**
> ♦ Follow the rules in the chart to use commas correctly.

## Independent Practice

**B. Using Commas in Sentences** Write each sentence, adding commas where they are needed.

6. Leo tell me about your life as a puppet.
   MODEL> Leo, tell me about your life as a puppet.
7. My wife's name is Gigi and my baby's name is Polly.
8. We travel to England France and Italy.
9. Yes I am a star in three countries.
10. We will perform on Sunday July 14 1991 at the fair.
11. Gigi will you perform in Dallas Texas this summer?

**C. Proofreading: Rewriting Sentences with Commas** Rewrite each sentence, using commas correctly.

12. The puppets were large and, they were heavy.
    MODEL> The puppets were large, and they were heavy.
13. The puppets were made from, clay, rock, and wood.
14. Well can we buy puppets, there today?
15. My aunt bought a marionette on Thursday, February 15 1990 in Mexico City, Mexico.
16. Please Mrs. Juarez, can we put on a puppet show?
17. Lily Dave, and Marcie can help you.

## Application — Writing and Speaking

**Puppet Play** Write one short scene of a puppet play. Name the puppets, and have them address each other directly in their lines. Use commas correctly in your sentences. Perform your scene.

# 3 Capitalization of Proper Nouns, Proper Adjectives, and *I*

◆ **FOCUS** Proper nouns, proper adjectives, and the pronoun *I* are always capitalized.

Remember that a proper noun names a particular person, place, or thing. The proper nouns in these sentences are in color.

1. Ms. Julie will meet me on Citrus Street Saturday .
2. We will go to the Talent Review in Tampa .

| Proper Nouns | | |
|---|---|---|
| People, Pets | Barnard Maxwell | Tippy |
| Titles, Initials | Ms. Lolly S. Lewis | Dr. Forest Bebee |
| Places | Lake Erie Magnolia Street | Albany, New York Australia |
| Days, Months | Monday | October |
| Holidays | Halloween | Father's Day |
| Languages | Spanish | German |
| Buildings | Sears Tower | Buckingham Palace |
| Businesses | Balloons, Inc. | Paxton's Apparel |

A proper adjective is an adjective formed from a proper noun. A proper adjective is always capitalized.

3. F rench poodle    4. N orth A merican continent

The pronoun *I* is always capitalized.

5. I tell jokes.    6. Mary and I watch variety shows.

## Guided Practice

**A.** Write the following. Capitalize words which should be capitalized.

1. lake superior
2. st. louis
3. taconic parkway
4. jay levin
5. vermont
6. south american cities
7. mt. rushmore
8. memorial day
9. gulf of mexico
10. november

## Independent Practice

**B. Capitalizing Proper Nouns and Proper Adjectives**   Write each word or group of words, using capital letters where they are needed.

11. james madison

MODEL ▷ James Madison

12. isle of wight
13. central park
14. alex p. keaton
15. atlantic ocean
16. salt lake city

17. russian doll
18. canadian rockies
19. tuesday
20. tall tom's cafe
21. asia

22. rhode island
23. hayes theater
24. fourth of july
25. chinese silk
26. alaska

**C. Revising: Capitalizing Proper Nouns, Proper Adjectives, and *I* in Sentences**   Write each sentence, using capital letters where needed.

27. In the old days i worked at the long street theater.

MODEL ▷ In the old days I worked at the Long Street Theater.

28. My mother and i went every saturday night.
29. We saw charlie oaks, the chinese acrobats, and more.
30. In june, july, and august, we visited cape cod.
31. We attended performances at the melody tent.
32. George b. Adwell and i watched silent movies.
33. i took singing and dancing lessons at the carlson school of the arts in pittsburgh, pennsylvania.
34. In august i'm going to teach at the einhorn performing arts camp in concord, new hampshire.

## Application — Writing

**Show Program**   Imagine that you could arrange a performance by all your favorite actors, comedians, and musicians. Write a program for your show. Include the names of the performers and a description of what each will do. Be sure to capitalize proper nouns and proper adjectives correctly. Share your program with your classmates.

# 4 Abbreviations

◆ **FOCUS**  Most abbreviations begin with a capital
letter and are followed by a period.

Remember that an abbreviation is the shortened
form of a word. People often use abbreviations in
lists or addresses.

One kind of abbreviation is an initial. An initial is
the first letter of a person's name. An initial is always
a capital letter. Initials, and most other abbreviations,
are followed by periods.

Cartoon Festival
Sat., Sept. 21
The Funny Co.
1275 Quakertown Ave.

1. F.D.R. = Franklin Delano Roosevelt
2. John Q. Adams = John Quincy Adams

| Common Abbreviations of Proper Nouns | | | | | | |
|---|---|---|---|---|---|---|
| **Titles** | Ms. | Mrs. | Mr. | Dr. | Jr. | Sr. |
| **Days** | Sun. Mon. | Tues. | Wed. | Thurs. | Fri. | Sat. |
| **Addresses** | Street: St. Road: Rd. | Route: Rt./Rte. Avenue: Ave. | Drive: Dr. Boulevard: Blvd. | | | |
| **Months** | Jan. Feb. Sept. Oct. (May, June, and July are never abbreviated.) | Mar. Nov. | Apr. Dec. | Aug. | | |
| **Times** | before noon: A.M. | | after noon: P.M. | | | |
| **Business Words** | Company: Co. Corporation: Corp. | | Incorporated: Inc. Department: Dept. | | | |

## Guided Practice

**A.** Give the abbreviation for each underlined word.

1. <u>Sunday</u>, <u>June</u> 26
2. 101 Grassy Plain <u>Street</u>
3. Taft Bank, <u>Incorporated</u>
4. Thomas <u>Hopkins</u> Gallaudet
5. <u>Arthur Conan</u> Doyle
6. <u>Route</u> 33
7. Hollywood <u>Boulevard</u>
8. <u>February</u> 14
9. <u>Department</u> of the Interior
10. <u>Wednesday</u>, <u>March</u> 2

## Independent Practice

**B. Writing Abbreviations**   Read the following items. Write abbreviations for the underlined words.

11. George Washington Carver
MODEL > G. W. Carver
12. 1600 Pennsylvania Avenue
13. Elizabeth Barrett Browning
14. Perfect Poetry, Incorporated
15. Mister Todd Lincoln
16. East Side Drive
17. Sock and Stocking Department
18. Colorado Boulevard
19. April 24
20. Doctor Alana Robertson

21. Friday the 13th
22. Erik Eriksson, Senior
23. 4:18 before noon
24. The Grain Company
25. Route 66
26. 2:20 after noon
27. Martin Luther King, Junior
28. Willamette Street
29. October 31

**C. Proofreading: Writing Abbreviations and Initials in Addresses**
Rewrite each address. Use the correct abbreviations and initials for the underlined words.

30. Mister James Elsworth Barber
1150 South Street
Houston, TX 77024
MODEL > Mr. James E. Barber
1150 South St.
Houston, TX 77024
31. Doctor Erasmo Perez
4168 Holiday Road
Bloomington, IN 47400

32. Lester Chin, Junior
301 Underwood Avenue
Old Saybrook, CT 06854
33. Heather McLaughlin
92 Turquoise Drive
Casa Grande, AZ 85222
34. Chuckles Toy Corporation
Complaint Department
22 Giggles Drive
Manchester, NH 03287

## Application — Writing

**Personal Profile**   Imagine that you are filling out an application for a job in a comedy shop. Write your name, address, school name, birthday, and any other information about yourself. Be sure to capitalize and punctuate each abbreviation and initial correctly.

# 5 Letters

◆**FOCUS**   The parts of a friendly letter and a business letter follow rules of capitalization and punctuation.

The five parts of a friendly letter are the **heading**, the **greeting**, the **body**, the **closing**, and the **signature**. Read this friendly letter to Anna. Notice which parts of the letter are capitalized and how punctuation is used.

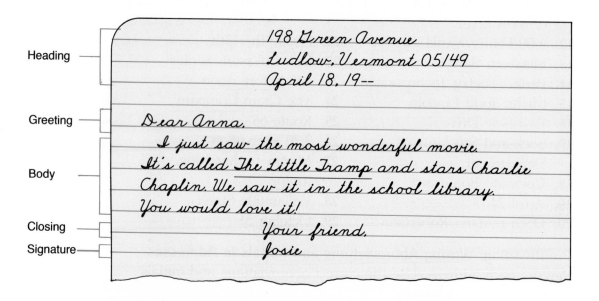

| Friendly Letter Parts | Capitalization | Comma |
|---|---|---|
| Heading | street, city state, month | between city and state between day and year |
| Greeting | first word | after last word |
| Closing | first word | after last word |
| Signature | proper noun | |

The six parts of a business letter are the **heading**, the **inside address**, the **greeting**, the **body**, the **closing**, and the **signature**. Notice that a colon follows the greeting in the business letter on page 419.

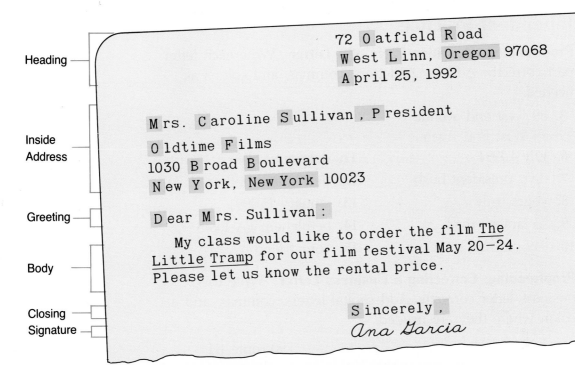

| Business Letter Parts | Capitalization | Punctuation |
|---|---|---|
| Heading | street, city state, month | comma between city and state and between day and year |
| Inside Address | proper name, title company name street, city | comma between name and title comma between city and state |
| Greeting | first word proper name, title | colon (:) after last word |
| Closing | first word | comma after last word |
| Signature | proper name | |

## Guided Practice

**A.** Tell how you would write each letter part correctly.

1. your son
2. dear funny film factory
3. with love
4. portland Maine

**THINK AND REMEMBER**
- Follow the rules in the charts to capitalize and to punctuate friendly letters and business letters correctly.

# Independent Practice

**B. Proofreading: Rewriting Parts of a Letter**   Write each letter part correctly. Add capital letters, commas, and colons as needed.

**5.** 89 west end avenue

MODEL> 89 West End Avenue

**6.** July 4 1991

**7.** dear president bush

**8.** yours truly

**9.** 55 lantern road

**10.** 949 old mill drive

**11.** dear aunt elsie

**12.** dear grandmother

**13.** january 15 1991

**14.** bethlehem PA 10818

**15.** your friend

**C. Proofreading: Correcting a Business Letter**   Write this business letter correctly. Add capital letters, commas, and a colon where they are needed.

> 790 route 111
> des moines Iowa 50336
> september 21 19– –

mr paul conrad manager
cape cod florist
78 seaside road
chatham Massachusetts 02658

dear mr. conrad

   Please send a bouquet of spring flowers to Mrs. Jennifer Flagg of Chatham. Mrs. Flagg lives at 12 West Harbor Lane, just around the corner from your shop. The enclosed check will cover the cost. Remember to sign the card "Your grandson, Sam."

> with thanks

> sam young

## Application — Writing

**Friendly Letter**   Write a friendly letter to a friend or a relative. Tell about something funny that you saw happen. Include the five parts of a friendly letter. Be sure to capitalize and punctuate each part of your letter correctly.

# 6 Envelopes

◆ **FOCUS** The return address and the receiver's address on an envelope follow rules of capitalization and punctuation.

The **return address** on an envelope is the name and address of the person or the business sending the letter. The **receiver's address** is the name and address of the receiver of the letter.

All proper names and abbreviations are capitalized. Remember that most abbreviations end with periods. Use the postal abbreviation for a state's name. This special abbreviation has two capital letters and no period.

## Postal Abbreviations

| | | | |
|---|---|---|---|
| Alabama AL | Idaho ID | Missouri MO | Pennsylvania PA |
| Alaska AK | Illinois IL | Montana MT | Rhode Island RI |
| Arizona AZ | Indiana IN | Nebraska NE | South Carolina SC |
| Arkansas AR | Iowa IA | Nevada NV | South Dakota SD |
| California CA | Kansas KS | New Hampshire NH | Tennessee TN |
| Colorado CO | Kentucky KY | New Jersey NJ | Texas TX |
| Connecticut CT | Louisiana LA | New Mexico NM | Utah UT |
| Delaware DE | Maine ME | New York NY | Vermont VT |
| District of | Maryland MD | North Carolina NC | Virginia VA |
|   Columbia DC | Massachusetts MA | North Dakota ND | Washington WA |
| Florida FL | Michigan MI | Ohio OH | West Virginia WV |
| Georgia GA | Minnesota MN | Oklahoma OK | Wisconsin WI |
| Hawaii HI | Mississippi MS | Oregon OR | Wyoming WY |

# Guided Practice

**A.** Tell how you would correct these parts of an envelope. Point out places where capital letters, commas, and periods are needed.

1. mr. cary kubek
2. ms mary ellen hatch
3. raleigh, n.c. 27605
4. miss kelly archer
5. 81 quabbin rd.
6. box top offers, inc
7. 799 thimblemill rd
8. leo battista, jr.
9. 52 wilson st
10. cambridge ma 02138
11. star records corp
12. 46 hail blvd
13. toy bird co
14. dr adam robert kendail

---

**THINK AND REMEMBER**

◆ Remember to capitalize proper names and abbreviations in addresses.
◆ Use postal abbreviations in addresses.

---

# Independent Practice

**B. Proofreading: Rewriting Parts of Envelope Addresses**
Rewrite these parts of an envelope. Use capital letters, commas, and periods as needed.

15. 15206 ripplewind dr
    MODEL  15206 Ripplewind Dr.

16. mrs betsy spath
17. gainesville fl 32605
18. dr fox cough drops inc
19. danny hilmer
20. maurice's book shop
21. houston tx 77068
22. miss nancy o'neill
23. 405 van buren st
24. orient map corp
25. petaluma ca 94953
26. 520 eleanor st
27. mrs helen bitner
28. west haven ct 06516
29. mr william stokes
30. miss jessica hartman
31. 5822 strasburg road
32. mercerville nj 08619
33. bonfield refrigeration corp
34. dr amanda bloor
35. huntington ny 11743
36. 694 creekwood dr
37. philadelphia pa 19145

**C. Proofreading: Correcting an Envelope**  Draw each envelope on another sheet of paper. Write the addresses correctly, adding capital letters, commas, and periods as needed.

38.
ms erica webb
1117 pond dr
east rutherford nj 07073

gardener's magazine co
12 rocky rd
indianapolis in 46268

39.
thelma toad
7 mushroom ave
milwaukee wi 53203

mr jay hopper
frog supply co
23 spring st
richmond va 23261

40.
putt putt power boats
17 ocean pines dr
ocean city md 21842

mr marvin dingy
818 rte 9
cincinnati ohio 45212

## Application — Writing

**Envelope**  Send your favorite joke to a classmate or relative. First, write the joke on a sheet of paper. Then, address an envelope. Use correct capitalization and punctuation as you write. Mail your joke.

# 7 Outlines

◆**FOCUS** An outline follows rules of capitalization and punctuation.

Writers need to organize their facts before they can write reports. One way to do this is to make an outline. Study this outline. Notice the placement of capital letters and periods.

*The Career of Mickey Mouse*
I. *Mickey's early years*
   A. *First drawn by Walt Disney on a train*
   B. *First film was silent, Plane Crazy*
   C. *First talkie, Steamboat Willie*
II. *Mickey's years as a movie star*
   A. *1930–1931 starred in 21 films*
   B. *Played fire chief, cowboy, soldier*
   C. *Won awards for films*
III. *Mickey's later years*
   A. *Mickey Mouse Club television show in 1955*
   B. *Celebrated 60th birthday in 1988*

In an outline, the **main topic,** or main idea, of each paragraph in a report is next to a Roman numeral. The details that support the main idea of each paragraph are **subtopics.** They are listed next to the capital letters under each Roman numeral.

A period follows each Roman numeral and each letter. Each main topic and subtopic begins with a capital letter. Main topics and subtopics need not be complete sentences. Notice that the subtopics are indented. The outline also has a title. Each important word in the title is capitalized.

## Guided Practice

**A.** Tell how to correct the mistakes in this outline.

silly superstitions
I   Good Luck
   a. hang up a horseshoe
   d. find a four-leaf clover
2   bad luck
A   open an umbrella inside the house
b   break a mirror

## Independent Practice

**B. Proofreading Outlines**   Rewrite these outlines. Use correct capitalization, punctuation, and indentation.

superman/clark kent

1   how he came to earth
a   born on planet Krypton
c   rocket escaped Krypton before it was destroyed
d   landed in Smallville, Illinois
2   life on Earth
a   worked as a reporter
b   had secret life fighting crime
c   known for being mild mannered
III super powers
b   can fly
c   can see through walls

snoopy, the wonder dog

I   early life
a   created by Charles M. Schulz
b   Born at Daisy Hill Puppy Farm
2   middle years
A   lives with Charlie Brown
b   sleeps on top of doghouse
C   World War I fighter pilot
3   most Recent events
a   lunar module named after him
B   met Woodstock, bird friend

## Application — Writing

**Outline**   Choose a character from a book, a television show, or a comic strip. Imagine that you will write a report about the character. Write an outline about the character's life. Use correct capitalization and punctuation in your outline.

# 8 Titles

◆ **FOCUS**   The title of a written work follows rules of capitalization and punctuation.

When you write, you should either underline or put quotation marks around a title. Underline the titles of books and movies and the names of newspapers and magazines. In printed material these titles appear in italics.

1. I look forward to reading <u>Parade</u>.   **magazine**
2. <u>Charlotte's Web</u> is about friendship.   **book**
3. Do you read the <u>Boston Globe</u>?   **newspaper**

Use quotation marks around the titles of stories, magazine articles, essays, songs, or poems.

4. "The Midnight Ride of Paul Revere" tells about the Revolutionary War.   **poem**
5. "The Fox and the Crow" has a moral.   **story**

Notice that all the important words in a title are capitalized. Do not capitalize *a, an, the, in, to,* and similar short words unless they are the first word of the title.

**Amy:** *Did you see the movie The Secret Garden?*

**Jan:** *The book was better.*

## Guided Practice

**A.** Tell whether each title should be underlined or enclosed in quotation marks.

1. Where the Sidewalk Ends (poem)
2. Where the Sidewalk Ends (book)
3. The Lion, the Witch and the Wardrobe (book)
4. Jokes Seldom Survive Translation (essay)
5. How the Fox Stole Fire from the Fireflies (story)
6. Cobblestone (magazine)

---

**THINK AND REMEMBER**

◆ Remember to capitalize the important words in a title.
◆ Underline the titles of books, movies, newspapers, and magazines.
◆ Use quotation marks around the titles of stories, magazine articles, essays, songs, or poems.

---

# Independent Practice

**B. Punctuating Titles**   Write each title. Underline or use quotation marks as needed.

   **7.** A Chair for My Brother (book)

MODEL <u>A Chair for My Brother</u>

   **8.** The Sidewalks of New York (song)

   **9.** The Bat (poem)

  **10.** The Bat Poet (book)

  **11.** The Thing About Monty the Pineapple (story)

  **12.** Maurice Sendak: King of All the Wild Things (essay)

  **13.** The Amazing, Riderless, Runaway Tricycle (movie)

  **14.** Ebony Jr! (magazine)

  **15.** The Oregonian (newspaper)

  **16.** Riding in My Car (song)

**C. Proofreading Titles**   Write each title. Capitalize the important words. Underline or use quotation marks as needed.

  **17.** highlights for children (magazine)

MODEL <u>Highlights for Children</u>

  **18.** the mummy, the will, and the crypt (book)

  **19.** nate the great and the snowy trail (book)

  **20.** the bear went over the mountain (song)

  **21.** why nobody pets the lion at the zoo (poem)

  **22.** the wizard of oz (movie)

  **23.** national geographic world (magazine)

  **24.** ranger rick (magazine)

  **25.** a taste of peace (essay)

  **26.** dear mr. henshaw (book)

  **27.** stopping by woods on a snowy evening (poem)

  **28.** daily mail (newspaper)

  **29.** lifeprints (magazine)

  **30.** the foolish frog (song)

# Application — Writing

**Titles**   Invent titles for a book, a story, a song, a movie, and a magazine that you might enjoy. Choose words that will interest students your age. Capitalize and punctuate your titles correctly.

# 9 Direct Quotations and Dialogue

◆ **FOCUS**   A direct quotation follows rules of capitalization and punctuation.

A **direct quotation** gives the exact words someone says. Notice how these sentences are capitalized and punctuated.

1. "Please tell me a joke," Luisa requested.
2. Jake said, "Knock, knock."
3. "Who's there?" Luisa inquired.
4. Jake exclaimed, "Who!"
5. "Who who?" asked Luisa.
6. "Hey, there's an owl in here!" shouted Jake.
7. "That," stated Luisa, "is the worst joke I've ever heard."
8. "I don't think so," said Jake. "It made me laugh."

Here are some guidelines to use when you write direct quotations.

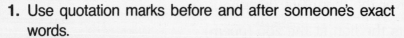

1. Use quotation marks before and after someone's exact words.
2. Capitalize the first word of a quotation, and put a punctuation mark for the quotation before the last quotation mark.
3. When the words that identify the speaker come before the quotation, put a comma after them. See sentence 2.
4. When the words that identify the speaker come after the quotation, use a comma, a question mark, or an exclamation point to separate the quotation from the rest of the sentence. See sentences 1, 3, and 6.
5. Sometimes a quotation is divided. If the quotation is one sentence, use a comma before and after the words that identify the speaker. See sentence 7.
6. If a divided quotation is two sentences, use a comma before and a period after the words that identify the speaker. Capitalize the first word of the second sentence. See sentence 8.
7. Begin a new paragraph when the speaker changes.

# Guided Practice

**A.** Identify where the quotation marks belong.

1. Why do you like knock-knock jokes? asked Tad.
2. I like to surprise people, answered Jake.
3. Mina complained, They're such corny jokes.
4. Most knock-knock jokes are puns, explained Mrs. Pool.
5. A pun is a play on words, she continued.

> **THINK AND REMEMBER**
> ◆ Remember to use quotation marks and proper punctuation to write direct quotations.

# Independent Practice

**B. Using Quotation Marks** Write each sentence. Add quotation marks where they are needed.

6. I'd like to tell you my favorite jokes, announced Al.
   MODEL "I'd like to tell you my favorite jokes," announced Al.
7. What looks like a duck, he began, but is not a duck?
8. Could it be a picture of a duck? I guessed.
9. You're a genius! said Al.
10. Please go on, I replied, but be quick about it.
11. What time is it when an elephant sits on your fence? Al giggled.
12. Time to buy a new fence, Michele suggested.

**C. Proofreading Quotations** Write each sentence. Use quotation marks, capital letters, and punctuation correctly.

13. Class, welcome the comedian Joe Lee said Mr. Ellis.
    MODEL "Class, welcome the comedian Joe Lee," said Mr. Ellis.
14. Gene asked how can I become a better comedian
15. That's very simple said Mr. Lee tell better jokes
16. Seriously Mr. Lee added, a straight man might help.
17. Lisa wondered what's a straight man
18. A straight man is a comedian's partner said Mr. Lee

# Application — Writing and Speaking

**Knock-Knock Joke** Make up a knock-knock joke for your classmates. Write your joke in direct quotation form. Be sure to use capital letters, quotation marks, commas, and periods as needed. Then, with a partner, read your joke aloud to the class.

# Building Vocabulary
## Idioms

An idiom is a phrase that has a special meaning. The special meaning is different from the ordinary meaning of the separate words. For example, the idiom *a bull in a china shop* does not refer to what is happening in the cartoon at the top of the page. The idiom means "a person who is clumsy and says or does upsetting things."

You probably hear many idioms every day. The idiom *to put my foot in my mouth* means "to say the wrong thing." The idiom *to have a heart of gold* means "to be extremely good and kind." Most idioms are used only in informal language.

Some idioms have interesting histories. For example, *to spin a yarn*

originally meant "to repair ropes." While sailors of long ago repaired ropes, they tried to make the time go faster by telling stories. Eventually the expression *to spin a yarn* became an idiom that means "to tell a story."

You can usually guess the meaning of an idiom by looking at the context in which it is used. Guess the meaning of the underlined idiom in the following sentence.

It took so long for your letter to arrive that it seemed like <u>a month of Sundays.</u>

From the context clue *took so long,* you probably guessed that *a month of Sundays* means "a very long time."

# Reading Practice

Read each sentence. Study the underlined idioms. Then, write the letter of the sentence that correctly defines the idiom.

1. On Halloween Beth told Anita her costume was <u>for the birds</u>.
   a. decorated with too many feathers    b. not very good
2. "You must be <u>off your rocker</u> to think your costume is scary," Beth said.
   a. crazy                               b. tired
3. When Billy Gonzalez saw Anita in her costume, <u>his hair stood on end</u>.
   a. He combed his hair back.    b. He was terrified.
4. Beth said, "After seeing Billy's reaction to your costume, I guess I have to <u>eat humble pie</u>."
   a. admit my mistake and apologize    b. take you out for dessert

# Writing Practice

Rewrite the sentences. Replace the underlined idioms with formal language that means the same thing.

5. When Anita entered the Halloween costume contest, she <u>had butterflies in her stomach</u>.
6. Beth said something to her, but <u>it went in one ear and out the other</u>.
7. The judge said, "I know you want to hear the results, but you'll have to <u>hold your horses</u>."
8. "I'll never win," said Anita, "so I might as well <u>throw in the towel</u> and stop hoping."
9. Anita was <u>in seventh heaven</u> when she won first prize for the scariest costume.

# Project

Choose five idioms that do not appear in this lesson. Write each idiom and its definition. On one sheet of paper, write sentences using the idioms. On another sheet of paper, write sentences using formal language that expresses the same meanings as the idioms. Show your two sets of sentences to a classmate. See if your partner can match each sentence that has an idiom with the sentence that uses formal language to express the same idea.

# Language Enrichment
## Mechanics Wrap-up

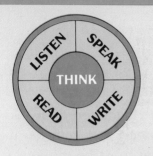

Use what you know about mechanics to complete these activities.

### In the Top Ten

Make a list of movies you'd like to see, books you hope to read, and current songs that you enjoy. Write their titles, using correct capitalization and punctuation. Then compare your list with classmates' lists. Make a class graph showing the most popular movies, books, and songs.

### Fan Mail

Everyone needs a fan. Place the names of all your classmates in a hat. Then choose a name. Write a short friendly letter to the person whose name you chose. Tell the person what you like about him or her. Don't sign your letter! To make yourself anonymous, type your letter. Your teacher will deliver the letters. Then sit back and enjoy your fan mail!

### Writing in the Air

Work with a partner to write a short conversation that the two of you might have together. Include punctuation marks such as periods, commas, question marks, and exclamation points. Then work together to come up with an appropriate hand or body signal to stand for each punctuation mark. For example, you might jump up and down to show an exclamation point. Practice performing your conversation, inserting punctuation-mark signals where they belong. After you perform your conversation for a small group of classmates, talk about what things people do as part of regular conversation to show the changes and feelings that punctuation shows in writing.

*That's great!*

# CONNECTING
## LANGUAGE ⟷ WRITING

In this unit you reviewed mechanics skills—capitalization, punctuation, and abbreviations. These are language skills that need to be learned for writing. They are not used in speaking and listening.

◆ **Using Mechanics in Your Writing** When you use mechanics correctly, your writing will be easier for readers to follow. For example, paragraph indentation lets the reader know when you are writing about a new topic. An exclamation point announces a strong idea or feeling. Capital letters indicate a specific person, place, or thing.

Pay special attention to the mechanics you use as you do these activities.

*Mr. Jones, you have a frog in your throat.*

 **Listening In**

Work in groups of three or four. One of you should choose a passage from a book to read aloud. This person should read slowly and clearly, allowing everyone time to write down what is being read. When everyone is finished, compare what you have written. Notice that you all used mechanics in different ways. Decide which copies are punctuated clearly, correctly, and in a meaningful way. Notice that there is often more than one right way. Finally, compare your writing to the original work. Write several sentences telling what this activity taught you about mechanics.

 **It Might Happen Like This . . .**

You learned about idioms on the **Building Vocabulary** pages. Now have fun with this idiom activity.

Choose three or more idioms that make you laugh. Then draw a quick sketch of what each idiom might look like if it could really happen. On the back of each sketch, write the idiom and its meaning. Also, use the idiom in a sentence.

Show your sketches to a classmate. See if he or she can guess the idiom.

# Unit Checkup

| Think Back | Think Ahead |
|---|---|
| ◆ What did you learn about humorous stories? What did you do to write one? | ◆ How will what you learned about humorous stories help you when you read a tall tale? |
| | ◆ How will exaggeration help you write a humorous story? A comic strip? A descriptive paragraph? |
| ◆ What did you learn about punctuation marks and capitalization? How did that help you with what you wrote? | ◆ What is one way you can use punctuation marks and capitalization to improve your writing? |

**Humorous Stories** *pages 392–394*

Look at the story map. Then follow the directions.

The Cat's Out of the Bag

**Characters**
Martin
Martin's mother

**Setting**
a neighborhood in a modern city

**Problem That Starts the Story**
Martin's mother dislikes Martin's cat, Itsy Bitsy.

**Additional Events**
1. Martin hides Itsy Bitsy in the closet.
2. Martin secretly feeds his cat, but Itsy Bitsy refuses to eat anything but beef.
3. Martin watches in horror as Itsy Bitsy becomes huge.

**Turning Point**
Itsy Bitsy gets away.

**Conclusion**
Martin finds Itsy Bitsy at grocery store, where the cat is happy and safe.

1. Write the time and place of the story.
2. State the problem the main character has in the story.
3. Write what will probably be humorous about the story.

## Figures of Speech   *pages 393–394*

Read the following sentences. Revise the sentences by adding a simile, metaphor, or exaggeration to each description.

4. Itsy Bitsy was a large cat with white fur and big black spots.
5. Martin's cat was very fond of beef.
6. As Martin struggled to hold his cat, Itsy Bitsy howled loudly.

## Using Details and Dialogue to Create Good Characters   *page 395*

Write a sentence about each character described. Use dialogue, details of action, or comments from other characters.

7. Barney's friends admired his boldness.
8. Mr. Boone was feared by most of the neighborhood children.
9. Cassandra told her brother he couldn't borrow her book.
10. Sam begged his mother to let him go swimming.

## The Writing Process   *pages 396–406*

11. Which topic for a tall tale would you cross off your list?
    a. a funny one          b. an exaggerated one
    c. one with ordinary people
12. How should information for a tall tale be gathered?
    a. List exaggerated events.    b. List facts.
    c. Draw pictures.
13. Why should the writer make a story map for a tall tale?
    a. to lengthen the story    b. to fit pictures with the story
    c. to show how the beginning, middle, and ending fit together
14. What is the major consideration for presenting a tall tale?
    a. to inform        b. to entertain        c. to persuade

## Capitalization and End Punctuation in Sentences ✓
*pages 410–411*

Write each sentence. Capitalize the first word of each sentence, and add the correct end punctuation.

15. lucius loved telling jokes to his friends
16. what kind of jokes did he like to tell
17. the one he just told me was so funny
18. tell me his latest joke
19. "hot dogs wear sweaters when they're chili dogs"

## Commas Within Sentences √ *pages 412–413*

Write each sentence, adding commas where they are needed.

20. Tom George and Juan wanted to earn some extra money.
21. They decided to collect old newspapers sell them to a recycling company and split the money they made.
22. Tom why do you wear a helmet when you go out to collect papers?
23. Well there are a lot of big dogs on my block.
24. You certainly look silly but I guess it works.

## Capitalization of Proper Nouns, Proper Adjectives, and *I*  *pages 414–415*

Write each sentence, using capital letters where needed.

25. Some tall tales feature paul bunyan.
26. He had a swedish ox, and he lived in wisconsin.
27. Babe could eat enough food to cover all of texas!
28. She could drink enough water to dry up lake superior!
29. On columbus day i read a book of tall tales.

## Abbreviations  *pages 416–417*

Read the following items. Write abbreviations for the underlined words.

30. San Mateo <u>Avenue</u>
31. William <u>Penn</u> Rogers
32. The Humor Book <u>Company</u>
33. <u>Friday</u>, <u>April</u> 10
34. 9:15 <u>before</u> <u>noon</u>
35. <u>year</u>

## Letters  *pages 418–420*

Write each letter part correctly. Add capital letters, commas, and colons as needed.

36. dear pedro
37. jorge rodriguez
38. dear mayor andrews
39. 28 oak Street
40. san Antonio texas 78203
41. Yours truly

## Envelopes  *pages 421–423*

Rewrite these parts of an envelope. Use capital letters, abbreviations, commas, and periods.

42. nancy thompson
43. jokes incorporated
44. mr william jackson senior
45. denver co 80219
46. 399 red river road
47. mobile al 36610

## Outlines   *pages 424–425*

Rewrite the outline below. Use correct capitalization, punctuation, and indentation.

will rogers, the humorist
1 his early years
a born 1879 near oologah ok of cherokee indian parents
b left school in 1898 and became a cowboy
2 his career as entertainer
a made first stage appearance in 1905 in new york city
b started movie career in 1918

## Titles √  *pages 426–427*

Write each title. Capitalize the important words. Underline or use quotation marks as needed.

**48.** a wrinkle in time (book)
**49.** pippi longstocking (book)
**50.** my greatest adventure in reading (article)
**51.** louisville courier (newspaper)
**52.** cinderella (movie)

## Direct Quotations and Dialogue √ *pages 428–429*

Write each sentence. Use quotation marks, capital letters, and punctuation correctly.

**53.** Mike said his friend Joey let's buy this book.
**54.** Why do you want that book asked Mike.
**55.** There are some funny riddles in it responded Joey
**56.** Look at this one exclaimed Joey.
**57.** You're right his friend said This is a great book

## Idioms √  *pages 430–431*

Write the letter of the item that correctly defines each idiom.

**58.** Karen and Jimmy were late, and their brother told them to <u>shake a leg</u> or he would leave them behind.
　　**a.** hurry up　　　　　　**b.** wave their feet
**59.** "When we get there," Jimmy warned Karen, "<u>hold your tongue</u> about our surprise."
　　**a.** grab your mouth　　　**b.** don't talk
**60.** They almost didn't make it to their aunt's house because the directions were <u>over their heads</u>.
　　**a.** in the sky　　　　　　**b.** too complicated

# Cumulative Review

## Sentences   *pages 34–37*

Write each group of words that is a sentence. Then, write *declarative, interrogative, imperative,* or *exclamatory.* Write *not a sentence* for each group of words that is not a sentence.

1. Homing pigeons have been used to carry special messages.
2. Their speed.
3. The Romans used homing pigeons to send important news.
4. How quickly the birds must have flown!
5. Find a book about the history of homing pigeons.
6. Why are they called homing pigeons?
7. Can fly thousands of miles and find their way home.

## Subjects and Predicates   *pages 38–43*

Add a simple subject to each group of words. Underline the simple predicate. Write the new sentence.

8. _____ grabbed the message pad.
9. The _____ on the telephone gave him a message.
10. The _____ on the table ran out of ink.
11. The _____ of the caller was very soft.
12. _____ took the message for his sister.
13. _____ used the last sheet on the pad.
14. Sometimes, the _____ rang too much.

## Avoiding Sentence Fragments and Run-on Sentences   *pages 52–53*

Make each sentence fragment a sentence by adding a subject or a predicate as needed.

15. The meaning of highway signs.
16. Is important for drivers to remember.
17. The speed limit.
18. Warn travelers about highway construction.
19. Is posted on some signs.
20. The advertisements along a highway.
21. Carry great meaning for careful observers.
22. Special paint.
23. Helps people see signs clearly at night.
24. Special symbols on signs.
25. Are useful to people visiting from foreign countries.

## Common and Proper Nouns   *pages 94–95*

Write each sentence. Underline the common nouns once.
Underline the proper nouns twice.

26. A mural is being built near Josephina's home.
27. She watches the workers draw the outline of several objects for the mural.
28. One worker walks to his truck to get some buckets of paint.
29. Another person begins to apply red paint to some parts of the wall.
30. Josephina is wondering why the mural is being created on one wall of Uncle Pepe's grocery store.
31. Her uncle tells her that he wants to make the neighborhood more beautiful.

## Singular and Plural Possessive Nouns   *pages 100–103*

Rewrite each sentence. Replace the underlined words with a singular possessive noun or a plural possessive noun.

32. The exhibits of the art fair inspired us.
33. The skill of each artist was impressive.
34. At the beginning of the fair, there were only a few people in attendance.
35. Several food stands of businesses sold hot dogs, lemonade, balloons, and souvenirs.
36. They proudly wore shirts decorated with the designs of their parents.
37. The balloons belonging to the children floated gaily above the crowd.
38. The artists in the fair sold most of their work.

## Action and Linking Verbs   *pages 138–141*

Write an action verb or a linking verb to complete each sentence. Then, write *action verb* or *linking verb*.

39. Betty _____ proud of her calf, Belle.
40. She _____ Belle in the county fair this summer.
41. Betty's cousin _____ a great sign for Belle to carry at the fair.
42. The contest judges _____ her calf for any signs of disease.
43. Betty's father _____ her lots of advice about raising calves.
44. Belle's sign _____ so unusual that it helped her win.

## Irregular Verbs  *pages 184–187*

Write the correct form of the verb in parentheses ( ).

45. We met an astronaut who has _____ on a space shuttle. (ride)
46. He _____ the journey into space was a memorable one. (say)
47. Trips into outer space have _____ us curious about living on another planet someday. (make)
48. What kinds of meals were _____ by the astronauts as they zoomed through space? (eat)
49. The astronaut's description sounded as if he had _____ better-looking meals. (see)
50. Astronauts have _____ thousands of miles in space shuttles. (fly)

## Easily Confused Verb Pairs  *pages 190–191*

Read each sentence. Write the correct verb in parentheses.

51. The librarian _____ a pile of books on various topics at each table. (sat, set)
52. The students _____ at long tables by the window. (sat, set)
53. If you know how to use the card catalogue, you _____ find several other books about a topic. (can, may)
54. There are many available, but you _____ each select just one of them. (can, may)
55. You will _____ the arrangement of the Dewey Decimal System. (teach, learn)
56. This visit will _____ you how to use the card catalogue. (teach, learn)

## Subject or Object Pronoun?  *pages 234–235*

Read each sentence. Write the correct pronoun in parentheses.
Then write *subject pronoun* or *object pronoun*.

57. The lady next door waved to Pete and (I, me).
58. (We, Us) visited her every day.
59. She offered (they, them) something to eat.
60. The lady stumbled, and (they, them) rushed to her side.
61. Pete and (I, me) helped her to a chair.
62. She thanked (they, them) for their assistance.
63. Without (they, them), she might have injured herself.

## Reflexive Pronouns   *pages 238–239*

Write each sentence. Use a reflexive pronoun in the blank.

**64.** We tested _____ to get ready for the history contest.

**65.** The team _____ has six members.

**66.** The opposing team members have probably prepared _____ too.

**67.** My older brother helped me time _____ while I studied.

**68.** He will be one of the judges, so he _____ has to know all the answers to the questions.

**69.** When the judges begin the contest, we caution _____ to listen carefully to each question.

## Agreement of Pronouns   *pages 240–241*

Write each sentence, choosing a pronoun to fill each blank. Underline the pronoun's antecedent.

**70.** Sequoya was a Cherokee Indian. _____ invented a form of writing for Cherokees to use.

**71.** Like most Indians of Sequoya's day, Cherokees did not use writing to communicate. _____ depended mainly on speaking and pictures.

**72.** For 12 years Sequoya worked on a system of writing. _____ had to fit his people's ways and traditions, so he created special symbols.

**73.** In 1821 he completed the new written language for Cherokees. Now _____ could publish and read their own newspapers and books.

**74.** Sequoya's search for a suitable written language made him a great man among his people. _____ speak of him proudly as a hero.

## Adjectives   *pages 274–275*

Write the adjectives in each sentence. Then write whether they tell *what kind* or *how many*. Use commas to separate two adjectives that tell *what kind*.

**75.** Benito went camping with his three brothers.

**76.** At night they slept beneath a moonlit starry sky.

**77.** The stars seemed like a thousand nightlights.

**78.** A wolf howled, and Benito shivered in his green pajamas.

**79.** He clutched the warm cozy blanket and hoped this night would pass quickly.

## Comparison with Adjectives   *pages 282–287*
Write the correct form of the adjective in parentheses ( ).

80. Sharon was known for being _____ than most children her age. (bold)
81. She loved to climb the _____ tree in her neighborhood. (tall)
82. None of her friends had _____ courage than Sharon did. (great)
83. Sharon discovered that climbing mountains is _____ than climbing trees. (dangerous)
84. Of all the exciting experiences in her life, she felt _____ when she climbed mountains. (alive)
85. Being on a mountain felt _____ than being at sea level. (good)
86. The view from the mountain she climbed last summer was the _____ sight she had ever seen. (breathtaking)

## Adverbs   *pages 320–321*
Write the sentences. Underline the adverb in each, and draw an arrow to the verb it describes.

87. Bob carefully drew a line on the piece of lumber.

88. His father held the saw firmly and cut the lumber.

89. Place the lumber there until we are ready to use it.

90. Bob applied the glue smoothly to the wood.

91. The new table will be finished soon.

92. Bob helped his father put the tools away.

93. They looked approvingly at the table they had made.

## Adverb or Adjective?   *pages 328–329*
Write the word in parentheses that correctly completes each sentence.

94. Wanda and Carla _____ displayed the jewelry they had made. (neat, neatly)
95. They were _____ to see lots of people at the fair. (glad, gladly)
96. They sold _____ colored necklaces. (bright, brightly)
97. One woman said they had _____ skill with jewelry. (remarkable, remarkably)
98. The two girls _____ split the money they made. (even, evenly)

## Prepositions and Prepositional Phrases   *pages 366–369*

Write each sentence. Underline each prepositional phrase once. Underline the preposition twice.

99. President Benito Juarez gave more power to poor Mexicans.

100. Under his leadership, Mexico became a more democratic nation.

101. Many wealthy Mexicans disliked his decisions, and they fought him with all their might.

102. President Juarez defeated a bloody takeover attempt by France's ruler.

103. There were many fierce battles between the Mexicans and the French.

104. The French army finally withdrew from Mexico and peace returned.

105. Juarez continued his presidency until his death.

## Conjunctions   *pages 372–373*

Write the conjunction in each sentence.

106. Our school is having a history fair, and each of us will bring objects from home.

107. Stella has borrowed an old clock and a pair of embroidered suspenders from her great-uncle.

108. Timothy will bring a collection of postage stamps, but they will be sealed in plastic.

109. Tanya wants to display her grandmother's set of dolls or her grandfather's photograph album.

110. I asked my parents to let me bring their old records, but they would not part with them.

111. Felicia plans to display a lace shawl, a handmade blouse, and a pretty skirt from Mexico.

## Interjections   *pages 374–375*

Write each sentence. Use an interjection to fill the blank.

112. _____ ! My parents agreed to buy me an Irish setter puppy.

113. _____ ! The puppy is lively.

114. _____ ! His teeth are as sharp as little razor blades!

115. _____ ! I'd better put the registration papers in a safe place.

116. _____ ! I can't find the papers.

# STUDY SKILLS

## Contents

# 1 Finding Words in a Dictionary

A **dictionary** is a book that lists words and gives their pronunciations and their meanings. The words listed in a dictionary are arranged in **alphabetical order,** from *A* through *Z.*

astronaut    fantasy    magnificent    special    zoology

All the words that begin with the same letter are listed together. They are alphabetized by the second letter in each word. If the first two letters are the same, they are alphabetized by the third letter. If the first three are the same, the fourth letter is used, and so on.

| dance | deposit | distant | donate | draft |
|-------|---------|---------|--------|-------|
| madras | magazine | malaria | marvel | mast |
| space | spaghetti | span | spare | spatula |

How can you find words quickly? Think of the dictionary as being divided into three parts, like this.

| **front** | **middle** | **back** |
|-----------|------------|----------|
| abcde | fghijklmnop | qrstuvwxyz |

Decide whether the word you want is in the front, the middle, or the back of the dictionary, and open to that section. Then turn forward or back until you have found the word.

Every word listed in the dictionary is called an **entry word.** The **guide words** at the top of each page show which words are defined on that page. The guide word on the left is the first entry word on the page, and the one on the right is the last. All the words listed on that page come between the guide words alphabetically.

## Practice

**A.** Write *front, middle,* or *back* to show in which part of a dictionary these words would be found.

1. wallet
   MODEL ⟩ back
2. orbit
3. shy

4. wand
5. gander
6. cargo
7. theory

**B.** List the words in each group in alphabetical order. Underline the entry words in each group that would be found on a page with the guide words *pencil* and *plastic.*

8. plaster, parrot, plan
   MODEL ⟩ parrot, plan, plaster
9. pinch, phone, prance
10. penguin, pecan, pendant

11. pelican, planet, ply
12. phantom, pearl, phrase
13. plaid, playful, plaque
14. phoenix, pharynx, platypus

# 2 Using a Dictionary Entry

Each entry word in the dictionary is followed by its **definition,** or meaning. A word often has more than one related meaning. Sometimes, however, two words that are spelled alike are listed separately. They are called **homographs,** words that are spelled the same but that have different meanings and sometimes different pronunciations. The definition may include an **example sentence** that shows how to use the entry word.

> **con·tent¹** [kən·tent'] *adj.* Happy with what one is or has. Are you *content* with your new neighborhood?
>
> **con·tent²** [kon'tent] *n.* The amount contained. This cereal has a high sugar *content.*

The dictionary also tells what **part of speech** a word is, or how it is used. The abbreviation *adj.* in the model above shows that, as defined there, the word *content* is an adjective. A list of abbreviations for the parts of speech is often found at the front of a dictionary.

| | | | | | |
|---|---|---|---|---|---|
| *n.* | noun | *adj.* | adjective | *conj.* | conjunction |
| *pron.* | pronoun | *adv.* | adverb | *interj.* | interjection |
| *v.* | verb | *prep.* | preposition | | |

## Practice

Use these entries to answer the following questions.

> **scent** [sent]  **1** *n.* A particular odor or smell.  **2** *n.* Perfume.  **3** *v.* To make fragrant.  **4** *n.* The sense of smell.
>
> **scour¹** [skour] *v.* To clean by scrubbing hard.
>
> **scour²** [skour] *v.* To make a complete search.

1. How many definitions are given for the word *scent?*
   MODEL > four
2. Which words are spelled alike but listed separately? What are they called?
3. Write the number of the definition for *scent* as it is used in each of the following sentences.
      This perfumed oil *scents* the whole house.
      The *scent* Gina wears has a fruity fragrance.
      The cooking spices give the kitchen a sweet *scent.*
4. What part of speech is *scent* when it means "to make fragrant"?
5. Which homograph of *scour* is used in this sentence?
      I will scour the neighborhood until I find my puppy.

# 3 Using a Dictionary for Pronunciation

Each entry word in the dictionary is followed by a combination of letters and symbols called a **phonetic respelling**. The phonetic respelling shows how to pronounce the word. It is usually set between brackets [ ] and is divided into syllables. A **syllable** is a word part with only one vowel sound. In many dictionaries, dots and accent marks are used to separate the syllables in the respelling.

**sec·re·tar·y** [sek′rə·ter′ē]

An **accent mark** is a mark in the respelling that shows how much stress each syllable gets. A syllable with a **primary accent** (′) is pronounced with more force than a syllable with a **secondary accent** (′).

By looking at an entry word, you can see how it is spelled. You can also tell if it has any **variant,** or alternate, spellings. Note this variant spelling.

**ad·vis·er** or **ad·vis·or** [ad·vī′zər] *n.*

A **pronunciation key** explaining the symbols in the respelling appears frequently on the dictionary pages.

| | | | | | | | |
|---|---|---|---|---|---|---|---|
| **a** | add | **i** | it | $\overset{\smile}{oo}$ | took | **oi** | oil |
| **ā** | ace | **ī** | ice | $\overline{oo}$ | pool | **ou** | pout |
| **â** | care | **o** | odd | **u** | up | **ng** | ring |
| **ä** | palm | **ō** | open | **û** | burn | **th** | thin |
| **e** | end | **ô** | order | **yoo** | fuse | **t̶h̶** | this |
| **ē** | equal | | | | | **zh** | vision |

ə = { a in *above*   e in *sicken*   i in *possible*
      { o in *melon*   u in *circus*

## Practice

**A.** Write the words for these phonetic respellings.

1. ik·sīt′
   MODEL > excite
2. mag′ə·zēn′
3. doo′əl
4. pûr′fikt
5. gaj′it
6. ak′rə·bat′
7. in′də·kāt′
8. kûr′ij
9. ruf′əl
10. kə·rekt′
11. fiz′i·kəl

**B.** Divide these words into syllables. Write their primary and secondary accents as well. Use a dictionary for help.

12. muddy
    MODEL > mud′dy
13. accident
14. serious
15. bellowing
16. invite
17. finally
18. irritation
19. bicycle
20. recognize

# 4 Using a Title Page, a Copyright Page, and a Table of Contents

Most books have special pages in the front that help you find information about the book quickly and easily. The **title page,** for example, gives the title of the book. It also gives the author, the publisher, and the city in which the book was published. The **copyright page** tells when the book was published. It sometimes lists the titles of other books from which material was used with permission.

The **table of contents** lists units, chapters, or stories in the order in which they appear in the book. It also lists the pages on which all parts of the book begin. Study this title page, copyright page, and table of contents.

Animal
Builders

by
Lew Tyson

Greenleaf Publishing Company
New York

**title page**

Copyright © 1989
by Greenleaf Publishing Company
Acknowledgments
Penny Press, from *Animal Life*
   by Jane Soo.
All rights reserved.
Printed in the United States of America.

**copyright page**

| CONTENTS | |
|---|---|
| 1. Mound Builders | 1 |
| 2. Weavers and Platform Builders | 15 |
| 3. Silk Spinners | 28 |
| 4. Mud Users | 40 |
| 5. Makers of Paper | 54 |
| 6. Diggers | 68 |
| Glossary | 80 |
| Index | 86 |

**table of contents**

## Practice

Use the example pages to answer the following questions.

1. What is the title of the book?

MODEL  Animal Builders

2. Who is its author?
3. What company published the book?
4. When and where was the book published?
5. What is the name of the book from which the publisher borrowed some material?
6. Who wrote the book from which information was taken?
7. How many chapters does <u>Animal Builders</u> have?
8. Which chapter discusses animals that build with mud?
9. On what page does the chapter on mound builders end?

# 5 Using a Glossary and an Index

The **glossary** of a book gives the meanings of some words used in the book that might be unfamiliar. The words in a glossary are listed in alphabetical order.

The **index** lists the topics in a book in alphabetical order and gives the numbers of the pages on which each topic appears. Some topics are divided into **subtopics,** which are smaller divisions of the topic. The index also lists page numbers for each subtopic. Study these parts of a glossary and an index that might appear in *Animal Builders.*

glossary

**marmot** [mär′mət]. A rodent with a bushy tail; a prairie dog.
**membrane** [mem′brān′]. A thin, soft sheet or layer.
**miniature** [min′(ē·)ə·chər]. A tiny copy.
**mound** [mound]. A small pile of stones, twigs, or earth.
**mud dauber** [dôb′er]. Wasp. A wasp that makes mud cells on a solid base.

index

**Warren** (underground nest), 70−72
**Wasps,** 40−59
  cocoons, 48−50
  little hornets, 55−56
  mud daubers, 40−43
  nests, 45
  yellow jackets, 57−59. *See also*
    **Yellow jackets**
  wax users. *See* **Bees**
**Weaverbirds,** 18−23
**Webs.** *See* **Spiderwebs**
**Woodpeckers,** 73−87
  acorn storage, 76

## Practice

Use the example pages to answer the following questions.

1. What is another name for a prairie dog?
   MODEL⟩ marmot
2. What is the pronunciation of that name?
3. Under what topic would you look for information on webs?
4. What animal builds with mud?
5. Which glossary entry has the fewest syllables?
6. On what pages would you find information about wasps' cocoons?
7. What pages would you read to get general information about woodpeckers?
8. Where would you look to read about how woodpeckers store acorns?
9. Under which heading would you look to find information about wax users?
10. On how many pages could you read about little hornets?
11. Which glossary word means "a tiny copy"?
12. How many pages have information on weaverbirds?

STUDY SKILLS

# 6 Using the Dewey Decimal System

All the nonfiction books in the library are arranged according to the **Dewey Decimal System.** In this system, books are numbered and organized by subject area. There are 10 main subject areas. Next to each main subject in the box are topics or kinds of books that might be found under that heading. Each book has a **call number.** The call number tells you what subject area the book is about. The numbers in the box are **call numbers.** They are the numbers between which books in that subject area will be found. Libraries use call numbers to organize the books on the shelves. Each shelf is labeled with the call numbers of the books it contains.

| | |
|---|---|
| 000–099 | General Works (encyclopedias, atlases, newspapers) |
| 100–199 | Philosophy (ideas about the meaning of life, psychology) |
| 200–299 | Religion (world religions, mythology) |
| 300–399 | Social Science (government, law, business, education) |
| 400–499 | Language (dictionaries, grammar books) |
| 500–599 | Pure Science (mathematics, chemistry, plants, animals) |
| 600–699 | Applied Science (how-to books, engineering, radio) |
| 700–799 | Arts and Recreation (music, art, sports, hobbies) |
| 800–899 | Literature (poems, plays, essays) |
| 900–999 | History (travel, geography, biography) |

## Practice

Write the range of Dewey Decimal System numbers in which each of the following selections might appear.

1. *The Psychology of Teaching*
   MODEL ▷ 100–199
2. *A Dictionary for Elementary School*
3. "A Country School" (poem)
4. *Religious Schools in America*
5. *Laws for Public School Education*
6. *McGuffey's Reader, An Early School Reader*
7. *A Fifth-Grade Class Visits the White House* (true photo story)
8. *The American School in the 1800's*
9. "My Boyhood in a One-Room Schoolhouse" (essay)
10. *Modern School Mathematics*
11. *A Book of Synonyms and Antonyms*
12. *Activities for Physical Education*
13. "Computers in the Classroom" (encyclopedia article)
14. *The Day Kids Taught Teachers* (play)

# 7 Using the Card Catalogue

Every library has a **card catalogue,** which is usually stored in a cabinet of small drawers. Every book in the library is given a **call number** and is listed on a card in at least two of the drawers. The cards are arranged alphabetically. Guide letters on each drawer tell what cards are inside.

The card catalogue contains three kinds of cards. The **title card** lists the title of the book first. The **author card** lists the author's last name first. The **subject card** lists the subject of the book first. The subject card is useful when you want a book on a subject but do not have a particular book in mind. Every book in the library has an author card and a title card. Most books have at least one subject card.

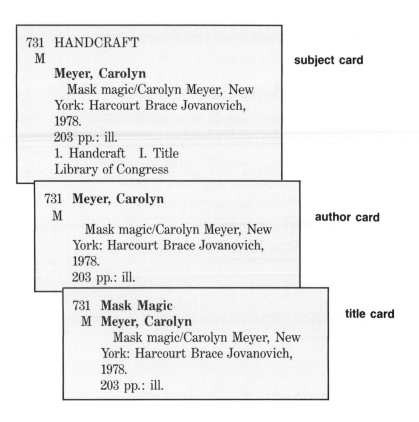

731 HANDCRAFT
M
    **Meyer, Carolyn**
      Mask magic/Carolyn Meyer, New York: Harcourt Brace Jovanovich, 1978.
    203 pp.: ill.
    1. Handcraft  I. Title
Library of Congress

**subject card**

731 **Meyer, Carolyn**
M
      Mask magic/Carolyn Meyer, New York: Harcourt Brace Jovanovich, 1978.
    203 pp.: ill.

**author card**

731 **Mask Magic**
M  **Meyer, Carolyn**
      Mask magic/Carolyn Meyer, New York: Harcourt Brace Jovanovich, 1978.
    203 pp.: ill.

**title card**

## Practice

Use the example cards to answer these questions.

**1.** What is the title of the book?

MODEL  Mask Magic

**2.** Who is the author?

**3.** Which company published the book?

**4.** In what year was the book published?

**5.** Where was the book published?

**6.** How many pages are in the book?

**7.** Under what subject is the book listed?

**8.** What is the call number of the book?

# 8 Identifying Kinds of Books

The library contains reading materials of all kinds. To make it easy for people to find the types of books they want, the library is divided into sections. The most common sections are the fiction section, the nonfiction section, the biography section, and the reference section. Some libraries also have sections for juvenile, or children's, books and for videocassettes and audiocassettes.

A **fiction** book tells a story of imaginary people and events. Fiction books are arranged alphabetically by the author's last name. A **nonfiction** book tells about real people, events, or things. Most nonfiction books are numbered and shelved according to the Dewey Decimal System.

A **biography** is a special kind of nonfiction book. It tells the story of a person's life. Biographies are shelved in alphabetical order by the subject's last name.

**Reference** books such as dictionaries, encyclopedias, almanacs, and atlases are kept together in one section. Because reference books are used so often by so many people, most libraries do not allow people to check them out.

## Practice

Name the section of the library in which you would find each of the following materials.

1. an encyclopedia article about the planet Mars
MODEL > reference

2. the novel *Norby, the Mixed-Up Robot*
3. the life story of Robert Goddard, inventor of the rocket
4. a book of words that have come into the English language since the beginning of the Space Age
5. a book of star maps
6. a book called *The Origin and Early History of Communication Satellites in Space*
7. a recent dictionary
8. a book about the history of space travel
9. a novel about a time traveler who sails with Christopher Columbus in 1492
10. a book about the life of astronomer Maria Mitchell
11. a book called *The First American Astronauts*
12. a book called *Mystery of the Missing Moon Rocks*
13. a book of photographs taken by astronauts during space flights
14. a book in which a famous astronaut tells about her experiences
15. a book about the time when an invading army of Martians took over the earth

# 9 Using an Encyclopedia

Most encyclopedias are sets of books. Each book is called a **volume,** and the volumes in the set are arranged in alphabetical order. The first letter or letters of the subjects in each volume are printed on the spine, or side, of the book. A set of encyclopedias might look like this.

Encyclopedia entries are called **articles.** They are arranged in each book alphabetically by topic. At the top of every page are **guide words,** which indicate the starting letters of articles found on that page. **Key words,** or terms important to an understanding of a particular article, are often printed in italic or boldface type.

## Practice

**A.** Use the example encyclopedias to identify the number of the volume in which you would find each of these subjects.

1. whales
   MODEL▷ 21
2. Greenland
3. zebras
4. crocodiles
5. India
6. cattle
7. George Washington
8. baseball
9. kangaroos
10. electricity
11. diamonds
12. telephones
13. helicopters

**B.** Write the key word or words you would look up to get information about each topic.

14. the early life of Abraham Lincoln
    MODEL▷ Lincoln, Abraham
15. the first automobile
16. the care and feeding of boa constrictors
17. the history of the telescope
18. rivers of China
19. the routes of the Pony Express
20. the leading export of Mexico
21. the Sonora Desert region in Arizona

# 10 Using an Encyclopedia Index

An encyclopedia **index,** often the last volume in the set, lists all the entries in the encyclopedia in alphabetical order. The index gives several types of information. For a long article, subtopics of the article are listed with their page numbers. Since information about a particular subject is often found in more than one encyclopedia article, the index also gives **cross-references** to articles on related topics. Other related topics may also be listed at the end of an index entry.

---

**Australia** A:764 with illustrations
  Agriculture
    Australia (Agriculture) A:768
    Sheep S:255 (table) S:254
  Education
    Australia (Education) A:772
  Government
    Australia (Government) A:771
    Parliament P:98
  History
    Australia (History) A:764−766
  Natural resources
    Australia (Natural resources) A:773−774
    Conservation C:558
    Mining M:334
  People
    Australia (People) A:779
    Aborigines A:101
  Physical features
    Great Barrier Reef G:775
*See also* Great Britain

---

## Practice

Use the example index to answer the questions.

1. In what volume and on what pages would you find information on sheep in Australia?

   MODEL ⟩ Volume S, pages 254 and 255

2. In what volume does information about the Great Barrier Reef appear?

3. In what volume can you find a history of Australia?

4. In what volumes does information about natural resources in Australia appear?

5. Besides the main article on Australia, what other entry related to Australia would be included in Volume A?

6. What cross-reference is given in this example index?

7. According to the index, how many subtopics are included in the article on Australia?

# 11 Using an Atlas and an Almanac

An **atlas** is a reference book that contains maps of every region of the world. Many maps show a region's size, population, and natural features. In addition, most atlases also show national and regional capitals and major traffic routes. Study this example atlas page.

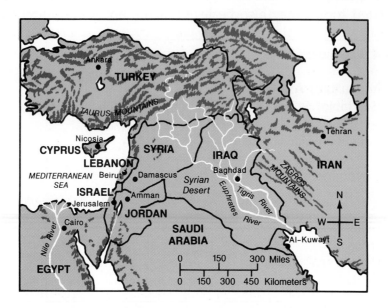

Almanacs are found in the reference section of a library, along with dictionaries, encyclopedias, and atlases. An **almanac** is a book that provides the latest information on many topics, including famous people, business trends, government, and sports. Items of cultural interest are also included. Most almanacs are revised and reprinted every year to be kept up to date.

## Practice

Write *atlas* or *almanac* as a source of the answer to each item.

1. Which country is further north, Poland or Hungary?
   MODEL> atlas
2. What was the rainfall in Florida in 1987?
3. How far is it from Denver to Los Angeles?
4. How high is Mount Whitney?
5. Who is the governor of Hawaii?
6. How many newspapers were published in the United States in 1988?
7. Which rivers are located in the state of Indiana?
8. Which horse won the Kentucky Derby last year?
9. Who are the two U.S. senators from your state?
10. In which state is the Liberty Bell located?
11. Which state is larger, Alabama or Mississippi?
12. What are the major highways connecting Minneapolis and St. Paul?

# 12 Using Periodicals and Newspapers

Magazines and other publications appearing at regular intervals are called **periodicals.** They may be printed weekly, monthly, every few months, or yearly. Because periodicals are published in less time than books, they usually offer more up-to-date information. In libraries, back issues of magazines and other periodicals are usually put into large jackets or boxes and are located by volume number.

A newspaper is a periodical that contains three main kinds of articles: news stories, feature articles, and editorials. A **news story** gives information about a specific event. It reports what happened, who was involved, when and where the event took place, and how it happened. News stories present facts, not opinions.

A **feature article** also presents facts. Unlike a news story, a feature article concentrates on only one or two angles, or parts, of a story. However, it covers these parts in more depth than is appropriate for a news story. For example, an article about the visit of the President to the state capital would be a news story. An article about the President's home and family would be a feature article. There are differences between newspaper feature articles and magazine articles as well. Usually newspaper feature articles are shorter and cover a narrower scope of information than articles in magazines.

An **editorial** is an article expressing an opinion, usually that of the newspaper's editors, about an issue in the news. Editorials are published regularly in most newspapers.

Many newspapers print news stories, features, and editorials in separate sections. Many papers also offer special sections on business, lifestyles and homes, and sports.

## Practice

Write *magazine* or *newspaper* to identify the source of each of these articles. For a newspaper, write what kind of article each one is.

1. an article giving an opinion on a proposed state highway
   MODEL newspaper—editorial
2. an article on a sinkhole that swallowed a local post office yesterday
3. an article on bills that became laws in several states during the past year
4. an article expressing the editor's feelings about building an expressway around the city
5. an article about yesterday's local warehouse fire
6. an article about the problems of the owner of the burned warehouse
7. an article on the alarming number of fires occurring in the nation's warehouses
8. an article on celebrities who make campaign appearances in support of candidates
9. an article on a singer who performed at a rally in town yesterday

# 13 Taking Notes

**Taking notes** is a way of recording information. Writing reports and studying for tests are always made easier with a good set of notes. Read these tips for taking notes.

| Tips for Taking Notes |
| --- |
| 1. Take notes on 3" × 5" cards. Later you can arrange them in any order you wish. |
| 2. Write the topic of each card first. Then add the facts. |
| 3. Paraphrase, or record the writer's ideas in your own words. Use phrases instead of sentences. Write key words. |
| 4. List the source from which you obtained the facts you wrote. |

When you have finished taking notes, make sure you can read and understand what you have written. Remember to write the name of the source from which you took notes.

## Practice

**A.** Use this paragraph in writing answers to the questions.

> The giant sequoia is the world's largest tree. It belongs to the cypress family and grows in forests in the Sierra Nevada Mountains of California. The General Sherman Tree is the largest sequoia. It grows in Sequoia National Park in California. It is 9.8 m (32.3 ft.) through the middle and 30.9 m (101.5 ft.) around the bottom. Some sequoias are taller than this one, but none are as wide.

1. What is the main subject of the paragraph?
   MODEL⟩ giant sequoias
2. What are some facts you might want to remember?
3. What key words will help you remember these facts?
4. What details tell more about these facts?
5. Which words in your notes could be abbreviated?

**B.** Take some notes on this paragraph.

> Apes are primates. Their arms, fingers, and toes are long, and their hairy bodies have no tails. Apes have flat nails on their fingers and toes. They can hold their arms sideways and move them in circles. They have large brains and may be the smartest animals other than human beings.

# 14 Writing an Outline

When you plan a report, it is wise to write an outline first. An **outline** gives the main ideas and the important details of a topic. It organizes the facts so your report will make sense. Study this example outline.

| Dinosaurs | |
|---|---|
| I. The world of the dinosaurs<br>  A. Land and climate<br>  B. Plant and animal life<br>II. Kinds of dinosaurs<br>  A. Lizard-hipped dinosaurs<br>  B. Bird-hipped dinosaurs | III. How dinosaurs lived<br>  A. Birth and growth<br>  B. Food |

| Tips for Writing Outlines |
|---|
| 1. Use Roman numerals in front of main ideas. Use capital letters in front of important details.<br>2. Indent each letter that appears below a number. Add a period.<br>3. Capitalize the first letter of each entry.<br>4. Keep outline entries short.<br>5. Do not write a *I* without a *II* or an *A* without a *B*. |

## Practice

Use this information as a basis for completing the outline below.

> Potatoes are plants. The part that you eat, called a *tuber*, grows underground. Potatoes are round or oval and hard. They have a thin skin that may be brown, red, light brown, or reddish-brown. The inside of a potato is white.
>
> Potatoes are 80 percent water and 20 percent starch, containing vitamins and such minerals as calcium and potassium.
>
> They can be prepared in many delicious ways. They can be baked, fried, boiled, roasted, or mashed.

Potatoes
I. Description
  A. Plant—tuber grows underground

# 15 Skimming and Scanning

Skimming and scanning are two useful ways of reading for information. To **skim** is to look over material in order to note its general subject, its divisions, and its major headings. To **scan,** on the other hand, is to look quickly at a particular passage, searching for key words. You would skim, for instance, if you were looking for general information on machines. However, you would scan to find out what axles, rotors, and condensers are.

## Practice

Skim the table of contents to write answers to questions 1–4. Scan the book page to answer questions 5–8.

Robots "learn" in various ways. First, a robot can be led through certain movements (for example, picking up a tool), and it will record what it has learned. Second, it can also be programmed by remote control. Third, a computer program can be put onto a microcomputer chip and placed inside a robot to allow it to be controlled. Most robots don't really think for themselves. One robot, named Shakey, was built to solve some problems by itself. At present, though, most robots do only what they have been programmed to do.

1. What general subject is the book about?
MODEL >  robots
2. Into what two parts is the book divided?
3. Which chapter tells about robots in stories?
4. Which chapter gives the advantages of robots?
5. How can computers be used with robots?
6. What can robots do that most machines cannot?
7. What is the second way that robots can be programmed?
8. What is the name of the robot that solved problems by itself?

# 16 Summarizing Information

To **summarize** something is to explain it in a very brief way. A summary contains only a main idea and a few related details. It is written in the writer's own words. Being able to summarize what you read is helpful because it helps you understand and remember the material.

Study the following paragraph. Try to find the main idea, and think about how you might summarize it. If you have trouble, look at the possible response below the paragraph.

> The Portuguese were the first Europeans to establish important trade links with China in the 1500's. The British, French, and Germans soon followed. Europe wanted Chinese silk, tea, porcelain, and ivory, but it had little to offer in return except cotton textiles and opium. Although the Chinese tried to ignore or resist the foreign traders, two factors worked against them. The central government in China was weak, and the Europeans had superior weapons and ships. By the beginning of the twentieth century, the Chinese were unable to stop foreign interests from influencing their country.

The main idea of the paragraph is that China could not keep foreigners away. Here is one way to summarize it.

> Although China tried to resist the foreign trade that began as early as the 1500's, by 1900 the Chinese were unable to stop foreign interests from influencing them.

Notice that this summary concentrates on main ideas and includes only two dates as details. It avoids any mention of such ideas as what the Europeans wanted from China and what they could trade in return.

## Practice

Read these paragraphs. Summarize the most important ideas.

> Cowboys in the American West worked long and hard. On the ranch, their biggest job was to watch over the cattle. They also did other chores such as mending fences and repairing equipment, training horses for riding, and pitching hay.
>
> Another job was handling the cattle drive. Cowboys had to lead hundreds of cattle from the ranch to the nearest railroad town. They had to cross rivers, keep the cattle from harm, and stop them from stampeding.
>
> Twice a year cowboys took part in a roundup. They gathered the cattle into one place to count them, to brand the new calves, and to choose older cattle for market.

# 17 Studying for a Test

Taking tests is not so difficult if you study for them a little every day. Read over these tips for studying, and ask yourself how your study habits compare with them.

| **Tips on Studying for Tests** |
| --- |
| 1. Listen carefully to what the teacher says. Pay attention to class discussions. |
| 2. If something is not clear, ask questions. |
| 3. Give yourself time to study at least a little of every subject every day. |
| 4. Work in a quiet, well-lighted, comfortable place. |
| 5. Be sure you have all the books and other materials you need. |
| 6. Take notes on important facts. |
| 7. Take a break every once in a while. |
| 8. Review what you have learned. |

## Practice

Read these study tips. Write *good study tip* for each one that is helpful. Correct those that are not.

1. Listen when the teacher is talking.
   `MODEL>` good study tip
2. Write letters to a friend during class discussions.
3. Don't ask a question in class unless you are sure that everyone else has the same question.
4. Study the subjects you like every day.
5. Work wherever you feel like working.
6. If you are watching television as you work, keep the sound low.
7. When you read a book for school, try to memorize everything.
8. When you write study notes, include every detail that you have room for.
9. Allow at least a little time to study every subject every day.
10. If your ballpoint pen runs dry, borrow one the next day and finish your work at school.
11. The night before a test, try to cram everything into your head. Work nonstop.
12. Take breaks every now and then so you can return to your work refreshed.

# 18 Taking a Test

If you have studied for a test, taking it should not be difficult. However, these guidelines might help you to keep calm and use your test time wisely.

---

### Tips for Taking Tests

1. Listen as the directions are given. If you do not understand something, ask questions.
2. If the directions are printed on the test, read them carefully.
3. Look over the entire test before you begin to work. Plan how much time you will spend on each question.
4. Answer all the easy questions first. Then go back and do the ones that are more difficult.
5. If you are filling in spaces on an answer sheet, be sure the number of the question and the number of the answer space are the same.
6. Watch the time carefully.
7. If you finish early, go back over the test and check your answers.

---

## Practice

**A.** Use the test-taking tips to answer questions 1–5.

 1. What should you remember about test directions?
   MODEL> Listen to them or read them carefully. Be sure you know what to do.

 2. Before you begin to write, what should you do?
 3. Which questions should you answer first—the easy ones or the hard ones? Why?
 4. Why should you be concerned about time?
 5. What should you do if you finish the test before the time is up?

**B.** Write *good tip* if a test-taking idea is good. If it is not, rewrite it to make it a good one.

 6. Don't bother to write your name on the test.
   MODEL> Write your name on the test.
 7. Answer the questions in the order they are given.
 8. Plan to use your time carefully so that you can complete the entire test.
 9. Do the hard questions first to get them over with.
 10. Don't worry about how many minutes are left. The teacher will tell you when time is up.

STUDY SKILLS Test **463**

# 19 Taking an Essay Test

Essay questions require thought and planning. Before you begin to write the answer to an essay question, it is a good idea to stop and think about how you will organize it. Read these tips for taking essay tests.

---

**Tips for Taking Essay Tests**

1. Read each question carefully.
2. Watch for word clues that tell you what kind of answer to write. Here are some clues.
   *Explain* . . . (tell how and why)
   *Compare* . . . (show likenesses)
   *Contrast* . . . (show differences)
   *Describe* . . . (tell how it affects the senses)
   *Solve* . . . (figure out an answer)
   *Give an opinion* . . . (tell what you think—and give reasons)
3. Try to remember what you know about the topic.
4. Organize ideas for your answer. Then write your response.
5. Read the question again, and reread your answer, correcting it if necessary.

---

On one test students were asked to identify the problems with and suggest solutions for keeping our highways beautiful. Here is what one student wrote.

---

There are three main problems with keeping our highways beautiful. First, our rest stops are full of litter. Second, people throw trash from car windows. Third, there are too many billboards along the roads.

We can all help solve these problems. There should be more trash barrels at every rest area. Businesses should give away litter bags to drivers. The fine for littering should be higher, and each state should cut back the number of billboards.

---

## Practice

Use the tips in the box as well as the student response to write answers to these questions.

1. What main idea were the students asked to discuss?
   MODEL > problems with and solutions for keeping highways beautiful
2. What letter grade would you give to the answer to question 1? Why?
3. What key words did the student use to figure out how to answer the question?
4. How did the student organize the answer?
5. Why do you think the student wrote a two-paragraph answer? Why was it a good strategy for that question?

## 20 Writing a Social Note

Notice the information Tony includes in this invitation.

385 East Avenue
Richmond, Virginia 23220
October 5, 19— —

— heading

Dear Tamara,

— greeting

    I hope you can come to my Halloween
party. It's on Friday, October 30, at my
house, starting at 7:30 P.M. If possible,
please come dressed as your favorite
cartoon character. I'm looking forward
to seeing you.

— body

Your friend,
Tony

— closing
— signature

R.S.V.P.

An invitation is an example of a social note. **Social notes** are friendly letters written for specific purposes. Like friendly letters, social notes have five parts. Read these tips for writing social notes correctly.

---

### Tips for Writing Social Notes

1. Write the heading in the upper right corner of the page.
2. Write the greeting under the heading at the left margin.
3. Organize the body of the note into paragraphs. If you are issuing an invitation, be specific about dates and times as well as the address at which the event will be held.
4. Put the closing at the same point on the line as the heading.
5. Begin the signature on a line with the closing.
6. If you wish, put *R.S.V.P.* at the left margin, to request a response to your invitation.

---

## Practice

Write an invitation to your birthday party. The party is to be held on [your birth date] at 6:00 P.M. at your house.

# 21 Writing a Friendly Letter

Read this friendly letter from Mike to Phil.

209 West Grove Street
Lebanon, Ohio 45036
August 15, 19-- — **heading**

Dear Phil, — **greeting**

How has your summer been? Not too hot, I hope. Did you get to visit your grandparents? Did you go on your trip to Toronto as you had hoped? They say Toronto is a beautiful city!

This is my second season at Camp Bellaire. I just passed my swimming test. Now I can swim out to the raft and also use the boats. To pass, I had to jump into the water with my clothes on (as if I had just fallen out of a boat). Then I had to take them off down to my swim trunks, even my shoes and socks, and finally swim back to shore. It was tough, but I did it!

Last weekend we went on our first camping trip. We slept overnight at Lookout Mountain. Naturally it rained, but not enough to make the trip a washout. I'm looking forward to seeing you soon. There is lots of news to catch up on! — **body**

Sincerely, — **closing**
Mike — **signature**

A **friendly letter** is a letter written to someone you know well. Friendly letters are written to exchange news or send greetings. It is clear from Mike's letter that he had a lot of news to share with Phil, but he couldn't talk to him directly. Mike's letter took the place of a personal or telephone conversation.

Friendly letters have five parts. The *heading* gives the sender's address and the date on which the letter was written. The *greeting* addresses the person to whom the letter is written. The *body* of the letter contains the questions, news, and comments that the letter writer wants the receiver to know. The *closing* is the "sign-off," or the letter writer's way of saying that the letter has come to an end. The *signature,* as a rule, consists only of the writer's first name. Now read these tips for writing friendly letters in the proper format.

| **Tips for Writing Friendly Letters** |
|---|
| 1. Write the heading in the upper right corner of the page. The heading contains the writer's address, including street address, city, state, and ZIP code, and the date on which the letter is written. |
| 2. Write the greeting under the heading and at the left margin. It begins with a capital letter and ends with a comma. |
| 3. Organize the body in paragraph form, indenting the first line of each paragraph. |
| 4. Put the closing at the same point on the line as the heading. It begins with a capital letter and ends with a comma. |
| 5. Write your signature directly under the closing. |
| 6. Prepare an envelope with your full name and address in the upper left corner and the receiver's full name and address in the lower middle. |

## Practice

**A.** Rewrite the following friendly letter using the five-part form described above.

395 River Avenue, St. Louis Missouri 63155 August 10 19--. Dear Joan You will never guess whom I saw today. Do you remember Ivy Partridge, who moved away after fourth grade? Well, she's back, visiting her aunt. Another unusual thing happened yesterday. I forgot the keys to our house and had to climb in the window when I got home from day camp! I guess I won't forget my keys next time. I miss you this summer. How are your grandparents? Please write. Love Mary.

**B.** Write a letter to a friend telling him or her that you have just found a new pen pal. Tell the friend that you will now be writing to both of them and will therefore have twice the news to tell. Be sure to follow the correct format for a friendly letter.

# 22 Writing a Business Letter

Liz Berliner wanted to learn to make bread. A friend gave her the address of a company that might give her some useful bread-baking ideas. Read the letter Liz wrote to the company.

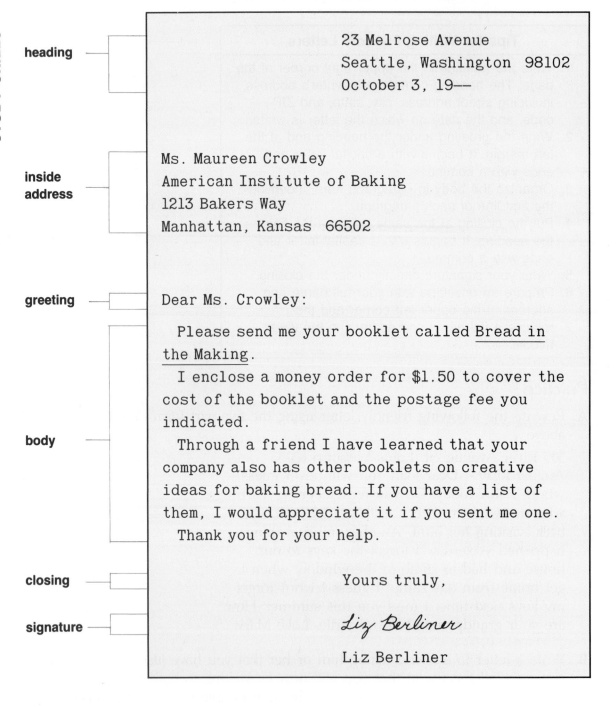

**heading**

23 Melrose Avenue
Seattle, Washington  98102
October 3, 19—

**inside address**

Ms. Maureen Crowley
American Institute of Baking
1213 Bakers Way
Manhattan, Kansas  66502

**greeting**

Dear Ms. Crowley:

**body**

Please send me your booklet called <u>Bread in the Making</u>.

I enclose a money order for $1.50 to cover the cost of the booklet and the postage fee you indicated.

Through a friend I have learned that your company also has other booklets on creative ideas for baking bread. If you have a list of them, I would appreciate it if you sent me one.

Thank you for your help.

**closing**

Yours truly,

**signature**

*Liz Berliner*

Liz Berliner

There are several different kinds of business letters. Some are written to companies to order gifts and supplies, to complain about late or damaged merchandise, or to request a refund. Business letters are also written to citizens' groups and to newspapers to express opinions on local news. No matter what the purpose of a business letter, however, all business letters should have the same format. Study these tips for writing business letters in the proper format.

| Tips for Writing Business Letters |
|---|
| 1. Write the heading in the upper right corner of the page. |
| 2. Write the inside address below the heading and at the left margin. |
| 3. Write the greeting under the inside address. It begins with a capital letter and is followed by a colon. |
| 4. Write the body in paragraph form. |
| 5. Write the closing and your full signature in line with the heading. |
| 6. Prepare an envelope with your full name and address in the upper left corner and the receiver's full name and address in the lower middle. |

## Practice

**A.** Write this business letter in the correct format. Use your name and address and the current date.

United Beverage Corporation, Recycling Department, 200 West Pine Street, St. Louis, Missouri 63108. Dear Sir or Madam Please send me any materials you have on recycling. Our class would like to sponsor a recycling drive to earn money for our next trip. We would be able to recycle aluminum cans as well as glass. Thank you for your help.

**B.** Write a business letter to Ellen Smith at the National Park Service, U.S. Department of the Interior, Washington, D.C. 20025. Request a brochure or other printed material.

Explain that you and your classmates are gathering facts about national parks in your own area. Be sure to follow the correct format for a business letter.

# 23 Writing a Book Report

A **book report** is a way to tell other people about a book you have read. It gives them an idea of what the book is about and helps them decide whether to read it. Study this example book report.

*Tim's Real Adventure,* by Lee Shelton, is about a boy named Tim who thinks his family treats him like a baby. One day Tim rows out to an island in the lake near his home. On the island he feels that he can be the boss.

Things get exciting the day Tim learns that his mother is going to have a baby. That night, Tim rows to the island. What he finds there is totally unexpected.

I really enjoyed this book. One reason is that I like Tim. Another is that the suspense is great!

---

### Tips for Writing Book Reports

1. Give the title and author of the book. Give the setting (when and where the action takes place).
2. Tell who the main characters are.
3. Give a brief summary of the action, but do not give away the ending.
4. Give your opinion of the book and one or two good reasons for how you feel.

## Practice

Write answers to complete these sentences.

1. Giving the title and author of the book is important in a book report because

 a person who became interested in reading the book would need to know the title and author to request it.

2. It is important not to give away the ending of a book because

3. In the example book report, Tim rows out to the island in the lake because

4. By telling that Tim rows out to the island one night, the book report writer is able to show

5. The writer's summary of the book makes me think I would like to read it (or not read it) because

6. The section giving the writer's opinion of the book could have been improved by saying

7. If the book report writer had not included the setting in his or her report, we would not know

# 24 Using a Map

A **map** is a drawing of an area, such as a country or a city. The **distance scale** on a map shows how many miles or kilometers are represented by an inch or a part of an inch. The **compass rose** shows which directions are north, south, east, and west. Sometimes **symbols,** or special marks, are used to show areas where certain crops, industries, or public facilities are located. The meaning of each symbol used on a map is shown in a **legend,** or key, in one of the corners of the map.

Study this map of a small town in Maine. Use the distance scale, compass rose, and the symbols on the legend to try to understand what the map shows.

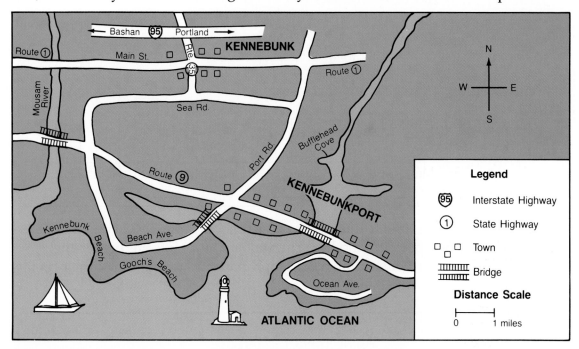

## Practice

Use the example map to write the answers to these questions.

1. What two towns are shown on the map?
   MODEL▷ Kennebunk and Kennebunkport
2. Which town is farther north?
3. To which city does Interstate 95 East go?
4. How many state highways are shown on the map?
5. Does Route 1 run north and south, or does it run east and west?
6. To what street name does Port Road change as you travel southwest?
7. What road is closest to Bufflehead Cove?
8. Into what body of water does Mousam River empty?
9. Which is located farther to the west, Gooch's Beach or Kennebunk Beach?
10. What landmark is in the water southeast of Gooch's Beach?

# 25 Using a Bar Graph and a Line Graph

A **graph** is a drawing that gives information having to do with numbers. It is a way of showing how items compare and contrast with one another.

Two kinds of graphs you should know about are bar graphs and line graphs. A **bar graph** shows numbers of items with long bars, or bands, of color. The longer the bar, the higher the number. Bar graphs may run horizontally (from side to side) or vertically (up and down), as this one does.

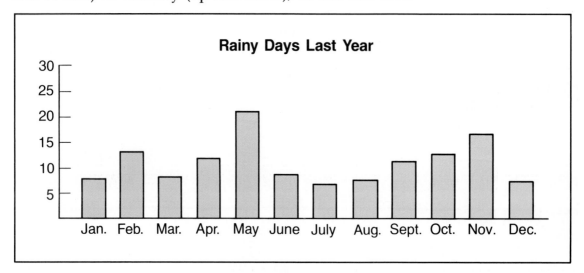

Another kind of graph is a **line graph,** which shows numbers with straight lines drawn from one point to another. The higher the point, the higher the number. Line graphs are often drawn on graph paper to assure that certain points are very clear. Study this line graph.

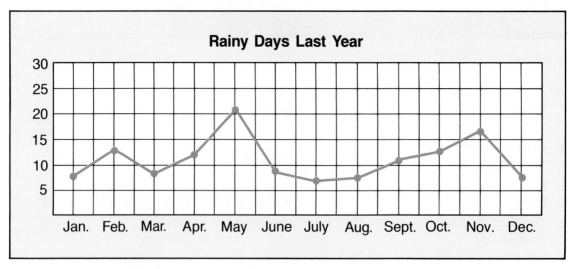

To read a graph, first look at the title to see what it measures. Next, read the words and/or numbers that run across the bottom and along one side of the graph. The numbers at which the bars and lines stop on these two graphs show the number of days on which rain fell in each month last year.

## Practice

Use this example bar graph to write the answers to questions 1–3. Use the example line graph below to answer questions 4–6.

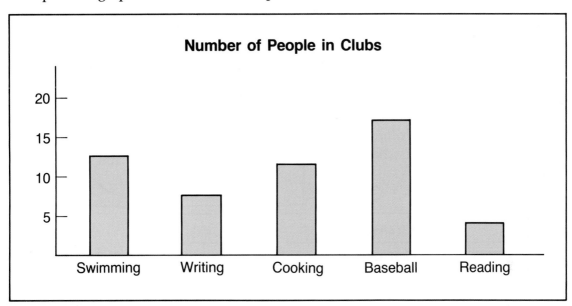

Number of People in Clubs

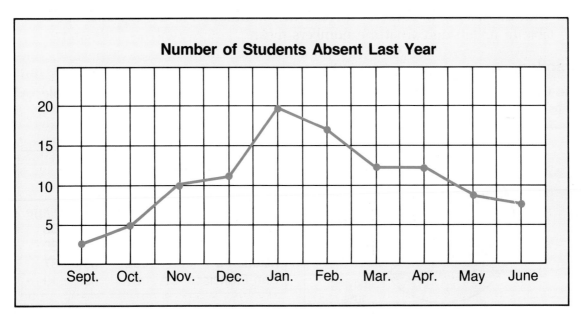

Number of Students Absent Last Year

1. Which club has the fewest members?
   MODEL ▷ Reading Club
2. What are the two most popular clubs?
3. What are the two next most popular clubs?
4. During which month was class attendance best?
5. During which month were the most students absent?
6. In which season is attendance better, winter or spring?

# 26 Using a Pie Chart and a Table

A **pie chart** is a circle graph. Each piece of the graph, like a piece of pie, is a part of the whole.

The pie chart at the right shows how Class 5-2 earned money for a trip. For example, you can see that the bake sale earned 40% of the money and the raffle earned 10%.

A **table** gives information as a list of numbers arranged in columns. The column headings tell you what the numbers stand for.

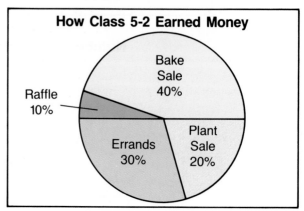

**How Class 5-2 Earned Money**

Bake Sale 40%
Raffle 10%
Errands 30%
Plant Sale 20%

| Push-up Record | | |
|---|---|---|
| *Name* | *First Week* | *Second Week* |
| Tina | 5 | 10 |
| Lois | 2 | 9 |
| Neal | 6 | 7 |

To read pie charts, compare the numbers in each section with other sections and with the whole. To read tables, read the information at the top and side of the table to understand what the numbers mean.

## Practice

Use the example pie chart to write answers to questions 1–3. Use the example table to write answers to questions 4–6.

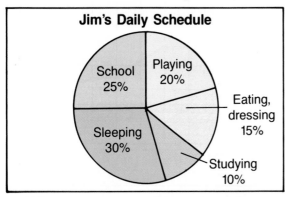

**Jim's Daily Schedule**

School 25%
Playing 20%
Eating, dressing 15%
Sleeping 30%
Studying 10%

| Temperatures (in Degrees Fahrenheit) Today | | | |
|---|---|---|---|
| *City* | *High* | *Low* | *Change* |
| Anchorage, AK | 25 | −10 | 35 |
| Las Vegas, NV | 110 | 80 | 30 |
| Miami, FL | 102 | 65 | 37 |
| San Francisco, CA | 81 | 62 | 19 |

**1.** What percentage of Jim's time does he spend in school?

MODEL▷ 25 percent

**2.** In what activity does Jim spend the most time?

**3.** What is the total of all the percentages on the pie chart?

**4.** What city had the lowest temperature?

**5.** What two cities had the highest temperatures?

**6.** In what city did the temperature change the least?

# 27 Taking a Telephone Message

Knowing how to write a telephone message is a valuable skill. Like taking notes for class, it involves writing only the important facts and leaving out small details. Study these tips for taking accurate telephone messages.

---

### Tips for Taking Telephone Messages

1. Write the date and time of the call.
2. Write the name of the person the message is for.
3. Write the name and phone number of the caller, and jot down the important facts the caller tells you.
4. If you don't understand something, ask the caller to explain. If you don't know how to spell something, ask the caller to spell it for you.
5. Write your name at the end of the message.
6. If your writing is not clear, recopy the message neatly.

---

## Practice

Read the following conversations. Write the telephone messages clearly and accurately. Use today's date and the current time. Use your own name as that of the message taker.

1. This is Jeff Meyers. Please tell Jimmy I called to invite him to my party. It is next Sunday afternoon at one o'clock. Please have him call me at 555-5632 and tell me if he can come.

> MODEL

> 10/24
> 7:00 P.M.
> Jimmy—
> Jeff Meyers called. He wants to invite you to a party next Sunday afternoon at one o'clock. Call him at 555-5632.
> Lenny

2. This is Sandy Bloom. Please ask Luis to call me when he gets in. I would like to stop over there for a few minutes tonight and borrow his copy of the class magazine. My number is 555-0091.

3. This is Jill Bass. Please remind Sherry to wear her new running shoes to school tomorrow. She'll know what I mean. If she wants to call me, my number is 555-6653.

4. This is Fire Chief Mason. I want to thank Ernie personally for sounding the fire alarm on Blaine Street yesterday. Ernie's quick thinking may have prevented a tragic fire. If it is all right with him, I would like to thank Ernie in person tomorrow evening. I plan to come to your house about 7:00. Tell him to call me at 555-3498 if this is inconvenient.

# 28 Completing a Form

People are often asked to complete forms. **Forms** are sheets of paper that require a person to write information in blanks. For example, a fifth-grade student might need to fill out a form to apply for a Social Security card or a library card. Forms ask for basic information such as **name, address,** and **phone number.** Other kinds of information, such as grade and school, might also be necessary.

It is important to fill out forms correctly. These tips may help you to complete forms correctly the first time.

| Tips for Completing Forms |
| :--- |
| 1. Read over the entire form before you begin to write. Note important points, such as a request to print. |
| 2. Give as much information as you can. |
| 3. Be sure to put each part of the information on the correct line. |
| 4. Write small enough to fit everything onto the available lines. Be sure to write as clearly as you can. |
| 5. When you have finished, check to be sure you haven't left anything out. |

## Practice

Use this model library card application to print the answers to the questions.

_____Anna_____ Please print. _____Lopez_____
   last name                               first name

1. When is your birthday? __May__   __24__
                              month       day

2. How old are you? _10_____

3. What grade are you in? _5_____

4. What is the name of your homeroom teacher? __Mr. King__

1. Did Anna write her name correctly? Explain.
2. The form that Anna completed was for her school library. What part of the form gave you a hint about that?
3. Why did the form ask for the homeroom teacher's name rather than the student's home address?

# EXTRA PRACTICE

## Contents

# UNIT 1

## 1 Sentences *pages 34–35*

**A.** **Identifying Sentences**   Read each group of words. Then write *sentence* or *not a sentence.*

   **1.** Linda has a friend in England.

MODEL⟩ sentence

   **2.** The telephone is ringing.

   **3.** The operator asks for Linda.

   **4.** A long-distance call.

   **5.** Margaret is calling from England.

   **6.** The girls are friends.

   **7.** Pen pals for three years.

   **8.** Margaret invites Linda for a visit.

   **9.** A trip to England.

  **10.** Has never been away from home before.

  **11.** The girls will meet each other at last.

**B.** **Completing Sentences**   Choose the word or words in parentheses ( ) that will make a complete sentence. Write the sentence.

  **12.** (Linda, At noon) leaves for England.

MODEL⟩ Linda leaves for England.

  **13.** (Linda, Today) is ready for the trip.

  **14.** Her suitcases (are packed, at the door).

  **15.** Linda (takes a taxi, in a hurry).

  **16.** The traffic (is very heavy, at this hour).

  **17.** (A man, On a cart) carries her suitcases.

  **18.** (People, Everywhere) wait for their flights.

  **19.** Linda (boards the plane, in the terminal).

  **20.** The pilot (before long, makes an announcement).

  **21.** The plane (will take off, into the clouds).

**C.** **Writing Sentences**   Add a word or words to each sentence to make it complete. Write each sentence.

  **22.** The passengers _____ .

MODEL⟩ The passengers get ready for landing.

  **23.** _____ waits for Linda's flight.

  **24.** The plane _____ .

  **25.** _____ announces its arrival.

  **26.** Margaret _____ .

  **27.** _____ see each other.

## 2 Four Kinds of Sentences *pages 36–37*

**A. Identifying the Four Kinds of Sentences**   Write *declarative, interrogative, imperative,* or *exclamatory* to identify each sentence.

**1.** Did the telegraph improve communication?
MODEL> interrogative
**2.** Think about life before the telephone.
**3.** How could you get a message to someone quickly?
**4.** Mail often did not arrive for weeks.
**5.** Samuel Morse developed the telegraph.
**6.** What an amazing invention it was!
**7.** How excited people must have been in 1840!
**8.** A message could be sent and received in seconds.
**9.** How does the telegraph work?
**10.** Read more about the telegraph in the encyclopedia.

**B. Correcting the Four Kinds of Sentences**   Add capital letters and the correct end punctuation. Write each sentence.

**11.** you can make a telegraph set
MODEL> You can make a telegraph set.
**12.** have you ever made a telegraph set
**13.** it is really not so difficult
**14.** we made our own set in class
**15.** what fun we had
**16.** the directions are easy to follow
**17.** don't forget the battery
**18.** use Morse code and send out your message
**19.** do you think your friends will guess
**20.** oh, how confusing the dots and dashes are
**21.** there must be an easier way to send a message

**C. Writing the Four Kinds of Sentences**   Add words to each item to make the kind of sentence named in parentheses ( ). Write each sentence.

**22.** the telephone (interrogative)
MODEL> How does the telephone work?
**23.** the television set (imperative)
**24.** this new clock radio (interrogative)
**25.** some tape recorders (declarative)
**26.** pushed the wrong button (exclamatory)

# UNIT 1

## 3 Subjects and Predicates *pages 38–39*

**A. Identifying Complete Predicates** Write each sentence. Underline the complete predicate.

  **1.** The newspaper is a form of communication.

  MODEL ⟩ The newspaper <u>is a form of communication.</u>

  **2.** People have always been interested in the news.

  **3.** Ancient Romans read handwritten news sheets.

  **4.** The sheets were posted in public places.

  **5.** Newspapers keep us informed today.

  **6.** A person can buy a paper every day of the week.

  **7.** Stories cover local, national, and world events.

  **8.** Editorials present opinions on important issues.

  **9.** Readers learn many things in feature articles.

  **10.** Most daily papers include entertainment items.

**B. Distinguishing Between Subjects and Predicates**
Read each sentence. Write *subject* or *predicate* to describe the underlined words.

  **11.** <u>Our school</u> has a student newspaper.

  MODEL ⟩ subject

  **12.** *Park School Review* <u>is the name of our paper.</u>

  **13.** The paper <u>comes out at the end of each month.</u>

  **14.** <u>Everyone on the staff</u> works hard.

  **15.** Teachers <u>help the students with their jobs.</u>

  **16.** <u>Mr. Johnson</u> takes pictures for the paper.

  **17.** <u>The photography club</u> develops the film.

  **18.** <u>Our paper</u> will include a new feature next month.

  **19.** A reporter <u>will interview an outstanding student.</u>

  **20.** <u>The first interview</u> will be with Megan Smith.

  **21.** Megan <u>won an award for helping senior citizens.</u>

**C. Writing Sentences** Add a complete subject or a complete predicate to each group of words. Write each sentence.

  **22.** _____ delivers newspapers.

  MODEL ⟩ My brother delivers newspapers.

  **23.** This article _____ .

  **24.** _____ likes the comics.

  **25.** _____ is interesting.

  **26.** Newspapers _____ .

  **27.** _____ is a reporter.

  **28.** Reporters _____ .

# 4 Complete and Simple Subjects *pages 40–41*

**A. Identifying Complete and Simple Subjects**  Write the complete subject in each sentence. Then underline the simple subject.

   1. My best friend is away for two weeks.

   MODEL > My best <u>friend</u>

   2. Beth's family went to New York City.
   3. Her grandparents live near the city.
   4. Some interesting buildings are in New York City.
   5. Many people from around the world visit each year.
   6. Numerous tourists go to the Empire State Building.
   7. Beth rode an elevator to the top floor.
   8. Tomorrow the family visits the Statue of Liberty.
   9. A boat will take them to and from the island.
   10. Then the group will visit several of the museums.
   11. All the relatives are having a good time.

**B. Choosing Simple Subjects**  Complete each sentence with a simple subject from the box. Use each subject only once. Write each sentence.

| |
|---|
| people |
| vendor |
| line |
| cast |
| lights |
| variety |
| box office |
| audience |
| family |
| usher |
| program |

   12. Many _____ go to the Theater District.

   MODEL > Many people go to the Theater District.

   13. A _____ of plays and comedies can be seen.
   14. Beth's _____ decided to see a musical.
   15. The _____ opened early.
   16. A long _____ of people was already waiting.
   17. A street _____ sold fruit juice.
   18. An _____ showed people to their seats.
   19. A _____ listed each song in the show.
   20. The bright _____ dimmed slowly.
   21. The entire _____ came on stage.
   22. The _____ applauded wildly.

**C. Writing Sentences**  Write a sentence using each complete subject. Then underline the simple subject.

   23. the newspaper reviews

   MODEL > The newspaper <u>reviews</u> were good.

   24. opening night
   25. many cast members
   26. the star of the show
   27. the colorful costumes
   28. twenty-five musicians
   29. the musical score

# 5 Complete and Simple Predicates *pages 42–43*

**A. Identifying Simple Predicates**  The complete predicate in each sentence is underlined. Write the simple predicate.

  1. Mail delivery <u>changed over the years</u>.

MODEL  changed

  2. The pony express <u>was a mail-delivery service</u>.
  3. It <u>operated during the 1860's</u>.
  4. Riders on horseback <u>carried letters and packages</u>.
  5. They <u>rode between Missouri and California</u>.
  6. The trail <u>was over 1,900 miles long</u>.
  7. The pony express <u>had 190 stations</u>.
  8. The stations <u>were up to 15 miles apart</u>.
  9. A rider <u>switched ponies at each station</u>.
 10. It <u>took only two minutes to change ponies</u>.
 11. Each rider <u>covered 75 miles or more in a trip</u>.

**B. Distinguishing Between Complete and Simple Predicates**  Write the complete predicate in each sentence. Then underline the simple predicate.

 12. Riders earned over 100 dollars a month.

MODEL  <u>earned</u> over one hundred dollars a month

 13. The pony express was the best service available.
 14. The service ran throughout the day and night.
 15. Horses and riders worked in all kinds of weather.
 16. They moved the mail over 200 miles a day.
 17. Mail reached California within ten days.
 18. Many of the riders were teenage boys.
 19. They used special saddlebags for the mail.
 20. It cost five dollars for half an ounce of mail.
 21. Later the rate dropped to one dollar.

**C. Writing Sentences**  Add a complete predicate to make each group of words a complete sentence. Then underline the simple predicate.

 22. Today's mail _____ .

MODEL  Today's mail <u>moves</u> much faster.

 23. A letter _____ .
 24. The post office _____ .
 25. A mailbox _____ .
 26. Postage stamps _____ .
 27. A letter carrier _____ .
 28. Mail trucks _____ .

# 6 Subject in Imperative Sentences pages 44–45

**A. Identifying Imperative and Declarative Sentences** Read each sentence. Then write *imperative* or *declarative.*

1. Evelio is ready to speak.
MODEL⟩ declarative
2. I remember how to speak to an audience.
3. Stand up straight.
4. Breathe deeply and evenly.
5. Evelio will talk about the new computers.
6. He went to the computer center for information.
7. Don't be nervous.
8. It seems that he is calm and prepared.
9. Listen and take good notes.
10. Ask questions if you do not understand.
11. He is a confident speaker.

**B. Choosing Predicates for Imperative Sentences** Write the correct form of the verb for each imperative sentence.

12. (Sit, Sits) in groups of four.
MODEL⟩ Sit
13. (Chooses, Choose) a partner.
14. (Say, Says) these tongue twisters.
15. (Switch, Switches) partners.
16. (Uses, Use) the breathing exercises we learned.
17. (Concentrate, Concentrates) on each word.
18. (Listen, Listens) to your partner.
19. (Holds, Hold) your head straight.
20. (Do, Does) this exercise one more time.

**C. Writing Imperative Sentences** Complete each imperative sentence with a verb from the box. Use each verb only once. Write each sentence.

| write |
| speak |
| take |
| practice |
| stand |
| check |
| find |

21. _____ an outline for your speech.
MODEL⟩ Write an outline for your speech.
22. _____ the outline home.
23. _____ some more information for the outline.
24. Please _____ my work.
25. _____ your speeches this afternoon.
26. Never _____ softly when giving a speech.
27. _____ in front of the room.

**UNIT 1**

# 7 Compound Subjects *pages 46–47*

**A. Identifying Compound Subjects** Write the compound subject in each sentence. Underline the word that joins the subjects.

**1.** Students and teachers are putting on a show.

MODEL > Students and teachers

**2.** Mr. Allison and Ms. Harmon will organize everyone.
**3.** Signs and posters announce the date and time.
**4.** Parents, relatives, and friends are invited.
**5.** Marianne or Andy can type the program.
**6.** The art teacher and her students can paint scenery.
**7.** Mr. Polk or Ms. Thomas will operate the curtain.
**8.** The lights and microphones will be checked.
**9.** Marty, John, or Bill will help with the props.
**10.** Jan and Al need a tape recorder for their act.

**B. Distinguishing Between Simple Subjects and Compound Subjects** Write the complete subject of each sentence. Write *compound* if the subject is compound. Write *not compound* if the subject is not compound.

**11.** The days and weeks went by quickly.

MODEL > The days and weeks    compound

**12.** The dress rehearsal was fun and exciting.
**13.** The day of the show finally arrived.
**14.** The props and the scenery were in place.
**15.** Martha or Rosa would hand out the programs.
**16.** Parents, friends, and children filled the auditorium.
**17.** The singers, dancers, and musicians performed well.
**18.** The audience and the performers had a good time.
**19.** An article and a picture appeared in the newspaper.
**20.** The talent show was a big success!

**C. Writing Sentences with Compound Subjects** Complete the sentences with compound subjects. Write each sentence.

**21.** _____ and _____ plan for next year.

MODEL > Actors and musicians plan for next year.

**22.** _____ and _____ want to do a magic act.
**23.** _____ or _____ can assist them.
**24.** _____ , _____ , and _____ will put on a skit.
**25.** _____ and _____ want to sing a duet.

EXTRA PRACTICE

EXTRA PRACTICE    **9**

# 8 Compound Predicates *pages 48–49*

**A. Identifying Compound Predicates**   Write the compound predicate in each sentence. Underline the word that joins the predicates.

1. Ann prepared and gave a speech about Bigfoot.
   MODEL > prepared <u>and</u> gave
2. Ann gathered materials and interviewed people.
3. She read many books and took pages of notes.
4. She wrote a draft, revised it, and proofread it.
5. Ann stood before a mirror and practiced.
6. Her parents always listened or made suggestions.
7. She made some more changes and tried again.
8. Ann walked on stage, faced the audience, and began.
9. Everyone looked at her and listened carefully.
10. People made comments or asked questions afterwards.
11. The audience smiled and applauded loudly.

**B. Distinguishing Between Simple Predicates and Compound Predicates**   Write the complete predicate in each sentence. Write *compound* if the predicate is compound. Write *not compound* if the predicate is not compound.

12. Ann heard and learned about Bigfoot.
    MODEL > heard and learned about Bigfoot    compound
13. Ann wanted more information about Bigfoot.
14. She saw a film, read reports, and gathered data.
15. Does Bigfoot walk like a man and have fur like an ape?
16. It is very tall and has long arms.
17. Ann flew to the mountains of Oregon and Washington.
18. She searched, observed, and spoke to witnesses.
19. She never really saw the creature herself.

**C. Writing Sentences with Compound Predicates**   Combine the predicates in each group of sentences to make one sentence with a compound predicate.

20. Ann saw footprints. Ann followed them.
    MODEL > Ann saw footprints and followed them.
21. She explored. She took photos. She spoke to people.
22. Bigfoot is very tall. Bigfoot weighs 500 pounds.
23. Ann wants to know. Ann needs more evidence.
24. Some people aren't sure. Some people don't believe.

EXTRA PRACTICE

# 9 Compound Sentences *pages 50–51*

**A. Identifying Compound Sentences**  Write whether each sentence is a *compound sentence* or *not a compound sentence.*

1. It is Saturday, and everyone is asleep.
   `MODEL` compound sentence
2. Ben gets up early, but he must be quiet.
3. He is also very hungry and wants to eat breakfast.
4. Ben likes pancakes but isn't sure how to make them.
5. He can find a recipe, wait for help, or eat cereal.
6. His sister comes to the kitchen and offers her help.
7. Ben thanks Jan, but he does it by himself.
8. Jan can set the table, or she can find a recipe.
9. Jan sets the table, and Ben looks for the cookbook.
10. He checks the index, finds a recipe, and is ready.

**B. Correcting Compound Sentences**  Write each sentence. Add commas where they are needed.

11. The directions are easy and Ben follows them.
    `MODEL` The directions are easy, and Ben follows them.
12. Ben measures some flour and he puts it in a bowl.
13. He cracks an egg and he mixes it with the flour.
14. Ben wants to heat the griddle but Jan does it.
15. The griddle is hot but Ben is very careful.
16. The pancakes bubble and Ben flips them.
17. He puts the pancakes on plates and Jan pours juice.
18. Ben calls his parents and they come to the table.
19. His parents are pleased and Ben is quite proud.
20. Ben can make pancakes again or he can try waffles.

**C. Writing Compound Sentences**  Combine each pair of sentences to make a compound sentence using *and, but,* or *or.* Add commas where they are needed.

21. A recipe lists ingredients. It tells how to prepare a dish.
    `MODEL` A recipe lists ingredients, and it tells how to prepare a dish.
22. This recipe calls for sugar. You can use honey instead.
23. You can roast the meat. You can grill it.
24. Preheat the oven. Grease the pan.
25. We can have salad. We can have soup.

## 10 Avoiding Sentence Fragments and Run-on Sentences *pages 52–53*

**A. Identifying Simple Sentences, Sentence Fragments, and Run-on Sentences** Read each word group. Write *simple sentence, sentence fragment,* or *run-on sentence.*

1. The United Nations works toward world peace.
   MODEL〉 simple sentence
2. The UN is in New York it is along the East River.
3. Delegates from 159 nations.
4. It was established in 1945.
5. Tries to solve problems throughout the world.
6. Members must communicate with each other.
7. Speaks dozens of different languages.
8. The UN uses six official languages.
9. Many interpreters speaking through earphones.
10. Translating a speech into each official language.
11. Listeners have earphones they hear the translation.

**B. Correcting Sentence Fragments and Run-on Sentences** Add a subject or a predicate to make each sentence fragment into a sentence. Make each run-on sentence into two sentences or a compound sentence.

12. I counted the flags there are over 100.
    MODEL〉 I counted the flags, and there are over 100.
13. I visited the UN it is an interesting place.
14. Consists of three main buildings and a library.
15. A guide gave us a tour she told us about the UN.
16. Walked through the General Assembly Building.
17. We heard many languages I understood only English.
18. Is one of the six official languages.
19. Is important for delegates to understand one another.
20. Problems can be solved this requires communication.

**C. Writing Sentences Correctly** Use each group of words in a complete sentence. Avoid sentence fragments and run-on sentences.

21. members of the UN
    MODEL〉 Members of the UN come from around the world.
22. English and Spanish
23. the United Nations
24. communication with others
25. many countries

## UNIT 2

## 1 Nouns *pages 88–89*

**A. Identifying Nouns** Write the nouns in each sentence. Then write *person, place, thing,* or *idea* for each noun.

1. The boys are playing a game.
   MODEL⟩ boys—person    game—thing
2. Adam climbs the ladder to his secret hideout.
3. It is really a tree house in his backyard.
4. The floor is supported by two branches.
5. It has windows, a door, and room for a table.
6. The children in the neighborhood have a good time.
7. They play in the tree house after school.
8. One day they are sailors on a ship.
9. Next they are astronauts traveling in space.
10. Sometimes the boys listen to the radio.
11. On some afternoons they even do their homework!

**B. Using Nouns** Replace the underlined noun in each sentence with a more exact noun or a more vivid noun.

12. Adam painted his tree house a dark color.
    MODEL⟩ Adam painted his tree house a dark brown.
13. Adam and his friend slept in the place one night.
14. They ate a snack and told scary stories.
15. Did you hear that sound?
16. I think I saw something moving in that bush!
17. Do you think it could be a wild animal?
18. Then they saw that it was only Adam's relative.
19. He was just checking on the two children.

**C. Writing Nouns** Complete each sentence with the kind of noun named in parentheses ( ).

20. My _____ and I do things together. (person)
    MODEL⟩ My sister and I do things together.
21. Sometimes we like visiting the _____ . (place)
22. What _____ we have there! (idea)
23. Last week, we saw a _____ . (thing)
24. It had two great big _____ . (thing)
25. We told our _____ about it. (person)
26. It was gone the next time. What a _____ ! (idea)

# 2 Singular and Plural Nouns *pages 90–91*

**A.** **Identifying Singular and Plural Nouns** Write *singular* or *plural* for each underlined noun.

1. Amy followed the <u>path</u> through the <u>dunes</u>.
   MODEL ▷ path—singular   dunes—plural
2. She sat on one of the <u>benches</u> and ate her <u>lunch</u>.
3. Huge <u>waves</u> crashed against the <u>shore</u>.
4. Several <u>birds</u> were fighting over a <u>fish</u>.
5. Amy watched a passing <u>ship</u> on the horizon.
6. She tried to imagine <u>life</u> on the <u>sea</u> long ago.
7. Her <u>ancestor</u> had been a sea <u>captain</u>.
8. He lived during the <u>days</u> of the <u>clipper</u> ships.
9. Clipper ships had six <u>rows</u> of <u>sails</u> on each <u>mast</u>.
10. They could travel through the <u>water</u> at 20 <u>knots</u>.
11. <u>Passengers</u> as well as <u>cargo</u> were transported.

**B.** **Writing Plural Nouns** Write the plural form for the underlined nouns in each sentence.

12. Amy heard a <u>tale</u> or two about the <u>sailor</u>.
    MODEL ▷ tales   sailors
13. Amy found her grandparents' <u>trunk</u> in the <u>attic</u>.
14. It contained a <u>box</u> of books and a <u>pack</u> of letters.
15. There was a <u>spyglass</u> in a leather <u>case</u>.
16. Amy also discovered a <u>diary</u> and an old <u>uniform</u>.
17. She read each <u>entry</u> of the diary, <u>page</u> by page.
18. This <u>journal</u> had been written by her <u>grandfather</u>.
19. A great <u>clipper</u> sank during a terrible <u>storm</u>.
20. Only one <u>witness</u> survived to tell the <u>story</u>.
21. He reached the <u>beach</u> by clinging to a <u>plank</u>.

**C.** **Writing Singular and Plural Nouns** Write the correct form of the word in parentheses ( ). Write the sentence.

22. He worked for a shipping _____ . (company)
    MODEL ▷ He worked for a shipping company.
23. The captain made 30 _____ . (voyage)
24. He had an interesting _____ . (experience)
25. Sometimes there were terrible _____ . (storm)
26. Sailors packed their _____ in a trunk. (necessity)
27. England was the captain's favorite _____ . (country)

# 3 More Plural Nouns *pages 92–93*

**A. Identifying Plural Nouns** Write *singular* or *plural* for each underlined noun.

**1.** Ben wrote a <u>series</u> of stories.
MODEL⟩ series—singular
**2.** The first story is about a <u>man</u> and his family.
**3.** There is very little left on their <u>shelves</u> to eat.
**4.** His wife has enough flour for a <u>loaf</u> of bread.
**5.** The man sends his <u>sons</u> out fishing.
**6.** He must stay and tend his crop of <u>potatoes</u>.
**7.** The stream is about a mile and a <u>half</u> away.
**8.** "Try to catch a big <u>fish</u>," says their father.
**9.** They meet a pair of <u>moose</u> and three <u>mice</u>.
**10.** One <u>moose</u> warns them not to go near Rapid Falls.
**11.** "You will be sorry if you do," says a <u>mouse</u>.
**12.** The <u>brothers</u> look at each other.
**13.** All the <u>animals</u> run away into the <u>forest</u>.

**B. Using Plural Nouns** Complete each sentence with the plural form of the noun in parentheses ( ).

**14.** The _____ go to Rapid Falls anyway. (child)
MODEL⟩ The children go to Rapid Falls anyway.
**15.** They cut fishing lines with their _____ . (knife)
**16.** They catch some _____ in no time. (fish)
**17.** The boys will be _____ . (hero)
**18.** Suddenly, they hear the sounds of _____ . (hoof)
**19.** "Stop, you _____!" bellows a voice. (thief)
**20.** The boys move several _____ from the falls. (foot)
**21.** They drop the fish and run for their _____ . (life)
**22.** Our _____ will never believe this! (parent)
**23.** We should have listened to the _____ . (mouse)
**24.** It will be bread and _____ for supper tonight. (potato)

**C. Writing Plural Nouns** Write a humorous sentence using the plural form of each noun.

**25.** radio
MODEL⟩ The rodeo rider's radios broke.
**26.** goose
**27.** calf
**28.** woman
**29.** wife
**30.** stereo
**31.** tomato

# 4 Common and Proper Nouns *pages 94–95*

**A. Identifying Common and Proper Nouns**   Write *common* or *proper* for each underlined noun.

  1. Our <u>city</u> will soon celebrate <u>Kite Day</u>.
  `MODEL` city—common     Kite Day—proper
  2. This <u>year</u> it will be held on <u>Saturday</u>, <u>March</u> 26.
  3. Each <u>contestant</u> must design, make, and fly a <u>kite</u>.
  4. The kites will be displayed from <u>Monday</u> to <u>Friday</u>.
  5. You can see them in the main <u>lobby</u> of <u>City Hall</u>.
  6. The <u>building</u> is on <u>Main Street</u>.
  7. The <u>contestants</u> will be at <u>Miller's Field</u>.
  8. Go north on <u>Mill Road</u> past <u>Twin Lakes</u>.
  9. <u>Mr. Munson</u> and his <u>assistant</u> will judge the <u>event</u>.
 10. The <u>Merchants' Association</u> is offering a <u>prize</u>.
 11. I hope my brother <u>Chris</u> wins the <u>contest</u>.

**B. Correcting Proper Nouns**   Capitalize the proper nouns in each sentence. Write the sentences correctly.

 12. Kite day began in greensburg two years ago.
 `MODEL` Kite Day began in Greensburg two years ago.
 13. The greensburg museum of art had a kite exhibit.
 14. mr. lewis took his art students to see it.
 15. There were kites from asia and north america.
 16. Kites date back 3,000 years to china.
 17. In america, ben franklin and the wright brothers used kites in their experiments.
 18. In japan there is a special kite festival.
 19. It began over 400 years ago in hamamatsu.
 20. The students of hill school wanted a festival.
 21. mrs. wilson said the museum would help.
 22. This kite day in greensburg was a huge success.
 23. The first-place prize will be awarded on sunday.

**C. Writing Common and Proper Nouns**   Write a sentence using each pair of common and proper nouns.

 24. day, Friday
 `MODEL` Friday is the best day of the week.

 25. country, Canada
 26. holiday, Fourth of July
 27. state, Pennsylvania
 28. ocean, Atlantic Ocean
 29. building, White House
 30. continent, North America

EXTRA PRACTICE

## UNIT 2

# 5 Capitalization of Proper Nouns *pages 96–97*

**A. Identifying Proper Nouns**   Write the proper noun or nouns in each sentence.

1. My parents took us on a vacation in July.

MODEL⟩ July

2. Our family visited the city of Boston.
3. Miss Lee took care of our cats, Fritz and Boots.
4. We flew to Logan International Airport on Sunday.
5. The city is on the Massachusetts Bay.
6. The British founded the city on a peninsula in 1630.
7. John Winthrop and some Puritans settled there.
8. It is between the Charles River and Boston Harbor.
9. The city is one of the largest in New England.
10. My cousins live in nearby Lexington.
11. We went to a park called the Boston Common.

**B. Correcting Proper Nouns**   Add capital letters to the proper nouns. Write each sentence correctly.

12. Many historical events took place in boston.

MODEL⟩ Many historical events took place in Boston.

13. Colonists wanted independence from great britain.
14. They protested the british tax on tea.
15. Colonists dressed as indians and raided three ships.
16. They dumped 340 chests of tea into boston harbor.
17. Today, visitors can walk along the freedom trail.
18. It passes many historic landmarks in boston.
19. A sign on milk street marks the birthplace of ben franklin.
20. You can see the house in which paul revere lived.
21. Do you know where faneuil hall is?

**C. Writing Proper Nouns in Sentences**   Write a sentence using a proper noun for each of the items below.

22. your name

MODEL⟩ My name is Greg Christopher Adams.

23. your favorite holiday
24. the name of a family pet
25. a famous landmark
26. your city and state
27. the nearest ocean
28. someone you admire

## UNIT 2

# 6 Abbreviations *pages 98–99*

**A. Identifying Abbreviations**  Write the complete word for each underlined abbreviation.

1. Chicago, <u>IL</u>

MODEL ▷ Illinois

2. Madison, <u>WI</u>
3. <u>Rev.</u> Allen
4. First <u>Ave.</u>
5. <u>Rte.</u> 66
6. 1:56 <u>P.M.</u>
7. Roselle, <u>NJ</u>
8. Sat., <u>Aug.</u> 31
9. Wilson Ames, <u>Jr.</u>
10. Ace Packing, <u>Inc.</u>

11. <u>Dr.</u> Alan Anders, <u>Sr.</u>
12. <u>Dept.</u> of Sanitation
13. Pleasant <u>Dr.</u>
14. Westmill <u>Corp.</u>
15. Pittsburgh, <u>PA</u>
16. <u>Mr.</u> Michael James
17. <u>Jan.</u>
18. Boise, <u>ID</u>
19. Washington, <u>DC</u>

**B. Writing Abbreviations and Initials in Addresses**  Use the correct abbreviations and initials for the underlined words. Rewrite each item.

20. <u>Reverend</u> Lewis Smith
    33 Charles <u>Street</u>
    Aberdeen, <u>Maryland</u> 21001

MODEL ▷ Rev. Lewis Smith
    33 Charles St.
    Aberdeen, MD 21001

21. (married woman) Martha
    Lee Johns
    14 Elm <u>Boulevard</u>
    Akron, <u>Ohio</u> 44304

22. Kathy Bernard
    19 Beacon <u>Street</u>
    Boston, <u>Massachusetts</u>
    02130

23. ABC Tire <u>Company</u>,
    <u>Incorporated</u>
    1239 Westwood <u>Drive</u>
    Flint, <u>Michigan</u> 48592

24. (man) James <u>Lee</u> Hanks
    3421 Third <u>Avenue</u>
    New York, <u>New York</u> 10022

25. Holiday <u>Corporation</u>
    8315 Prospect <u>Street</u>
    Orlando, <u>Florida</u> 32819

26. Highway <u>Department</u>
    <u>Route</u> 22, Somerset, <u>New
    Jersey</u> 08873

**C. Writing Abbreviations and Initials**  Use abbreviations and initials to write these items.

27. the name of a friend

MODEL ▷ Sherry N. Evans

28. your name and address
29. the name and address of a friend
30. today's date
31. the exact time
32. the name of a company in your town

**UNIT 2**

# 7 Singular Possessive Nouns *pages 100–101*

**A. Identifying Singular Possessive Nouns**  Read each sentence. Write the possessive noun in each.

1. My friend's birthday is October 30.

MODEL > friend's

2. Ann's invitation came in the mail today.
3. Jenny's parents are having a costume party.
4. The family's address is on the invitation.
5. Next Saturday's party should be lots of fun.
6. Dan's father will drive us to the party.
7. His father's car is big enough for all of us.
8. Megan will wear her sister's Halloween costume.
9. Dan can borrow his uncle's uniform.
10. Ben asked for one of his father's hats.
11. I can't wait to see everyone's costume.

**B. Using Singular Possessive Nouns**  Complete each sentence with the possessive form of the noun in parentheses ( ).

12. _____ birthday was last week. (Jenny)

MODEL > Jenny's

13. It was her _____ idea to wear costumes. (brother)
14. Joey wore his _____ suit backwards. (father)
15. _____ makeup was incredible! (Megan)
16. The _____ dog even barked at Megan. (family)
17. _____ huge tie came down to his knees. (Brendan)
18. We all laughed at _____ wild hairdo. (Denise)
19. It looked like a huge _____ nest. (bird)
20. _____ top hat was too big for his head. (Luis)
21. Ann wore her _____ old fur coat. (grandma)

**C. Writing Singular Possessive Nouns**  Write each sentence in another way. Change the underlined words to a phrase containing a singular possessive noun.

22. The friends belonging to Jenny had fun.

MODEL > Jenny's friends had fun.

23. Jenny used the camera belonging to her father.
24. The costume of each person was different.
25. The mask that Mike had slipped off.
26. The gift that Maria gave was really nice.
27. The mother of Maria had made it for Jenny.
28. How did the family of Jenny surprise her?

# 8 Plural Possessive Nouns *pages 102–103*

**A. Identifying Plural Possessive Nouns**  Write the plural possessive noun in each sentence.

1. The marching bands' contest is today.
MODEL> bands'
2. Volunteers loaded the musicians' instruments.
3. Next they loaded the band members' uniforms.
4. The hats' plumes were packed in a special case.
5. The uniforms' colors are blue and gold.
6. The twirlers' batons have stripes.
7. The two drum majors' uniforms are exactly alike.
8. It was the drivers' decision to take Route 9.

**B. Using Plural Possessive Nouns**  Complete each sentence with the plural possessive form of the noun in parentheses ( ).

9. Our band accepted the two _____ invitations. (competitions)
MODEL> Our band accepted the two competitions' invitations.
10. The two brass _____ rehearsal is at noon. (sections)
11. The _____ practice area is soundproof. (drummers)
12. Mr. Allen is the woodwind _____ teacher. (players)
13. The _____ coach is Miss Emery. (twirlers)
14. Ms. Lee is both the flag and the rifle _____ coach. (squads)
15. The _____ energy and enthusiasm is only surpassed by their talent. (students)
16. The _____ association sponsored a bake sale to help raise money. (parents)
17. Two local _____ groups heard about the invitation and donated funds. (citizens)

**C. Writing Plural Possessive Nouns**  Write each sentence in another way. Change the underlined words to a phrase containing a plural possessive noun.

18. The rules of both competitions are strict.
MODEL> Both competitions' rules are strict.
19. The routines of all the marching bands were good.
20. The parents of the band members cheered.
21. The crowds appreciated the talents of the bands.
22. The results of the competitions surprised us.
23. The excitement of the students was pleasing.

## UNIT 3

# 1 Action Verbs *pages 138–139*

**A. Identifying Action Verbs**  Write the action verb in each sentence.

1. Some architects join a firm.
> MODEL ▷ join
2. Architects attend school for five years.
3. In school they work as interns in offices.
4. An intern learns how to design buildings.
5. The school gives a test to the student.
6. The student passes in order to graduate.
7. Architects design buildings.
8. An architect makes blueprints of buildings.
9. A builder uses blueprints to build houses.

**B. Finding Action Verbs in Complete Predicates**  Write the complete predicate in each sentence. Then underline the action verb in each complete predicate.

10. Val drafts blueprints for houses.
> MODEL ▷ drafts blueprints for houses
11. She makes a blueprint of the house.
12. The builder plans the job.
13. Blueprints guide the builder.
14. The workers study the blueprints.
15. Home construction requires many workers.
16. Workers dig the foundation.
17. The frame, walls, and roof come next.
18. An electrician installs the wiring.
19. Workers finish the inside of the house.
20. The family moves into its new home.

**C. Writing Action Verbs**  Complete each sentence with an action verb. Write each sentence.

21. The workers _____ the roof.
> MODEL ▷ The workers finish the roof.
22. She _____ the first coat of paint.
23. My family _____ into the house next month.
24. His boss _____ the wiring and plumbing.
25. The owner _____ to the plasterer.

**UNIT 3**

# 2 Linking Verbs *pages 140–141*

**A. Identifying Linking Verbs** Write the linking verb in each
sentence.

1. The telephone was an important invention.

MODEL ⟩ was

2. Alexander Graham Bell was the inventor.
3. He became a famous scientist.
4. His dedication to his work was obvious.
5. At first people seemed uninterested.
6. They were unaware of the telephone's importance.
7. Gradually, its value became clear.
8. Massachusetts was the site of the first commercial
   telephone line.
9. Today the telephone is a necessity.
10. It is essential to our way of life.
11. Life without a telephone seems unimaginable.

**B. Choosing Linking Verbs** Write the linking verb in
parentheses ( ) that completes each sentence correctly.

12. Ed _____ excited about the computer. (is, am)

MODEL ⟩ is

13. The computer _____ a birthday gift. (was, were)
14. Ed _____ eleven years old last week. (was, were)
15. He _____ old enough to use a computer. (is, are)
16. His parents _____ sure he would enjoy it. (was, were)
17. Computer games _____ fun. (is, are)
18. Ed and his mom _____ eager to try them. (am, are)
19. "Space Raiders" _____ their favorite. (is, are)
20. Computers _____ useful for other things. (is, are)
21. Many types of programs _____ available. (is, are)
22. The computer _____ an amazing invention. (is, are)

**C. Writing Linking Verbs** Complete each sentence
with a linking verb from the box. Write each
sentence.

23. Computers _____ smaller and faster today.

MODEL ⟩ Computers are smaller and faster today.

24. The uses of a computer _____ endless.
25. Many people _____ uneasy with a computer.
26. Computer jargon _____ difficult.
27. Computers _____ important to our society.
28. This computer _____ easy to use.

| are |
| sounds |
| is |
| became |
| feel |
| seem |

**EXTRA PRACTICE**

**22** EXTRA PRACTICE

# 3 Main Verbs and Helping Verbs *pages 142–143*

**A. Identifying Main Verbs and Helping Verbs** Write the main verb and the helping verb in each sentence.

1. I am looking for Dad's yearbook.

[MODEL]> am looking

2. Danny will help me in my search.
3. I shall look for the yearbook in the attic.
4. Mom is checking the bookshelf.
5. I have searched there already.
6. Danny and I are looking in the trunk.
7. I have found it!
8. We were laughing at Dad's photo.
9. Dad sure has changed since high school.
10. His hair has turned gray.
11. Dad has put the yearbook away.

**B. Choosing Helping Verbs** Write the helping verb that completes each sentence correctly.

12. We (are, will) cleaning out the attic.

[MODEL]> are

13. Mom (will, had) asked us for help.
14. It (will, is) take several days.
15. Jim and I (am, are) packing all the books.
16. Mom (is, has) found an old trunk.
17. It (had, was) belonged to her grandmother.
18. She (had, is) unlocking it.
19. I (are, am) trying on a very old dress.
20. Everyone (is, have) laughing at me.
21. How styles (is, have) changed!
22. My great-grandmother (is, had) worn that dress once.

**C. Writing Helping Verbs** Complete each sentence with a helping verb from the box. Write each sentence.

23. My mother _____ worn this gown.

[MODEL]> My mother has worn this gown.

24. Now I _____ wearing the gown.
25. My sister _____ trying on a hat.
26. Mother _____ take our pictures soon.
27. We _____ found photos of our aunt.
28. She _____ worn the same hat and gown.
29. Mom and I _____ looking for other photos.

| |
|---|
| has |
| am |
| have |
| will |
| had |
| are |
| is |

# 4 Present Tense *pages 144–145*

**A. Identifying Present-Tense Verbs**  Complete each sentence with the correct present-tense form of the verb in parentheses ( ).

  1. The Murphys (move, moves) away today.
  MODEL>  move
  2. The family (need, needs) a bigger home.
  3. They (have, has) a new baby.
  4. Mr. Murphy (pack, packs) the china.
  5. The van (come, comes) early in the morning.
  6. The workers (load, loads) the furniture.
  7. Dan (carry, carries) a box from the basement.
  8. Mr. Murphy (follow, follows) the van.
  9. They (arrive, arrives) at their new home.
  10. The neighborhood (have, has) many children.
  11. The Murphys (like, likes) their new community.

**B. Using Present-Tense Verbs**  Change the underlined verb in each sentence to the present tense.

  12. Mr. Murphy <u>found</u> a new job.
  MODEL>  finds
  13. He <u>worked</u> for the *News Press*.
  14. Mr. Murphy <u>wrote</u> a daily column.
  15. He <u>interviewed</u> many interesting people.
  16. The reporter <u>covered</u> the election.
  17. The candidates <u>held</u> a press conference.
  18. The reporters <u>questioned</u> the candidates.
  19. Mr. Murphy <u>asked</u> for their views on education.
  20. A photographer <u>took</u> many pictures.
  21. The press conference <u>ended</u> at noon.
  22. The reporter <u>called</u> in his story.

**C. Writing Present-Tense Verbs**  Complete each sentence with the present-tense form of the verb in parentheses ( ). Write each sentence.

  23. The Murphys _____ the living room. (paint)
  MODEL>  The Murphys paint the living room.
  24. Mr. Murphy _____ the furniture. (cover)
  25. Mrs. Murphy _____ the paint. (mix)
  26. Their son _____ them. (watch)
  27. Some of the paint _____ on the floor. (splash)
  28. Dan _____ up the paint. (wipe)

# UNIT 3

## 5 Past Tense *pages 146–147*

**A. Identifying Past-Tense Verbs** Write the past-tense verb in each sentence.

1. My brothers and I finished our chores.

MODEL > finished

2. We warmed ourselves by the fire.
3. John studied his lessons.
4. The schoolmaster loaned him a book.
5. Father dozed in his chair.
6. His book slid to the floor.
7. I picked it up quietly.
8. Beth worked on her homework.
9. Mother checked the answers.
10. My brother Matthew counted his marbles.
11. He traded some with his friends today.

**B. Using Past-Tense Verbs** Complete each sentence with the past-tense form of the verb in parentheses ( ).

12. Some children _____ a dame school. (attend)

MODEL > attended

13. A woman _____ the children. (instruct)
14. They _____ to her house each day. (come)
15. Boys and girls _____ reading and writing. (study)
16. They _____ hornbooks. (use)
17. Boys _____ their education after dame school. (continue)
18. They _____ another school. (attend)
19. The boys _____ the *New England Primer.* (use)
20. The girls _____ at home. (stay)
21. Some parents _____ their daughters. (educate)

**C. Writing Past-Tense Verbs** Change the underlined verb in each sentence to the past tense. Write the sentence.

22. Emily <u>sews</u> a sampler.

MODEL > Emily sewed a sampler.

23. Mother <u>helps</u> her with the stitches.
24. Emily <u>needs</u> more blue thread.
25. Emily <u>threads</u> the needle.
26. She <u>makes</u> the letters of the alphabet.
27. Emily <u>shows</u> the sampler to her father.

# 6 Future Tense *pages 148–149*

**A. Identifying Future-Tense Verbs**   Write each verb that is in the future tense. If the verb is in the present tense, write *present.* If the verb is in the past tense, write *past.*

1. This volcano will erupt soon.
MODEL⟩ will erupt
2. Scientists warned the people.
3. We begin the evacuation today.
4. Residents will leave the area.
5. Tons of rock will fly into the air.
6. Lava will flow down the sides of the volcano.
7. Volcanic ash will travel thousands of miles.
8. This volcano was quiet until recently.
9. It erupted over 100 years ago.
10. Then it destroyed the surrounding towns.

**B. Using Future-Tense Verbs**   Change the underlined verb in each sentence to the future tense.

11. We <u>observe</u> the eagles.
MODEL⟩ will observe
12. They <u>nest</u> on the cliff.
13. The eagles <u>use</u> sticks and green leaves.
14. The female <u>lays</u> two eggs.
15. She <u>sits</u> on the eggs most of the time.
16. The male <u>keeps</u> them warm occasionally.
17. He <u>brings</u> food to the female.
18. The eaglets <u>hatch</u> in 40 days.
19. Both parents <u>feed</u> them.
20. They <u>leave</u> the nest after 12 weeks.
21. Some eagles <u>live</u> up to 50 years.

**C. Writing Future-Tense Verbs**   Change the verb in parentheses ( ) to the future tense. Write each sentence.

22. Monarch butterflies _____ the winter. (escape)
MODEL⟩ Monarch butterflies will escape the winter.
23. They _____ to a warmer area. (migrate)
24. A swarm of monarchs _____ 2,000 miles. (travel)
25. The butterflies _____ for the winter. (rest)
26. In the spring they _____ to the north. (return)
27. Females _____ eggs along the way. (lay)
28. The new butterflies _____ the journey. (continue)

# UNIT 3

## 7 Be and Have pages 150–151

**A. Identifying Forms of Be and Have** Write the form of *be* or *have* in each sentence. Then write *helping verb* or *main verb* to identify how it is used in the sentence.

1. Jean Alexander is our mayor.

> MODEL  is—main verb

2. She is speaking at noon today.
3. Mayor Alexander has one year left in office.
4. She is announcing her plans for reelection.
5. We were hoping for a large crowd.
6. The mayor's programs have improved our city.
7. We have a new senior citizens' center.
8. Senior citizens are living there now.
9. Mayor Alexander is an impressive person.
10. The city is planning a banquet in her honor.
11. I am going with my family.

**B. Using Be and Have** Complete each sentence with the correct form of *be* or *have* in parentheses ( ).

12. Students _____ helping Ms. Cahn. (is, are)

> MODEL  are

13. She _____ organizing the school fair. (is, are)
14. We _____ a month left until the fair. (have, has)
15. Ms. Cahn _____ planning some games. (was, were)
16. She _____ the prizes already. (has, have)
17. Many parents _____ offered to help. (has, have)
18. My mother _____ baking cookies this year. (is, are)
19. We _____ having a pony ride. (is, are)
20. Mr. Alan _____ several ponies. (has, have)
21. They _____ always a big attraction. (is, are)

**C. Writing Be and Have** Choose the correct form of *have* or *be* in the box to complete each sentence.

22. Our school fairs _____ always been a success.

> MODEL  Our school fairs have always been a success.

23. Ms. Cahn _____ not expected such a crowd yesterday.
24. She _____ planned the fair for next year.
25. We _____ offered our help.
26. We _____ talking about it yesterday.
27. I _____ taking notes during the meeting.

| |
|---|
| have |
| were |
| was |
| has |
| had |

# 1 Irregular Verbs *pages 184–185*

**A. Identifying Irregular Verbs**   Write the irregular verb in each sentence.

**1.** My family went on a hike.

MODEL⟩ went

**2.** We chose a trail called "Winding Path."
**3.** Once we rode on horseback.
**4.** My father took notes on the wildlife.
**5.** He did this for many years.
**6.** We saw many different wildflowers.
**7.** I thought about picking some for my mother.
**8.** Dad spoke to me about preserving nature.
**9.** We ate lunch beside a stream.

**B. Choosing Irregular Verbs**   Write the correct past-tense form of the verb in parentheses ( ) that completes each sentence.

**10.** Our teacher (took, taken) us to a botanical garden.

MODEL⟩ took

**11.** Mr. Abbott also (come, came) along.
**12.** I had (think, thought) it might be boring.
**13.** I had never (went, gone) there before.
**14.** We (saw, seen) many interesting plants.
**15.** Have you ever (saw, seen) an artichoke?
**16.** Our guide (gave, given) us a taste of one.
**17.** Next we (ate, eaten) fried squash flowers.
**18.** Most of us have never (ate, eaten) these things.
**19.** Then we (went, gone) to the desert and (saw, seen) the plants and flowers.
**20.** The next day we (wrote, written) about our trip.

**C. Writing Irregular Verbs with Helping Verbs**   Complete each sentence with the correct past-tense form of the verb in parentheses ( ). Write each sentence.

**21.** I have _____ to the Japanese gardens. (go)

MODEL⟩ I have gone to the Japanese gardens.

**22.** Dad had _____ us a year ago. (take)
**23.** The gardeners have _____ interesting things. (do)
**24.** They have _____ a bonsai garden. (make)
**25.** A gardener had _____ they need much care. (say)
**26.** My aunt had _____ a bonsai tree to me. (give)

# UNIT 4

## 2 More Irregular Verbs *pages 186–187*

**A. Identifying Irregular Verbs**   Write *correct* if the underlined verb in each sentence is the correct past-tense form of the irregular verb. If the form of the verb is *incorrect,* write the correct form.

   **1.** Yesterday we <u>found</u> a baby robin.

> MODEL  correct

   **2.** The wind must have <u>blew</u> it from the nest.
   **3.** We <u>knew</u> that it couldn't fly yet.
   **4.** Maybe it had <u>broke</u> its wing.
   **5.** The parents must have <u>flown</u> away.
   **6.** My mother <u>begun</u> feeding it.
   **7.** Maggie <u>brought</u> some worms.
   **8.** I <u>caught</u> insects in the grass.
   **9.** The robin had <u>grew</u> to full size in a month.
 **10.** It chirped and <u>sung</u> when we talked to it.
 **11.** One morning the robin <u>flew</u> off.

**B. Choosing Irregular Verbs**   Write the verb in parentheses ( ) that completes each sentence correctly.

 **12.** We (knew, known) there were animals nearby.

> MODEL  knew

 **13.** Something has (tore, torn) into the garbage again.
 **14.** We also have (find, found) paw prints.
 **15.** We have (began, begun) a night watch.
 **16.** It was chilly, so we (wore, worn) jackets.
 **17.** Dad pointed and (spoke, spoken) in a whisper.
 **18.** We (froze, frozen) in our tracks.
 **19.** A large raccoon had (bring, brought) its family!
 **20.** They (drank, drunk) from the pond in our yard.
 **21.** We (did, done) not frighten them away.

**C. Writing Irregular Verbs with Helping Verbs**   Complete each sentence with the correct past-tense form of the verb in parentheses ( ). Write each sentence.

 **22.** We have _____ the wounded goose. (find)

> MODEL  We have found the wounded goose.

 **23.** It had _____ as far as it could. (fly)
 **24.** We had _____ sight of it for a while. (lose)
 **25.** Mike has _____ to the veterinarian. (speak)
 **26.** The goose may have _____ a leg. (break)
 **27.** Its wounds have _____ to heal. (begin)

# UNIT 4

## 3 Direct Objects *pages 188–189*

**A. Identifying Action Verbs and Direct Objects** Write each sentence. Underline the action verb once. Underline the direct object twice.

    **1.** Alan visited the aquarium.

Alan <u>visited</u> the <u>aquarium</u>.

    **2.** He observed the energetic sea otters.

    **3.** Sea otters eat shellfish.

    **4.** The otters amused Alan.

    **5.** One of the otters completed a dive.

    **6.** It grabbed two large clams in its paws.

    **7.** The otter pounded the clams together.

    **8.** Another otter balanced a rock on its belly.

    **9.** Fur traders once hunted these creatures.

  **10.** In 1911 four countries signed a treaty.

  **11.** The treaty protects the animals.

**B. Identifying Direct Objects** Write the direct object in each sentence.

  **12.** The ship left the harbor.

harbor

  **13.** The captain set the course.

  **14.** Several crew members sighted whales.

  **15.** The ship approached the huge animals.

  **16.** They did not fear the ship.

  **17.** The captain watched them cautiously.

  **18.** One leaping whale pounded the water.

  **19.** Waves splashed the deck of the ship.

  **20.** Water soaked the observers.

  **21.** A baby whale imitated its mother.

  **22.** Cameras recorded the amazing sight.

**C. Writing Direct Objects** Complete each sentence with a direct object. Write each sentence. Then write whether the direct object tells *whom* or *what*.

  **23.** People on the beach saw _____.

People on the beach saw a strange fish.   what

  **24.** We heard _____.

  **25.** I photographed _____.

  **26.** The lifeguard warned _____.

  **27.** The next day we read _____.

  **28.** A reporter had interviewed _____.

# 4 Easily Confused Verb Pairs *Pages 190–191*

**A. Identifying Verbs**   Write the correct sentence in each pair.

1. We sit and watch the stars.
   We set and watch the stars.

   MODEL ⟩ We sit and watch the stars.

2. Please come and set over here.
   Please come and sit over here.

3. Set the telescope on the table.
   Sit the telescope on the table.

4. May I look through the telescope?
   Can I look through the telescope?

5. Can you see the planet Venus?
   May you see the planet Venus?

6. I will learn you about Venus.
   I will teach you about Venus.

7. Leave me look again, please.
   Let me look again, please.

**B. Choosing Verbs**   Complete each sentence with the correct form of the verb in parentheses ( ). Write the verb.

8. (Can, May) you be ready in an hour?

   MODEL ⟩ Can

9. Our parents will (leave, let) us take the bus.
10. Dr. Lee will (teach, learn) us about the stars.
11. We will (teach, learn) how stars were formed.
12. Did you (leave, let) your glasses at home?
13. I think I (sit, set) them on the table.
14. I hope we (can, may) see the stars tonight.

**C. Writing Verbs**   Choose a verb from the box to complete each sentence. Write each sentence.

15. Lunar rocks _____ us about the moon.

    MODEL ⟩ Lunar rocks teach us about the moon.

16. We can _____ about the surface of the moon.
17. What _____ you tell us about it?
18. _____ in this seat, please.
19. _____ I look at the rock?
20. Will you _____ me hold it?
21. Please _____ it down on the table.
22. We will _____ it on display.

| teach |
| sit |
| learn |
| let |
| leave |
| can |
| may |
| set |

## UNIT 4

## 5 Contractions *pages 192–193*

**A. Identifying Contractions**   Write the contraction that can be made from the underlined words in each sentence.

1. It is almost springtime.
MODEL  It's
2. You would never know it, though.
3. We have not seen one robin yet.
4. The daffodils are not in bloom, either.
5. They have even called for more snow.
6. We are turning the clocks ahead tomorrow.
7. Soon I will be mowing the grass.
8. That is not my favorite job.
9. Dad says I should not complain.
10. He will not increase my allowance.
11. My sister said she would help me.

**B. Choosing Contractions**   Choose the correct contraction for each sentence. Write the contraction.

12. It (isn't, aren't) raining yet.
MODEL  isn't
13. We (doesn't, don't) want any rain.
14. Grandpa said it (wouldn't, weren't) rain today.
15. I (wasn't, weren't) convinced.
16. Weather reports (aren't, isn't) always correct.
17. Grandpa (don't, doesn't) believe in them.
18. He (hasn't, haven't) listened to them in years.
19. Grandpa (wasn't, weren't) wrong this time, either.
20. Grandpa (isn't, aren't) wrong very often.

**C. Writing Contractions**   Make each sentence less formal. Use a contraction in place of some words. Write each sentence.

21. I would go skiing with you.
MODEL  I'd go skiing with you.
22. We do not own skis.
23. We have not been to the mountain.
24. Maybe we will try later.
25. You will enjoy skiing.
26. Do not forget your gloves.
27. I wish we had learned sooner.
28. He is a good instructor.
29. She has not fallen once!

EXTRA PRACTICE

# UNIT 5

## 1 Pronouns *pages 228–229*

**A. Identifying Pronouns**   Write the pronoun or pronouns in each sentence.

**1.** He chose the crew for the race.

MODEL ▷ He

**2.** He has the best sailing crew in the country.
**3.** They have many years of sailing experience.
**4.** The crew members work hard for him.
**5.** They anchored the yacht in the harbor.
**6.** They are preparing it for the race.
**7.** The crew checks the sails and rigging on it.
**8.** They will soon compete for the America's Cup.
**9.** We wish them good luck.
**10.** Have you ever sailed in a race?
**11.** My dream is that I will be in this race someday.

**B. Choosing Pronouns**   Write the pronoun in parentheses ( ) that completes each sentence correctly.

**12.** (We, Us) will have our own race.

MODEL ▷ We

**13.** (My, Me) sister and I will be in the race.
**14.** Most of our friends built (their, them) own boats.
**15.** We built (our, us) boats, also.
**16.** (Them, They) each have one mast and two sails.
**17.** Our parents helped (we, us).
**18.** Do (you, your) think I will win?
**19.** (I, Me) am determined to come in first.
**20.** My sister thinks (she, her) will win.
**21.** (Her, She) boat is the fastest.
**22.** (We, Us) will see tomorrow.

**C. Writing Pronouns**   Replace each underlined word or words with a pronoun from the box. Write each sentence.

**23.** The race is about to start.

MODEL ▷ It is about to start.

**24.** The boat passed the first marker.
**25.** Mom yelled to me.
**26.** Trim the sails!
**27.** Watch out for Ann's boat!
**28.** My sister and I finished together.
**29.** The judges congratulated the two of us.

| |
|---|
| it |
| they |
| her |
| them |
| we |
| she |

## 2 Subject Pronouns *pages 230–231*

**A. Identifying Subject Pronouns** Write the subject pronoun in each sentence.

1. You should meet Mr. Crump.

MODEL> You

2. He and his wife just learned to ski.
3. They are both in their sixties.
4. We met in ski class yesterday.
5. I am their instructor.
6. She has always enjoyed sports.
7. They had never tried skiing before.
8. It surprised them.
9. She skis very well.
10. You should see the mountain today.
11. It looks treacherous.

**B. Choosing Subject Pronouns** Choose a pronoun from the box to complete each sentence correctly.

12. _____ use this rope for climbing.

MODEL> We

13. _____ is very strong.
14. Do _____ know how to climb?
15. _____ always climb with my father.
16. _____ is an expert climber.
17. He and _____ have climbed for years.
18. Would _____ like to climb with us?
19. _____ are leaving in the morning.
20. _____ can use my sister's equipment.
21. _____ can't go this time.
22. _____ will have a good time.

| |
|---|
| we |
| he |
| I |
| it |
| you |
| she |

**C. Writing Subject Pronouns** Replace the underlined word or words in each sentence with a subject pronoun.

23. Skiing is popular in many countries.

MODEL> It is popular in many countries.

24. Competitive skiers must train and practice.
25. The sport is challenging and strenuous.
26. My sister is training for the Olympics.
27. Her coach lives in Colorado.
28. My parents and I will cheer her on.
29. My mom and dad are proud of my sister.

# UNIT 5

## 3 Object Pronouns *pages 232–233*

**A. Identifying Object Pronouns**  Write the object pronoun in each sentence.

1. Jon joined us at the campground.

MODEL ▷ us

2. We invited him to come along.
3. Jon helped me set up the tent.
4. We put it near the stream.
5. My sister called Jon and me.
6. A camper told her about some bears.
7. Later, a park ranger warned us.
8. Don't leave food out or feed them.
9. The bears could harm you.
10. All the campers thanked him.
11. Mom and Dad reminded us.

**B. Using Object Pronouns**  Replace the underlined word or words with an object pronoun. Write each sentence.

12. Tammy wanted to follow the trail.

MODEL ▷ Tammy wanted to follow it.

13. The trail leads to the stream.
14. Tammy asked Jon and me to go along.
15. We told Tammy yes.
16. We got permission from Mom and Dad.
17. They told Jon, Tammy, and me to be careful.
18. We saw bears at the stream.
19. One bear had caught a fish.
20. Another bear was eating berries.
21. We ran back and warned the campers.
22. Dad notified the ranger.

**C. Writing Object Pronouns**  Use an object pronoun in place of the word or words in parentheses ( ). Write each sentence.

23. We thanked _____ for his help. (the ranger)

MODEL ▷ We thanked him for his help.

24. Dad spoke to _____. (Tammy)
25. Did you pack _____? (the sleeping bags)
26. Mom asked _____ to help. (Jon and me)
27. Please carry _____ to the car. (the suitcases)
28. Make sure _____ is out completely. (the fire)
29. Put _____ in the trash container. (the trash bags)

# 4 Subject or Object Pronoun? *pages 234–235*

**A. Identifying Subject and Object Pronouns**   Write the pronoun in each sentence. Then write whether the pronoun is a *subject pronoun* or an *object pronoun*.

1. We may go to the museum tomorrow.
MODEL > We—subject pronoun
2. Mom and Dad will take us.
3. Bob told me about the dinosaur exhibit.
4. He said the exhibit was fascinating.
5. I am very interested in dinosaurs.
6. Bob's sister introduced him to the curators.
7. They let Bob hold some dinosaur fossils.
8. Bob examined them carefully.
9. He had a terrific time.
10. We can't wait to see the exhibit.

**B. Choosing Correct Pronouns**   Write the pronoun in parentheses ( ) that completes each sentence correctly.

11. Our parents took (we, us) to the museum.
MODEL > us
12. (We, Us) spoke to a curator.
13. The curator discussed dinosaurs with (we, us).
14. Bob asked (her, she) why the dinosaurs disappeared.
15. (He, Him) learned there had been a change in climate.
16. (She, Her) discussed several other theories.
17. (I, Me) wanted to look at the fossils.
18. The curator took (I, me) to a special room.
19. (They, Them) had fossils everywhere.
20. Scientists found (they, them) all over the world.
21. Fossils tell (we, us) many things about dinosaurs.

**C. Writing Correct Pronouns**   Choose a subject pronoun or an object pronoun to complete each sentence correctly. Write the sentence.

22. _____ bought a book about dinosaurs.
MODEL > I bought a book about dinosaurs.
23. _____ lived millions of years ago.
24. Something caused _____ to become extinct.
25. Dinosaurs left _____ some clues.
26. What do _____ think happened?
27. Can you tell _____?

# UNIT 5

## 5 Possessive Pronouns pages 236–237

**A. Identifying Possessive Pronouns**  Write the possessive pronoun in each sentence.

1. My friend Mike taught me to swim.
MODEL> My
2. I was visiting his family at the time.
3. We were invited to swim in their pool.
4. Ellen jumped in after her brother.
5. "It's your turn," they told me.
6. I had forgotten my float.
7. "Use ours, or I'll teach you to swim," said Mike.
8. "The choice is yours," he added.
9. I finally overcame my fears.
10. Now I swim on our school team.
11. Does your school have a swim team?

**B. Using Possessive Pronouns**  Write the possessive pronoun in parentheses ( ) that completes each sentence correctly.

12. (Our, Ours) school has a big pool.
MODEL> Our
13. Do many schools have a pool like (your, yours)?
14. (Our, Ours) measures 50 meters.
15. (Our, Ours) swim team practices begin after school.
16. First we do (our, ours) warm-ups.
17. Then I practice (my, mine) starts.
18. What is (your, yours) best stroke?
19. (My, Mine) is the backstroke.
20. Lois is (their, theirs) best swimmer.
21. What is (her, hers) fastest time?
22. Who is (our, ours) best swimmer?

**C. Writing Possessive Pronouns**  Write a possessive pronoun to complete each sentence correctly. Write each sentence.

23. Lois swam _____ best at the meet.
MODEL> Lois swam her best at the meet.
24. Mike swam against _____ brother.
25. The judges watched _____ strokes and turns.
26. The students cheered for _____ team.
27. Several swimmers broke _____ own records.
28. The trophy is _____.
29. The coach thanked _____ team.

# 6 Reflexive Pronouns *pages 238–239*

**A. Identifying Reflexive Pronouns** Write the reflexive pronoun in each sentence.

1. We read ourselves the legend of King Arthur.
> MODEL> ourselves
2. We imagined ourselves in Arthur's court.
3. The king showed himself to us at once.
4. I asked myself if it could be a dream.
5. "Tell yourself you are dreaming," I thought.
6. We found ourselves seated at the Round Table.
7. It was hard to see how a table so large could support itself.
8. Queen Guinevere seated herself next to me.
9. The knights introduced themselves to us.
10. Sir Lancelot considered himself to be the greatest knight.
11. Read the legend and decide for yourself.

**B. Using Reflexive Pronouns** Choose a reflexive pronoun from the box to complete each sentence correctly. Write each sentence.

12. The king presented _____ at the tournament.
> MODEL> The king presented himself at the tournament.
13. The queen seated _____ next to us.
14. The knights divided _____ into groups.
15. Each group prepared _____ to fight.
16. Each knight prided _____ on his courage.
17. One horse displayed _____ before the king.
18. Imagine _____ on horseback.
19. One knight hurt _____ when he fell.
20. We enjoyed _____ at the tournament.

| himself |
| ourselves |
| yourself |
| herself |
| itself |
| themselves |

**C. Writing Reflexive Pronouns** Complete each sentence with a reflexive pronoun. Write each sentence.

21. The legend sustains _____.
> MODEL> The legend sustains itself.
22. Arthur proved _____ fit to be king when he removed the sword from the stone.
23. You must ask _____ if it is true.
24. I find _____ believing it.
25. We tell _____ that an Arthur probably did exist.
26. Historians with other theories need to explain _____.

**EXTRA PRACTICE**

# UNIT 5

## 7 Agreement of Pronouns *pages 240–241*

**A. Identifying Agreement of Subject Pronouns and Verbs**
Write *correct* if the underlined verb in each sentence agrees with the subject pronoun. Write *incorrect* if it does not.

1. He <u>rides</u> his bicycle to basketball practice.
   MODEL > correct
2. It <u>begin</u> at 3:30.
3. We <u>practice</u> every day.
4. I <u>listens</u> to the coaches.
5. They <u>teach</u> us new plays.
6. It <u>is</u> hard work.
7. I <u>ask</u> the coach for help with my game.
8. He <u>dribble</u> the ball.
9. You <u>try</u> to steal it.
10. He <u>toss</u> it to me.
11. I <u>pass</u> it to Al.
12. He <u>misses</u> the basket.
13. You <u>makes</u> the rebound.

**B. Choosing Pronouns That Agree with Antecedents** Write the pronoun that agrees with the underlined antecedent.

14. <u>Basketball</u> is an exciting sport. _____ is very popular.
    MODEL > It
15. <u>My friends and I</u> play. _____ are a team.
16. <u>My sister</u> plays, also. My dad taught _____.
17. She plays with <u>the Rockets</u>. _____ are a good team.
18. Tonight was <u>the big game</u>. _____ was exciting.
19. Coach talked to <u>the players</u>. He wished _____ luck.
20. <u>Mom, Dad, and I</u> went. Laura waved to _____.
21. <u>Susan</u> fell on the court. She hurt _____ knee.
22. The coach signaled <u>Laura</u>. _____ called a time-out.
23. They needed <u>one point</u> to win. Laura made _____.
24. The crowd cheered for <u>the girls</u>. _____ won the game.

**C. Writing Verbs That Agree with Subject Pronouns** Complete each sentence with the correct present-tense form of the verb in parentheses ( ). Write each sentence.

25. We _____ basketball. (like)
    MODEL > We like basketball.
26. We _____ a team. (want)
27. I _____ Ben to help. (ask)
28. He _____ basketball. (coach)
29. We _____ the players. (organize)
30. They _____ at his house. (meet)
31. We _____ at the playground. (practice)
32. Ben _____ us in many ways. (help)
33. We _____ him every day. (thank)

## UNIT 6

# 1 Adjectives *pages 274–275*

**A. Identifying Adjectives** Write the adjectives that describe the underlined nouns in the sentences.

1. An experienced guide led the small group.
   MODEL▷ experienced, small
2. She told us many interesting facts during our walk through the wilderness.
3. The narrow trail winds along for five miles.
4. Pretty wildflowers dot the rocky hillside.
5. Did you hear a strange sound?
6. Three frightened chipmunks darted quickly into the bushes.
7. I took two photographs of a beautiful hawk.
8. What a wonderful sight it was!
9. We stopped along an icy stream.
10. I touched the bubbling water.
11. The water soothed my tired, sore feet.

**B. Classifying Adjectives** Write the adjective or adjectives in each sentence. Then write whether each adjective describes *what kind* or *how many.*

12. Five mules bumped along the trail.
    MODEL▷ five—how many
13. It is two miles to the bottom of the canyon.
14. The trip will take one day.
15. The trail winds down a steep cliff.
16. They left at sunrise from the south rim.
17. The five riders rested after three hours.
18. The tired riders brushed off their dusty clothes.
19. They enjoyed the incredible view.
20. The guide pointed to the big snake.
21. It was a brown rattlesnake!

**C. Writing Adjectives** Add two adjectives to each sentence. Add commas where they are needed. Write each sentence.

22. The _____ _____ travelers stop for a rest.
    MODEL▷ The hot, thirsty travelers stop for a rest.
23. The _____ _____ canyon amazes them.
24. A _____ _____ river winds through the canyon.
25. _____ _____ clouds float across the sky.
26. A _____ _____ squirrel watches the travelers.

# UNIT 6

## 2 Articles and Demonstrative Adjectives *pages 276–277*

**A. Identifying Articles and Demonstrative Adjectives**  Write the article or demonstrative adjective in each sentence.

1. Let's explore that cave.
[MODEL] > that
2. We will go with an experienced guide.
3. What an exciting time we are having!
4. This cave is dark and damp.
5. Do you have a headlamp?
6. Watch out for those jagged rocks!
7. I want photographs of these formations.
8. What an incredible sight we saw!
9. What is that noise?
10. You hear sounds of an underground river.

**B. Choosing Articles and Demonstrative Adjectives**  Complete each sentence with the correct article or demonstrative adjective in parentheses ( ).

11. Look at _____ bats over there. (this, those)
[MODEL] > Look at those bats over there.
12. They roost in _____ cave. (this, these)
13. They hunt insects during _____ night. (the, a)
14. What is _____ strange formation? (that, those)
15. It is called _____ stalactite. (a, an)
16. The stalactite looks like _____ icicle. (a, an)
17. _____ formation here is a stalagmite. (This, That)
18. It resembles _____ pillar rising from the floor. (a, an)
19. Is there _____ exit to this cave? (a, an)
20. We will be outside in _____ hour. (a, an)

**C. Writing Articles and Demonstrative Adjectives**  Complete each sentence with the type of adjective named in parentheses ( ). Write each sentence.

21. Many people visit _____ cave. (demonstrative adjective)
[MODEL] > Many people visit this (*or* that) cave.
22. It is _____ longest cave ever explored. (article)
23. _____ cave has 20 miles of passages. (demonstrative adjective)
24. _____ rocks resemble flowers. (demonstrative adjective)
25. Fish live in _____ underground river. (article)
26. _____ fish are blind and colorless. (demonstrative adjective)
27. Did people once live in _____ cave? (demonstrative adjective)

# 3 Proper Adjectives *pages 278–279*

**A. Identifying Proper Adjectives**   Write the proper adjective in each sentence.

**1.** Canada is a North American country.

MODEL ▷ North American

**2.** The Canadian coastline is 155,000 miles long.

**3.** Northern Canada has many Eskimo tribes.

**4.** The Arctic wastelands are in the far north.

**5.** The Great Lakes region is highly industrialized.

**6.** A variety of Indian tribes inhabited Canada first.

**7.** The word *Canada* comes from an Iroquois word.

**8.** The vast majority of Canadians today are of European descent.

**9.** Most are of British ancestry.

**10.** Canadians descended from the French colonists make up a powerful minority.

**B. Using Proper Adjectives**   Write the proper adjective that can be made from the noun in parentheses ( ).

**11.** My family toured _____ countries. (Europe)

MODEL ▷ European

**12.** The tour was arranged by a _____ travel agency. (Canada)

**13.** An _____ airline flew us to London. (America)

**14.** I enjoyed the _____ museums and sights. (Britain)

**15.** Our _____ hosts were very helpful. (England)

**16.** Next we flew to the _____ capital. (France)

**17.** We toured the _____ countryside by car. (Italy)

**18.** The _____ ruins were very interesting. (Rome)

**19.** We saw our _____ friends a week later. (Germany)

**C. Writing Proper Adjectives**   Answer each question by writing a sentence that uses a proper adjective.

**20.** Have you ever visited the castles of Austria?

MODEL ▷ I have never visited the Austrian castles.

**21.** Did you visit the pyramids of Egypt last year?

**22.** Do you speak the language of Germany?

**23.** Do you have any relatives in Spain?

**24.** What is your favorite dish from Japan?

**25.** Do you know the capital of Turkey?

**26.** Is that a custom in South America?

# 4 Adjectives That Follow Linking Verbs *pages 280–281*

**A. Identifying Adjectives That Follow Linking Verbs** Write the adjective that describes the subject in each sentence. Then write the linking verb.

1. The stagecoach was crowded on this trip.

MODEL ⟩ crowded, was

2. The road was bumpy.
3. The seats were uncomfortable.
4. Everyone was dusty after an hour.
5. Sleeping seemed impossible to them.
6. One of the passengers appeared nervous.
7. She was afraid of a robbery.
8. The passengers were glad to stop.

**B. Finding Adjectives in Different Positions in a Sentence** Write each sentence. Underline each adjective once. Do not include *a, an,* or *the.* Draw an arrow from each adjective to the noun it describes. Underline the linking verb twice.

9. The notorious gang is eager to rob the train.

MODEL ⟩ The notorious gang is eager to rob the train.

10. The five masked men grow restless.

11. Even the horses are uneasy.

12. The old train is late.

13. The startled engineer grows pale when he sees them.

14. A young child becomes upset by the noise.

15. A brave sheriff is ready for the gang.

**C. Writing Adjectives in Different Positions in a Sentence** Add adjectives to complete each sentence. Then write each sentence.

16. That _____ story was _____.

MODEL ⟩ That mystery story was scary.

17. The _____ house was _____.
18. The _____ residents were _____.
19. A _____ sound grew _____.
20. The _____ father appeared _____.
21. What _____ creature was behind the _____ door?

# 5 Comparison with Adjectives: *er, est* pages 282–283

**A. Identifying Adjectives That Compare** Write the adjective that compares in each sentence. Then write whether the adjective is used to compare *two* or *three or more*.

1. Have you read a taller tale than this one?

MODEL > taller—two

2. Paul Bunyan is one of our greatest frontier heroes.
3. The legend of Paul Bunyan is the tallest tale of all.
4. His strength was greater than that of any other person.
5. Paul Bunyan was faster than you can imagine.
6. He was also the biggest lumberjack in America.
7. Paul's ox, Babe, was larger than any other ox.
8. In fact, Babe was the largest ox in the world.
9. Babe was bluer than the sky.
10. Babe could pull the heaviest load of logs.

**B. Choosing Adjectives That Compare** Write the form of the adjective in parentheses ( ) that completes each sentence correctly.

11. Today was the (scarier, scariest) day ever!

MODEL > scariest

12. The (bigger, biggest) of all tornadoes hit our town.
13. I had the (stranger, strangest) feeling all morning.
14. The afternoon sky grew (darker, darkest) than usual.
15. Lightning appeared (closer, closest) than before.
16. The wind grew (stronger, strongest) with each minute.
17. The hail was the (larger, largest) ever reported.
18. Then came the (odder, oddest) hissing sound of all.
19. It was the (louder, loudest) sound I've ever heard.
20. Our town had the (greater, greatest) damage of all.

**C. Writing Adjectives That Compare** Complete each sentence with the correct form of the adjective in parentheses ( ). Write each sentence.

21. This is the _____ book I've ever read. (sad)

MODEL > This is the saddest book I've ever read.

22. The main character is _____ than I. (young)
23. He is the _____ child in the world. (brave)
24. The boy is _____ than I would be. (strong)
25. I wish the ending were _____ than it is. (happy)
26. I will feel sad for the _____ time. (long)

EXTRA PRACTICE

# 6 Comparison with Adjectives: *More, Most*

*pages 284–285*

**A. Identifying Adjectives That Compare**  Write *more* or *most* to complete each sentence correctly.

1. This track meet was _____ exciting than last year's.

MODEL ▷ more

2. It was the _____ successful in our school's history.
3. We were _____ nervous than usual.
4. The athletes were _____ confident than before.
5. Track is the _____ popular of all sports in our school.
6. It is even _____ popular than basketball.
7. Winning is not the _____ important thing of all.
8. Doing our best is _____ important than winning.
9. We couldn't be _____ pleased than we are now.

**B. Using Adjectives That Compare**  Complete each sentence with the correct form of the adjective in parentheses ( ).

10. This year's fair is the _____ of all. (successful)

MODEL ▷ most successful

11. The crowds are _____ than usual. (enthusiastic)
12. The attractions are _____ than last year's. (unusual)
13. The magic show is the _____ attraction of them all. (exciting)
14. It is even _____ than the rides. (popular)
15. The disappearing elephant is the _____ feat in the show. (amazing)
16. I was the _____ member of the family. (impressed)
17. Greg the Great is the _____ magician of all. (popular)
18. Greg has a _____ act than the other magicians. (original)

**C. Writing Adjectives That Compare**  Add the correct form of an adjective from the box to complete each sentence. Write each sentence.

19. Mrs. Nakano organized the _____ show ever.

MODEL ▷ Mrs. Nakano organized the most amazing show ever.

20. The performers wore _____ costumes than any others we had ever seen.
21. The _____ costume was 20 feet long!
22. That girl danced to the _____ music.
23. That night, we saw _____ fireworks than ever before.
24. They provided the _____ entertainment of any show!

| amazing |
| beautiful |
| spectacular |
| colorful |
| unusual |
| enormous |

## 7 Comparison with Adjectives: Special Forms *pages 286–287*

**A. Identifying Adjectives with Special Comparison Forms**
Write the adjective in each sentence. Then write whether the adjective is used to compare *two* or *three or more*. If no comparison is made, write *none.*

1. My brother is a good skier.
MODEL > good—none
2. Amy is a better skier than Bob.
3. She has more experience than he.
4. Also, Amy has the best ski instructor.
5. It takes many hours of practice.
6. Bob has less time to practice than Amy.
7. This was a bad year for skiing.
8. There was so little snow.
9. We had the least amount of snow in years.

**B. Choosing Adjectives with Special Comparison Forms** Write the form of the adjective in parentheses ( ) that completes each sentence correctly.

10. Where is the (better, best) place in this area to ski?
MODEL > best
11. We are staying at the (better, best) resort of the three.
12. Do you have (many, most) slopes?
13. We have the (more, most) ski lifts of all.
14. The beginner slopes are the (less, least) difficult of all.
15. You have (little, least) chance of getting hurt there.
16. The intermediate slopes are (more, most) challenging than the beginner slopes.
17. Sam fell (more, most) often than Jenny did.

**C. Writing Adjectives with Special Comparison Forms**
Complete each sentence with the correct form of the adjective in parentheses ( ). Then write each sentence.

18. That was the _____ snowstorm I ever saw! (bad)
MODEL > That was the worst snowstorm I ever saw!
19. It grew steadily _____ as the day wore on. (bad)
20. The _____ place to be was inside. (good)
21. That was the _____ snow we had ever had. (much)
22. It took _____ time than usual to clear roads. (many)
23. With the new plows it will take _____ time. (little)

# UNIT 7

## 1 Adverbs *pages 320–321*

**A. Identifying Adverbs**   Write the adverb that describes the underlined verb in each sentence. Then write whether the adverb tells *how, when,* or *where.*

   **1.** Yesterday we <u>had</u> a science test.
MODEL Yesterday—when
   **2.** Everyone in the class <u>studied</u> diligently.
   **3.** Mike <u>reread</u> his notes silently.
   **4.** Then he <u>reviewed</u> the chapter.
   **5.** I <u>studied</u> quietly.
   **6.** We <u>waited</u> nervously for the test to begin.
   **7.** Mr. Jones quickly <u>handed</u> us the tests.
   **8.** He <u>gave</u> us directions carefully.
   **9.** <u>Bring</u> your tests here.
  **10.** We <u>have</u> no homework tonight.

**B. Connecting Adverbs and Verbs**   Write each sentence. Underline each adverb once. Then draw two lines under the verb it describes.

  **11.** We will get our test scores soon.
MODEL We <u>will get</u> our test scores <u>soon</u>.
  **12.** We waited patiently.
  **13.** Mr. Jones finally returned our papers.
  **14.** "I have your tests here," he said.
  **15.** I wondered anxiously about my grade.
  **16.** How slowly he distributed the tests!
  **17.** I bravely looked at my paper.
  **18.** I cheered happily to myself.

**C. Writing Adverbs**   Add an adverb to each sentence. Write each sentence.

  **19.** Graduation day _____ arrived.
MODEL Graduation day finally arrived.
  **20.** The students sat _____ on stage.
  **21.** They listened _____ to the principal's speech.
  **22.** _____ they received their diplomas.
  **23.** Sam smiled _____ at his parents.
  **24.** We cheered _____ at the end of the ceremony.
  **25.** The students displayed their diplomas _____ .

# UNIT 7

## 2 Comparison with Adverbs pages 322–323

**A. Identifying Adverbs That Compare**   Complete each set of sentences with the correct form of the adverb underlined in the first sentence.

MODEL **1.** I screamed loudly.
You yelled more loudly than I.
He yelled most loudly of all.

**2.** Jim worked hard.
Bob worked _____ than Jim.
We worked _____ of all.

**3.** Sue studied carefully.
Ed studied _____ than Sue.
Lee studied _____ of all.

**4.** Joe arrived late.
Jan arrived _____ than Joe.
Sam arrived _____ of all.

**5.** I walk slowly.
Mom walks _____ than I.
Al walks _____ of all.

**6.** He sang beautifully.
She sang _____ than Nell.
You sang _____ of all.

**7.** Mark climbed high.
Amy climbed _____ than he.
Ned climbed _____ of all.

**B. Choosing Adverbs That Compare**   Choose *more* or *most* to complete each sentence correctly. Then write the word that you chose.

**8.** Ann anticipates the spelling bee _____ eagerly than I.
MODEL more

**9.** She spells _____ accurately than most of us.

**10.** Max studies the words _____ carefully than he did last year.

**11.** Willy learns them _____ easily than Les does.

**12.** Jenny practices _____ often of all her friends.

**13.** Marty waits _____ nervously for his turn than Max.

**14.** Jim spells the word _____ slowly than before.

**15.** Susie speaks _____ softly than Sara.

**16.** Ann waits _____ anxiously of all for the last word.

**C. Writing Adverbs That Compare**   Complete each sentence with the correct form of the adverb in parentheses ( ). Write each sentence.

**17.** Dave spelled _____ than Jan. (fast)
MODEL Dave spelled faster than Jan.

**18.** Jim listened _____ than I. (careful)

**19.** I spelled my words _____ than Nancy. (slow)

**20.** I wait _____ of all for my last word. (impatient)

**21.** Ann accepted the award _____ of all. (gracious)

**22.** She smiled _____ of all. (happy)

# 3 Adverbs Before Adjectives and Other Adverbs *pages 324–325*

**A. Identifying Adverbs** Write the adverb that describes the underlined adjective or adverb in each sentence.

1. Immigration increased rather <u>dramatically</u> in the late 1800's.

MODEL⟩ rather

2. Many immigrants faced terribly <u>difficult</u> journeys.
3. Most of them were very <u>poor</u>.
4. They almost <u>always</u> traveled in the ship's steerage.
5. This section was incredibly <u>small</u>.
6. Families were uncomfortably <u>crowded</u>.
7. They faced rather <u>unsanitary</u> conditions.
8. There was too <u>little</u> light and air.
9. Passengers were hardly <u>ever</u> permitted on deck.
10. They must have been quite <u>happy</u> to reach America.

**B. Choosing Adverbs** Complete each sentence using an adverb from the box.

11. Ellis Island is _____ memorable to many.

MODEL⟩ quite

12. _____ all immigrants arrived at Ellis Island.
13. Amy's grandparents came _____ suddenly.
14. Hundreds stood in _____ long lines.
15. Amy's grandparents waited _____ patiently.
16. They must have been _____ confused.
17. Doctors examined everyone _____ carefully.
18. Some officials were _____ helpful to them.
19. They gathered their _____ meager belongings.
20. In the beginning, they were _____ nervous.
21. It didn't take them _____ long to get settled.

| |
|---|
| quite |
| too |
| so |
| terribly |
| slightly |
| almost |
| rather |
| extremely |
| incredibly |
| very |
| totally |

**C. Writing Adverbs** Complete each sentence with an adverb. Write each sentence correctly.

22. This photo album is _____ wonderful.

MODEL⟩ This photo album is truly wonderful.

23. Grandma's dress looks _____ beautiful.
24. Grandpa stands _____ proudly in front of their home.
25. Making a new home was _____ important to them.
26. It took them _____ 10 years to save enough money.
27. They both worked _____ hard.
28. I _____ admire my grandparents.

## UNIT 7

# 4 Negatives *pages 326–327*

**A. Identifying Negatives**   Identify the negative word in each sentence.

1. I had never been in the Olympic Games before.
   MODEL> never
2. I hoped this would not be the last time.
3. It was nothing like I had imagined.
4. Nobody could have told me how thrilling it would be.
5. No one knows until he or she experiences it.
6. There is nowhere more exciting to be.
7. No competition has ever been this important to me.
8. I haven't ever been this nervous.
9. None of my teammates was as nervous.
10. It wasn't easy being in front of the huge crowds.
11. I have never performed better!

**B. Correcting Double Negatives**   Each sentence has two negatives. Rewrite each sentence correctly.

12. The gymnast didn't have no fear.
    MODEL> The gymnast didn't have any fear.
13. Haven't you never seen her before?
14. The world has never seen no one like her.
15. There isn't nobody who can perform as well.
16. The arena wasn't never more packed.
17. We couldn't find nowhere to sit.
18. There wasn't no seat left anywhere.
19. We couldn't believe no one was that good.
20. Hasn't nobody ever gotten a perfect score before?
21. She hadn't never achieved such perfection.
22. Gymnastics hasn't never been so popular.

**C. Writing Negatives**   Answer each question. Use a sentence that contains a negative.

23. Have you ever won an Olympic gold medal?
    MODEL> I have never won an Olympic gold medal.
24. Do you know anyone who has won a gold medal?
25. Did you compete in the last Olympics?
26. Have you ever heard of Mark Spitz?
27. Did you know that he won seven medals?
28. Are the summer games your favorites?
29. Have you heard where the next games will be?

# 5 Adverb or Adjective? *pages 328–329*

**A. Identifying Adverbs and Adjectives** Write *adverb* or *adjective* for the underlined word in each sentence.

**1.** Amelia Earhart was a <u>skillful</u> pilot.

`MODEL` adjective

**2.** She became <u>very</u> famous during the 1930's.
**3.** As a <u>young</u> woman, Amelia worked hard to earn money.
**4.** She saved <u>diligently</u> for flying lessons.
**5.** Amelia was the <u>first</u> woman to fly successfully across the Atlantic Ocean.
**6.** It must have been <u>incredibly</u> exciting.
**7.** Amelia <u>proudly</u> accepted an award for flying.
**8.** Her <u>final</u> flight ended in tragedy.
**9.** The plane vanished <u>mysteriously</u> somewhere in the Pacific Ocean.

**B. Distinguishing Between *Good* and *Well*** Choose *good* or *well* to complete each sentence correctly. Then write the word that you chose.

**10.** I read a _____ book about Amelia Earhart.

`MODEL` good

**11.** Amelia flew her plane _____.
**12.** Amelia was a _____ pilot.
**13.** She learned her lessons _____.
**14.** She was as _____ a pilot as anyone.
**15.** Amelia had a _____ chance to set new records.
**16.** She planned her route _____.
**17.** She had a _____ flight to Europe.
**18.** It must feel _____ to fly above the clouds!
**19.** She wrote a _____ book about her experiences.
**20.** I hope to fly as _____ as Amelia Earhart did.

**C. Writing Adjectives and Adverbs** Complete each sentence with the correct word in parentheses ( ). Write each sentence.

**21.** Amelia prepared for her (final, finally) flight.

`MODEL` Amelia prepared for her final flight.

**22.** The route was planned (careful, carefully).
**23.** She checked the plane (thorough, thoroughly).
**24.** No one knows (exact, exactly) what happened.
**25.** The plane was (near, nearly) Howland Island.
**26.** How (terrible, terribly) it was when she disappeared!

# UNIT 8

## 1 Prepositions *pages 366–367*

**A. Identifying Prepositions** Write the preposition in each sentence.

    **1.** The Alamo is in San Antonio, Texas.

    MODEL in

    **2.** The Alamo got its name from cottonwood trees.

    **3.** It was built to be a mission during the 1700's.

    **4.** The mission was surrounded by high walls.

    **5.** A monastery and a church were built inside the walls.

    **6.** A battle was fought there between Texans and Mexicans.

    **7.** It took place during the Texas revolution.

    **8.** The Texans tried to break their ties with Mexico.

    **9.** They were not happy under Mexico's rule.

    **10.** General Santa Anna rode toward the Alamo.

    **11.** He brought nearly 5,000 soldiers with him.

**B. Distinguishing Between Prepositions and Their Objects** Write each sentence. Underline the preposition once. Underline the object of the preposition twice.

    **12.** The Texans had an army of 150 men.

    MODEL The Texans had an army <u>of</u> 150 <u><u>men</u></u>.

    **13.** They were under William Travis's command.

    **14.** Jim Bowie and Davy Crockett were among the men.

    **15.** Santa Anna's army moved toward San Antonio.

    **16.** Travis and his men retreated to the Alamo.

    **17.** The attack began on February 23, 1836.

    **18.** It continued through the month.

    **19.** By early March, the Texans were losing.

    **20.** They were nearly out of ammunition.

    **21.** The Mexicans climbed over the walls.

    **22.** The Texans fought bravely until the end.

**C. Writing Prepositions** Complete each sentence with one of the prepositions from the box.

| |
|---|
| by |
| at |
| on |
| during |
| to |

    **23.** General Sam Houston was then pursued _____ Santa Anna.

    MODEL General Sam Houston was then pursued by Santa Anna.

    **24.** Houston surprised the Mexican army _____ a siesta.

    **25.** This happened _____ San Jacinto, Texas.

    **26.** _____ the following day, Santa Anna was captured.

    **27.** He signed a treaty giving independence _____ the Texans.

EXTRA PRACTICE

# 2 Prepositional Phrases *pages 368–369*

**A. Identifying Prepositional Phrases**   The preposition in each sentence is underlined. Write the prepositional phrase.

    **1.** Last summer we drove <u>across</u> the country.

    MODEL ▷ across the country

    **2.** We left Pennsylvania and drove <u>to</u> Wyoming.

    **3.** <u>Before</u> the trip, I had never seen such scenery.

    **4.** Visiting Yellowstone National Park was the best part <u>of</u> the trip.

    **5.** It is the oldest national park <u>in</u> the United States.

    **6.** I enjoyed traveling <u>through</u> Yellowstone.

    **7.** We followed the Grand Loop <u>around</u> the park.

    **8.** Many cars are often <u>along</u> this road.

    **9.** I took a photograph <u>of</u> Old Faithful.

    **10.** The famous geyser erupted <u>after</u> a half hour.

    **11.** It shot boiling water 100 feet <u>into</u> the air.

**B. Identifying the Object of the Preposition**   Write the prepositional phrase in each sentence. Then underline the object of the preposition.

    **12.** Yellowstone covers over two million acres.

    MODEL ▷ over two million <u>acres</u>

    **13.** The park is famous for its natural wonders.

    **14.** Yellowstone was created by volcanic eruptions.

    **15.** Magma still lies beneath the park.

    **16.** It provides heat for the geysers and hot springs.

    **17.** A road loops around Yellowstone.

    **18.** Visitors enjoy the sights at observation points.

    **19.** They can also explore on foot or horseback.

    **20.** With a special permit visitors can fish.

**C. Writing Prepositional Phrases**   Add a prepositional phrase to each group of words. Use prepositions from the box or others you may know. Write each sentence.

    **21.** Are you going _____?

    MODEL ▷ Are you going to Yellowstone Park?

    **22.** We're planning a trip _____.

    **23.** We'll go _____.

    **24.** Dad says we'll stay _____.

    **25.** We'll fly _____.

    **26.** Then we'll rent a car _____.

| |
|---|
| to |
| during |
| for |
| at |
| from |
| by |

## 3 Preposition or Adverb? *pages 370–371*

**A. Identifying Prepositions and Adverbs** Write whether the underlined word in each sentence is a *preposition* or an *adverb*.

1. Have you been to this museum <u>before</u>?

MODEL ▷ adverb

2. Would you like to go <u>along</u>?
3. It's just <u>down</u> the block.
4. Let's go <u>inside</u>.
5. We can walk <u>around</u>.
6. We have two hours <u>before</u> closing time.
7. Stand <u>behind</u> that totem pole.
8. Look at the jewelry display <u>in</u> this corner.
9. This was made <u>by</u> the Northwest Coast Indians.
10. Look <u>above</u>.
11. What do you think <u>about</u> that enormous canoe?

**B. Using Prepositions and Adverbs** Complete each sentence with one of the words from the box. Then write whether the word is used as a *preposition* or an *adverb*.

12. Do you know _____ the Northwest Coast Indians?

MODEL ▷ about—preposition

13. Some tribes settled _____ the Pacific coast.
14. They lived _____ fishing and trading.
15. These Indians did not wander _____.
16. Instead, they built houses _____ the water.
17. Totem poles were erected _____.
18. They sailed to the sea _____ large wooden canoes.
19. Canoes were made _____ the trees of nearby forests.

| |
|---|
| along |
| around |
| inside |
| from |
| near |
| in |
| outside |
| by |

**C. Using Prepositions** Each sentence below has an adverb. Write a sentence using that same word as a preposition.

20. Anna and I walked along.

MODEL ▷ Anna and I walked along the street.

21. She and I went across.
22. We passed by.
23. The museum is near.
24. Let's go inside.
25. We walked around.
26. That painting hangs above.

# 4 Conjunctions *pages 372–373*

**A. Identifying Conjunctions**   Write the conjunction in each sentence.

1. Daniel Boone explored the wilderness and helped many settlers.

MODEL ▷ and

2. Daniel was born and raised in Pennsylvania.
3. He didn't go to school, but he learned to read.
4. The Boones farmed, and they had a blacksmith shop.
5. There was much work, and Daniel did his share.
6. He helped on the farm and tended cows.
7. Daniel watched and learned from the local Indians.
8. As a boy, he got a rifle and learned to hunt.
9. The area grew quickly, and the Boones felt crowded.
10. The Boones could stay, or they could move.
11. They packed and moved to North Carolina.

**B. Choosing Conjunctions**   Complete each sentence with the conjunction *and, but,* or *or.* Write the conjunction. Then write whether it joins *two subjects, two verbs,* or *two simple sentences.*

12. Daniel heard and enjoyed stories about Kentucky.

MODEL ▷ and—two verbs

13. Were they real, _____ were they tall tales?
14. Daniel wanted to know, _____ he wasn't sure of the best way to get there.
15. He knew of a trail, _____ could he find it?
16. No highways _____ maps existed in those days.
17. Daniel _____ several men set out for Kentucky.
18. Would they find the trail, _____ would they turn back?
19. They found the trail _____ followed it to Kentucky.
20. The stories were true, _____ he stayed for two years.

**C. Writing Conjunctions**   Use a conjunction to complete each sentence.

21. Daniel Boone hunted _____ farmed.

MODEL ▷ Daniel Boone hunted and farmed.

22. He was a peaceful man, _____ he fought when he had to.
23. Some Indians were hostile, _____ many were friendly.
24. He was once caught _____ held by the Indians.
25. His knowledge _____ bravery helped him survive.
26. Do we know the real Daniel Boone _____ the legendary Daniel Boone?

# 5 Interjections *pages 374–375*

**A. Identifying Interjections**   Write the interjection in each sentence.

1. Wow! Election day is here at last.

MODEL ▷ Wow!

2. Phew! I'm glad it's almost over.
3. Hey! Did you register to vote?
4. Oh, no! I forgot all about it.
5. Oh, dear! That means you can't vote.
6. Oh, my! I can't believe it.
7. Hooray! The election is over.
8. Wow! Can you believe who won?
9. Of course! Ms. Smith was the best candidate.
10. Well! I wanted Ms. Loomis to win.
11. Oh, well! You might have better luck in the next election.

**B. Choosing Interjections**   Complete each sentence with an interjection from the box.

12. _____, our school elections are next week!

MODEL ▷ Golly

13. _____! For whom are you voting?
14. _____! I'm voting for myself.
15. _____! I didn't realize you were running.
16. _____! Where have you been?
17. _____, I'm sorry!
18. _____, here's my campaign button anyway!
19. _____! I'll be sure to wear it.
20. _____! Do you think I'll win?
21. _____, you'll win!
22. _____! We wish you good luck.

| |
|---|
| Golly |
| Wow |
| Good grief |
| Hey |
| Oh |
| Gee |
| Oops |
| Of course |
| Well |
| Oh, my |
| Great |

**C. Writing Interjections**   Add an interjection to each sentence. Write the sentences.

23. _____! You should see all these ballots.

MODEL ▷ Gee! You should see all these ballots.

24. _____! Will you help me count them all!
25. _____! I'll be happy to help you.
26. _____! John received most of the votes.
27. _____! You have won the election.
28. _____! I'm really happy about it.

**UNIT 9**

# 1 Capitalization and End Punctuation in Sentences *pages 410–411*

**A. Identifying Sentences and End Punctuation**   Write whether each sentence is *declarative, imperative, interrogative,* or *exclamatory.* Then write the kind of punctuation needed.

   **1.** Have you ever been to Mexico

   MODEL⟩ interrogative—question mark

   **2.** We visited our relatives in Mexico last year

   **3.** Tell me all about your visit

   **4.** What a terrific time we had

   **5.** Do you speak Spanish

   **6.** I try, but I don't speak well

   **7.** Guess what I did at a restaurant

   **8.** I ordered fried shoes by mistake

   **9.** Were you embarrassed

**B. Capitalizing and Punctuating Sentences Correctly**   Write each sentence. Add capital letters and end punctuation.

   **10.** how long were you in Mexico.

   MODEL⟩ How long were you in Mexico?

   **11.** we were there for a month

   **12.** look at these photographs

   **13.** how pretty you looked

   **14.** what kind of outfit were you wearing

   **15.** why were you wearing it

   **16.** my cousin and I danced at a fiesta

   **17.** we did the *jarabe tapatio*

**C. Writing Sentences Correctly**   Write each sentence correctly. Then write whether it is *declarative, imperative, interrogative,* or *exclamatory.*

   **18.** do you know the *jarabe tapatio*

   MODEL⟩ Do you know the *jarabe tapatio?* interrogative

   **19.** it is the Mexican hat dance

   **20.** show me the steps, please

   **21.** dance with me

   **22.** will you turn on the music

   **23.** how easy this is

   **24.** what a good dancer you are

   **25.** do you know another dance

## 2 Commas Within Sentences *pages 412–413*

**A. Identifying Correct Usage of Commas** Write *correct* for each sentence in which commas are used correctly. Write *incorrect* for each one in which they are not.

1. Lianne, have you read this book yet?

MODEL ▷ correct

2. I want to, but the library has only one copy.
3. Ben Sandy and Al were talking about it in class.
4. It has the funniest jokes, riddles, and rhymes.
5. Sandy read a joke and I couldn't stop laughing.
6. Meg, may I read it when you're finished?
7. Yes, you may borrow it.

**B. Choosing Correct Usage of Commas** Write the sentence in each pair that is correct.

8. Mom drove Ann, Jim, and me to the library.
   Mom drove Ann Jim and me to the library.

MODEL ▷ Mom drove Ann, Jim, and me to the library.

9. Do you want me to help you Ann?
   Do you want me to help you, Ann?
10. No, I'll look for myself.
    No I'll look for myself.
11. I know I'm only five but I can read.
    I know I'm only five, but I can read.
12. We read about Flopsy, Mopsy, Cottontail, and Peter.
    We read about Flopsy, Mopsy, Cottontail, and, Peter.
13. Mom, Jim, and I loved the pictures.
    Mom Jim and I loved the pictures.
14. Let's finish the story, and then we'll know.
    Let's finish the story and then we'll know.

**C. Writing Sentences with Commas** Write each sentence correctly. Add commas where they are needed.

15. Did you like the story Ann?

MODEL ▷ Did you like the story, Ann?

16. Yes I thought it was funny.
17. Which story should I read Jim?
18. This one is good but I have read it.
19. Mr. Gregg may I check out both books?
20. No you may check out only one.
21. Mom Jim and Ann will wait for me outside.

# 3 Capitalization of Proper Nouns, Proper Adjectives, and *I* pages 414–415

**A. Identifying Proper Nouns and Proper Adjectives** Write the word or phrase in each pair that is written correctly.

1. Sunday   tuesday
MODEL▷ Sunday

2. San Diego   salt lake city
3. thanksgiving   Halloween
4. lake Erie   Hudson River
5. June   february
6. florida   Kentucky
7. argentina   Chile

8. German dolls   english tea
9. france   Spain
10. wednesday   Friday
11. August   october
12. First Ave.   hill st.
13. african   European

**B. Correcting Proper Nouns** Write each sentence correctly. Use capital letters where they are needed.

14. Our first volleyball game is on september 21.
MODEL▷ Our first volleyball game is on September 21.

15. It will be played at river city sports arena.
16. Our coach is mr. james l. smith.
17. He moved here from indiana last year.
18. My brother and i are on the team.
19. We practice every monday, wednesday, and friday.
20. Our team plays until the month of december.
21. We made the sports section of the *tribune review.*
22. The article was written by janet t. adams.
23. She said the river city rockets was a good team.

**C. Writing Sentences with Proper Nouns** Complete each sentence with the type of proper noun named in parentheses ( ). Write each sentence correctly.

24. Our baseball season begins in _____. (month)
MODEL▷ Our baseball season begins in April.

25. Baseball tryouts start _____. (day of the week)
26. We will meet at _____. (place)
27. It is near _____. (street)
28. _____ is the team coach. (person)
29. He played for the _____. (name of team)
30. _____ will sponsor the team. (business)
31. The play-offs will be in _____. (month)
32. _____ wants to be a pitcher. (person)

## 4 Abbreviations *pages 416–417*

**A. Identifying Abbreviations**  Write the abbreviation in each group of words. Then write what the abbreviation stands for.

**1.** Mr. Juan Ramirez

MODEL Mr.—Mister

**2.** Dr. Robert Keeler
**3.** 1221 East Idlewild St.
**4.** 704 East Third Ave.
**5.** Dept. of Recreation
**6.** Western Saddle Co.
**7.** Rte. 981
**8.** Mrs. Peg Alan
**9.** Northern Blvd.
**10.** 10:15 A.M.

**11.** Rev. Adam Lee, Sr.
**12.** New York City, NY
**13.** Bar Harbor, ME
**14.** Sept. 3
**15.** Maxwell Corp.
**16.** Ajax Ink, Inc.
**17.** 9:45 P.M.
**18.** Elizabeth, NJ
**19.** Winston-Salem, NC

**B. Choosing Abbreviations**  Read each sentence. Write the abbreviation in parentheses ( ) that would stand for the underlined word or words.

**20.** The letter was addressed to Dayton, Ohio. (OH, oh)

MODEL OH

**21.** We went to the state fair last year. (Yr., yr.)
**22.** Our county fair was in September. (Sep., Sept.)
**23.** Mister Jones drove the school bus. (MR, Mr.)
**24.** Doctor Lewis, our principal, went. (dr., Dr.)
**25.** We took Oak Drive for 10 miles. (Dr., DR.)
**26.** Then we got onto Route 9. (Rte., rte)
**27.** We arrived at 8:00 at night. (P.M., pm)
**28.** We spent all day Friday at the fair. (FRI, Fri.)
**29.** My brother and I went back on Sunday. (Sun., sun)

**C. Writing Abbreviations and Initials**  Rewrite each item, using an abbreviation or initial for the underlined word or words.

**30.** Midland Avenue

MODEL Midland Ave.

**31.** Terry Ann Tilson
**32.** Atlanta, Georgia
**33.** Northmont Road
**34.** Monday, October 2
**35.** Phoenix, Arizona
**36.** President Kennedy
**37.** Tuesday, March 4
**38.** Mister Kane

**39.** Doctor Janice Ward
**40.** Toddler Toys, Incorporated
**41.** Mister Alan Lee, Junior
**42.** Staten Island, New York
**43.** Brickridge Street
**44.** police department
**45.** 9:00 before noon
**46.** 11:00 at night

EXTRA PRACTICE

# UNIT 9

## 5 Letters *pages 418–420*

**A. Identifying Parts of a Letter**  For each pair, write the letter part that is correct.

  **1.** your friend,  Your friend,

`MODEL` Your friend,

  **2.** dear Luis  Dear Luis,

  **3.** January 9, 1991  january 9 1991

  **4.** Pittsburgh Pennsylvania  Pittsburgh, Pennsylvania

  **5.** 157 first avenue  157 First Avenue

  **6.** Mr. Ricardo Ramos  Mr. ricardo Ramos

  **7.** Burton Book company  Burton Book Company

  **8.** Sincerely yours,  sincerely Yours

**B. Capitalizing and Punctuating Parts of a Letter**  Write each letter part correctly.

  **9.** dear angela

`MODEL` Dear Angela,

  **10.** 3517 skyline drive

  **11.** august 1 1991

  **12.** bethlehem pennsylvania 18018

  **13.** j k murphy company

  **14.** 123 arrowhead drive

  **15.** prescott arizona 86301

  **16.** 112 east main street

  **17.** roselle new jersey 07203

  **18.** dear mr charles

  **19.** sincerely yours

  **20.** acme tire company

  **21.** yours truly

**C. Writing a Letter**  Add capital letters and punctuation where needed. Write the letter correctly.

        310 east hills road
        canton ohio 44711
        october 10 1990

mr c d allen

bits and bytes computer company

41 route 819

mount pleasant pennsylvania 15666

dear mr allen

    Enclosed is a check for the computer game Space Brigade. Thank you.

        sincerely
        sidney smith

## 6 Envelopes *pages 421–423*

**A. Identifying Parts of Addresses** For each pair, write the item that is correct.

1. 11 elm lane   670 Bay Street
MODEL> 670 Bay Street
2. 370 Myers Blvd.   14 northern road
3. orlando, fl   San Francisco, CA
4. mr. harvey t herman   Mrs. Grace A. Graham
5. The Toy Box, Inc.   alvin's antiques
6. miss megan alden   Dr. Daniel Davis, Sr.
7. 1459 rte. 66   1150 Jackson St.
8. Michael T. Jamison   robyn lynn lewis
9. Salt Lake City, UT   Wilmington, De
10. 1160 stone hill rd   1436 Rolling Rock Dr.
11. Mary Sue Bender   Bonnie l. christopher

**B. Capitalizing and Punctuating Addresses** Write the lines of each address in the correct order. Add capital letters and punctuation where necessary.

12. brooklyn ny 11012
    mrs. margaret doyle
    1500 flatbush ave
    MODEL> Mrs. Margaret Doyle
    1500 Flatbush Ave.
    Brooklyn, NY 11012
13. chatham nj 07928
    249 east hampton rd
    mr marvin mitchell sr.
14. box 324 rte 24
    mrs tina martinson
    baton rouge la 70821

15. dr john richards
    white plains ny 10602
    1361 martine ave
16. concord nc 28025
    ms allison smithly
    14 richland dr
17. miss mary dean
    indiana pa 15701
    14 maple st

**C. Writing Addresses** Write the address for each item below. Remember to use capital letters, correct punctuation, and abbreviations where needed. If possible, use a telephone directory or a personal address book.

18. a relative's home
19. your home
20. a neighbor's home
21. a classmate's home
22. your police station

23. your school
24. your family doctor's office
25. your public library
26. your town newspaper

## UNIT 9

# 7 Outlines *pages 424–425*

**A. Arranging Parts of an Outline**   Write the items for each outline in the correct order. Add capital letters where they belong.

1. B. the land before time
   A. the yearling
   I. favorite movies
   C. the wizard of oz

   MODEL ▷ I. Favorite movies
       A. The Yearling
       B. The Land Before Time
       C. The Wizard of Oz

2. B. cantaloupe
   IV. favorite foods
   C. beef stew
   A. rice and beans

3. C. Charles Lindbergh
   II. favorite heroes
   A. Sally Ride
   B. Alan Shepard

4. B. charleston
   A. los angeles
   III. favorite cities
   C. san antonio

5. A. baseball
   C. soccer
   VI. favorite sports
   B. archery

**B. Writing Information in Outline Form**   Write the information in each line in the correct outline form shown in parentheses ( ).

6. 1. tallest buildings (main topic)

   MODEL ▷ I. Tallest buildings

7. 3. prize-winning books (main topic)
8. b. lewis carroll (subtopic)
9. a. pablo picasso (subtopic)
10. 2. the smithsonian institution (main topic)

**C. Writing Outlines**   Change the information in each group of notes into correct outline form for the first main topic of a report.

11. American baseball players, Jackie Robinson, Mickey Mantle, Joe DiMaggio

   MODEL ▷ I. American baseball players
       A. Jackie Robinson
       B. Mickey Mantle
       C. Joe DiMaggio

12. American Presidents, Abraham Lincoln, Woodrow Wilson, Ronald Reagan
13. American inventors, The Wright brothers, Elias Howe, Eli Whitney
14. American painters, Andrew Wyeth, Frederic Remington, Georgia O'Keeffe

## 8 Titles *pages 426–427*

**A. Identifying Titles** For each pair, write the title that is correct.

  **1.** (book) <u>The Trumpet of the Swan</u>   Saturdays
  MODEL ▷ The Trumpet of the Swan
  **2.** (song) Sweet Adeline   "America"
  **3.** (magazine) national geographic   <u>Smithsonian</u>
  **4.** (story) "The Fun They Had"   The Foghorn
  **5.** (newspaper) <u>News Record</u>   "USA Today"
  **6.** (song) The Star-Spangled Banner   "Home on the Range"
  **7.** (poem) Running Away   "Elizabeth Blackwell"

**B. Correcting Titles** Write each title correctly.

  **8.** (song) oh, my darling clementine
  MODEL ▷ "Oh, My Darling Clementine"
  **9.** (book) dear mr. henshaw
  **10.** (poem) the song of hiawatha
  **11.** (story) something for davy
  **12.** (song) oklahoma!
  **13.** (magazine) good housekeeping
  **14.** (newspaper) asbury park press
  **15.** (song) texas, our texas
  **16.** (book) magellan: first around the world
  **17.** (magazine) cricket

**C. Writing Titles Correctly** Capitalize and punctuate each title. Write each sentence correctly.

  **18.** We read the poem if I were an elephant.
  MODEL ▷ We read the poem "If I Were an Elephant."
  **19.** I like the story called all summer in a day.
  **20.** Our newspaper, newsday, is delivered seven days a week.
  **21.** George Gershwin wrote the song Swanee.
  **22.** Have you read the book the incredible journey?
  **23.** The magazine motor trend features new cars.
  **24.** Robert Frost wrote the poem the secret sits.
  **25.** Do you have the book mary poppins?
  **26.** anything you can do is a song by Irving Berlin.
  **27.** I recommend the poem wilbur wright and orville wright.

# 9 Direct Quotations and Dialogue *pages 428–429*

**A. Identifying Direct Quotations**  Write each sentence.
Underline the direct quotation.

1. Henry said, "Here's a picture of me sleeping in a pile of hay."

MODEL> Henry said, "Here's a picture of me sleeping in a pile of hay."

2. "I went to stay at my aunt's farm for that entire summer," he said.
3. Angela asked, "How old were you?"
4. "I was twelve," Henry told us.
5. "We traveled part of the way by bus and part of the way by train to the farm," he added.
6. I exclaimed, "Your poor brother was so sick that they had to stop the bus!"
7. "He was so happy to get there that he kissed the ground!" Henry laughed.

**B. Forming Direct Quotations**  Capitalize and punctuate each direct quotation. Write each sentence correctly.

8. Robert sent these pictures said Connie

MODEL> "Robert sent these pictures," said Connie.

9. Henry asked when is he moving to Connecticut
10. Robert has moved there already she explained
11. is it far asked Sal
12. we will miss him I added
13. connie said I love these pictures
14. how nice of him to send a letter I exclaimed
15. do you think he will visit us soon asked Sal
16. connie suggested let's all visit Robert
17. this will be a big surprise exclaimed Henry

**C. Completing Direct Quotations**  Complete each direct quotation with a word that tells how the speaker talks. Write each sentence correctly.

18. Angela _____ Mystic Seaport is in Connecticut.

MODEL> Angela explained, "Mystic Seaport is in Connecticut."

19. She _____ perhaps we could stop there.
20. Wasn't Mystic Seaport a whaling village _____ Henry.
21. This ship is the Charles W. Morgan _____ our guide.
22. I am learning a lot about the sea _____ Sal.
23. This trip was a great idea we _____ .

# WRITER'S HANDBOOK

## Contents

# Sentences

- A **sentence** is a group of words that expresses a complete thought. Every sentence is made up of two parts, a *subject* and a *predicate*. Begin a sentence with a capital letter and end it with an end mark.

  T he actress performed without speaking .

The four kinds of sentences are *declarative, interrogative, imperative,* and *exclamatory.*

- A **declarative sentence** makes a statement. It ends with a period.

  Here is today's newspaper .

- An **interrogative sentence** asks a question. It ends with a question mark.

  What is your favorite section of the newspaper ?

- An **imperative sentence** gives a command or makes a request. It ends with a period.

  Read this editorial about the election .

- *You* **(understood)** is the subject of an imperative sentence.

  (you) Think about the editor's opinions.

- An **exclamatory sentence** expresses strong feeling or surprise. It ends with an exclamation point.

  What a strange opinion that is !

- A **simple sentence** expresses one complete thought.

  I will write a letter to the editor.

- A **compound sentence** is two or more simple sentences joined by a conjunction such as *and, or,* or *but.* When two or more simple sentences are joined to form a compound sentence, a comma comes before the conjunction.

  ⎡simple sentence⎤    ⎡simple sentence⎤
  Jim agrees with me , but    Sally doesn't.

**subject** • The **subject** tells whom or what the sentence is about.

A mime acts without using speech.

**complete subject** • The **complete subject** includes all the words that tell whom or what the sentence is about. It may be just one word or a group of words.

The young woman peeled a make-believe banana.

**simple subject** • The **simple subject** is the main word or words in the complete subject.

The clever mime pretended she was eating.

**compound subject** • A **compound subject** is two or more simple subjects that have the same predicate. The simple subjects in a compound subject are often joined by *and* or *or*. Commas are used to separate three or more simple subjects in a compound subject.

Mom, Dad, and I clapped for the performance.

**predicate** • The **predicate** is the part of a sentence that tells what the subject is or does.

The mime continued her performance.

**complete predicate** • The **complete predicate** is all the words in the predicate part of a sentence. It may be one word or a group of words.

She took another bite.

**simple predicate** • The **simple predicate** is the main word or words in the complete predicate.

The performer smacked her lips happily.

She has practiced her act many times.

**compound predicate** • A **compound predicate** is two or more simple predicates that have the same subject. The simple predicates in a compound predicate are often joined by *and* or *or*.

The mime bowed , curtsied , and waved .

**direct object** • A **direct object** receives the action of the verb. A direct object answers the question *Whom?* or *What?* after an action verb.

The audience enjoyed the act . **enjoyed *what?* the *act***

The performance amazed them . **amazed *whom? them***

# Nouns

- A **noun** is a word that names a person, a place, a thing, or an idea.

  **persons:** police officer, Officer Morris
  **places:** city, San Antonio
  **things:** chair, pencil
  **ideas:** freedom, honesty

- A **singular noun** names one person, place, thing, or idea.

  woman    mountain    book    justice

- A **plural noun** names more than one person, place, thing, or idea. For help with the spelling of plural nouns, see the *Spelling* section of this **Writer's Handbook.**

| Singular | Plural |
|----------|--------|
| explorer | explorers |
| forest | forests |
| lunch | lunches |
| class | classes |
| day | days |
| tragedy | tragedies |

- A **common noun** names any person, place, thing, or idea.

- A **proper noun** names a particular person, place, or thing. Each important word in a proper noun begins with a capital letter.

| Common Nouns | Proper Nouns |
|--------------|--------------|
| girl | Marcie |
| country | Costa Rica |
| language | English |
| day | Monday |
| continent | Asia |
| month | June |

- A **possessive noun** shows ownership.

  Larry's book    house's roof

noun

singular noun

plural noun

common noun

proper noun

possessive noun

WRITER'S HANDBOOK • Grammar

**singular possessive noun**
- A **singular possessive noun** shows ownership by one person or thing. To form the possessive of a singular noun, add an apostrophe and *s*.

  Wendy's dream is to fly away on a soft white cloud.

  What was James's dream about?

**plural possessive noun**
- A **plural possessive noun** shows ownership by more than one person or thing. To form the possessive of a plural noun that ends with *s*, add an apostrophe.

  You can see through the elves' wings.

  To form the possessive of a plural noun that does not end with *s*, add an apostrophe and *s* ('s).

  The men's race will start tomorrow.

## Pronouns

**pronoun**
- A **pronoun** is a word that takes the place of a noun or nouns.

  A space shuttle will be launched soon.

  It will be launched soon.

**antecedent**
- An **antecedent** is the noun or nouns to which a pronoun refers. A pronoun should agree with its antecedent in number and gender.

  Bobby wants to be an astronaut. He has written a letter to NASA.

  Jill and Sally watched a shuttle launch. They want to be astronauts too.

**subject pronoun**
- A **subject pronoun** takes the place of a noun or nouns in the subject of a sentence.

  The astronauts look forward to the journey.

  They look forward to the journey.

  Subject pronouns also take the place of nouns that follow forms of the linking verb *be*.

  A girl excited about space travel is Jill.

  A girl excited about space travel is she.

- An **object pronoun** takes the place of a noun that follows an action verb.

object pronoun

> We will watch the launch on television.

> We will watch it on television.

Object pronouns also take the place of nouns that follow words like *to, for, of, with, in, on,* and *at.*

> We have discussed the flight with a pilot .

> We have discussed the flight with him .

- A **possessive pronoun** shows ownership. There are two kinds of possessive pronouns. One kind is used before a noun.

possessive pronoun

> The climber's dream is to reach the top of the mountain.

> His dream is to reach the top of the mountain.

The other kind of possessive pronoun stands alone and replaces a noun in a sentence.

> This hiking gear is the instructor's .

> This hiking gear is hers .

- A **reflexive pronoun** refers to the subject.

reflexive pronoun

> The bears helped themselves to our food.

## Verbs

- A **verb** expresses action or being.

verb

- An **action verb** is a word that tells what the subject does, did, or will do.

action verb

> The chick hatches out of its shell.

- A **linking verb** connects the subject to a word or words in the predicate. A linking verb is followed by a word in the predicate that names or describes the subject. *Be* and forms of *be* are the most common linking verbs.

linking verb

> The chick's feathers are damp now.

Other linking verbs are *look, seem, feel, become, appear, taste, smell,* and *grow.*

> When they are dry, new chicks feel fluffy.

**main verb**
- The **main verb** is the most important verb in the predicate.

Many insects will go through changes in their lives.

**helping verb**
- A **helping verb** works with the main verb to show action.

helping verb main verb

A caterpillar is building a cocoon around itself.

**tense**
- The **tense** of a verb shows when the action happens.

**present-tense verb**
- A **present-tense verb** shows action that happens now. Add *s* or *es* to most verbs to show the present tense if the subject is singular.

A young butterfly grows .

**past-tense verb**
- A **past-tense verb** shows action that already happened. The past tense of most verbs is formed by adding *ed*.

The beautiful insect landed on a flower.

**future-tense verb**
- A **future-tense verb** shows action that will happen. To form the future tense of a verb, use the helping verb *will* with the main verb.

The seeds will sprout about a week after planting.

**subject-verb agreement**
- A verb must **agree** with the subject of the sentence. When a subject is singular, you usually add *s* or *es* to the main verb in the present tense.

A baby koala clings to its mother's back.

The baby reaches for a leaf.

When the subject is plural or *I* or *you,* the main verb does not change in the present tense.

Koalas drink no water.

You find koalas in Australia.

**agreement with *be* and *have***
- The verbs *be* and *have* change forms in special ways to agree with their subjects. The verb *be* or *have* may be the only word in the simple predicate, or the verb *be* or *have* may be a helping verb.

The kangaroo was hopping on Australia's grasslands.
**form of *be* as helping verb**

These animals **have** powerful legs for jumping.
**_have_ as main verb**

I **have admired** their beauty. **_have_ as helping verb**

| | be | | have | |
|---|---|---|---|---|
| **Singular** | **Present** | **Past** | **Present** | **Past** |
| I | am | was | have | had |
| you | are | were | have | had |
| he, she, it | is | was | has | had |
| singular noun | is | was | has | had |
| **Plural** | | | | |
| we | are | were | have | had |
| you | are | were | have | had |
| they | are | were | have | had |
| plural noun | are | were | have | had |

● An **irregular verb** does not end with *ed* in the past tense.    irregular verb

I **thought** baby frogs hatched from eggs.

They **have gone** through a tadpole stage first.

It **has taken** them a while to grow into frogs.

We **saw** tails disappear and legs grow on the tadpoles.

| Present | Past | Past with Helping Verb |
|---|---|---|
| come | came | (has, have, had) come |
| eat | ate | (has, have, had) eaten |
| give | gave | (has, have, had) given |
| go | went | (has, have, had) gone |
| make | made | (has, have, had) made |
| ride | rode | (has, have, had) ridden |
| run | ran | (has, have, had) run |
| say | said | (has, have, had) said |
| see | saw | (has, have, had) seen |
| take | took | (has, have, had) taken |
| think | thought | (has, have, had) thought |
| write | wrote | (has, have, had) written |

Some irregular verbs follow a pattern when they change form.

| Present | Past | Past with Helping Verb |
|---------|------|------------------------|
| blow | blew | (has, have, had) blown |
| fly | flew | (has, have, had) flown |
| grow | grew | (has, have, had) grown |
| know | knew | (has, have, had) known |
| tear | tore | (has, have, had) torn |
| wear | wore | (has, have, had) worn |
| begin | began | (has, have, had) begun |
| drink | drank | (has, have, had) drunk |
| ring | rang | (has, have, had) rung |
| sing | sang | (has, have, had) sung |
| swim | swam | (has, have, had) swum |
| break | broke | (has, have, had) broken |
| choose | chose | (has, have, had) chosen |
| freeze | froze | (has, have, had) frozen |
| speak | spoke | (has, have, had) spoken |
| steal | stole | (has, have, had) stolen |
| bring | brought | (has, have, had) brought |
| catch | caught | (has, have, had) caught |
| find | found | (has, have, had) found |
| lose | lost | (has, have, had) lost |

**verb contraction**

● A **contraction** is a shortened form of two words. Some contractions are formed by joining the words *I, you, he, she, it, we,* or *they* and a verb. Some contractions are formed by joining a verb and the word *not.* An apostrophe takes the place of the letter or letters that have been dropped to combine the two words.

| Some Common Contractions |
|--------------------------|
| you, he, she, they + will = you'll, he'll, she'll, they'll |
| he, she, it + is *or* has = he's, she's, it's |
| I, you, he, she + had *or* would = I'd, you'd, he'd, she'd |
| we, they + had *or* would = we'd, they'd |
| can + not = can't |
| will + not = won't |
| are + not = aren't |

WRITER'S HANDBOOK ● Grammar

# Adjectives

- An **adjective** is a word that describes a noun or a pronoun.

  Searching for clues, the students slowly entered
  the  dark  house.

  An adjective may tell *what kind.*

  The detectives could solve  tough  problems.

  An adjective may tell *how many.*

  The  four  students kept their wits about them.

  They had been through  several  adventures together.

- A **proper adjective** is formed from a proper noun. Some
  proper nouns do not change when used as proper adjectives.

  You can go whale-watching from ships along the
  New England  coast.

  Some proper adjectives are formed by adding endings to
  proper nouns.

  The  Alaskan  coast offers great views of whales.

- The adjectives *a, an,* and *the* are **articles.** The words *a* and *an*
  refer to any person, place, thing, or idea. The word *the* refers
  to a specific person, place, thing, or idea.

  The students had formed  a  detective club.

  The  club had solved many cases.

- *This, that, these,* and *those* are called **demonstrative adjectives**.
  *This* and *these* are used to describe nouns close to the speaker.
  *That* and *those* describe nouns that are farther away from the
  speaker.

  This  staircase is creaking.

  Who wants to search for clues in  those  closets?

- An **adjective that follows a linking verb** describes the subject.

  She is  wonderful .

  She became  frightened .

*Margin labels:*
adjective

proper adjective

articles

demonstrative adjectives

adjectives that follow linking verbs

**adjectives that compare**
- Adjectives can be used to **compare** people, places, things, or ideas. For help with spelling adjectives that compare, see the *Spelling* section of this **Writer's Handbook.**

**er**
- Add *er* to most adjectives to compare two things.

Tim's cat is younger than our cat.

**est**
- Add *est* to most adjectives to compare more than two things.

The lion is the largest animal in the zoo.

The spelling of some adjectives changes when *er* or *est* is added. For adjectives ending with *e,* drop the *e* and add *er* or *est.*

He sailed across the world's widest ocean.

For adjectives ending with a consonant plus *y,* change the *y* to *i* and add *er* or *est.*

The scariest thing is that he did it all alone.

For one-syllable adjectives ending with a vowel plus a consonant, double the last consonant and add *er* or *est.*

The weather was much hotter at the equator.

**more, most**
- *More* or *most* is used with adjectives of two or more syllables. When two people, places, things, or ideas are compared, *more* is used with the adjective. When three or more people, places, things, or ideas are compared, *most* is used with the adjective.

The second wave was more powerful than the first one.

The next wave was the most powerful one yet.

**special forms**
- Some adjectives that compare have **special forms.** The adjectives *good, bad, little, many,* and *much* have special forms for comparing nouns.

We had a good trip.

Ralph liked last year's trip better .

I think this was the best trip I have ever taken.

# Adverbs

- An **adverb** is a word that describes a verb, an adjective, or another adverb. An adverb tells *how, when, where,* or *to what extent.*

  adverb

  Lauren paints  beautifully .  **how**

  Yesterday  she entered an art contest.  **when**

  Her painting won a prize  there .  **where**

  She paints  very  slowly.  **to what extent**

- Adverbs can be used to **compare** two or more actions. When you compare two actions, add *er* to most short adverbs. When you compare three or more actions, add *est* to most short adverbs.

  **adverbs that compare**

  Hector worked  hard  at his schoolwork.

  Jeff worked  harder  than Hector.

  José worked the  hardest  of all three boys.

- Use *more* and *most* before adverbs that have two or more syllables or that end in *ly.*

  *more, most*

  Wendy worked  willingly  at the senior center.

  Kathy worked  more willingly  than Wendy.

  Tracy worked the  most willingly  of all three.

- A word that means "no" or "not" is called a **negative.** *Never, not, no, no one, nowhere, nothing, nobody,* and *none* are common negatives.

  negatives

  Mrs. Stein works at the school for  no  salary.

  She has  never  complained about the long hours.

Only one negative should be used in a sentence. It is incorrect to use a **double negative,** two negatives in one sentence.

  **incorrect:** Mrs. Stein  hasn't  let  no  bad weather stop her.

  **correct:** Mrs. Stein  hasn't  let bad weather stop her.

# Prepositions

**preposition**

- A **preposition** is a word that relates a noun or a pronoun to another word in a sentence.

Larry's grandparents described their lives in Russia.

He learned a foreign language from them.

| Common Prepositions | | | |
|---|---|---|---|
| about | below | in | over |
| above | beneath | inside | past |
| across | beside | into | through |
| after | between | near | to |
| along | by | of | toward |
| among | down | off | under |
| around | during | on | until |
| at | except | onto | up |
| before | for | out | with |
| behind | from | outside | without |

**object of the preposition**

- A preposition relates the noun or pronoun that follows it to other words in a sentence. The noun or pronoun that follows a preposition is the **object of the preposition.**

Carol visited a relative near London .

Upon arriving home, Carol sent a letter to her .

The object of the preposition can be a compound object.

Carol closed her letter with love and best wishes .

**prepositional phrase**

- A **prepositional phrase** is made up of a preposition, the object of the preposition, and all the words in between.

preposition     object of the preposition

Americans have come from many countries.

Prepositional phrases may be at the beginning, in the middle, or at the end of sentences.

In the early 1900's , many immigrants came.

Life on the crowded ships was often difficult.

The newcomers hoped for a better life .

## Conjunctions

● A **conjunction** is a word that connects words or groups of words in a sentence.

**conjunction**

My friend Sofia `and` her parents come from Greece.

The words *and, but,* and *or* are common conjunctions. Conjunctions may connect two or more subjects, two or more predicates, or two or more sentences.

Athens `and` its ancient ruins fascinate me.

Greece's friendly people smile `and` make visitors welcome.

Sofia's parents have accents, `but` they speak perfect English.

The conjunctions *and, but,* and *or* have different meanings. The word *and* is used to join together. The word *but* is used to show contrast. The word *or* is used to show choice.

Greek myths `and` legends are famous around the world.

The gods and goddesses do marvelous things, `but` they are like human beings too.

Is your favorite goddess Hera `or` Athena?

## Interjections

● An **interjection** is a word or group of words that expresses feeling.

**interjection**

`Wow`! I can't believe the *Mayflower* was so small!

| Common Interjections | | | | |
|---|---|---|---|---|
| hey | oh | ouch | my | aha |
| oops | wow | never | yikes | oh, dear |
| great | good grief | gee | yuck | eek |
| hooray | well, well | alas | oh, no | phew |

Interjections that show very strong feelings may stand alone. They are usually followed by an exclamation point.

`Yuck!` I don't think I could have made the trip.

Interjections that show milder feelings are separated from the beginning or end of a sentence by a comma.

`Oh, my,` they were strong-willed people.

## Capitalization

**sentences**
- Begin every sentence with a capital letter.

   A lmost everyone loves cartoons.

   D on't you enjoy a good laugh at the movies?

**proper nouns**
- Begin each important word in a proper noun with a capital letter.

- Capitalize the names of people and pets.

   H erman  P otter     R ita  G omez

   L assie

- Capitalize each important word in the names of particular places and things.

   L incoln  M emorial     E ngland     O hio

   M ojave  D esert     M etropolitan  M useum of  A rt

   L os  A ngeles     N ew  Y ork

- Capitalize the names of months, days, and holidays.

   T uesday     S eptember     T hanksgiving

   I ndependence  D ay     P residents'  D ay

**proper adjectives**
- Capitalize proper adjectives.

   F rench team     C anadian flag

**I**
- The pronoun *I* is always capitalized.

   Scott and  I  are learning to stand on our heads.

**abbreviations**
- Many abbreviations begin with a capital letter and are followed by a period.

   Mister— M r .     Doctor— D r .     Senior— S r .

   Avenue— A ve .     Street— S t .     Road— R d .

   February— F eb .     Tuesday— T ues .

   Company— C o .     Corporation— C orp .

   Department— D ept .     A.M. ,  P.M.

WRITER'S HANDBOOK • Mechanics

- Postal abbreviations for states have two capital letters and no periods.

    Indiana— IN      Connecticut— CT      Oklahoma— OK

- Capital letters are used in the heading, the greeting, and the closing of a letter.

| | |
|---|---|
| **heading** | 666 M aple R oad |
| | O gden, U tah 98765 |
| | O ctober 14, 19－－ |
| **greeting** | D ear S am, |
| **closing** | Y our pal, |

- Capitalize the first, last, and all other important words in the titles of books, movies, newspapers, magazines, stories, magazine articles, songs, and poems.

    A L ight in the A ttic (book)

    " T icklish T om" (poem)

    S pringfield T imes (newspaper)

    " O n T op of S paghetti" (song)

    S couting T oday (magazine)

- Capitalize the first word of each sentence within a direct quotation.

    " Y ou stepped on my nose!" cried Elmer the Elephant.

    " E xcuse me," replied Foxy. " A ctually, I was aiming for your toes."

- Capitalize the first word in the main topics and subtopics of an outline.

    I.  B reeds of dogs

        A.  T erriers

        B.  B eagles

        C.  P oodles

# Punctuation

sentences
- A sentence ends with a punctuation mark.

- A declarative sentence and an imperative sentence end with a **period.**

    You're a very funny person .

    Tell me that knock-knock joke again .

- An interrogative sentence ends with a **question mark.**

    Where is the zoo located ?

- An exclamatory sentence ends with an **exclamation point.**

    What a wonderful book that was !

period
- Use a period after an initial.

    Ruth Q . Martini    Hugo V . Farr    I . M . Grant

- Use a period after an abbreviation.

    Mrs . Montez    Toys, Inc .    Thurman Ave .

- Use a period at the end of a direct quotation if the quotation is a statement or a command and if no words follow it.

    José answered, "I'll be on time tomorrow . "

- Use a period after the speaker's name if a divided quotation is two sentences.

    "I don't get it," said Terry . "What's so funny?"

- Use a period after every Roman numeral and every letter in an outline.

    I . Humor on television

    A . Comedy shows

    B . Funny commercials

comma
- Use commas to separate three or more subjects in a compound subject.

    Jokes , riddles , and puns may make you laugh.

- Use commas to separate three or more predicates in a compound predicate.

    We smiled , giggled , and laughed at the funny show.

- Use a comma before the word *and* that joins two simple sentences in a compound sentence.

  We clapped , and the performers took an extra bow.

- Use a comma after each item except the last one in a series of three or more items.

  Funny ads for cereal , soap , and floor wax came on during the program.

- Use a comma to set off words such as *yes, no,* and *well* when they begin a sentence.

  Yes , she is the funniest comedian around.

- Use a comma to set off the name of a person who is spoken to directly in a sentence.

  Karen , what was the funniest scene in the movie?

- Use a comma to separate the name of the day from the date and the date from the year. Use a comma after the year when it appears with the date in the middle of a sentence.

  On Sunday , December 6 , 1989 , a clown performed at the child's birthday party.

- Use a comma to separate the names of a city and a state. Use a comma after a state when it appears with a city in the middle of a sentence.

  The comedian will do her act in Chicago , Illinois , next month.

- For both friendly letters and business letters, use a comma between the city and state names, between the day of the month and the year, and after the last word of the closing. For a friendly letter, use a comma after the last word in the greeting.

  Briarwood , New York 11435     June 27 , 19− −

  Your pal ,     Sincerely yours ,     Dear Wendy ,

- Use a comma to separate the quotation from the speaker. The comma comes before the quotation marks.

  Bob asked , "What's green and white and green and white?"

  "I don't know ," answered Mary.

- If a divided quotation is all one sentence, use another comma after the speaker's name.

  "The answer is , " said Don , "a pickle rolling downhill in the snow."

apostrophe - Use an apostrophe to form contractions of pronouns and verbs.

  We ' re going to learn how to scuba dive.

  Use an apostrophe to form contractions of verbs and the adverb *not.*

  Isn ' t that exciting?

- To form the possessive of a singular noun, add an apostrophe and *s.*

  Kim 's stories show off her good imagination.

  To form the possessive of a plural noun that ends with *s,* add an apostrophe.

  The stories ' plots are so interesting.

  To form the possessive of a plural noun that does not end with *s,* add an apostrophe and *s.*

  The women 's photographs won prizes in the contest.

quotation marks - Use quotation marks before and after someone's exact words. If the quotation is divided into two parts by other words, place quotation marks around the quoted words only.

  Carol said, " A dog and a tree have something in common. "

  " I know, " replied Sandy. " They each have a bark. "

- Use quotation marks around the titles of stories, magazine articles, essays, songs, and poems.

  " The Night the Ghost Got In " (story)

  " The Purple Cow " (poem)

underline - Underline the titles of books and movies and the names of newspapers and magazines.

  Where the Sidewalk Ends (book)
  Steamboat Willie (movie)
  Greenville News (newspaper)
  Life (magazine)

## Troublesome Words

- Use the word *there* to indicate placement. Use the pronoun *their* when you mean "belonging to them." Use the pronoun *they're* as a contraction for "they are."

*there, their, they're*

> There in the distance are the state's highest mountains.

> You can see their white peaks from miles away.

> They're going to attempt to climb to the very top.

- Use the word *too* when you mean "also" or "very." Use the adjective *two* to mean the number 2. Use the preposition *to* to show movement toward something.

*too, two, to*

> You, too, can learn how to ski.

> Skiing down a steep hill seems too frightening.

> I have worked out on the ski slopes for two weeks.

> Go to Aspen, Colorado, for some thrilling skiing.

## Easily Confused Verb Pairs

- Use *sit* when you mean "rest." Use *set* when you mean "place."

*sit, set*

> Sit, do not stand up, in the rowboat.

> Set the oars on the sides of the boat.

- Use *can* when you mean "able." Use *may* when you mean "allowed."

*can, may*

> I can swim fairly well.

> May I swim in your pool?

- Use *teach* when you mean "give instruction." Use *learn* when you mean "receive instruction."

*teach, learn*

> I will teach you how to do the butterfly stroke.

> With practice you will soon learn how to do it well.

**let, leave** ● Use *let* when you mean "permit." Use *leave* when you mean "go away from" or "let remain in place."

Please let me join the swimming club at school.

I must leave for practice at 3:30 today.

Don't leave your wet things in your locker.

**good, well** ● Use *good* as an adjective. Use *well* as an adverb to describe a verb or as an adjective to mean "healthy."

This is a good suspense story.

I read the story when I was not feeling well.

The author writes well.

## Pronouns

**its, it's** ● Use *its* when you mean "belonging to it." Use *it's* when you mean "it is."

Astronauts have visited the moon and walked on its surface.

It's amazing that humans have actually done this.

**your, you're** ● Use *your* when you mean "belonging to you." Use *you're* when you mean "you are."

Do your heroes come from the world of sports?

You're a very good athlete too.

**I, me** ● Use *I* as a subject and following a linking verb. Use *me* following an action verb and words like *at, for, to,* and *with.*

I want to search for Indian arrowheads.

It was I who suggested the field trip.

Please help me find artifacts of ancient people.

Sift this dirt with me.

**subject or object pronouns** ● Pronouns can be subjects or objects in sentences.

The girl is extremely brave.

She is extremely brave.  **subject pronoun**

The girl rescued the little boy from the water.

The girl rescued him from the water.  **object pronoun**

## Negatives

- Words that mean "no" or "not" are called **negatives.**

negatives

| | |
|---|---|
| no | nothing |
| not | nobody |
| none | nowhere |
| never | |

- Contractions made with the adverb *not* act as negatives.

| | |
|---|---|
| can't | couldn't |
| don't | shouldn't |
| won't | wouldn't |
| | haven't |

- Two negatives usually are not used in the same sentence.

**incorrect:** There wasn't nobody there.

**correct:** There wasn't anybody there.

There was nobody there.

## Agreement

- A verb agrees with the subject of the sentence.

subject-verb agreement

- When a subject is singular, you usually add *s* or *es* to the main verb in the present tense.

That tree grows very slowly.

The rain washes the leaves.

- When the subject is plural or *I* or *you,* the main verb usually does not change in the present tense.

The team members practice a lot.

I often study in the library.

You arrive on time every day.

WRITER'S HANDBOOK • Usage

# Expository Paragraph

expository
paragraph

- An **expository paragraph** is a group of sentences that tells about one main idea. A paragraph often begins with a **topic sentence,** which expresses the main idea of the paragraph. It tells what all the other sentences in the paragraph are about. These other sentences are called **detail sentences.** Detail sentences add information about the topic. They help the audience understand the main idea.

| Writer's Guide: Expository Paragraph |
|---|
| 1. Write a topic sentence that clearly tells the main idea of your paragraph. |
| 2. Indent the first line. |
| 3. Write clearly connected detail sentences that explain the main idea. |

**topic
sentence**

**detail
sentences**

An advertising copywriter writes all the words that appear in the ads you see in newspapers, magazines, and even on billboards! Good copywriters must understand their audience, which is the advertiser's customers. Most ads have two parts, the headline and the body. The headline must get the reader's attention. The body must tell the audience about the features and the benefits of the product. Product features, like "battery-operated," just tell about the product. Product benefits, like "battery-operated so you can take it anywhere," show how the product might appeal to the audience. An advertising copywriter works as "the writing part" of a team that also includes a creative director, an art director, and artists.

WRITER'S HANDBOOK • Composition

# How-to Paragraph

● In a **how-to paragraph** a writer gives directions or explains how to do something.

how-to
paragraph

| **Writer's Guide: How-to Paragraph** |
|---|
| 1. Write a topic sentence that identifies the process you are explaining. |
| 2. Write a detail sentence that lists the materials needed to complete the process. |
| 3. Write detail sentences that tell the steps in the process. Be sure the steps are in the correct order. |
| 4. Use time-order words such as *first*, *next*, *then*, and *finally* to show the order of the steps. |

A theme collage is a colorful way to express an idea. A collage is a group of pictures presented together. To make your collage, you will need to have scissors, old magazines, construction paper, and glue. First, pick a theme. Then, select magazine pictures that go with your theme. Next, cut them out. Finally, after you have arranged your pictures in a pleasing design, glue them to the construction paper.

This collage can be an excellent decoration for your room. You can also make a special holiday greeting by putting your theme collage on the outside of a card. At first, I planned just to show my collage in the crafts fair, but I ended up giving it to my aunt for her birthday.

topic
sentence

materials

steps in
time order

# Paragraph of Comparison

**paragraph of comparison**

- In a **paragraph of comparison,** a writer shows ways in which two subjects are alike. The subjects may be people, places, things, or ideas.

---

### Writer's Guide: Paragraph of Comparison

1. Think of ways your subjects are alike.
2. Write a topic sentence that identifies the two subjects and names the qualities you will compare.
3. In the detail sentences, give examples that clearly explain the qualities your subjects have in common.
4. Write about the qualities in the same order in which you introduced them in the topic sentence.

---

**topic sentence**

*The timber rattlesnake and the Gila monster are interesting but dangerous reptiles. They can be found in Texas and other parts of the United States and Mexico.*

**detail sentences that compare**

*They both are active at night and rest during the day. Though they look sluggish, they are still quick to attack, even when they are resting. The timber rattlesnake and the Gila monster both use venom to kill their prey. The timber rattlesnake's venom is forced through its hollow fangs, but the Gila monster's venom flows down a groove in its sharp teeth.*

## Paragraph of Contrast

- In a **paragraph of contrast,** a writer explains the key differences between two subjects. The subjects may be people, places, things, or ideas.

| **Writer's Guide: Paragraph of Contrast** |
| --- |
| 1. Think of ways your subjects are different. |
| 2. Write a topic sentence that identifies the two subjects and names the qualities you will contrast. |
| 3. In the detail sentences, give examples that clearly explain the differences between your subjects. |
| 4. Write about the differences in the same order in which you introduced them in the topic sentence. |

The timber rattlesnake and the Gila monster are alike in some ways, but they have different hunting styles and habitats. The timber rattlesnake can grab its prey only with its mouth, but the Gila monster can use its strong claws. The timber rattlesnake's habitat is more likely to be in a cool area with trees. The Gila monster lives in the dry, barren deserts of the southwestern United States and Mexico.

topic sentence

detail sentences that contrast

WRITER'S HANDBOOK • Composition

# Persuasive Paragraph

- In a **persuasive paragraph** a writer tries to convince the audience to agree with his or her opinion on an issue.

| Writer's Guide: Persuasive Paragraph |
| --- |
| 1. Write a topic sentence that states the issue and your opinion about it. |
| 2. Keep in mind the audience that you are trying to persuade. |
| 3. In the detail sentences, include at least three reasons that support your opinion. Explain your reasons with clear examples. Save your strongest reason for last. |
| 4. Write a concluding sentence that restates your opinion and asks the audience to accept it or to take action. |

**topic sentence**

*I think Miss Dixon should be nominated as the Maplewood School's Teacher of the Year.*

**detail sentences**

*She is an excellent teacher whose students always do well on our county tests. For the past three years, her students have gone on to the finals in state math competitions. In addition, her work with the girl's soccer team helped us to improve our record over last year's. Most important, however, she is a caring person who is always willing to give her time to a student who needs extra help.*

**concluding sentence**

*Please join me in nominating Miss Dixon as Maplewood's Teacher of the Year.*

WRITER'S HANDBOOK • Composition

# Descriptive Paragraph

descriptive paragraph

- In a **descriptive paragraph** a writer describes a person, a place, a thing, or an event by using specific details. The details should let the audience see, feel, hear, and sometimes taste and smell what is being described.

---

### Writer's Guide: Descriptive Paragraph

1. Write a topic sentence that tells what you will describe.
2. Write detail sentences that give specific information about your topic.
3. Choose details that contribute to the tone or mood you want to create.
4. Use vivid and colorful describing words that appeal to the audience's senses.

---

I am going to describe just one spot we stopped at on our boat trip into the Everglades. In the boat were my dad, my cousin Fred, and me. We turned off the engine so we would not frighten the animals away. It was a hot and humid day, so vapor was rising off the water everywhere we looked. A monstrous alligator sat on the left bank, and then it suddenly splashed into the water. We could see mosquito fish darting in front of the boat. A snowy egret soared ahead of us into the distance. Behind the mangroves on our right we heard cicadas humming like a radio that hasn't been tuned in right. On the banks behind the boat, frogs were croaking to each other. We ate our lunch on the boat and enjoyed this wonderful nature show.

# Dialogue

● In a **dialogue** a writer tells the exact words that one person says to another.

---

## Writer's Guide: Dialogue

1. Place quotation marks before and after the exact words of a speaker.
2. Use a comma to separate a quotation from the rest of the sentence unless a question mark or an exclamation point is needed.
3. Begin a new paragraph each time the speaker changes.
4. Be sure that the dialogue sounds like real people talking.
5. Use words such as *said, cried, answered,* and *shouted* to show how the speaker says the words.

---

**exact words**

**new speaker**

Hannah cried, "The British are coming! What will we do?"

"They are coming for the guns that are stored in Concord," answered Father, calmly.

"But when they get to Concord, there will be nothing there," added Mr. Gray.

"You see," said Father, "we moved the guns out. We've stored them in new hiding places in other villages!"

# Journal

- In a **journal** a writer keeps a daily record of events. Each record of events is called an **entry**. A journal can be a good source of writing ideas.

journal

---

### Writer's Guide: Journal

1. Begin each entry with the date.
2. Describe events that are important to you.
3. Tell *who, what, where, when,* and *why* about each event.
4. Tell your feelings about the event.

---

*August 27, 1990*  — date of entry

Boy, was I nervous about my first day at the new school, but I think everything is going to be all right. The teacher looks like she is going to be tough but fun. Then at recess two boys started talking about soccer. I kind of joined in, and they told me they were looking for kids to join their league. They told me the time of the first meeting and everything. They were really friendly. I guess I'm on my way.

— event

— feelings

# Personal Narrative

**personal narrative**
- In a **personal narrative** a writer tells about an experience in his or her life.

---

### Writer's Guide: Personal Narrative

1. Write a strong topic sentence to begin your narrative.
2. In the middle, write detail sentences that describe events in time order.
3. Write an ending that tells what happened as a result of the events.
4. Use cause-and-effect words like *because* and *so* to relate ideas.

---

My trip to Channel Islands National Park last month was full of surprises. I saw many new animals and learned many things. As soon as we had trudged up the 154 stairs to the main part of Anacapa Island, we saw dozens of seagull chicks just three or four weeks old. I had never seen so many baby animals before! I was surprised because they were brown and spotted. Adult gulls are white.

The ranger told us an interesting story about a building on the island that I thought was a church. Actually it is for storing water. The guide explained to my family and me that a long time ago, people used to shoot at the old water tower. Later, the building was constructed like a church to store the water because the people on the island figured no one would shoot at a church. So far the water has been protected!

My trip to the Channel Islands was fun. At the same time, it was educational. It showed me how important our wildlife parks are to us, and it made me think about the way we live with nature.

# Story

- In a **story** a writer tells about one main idea. A story has an introduction, a development, and a conclusion.

story

| Writer's Guide: Story |
|---|
| **1.** Name the main character and describe the setting in the introduction. |
| **2.** Tell the problem or challenge the main character faces in the development. |
| **3.** Write some conversation or dialogue between the main character and other characters. Use words that tell how the characters feel or speak. |
| **4.** Write an ending for the story. Show how the problem is solved or not solved. |
| **5.** Write an interesting title for your story. |

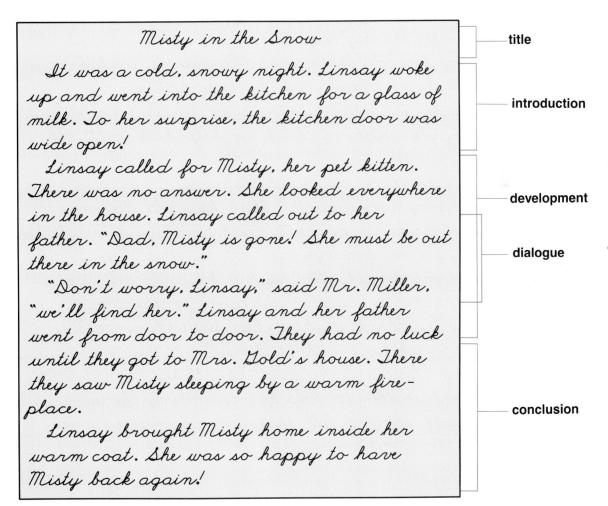

*Misty in the Snow* — title

It was a cold, snowy night. Linsay woke up and went into the kitchen for a glass of milk. To her surprise, the kitchen door was wide open! — introduction

Linsay called for Misty, her pet kitten. There was no answer. She looked everywhere in the house. Linsay called out to her father. "Dad, Misty is gone! She must be out there in the snow." — development

"Don't worry, Linsay," said Mr. Miller, "we'll find her." Linsay and her father went from door to door. They had no luck until they got to Mrs. Gold's house. There they saw Misty sleeping by a warm fireplace. — dialogue

Linsay brought Misty home inside her warm coat. She was so happy to have Misty back again! — conclusion

## Tall Tale

tall tale
- In a **tall tale** a writer uses characters, setting, and a plot to entertain the reader.

| Writer's Guide: Tall Tale |
| --- |
| **1.** Write a beginning in which you present the characters and the setting. |
| **2.** Write a middle that tells the events of the plot in order. |
| **3.** Write an ending that tells how the events turn out. |
| **4.** Use dialogue to bring your tall tale to life. |
| **5.** Write a title for your tall tale. |

### Clever Clarence

Once upon a time, Farmer McCoy had to leave his farm to go to the big city for three days.

His young friend Clarence had promised to take care of Farmer McCoy's chores, but Clarence had no experience with farming. Clarence was depending on Farmer McCoy's neighbor Chuck to help him with all the chores.

"You can depend on me," said Clarence.

Farmer McCoy was doubtful that he could depend on Clarence, but he knew he could depend on Chuck, so he smiled and waved goodbye.

Clarence went directly to Chuck's house to get him to help with the chores. Chuck's wife came to the door.

"I need to see Chuck right away," said Clarence. "We have to get cracking on those chores!"

"I'm sorry, Clarence," she said. "Chuck has a bad cold, and he won't be able to help you with any chores."

Clarence was shocked. All that day he worried and

wondered how he could do Farmer McCoy's chores all by himself. Suddenly, he had an idea. "That's it!" he shouted.

Three days later, Farmer McCoy returned home. He was amazed at what he found. His farm seemed to be running itself. The dogs were playing "fetch" with firewood and piling it by his back door. The horses were grooming themselves on huge brushes every time they walked into the stable. Even the hens, which never cooperated with him, had gotten into the act. They were laying eggs directly into the egg cartons that Clarence had provided for them.

"Welcome back!" Clarence called from the rocking chair on the porch.

Farmer McCoy joined him, still trying to believe his eyes. "How . . . How did everything go while I was gone?"

"Take a look," said Clarence. "Once I figured out what all these animals could do for themselves, there was nothing left for me to do but sit here. Even the pigs are taking care of themselves."

"No, no, no, no," Farmer McCoy replied. "I can believe the dogs, and the horses, and maybe even the hens. But how on earth did you get the pigs to help?"

"I lead them into the dining room after dinner," said Clarence. "The food is served on plates made of stale bread," he explained, "and the pigs eat the stale bread with all of the leftovers so there's no mess."

Farmer McCoy shook his head for a full five minutes. He could think of nothing else to say except, "You sure are clever, Clarence."

play ● In a **play** a writer tells a story that is meant to be acted out by performers. A play has characters, one or more settings, and a plot. The conversation between characters in a play is called **dialogue.** The writer includes **stage directions** that tell the characters how to move, act, and speak.

---

### Writer's Guide: Play

1. Use dialogue to tell the story. Let the characters' conversations show how the plot develops. In a play, do not use quotation marks to show what the characters will say.
2. Write clear stage directions that tell the characters exactly how to move, act, or speak. Put the directions in parentheses and underline them.
3. Be sure your play has interesting characters, believable dialogue, and a plot.
4. Give your play a title.

---

**title**

*The Championship*

**stage directions**

(Coach Reed walks to the pitcher's mound with a worried expression on his face.)

**dialogue**

Coach Reed (whispering to Jim): What's happening to you, Jim? You've just walked the last two batters. If you keep this up, I'll have to pull you out.

Jim (pounding the baseball into his glove): I just have to concentrate, Coach. I know I can do it. This championship is the most important game of my life. Just give me one more chance.

Coach Reed (with renewed confidence): Okay, Jim. I believe you. You're the best pitcher we have. Now, their best hitter is up next. Relax and bear down. You can do it. We only need one more out and the championship is ours.

# Poem

- In a **poem** a writer paints a picture or expresses a feeling with words. The writer uses unusual combinations of words to describe people, places, things, or ideas. A poem often has a definite rhyme and rhythm. See page 11 in the **Glossary** to learn more about rhyme and rhythm. To help the audience see and feel as the writer does, a poem often contains **figures of speech.** Similes and metaphors are figures of speech. In a **simile** a writer makes a comparison between two things, using the word *like* or *as.* In a **metaphor** a writer also makes a comparison but does not use *like* or *as.*

poem

| Writer's Guide: Poem |
|---|
| 1. Use strong and colorful descriptive words to describe your subject. |
| 2. To make your feelings clear to the audience, use similes and metaphors. |
| 3. Use rhyme and rhythm to construct your poem. |
| 4. Give your poem a title. |

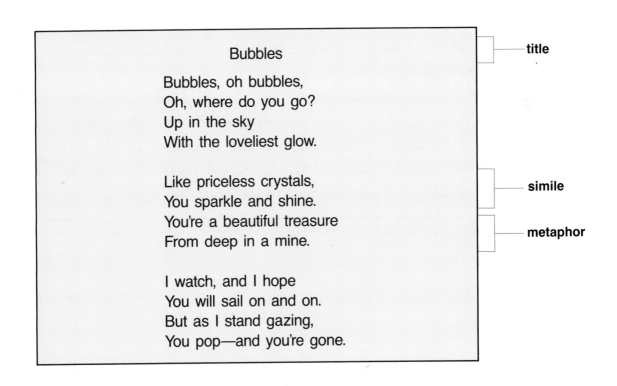

Bubbles

Bubbles, oh bubbles,
Oh, where do you go?
Up in the sky
With the loveliest glow.

Like priceless crystals,
You sparkle and shine.
You're a beautiful treasure
From deep in a mine.

I watch, and I hope
You will sail on and on.
But as I stand gazing,
You pop—and you're gone.

title

simile

metaphor

# Character Sketch

**character sketch**  ● In a **character sketch** a writer describes a real or an imaginary person.

---

### Writer's Guide: Character Sketch

1. Tell the person's name in your first sentence.
2. Describe how the person looks and moves.
3. Tell what the person does that makes him or her special.
4. Describe a situation in which the person showed his or her special qualities.

---

**name**

**description**

**what makes the person special**

Lisa Graham is my ballet teacher. She has dark brown hair that she keeps in a bun during class. She is tall, thin, and very graceful. Lisa used to be a professional ballet dancer.

I make a lot of mistakes in class, but Lisa never gets angry. She's very patient, and she shows me over and over the right way to do things.

Last year I tried out for a part in _The Nutcracker_. Lisa worked with me after class because she knew I really wanted to be in the ballet. I wouldn't have gotten the part without Lisa's special help.

## News Story

- In a **news story** a writer provides information for an audience. A news story has three parts—the lead, the body, and the headline. The **lead** is the first paragraph of a news story. It tells *who, what, where, when, why,* and sometimes *how* about something that happened. The rest of the news story is called the **body.** It gives more details about the lead. The title of a news story is called a **headline.**

---

### Writer's Guide: News Story

1. Write the lead. Be sure that it answers the questions *who, what, where, when,* and *why.*
2. In the body of the news story, give more details about the lead.
3. Write a short, interesting headline. Use a strong verb to attract the attention of the audience.

---

## Jackson Boy Wins Spelling Bee
— headline

Grover Lewis won the citywide spelling bee at Smith Hall last Friday. Grover is a fifth-grader at Jackson School.
— lead

Only two other students were good enough to last into the final round. They were last year's winner Lisa Rud and Paul Updike from Oakview School.

Grover won by spelling the word *accommodate.* Paul and Lisa lost the contest when they misspelled *accommodate.* Lisa spelled the word with only one *c.* Paul spelled the word with only one *m.* After the spelling bee was over, Grover relaxed with his family in the park. He explained his strategy for spelling. "If I've seen a word, I try to picture it in my mind. Then I just read off the letters," he said.
— body

# Research Report

• To write a **research report,** a writer gathers information from several sources, takes notes from the sources, and organizes the notes into an outline. Then he or she writes the report from the notes and outline.

---

### Writer's Guide: Research Report

1. Use your notes and outline to write your research report.
2. Write an introduction that identifies your topic. Make your sentences interesting to capture the attention of your audience.
3. Write one paragraph for each subtopic in your outline.
4. Follow your outline to write details about your topic.
5. Give your research report a title.

---

### Harriet Tubman

Before the Civil War, Harriet Tubman was very active in helping slaves escape. She escaped in 1849 from the plantation where she was a slave and went north by the Underground Railroad. The Underground Railroad was not really a railroad but a network of safe-houses for escaping slaves. She helped more than 300 slaves escape. She sometimes threatened frightened or tired slaves with a loaded pistol to keep them going. The slaves she helped called her "Moses," and abolitionist John Brown called her "General Tubman" because of her leadership and bravery.

Harriet Tubman continued to be very active both during and after the Civil War. She served as a cook, guide, and spy with the Union Army. During one military campaign she helped free 750 slaves.

Harriet Tubman's commitment to her fellow slaves went beyond just leading them to freedom in the north. She was a lifelong helper for black Americans, both young and old. She supported black schools by raising money for them. In 1908, she established a home for elderly and needy black people.

Harriet Tubman died in 1913. She had never been sure about the year of her birth, but she was approximately 93 years of age. By living her life as a brave and free woman, she had helped to bring courage and freedom to countless others.

# Book Report

book report
- In a **book report** a writer summarizes the important events in a book. The writer also gives his or her opinion of the book.

| Writer's Guide: Book Report |
| --- |
| 1. In your first sentence, give the title of the book and the name of the author. Remember to underline the title of the book. |
| 2. Write a summary of the important events. Include the main idea, the names of the main characters, and some interesting details. Do not tell the ending. |
| 3. Tell why a person might or might not like the book, or give your opinion of the book. Support your opinion with reasons. |

title/
author

summary

opinion

A Hunter Comes Home, by Ann Turner, tells about Eskimo life today. A boy named Jonas goes from a boarding school in the city back to his mother's home. Then he has a big decision to make. Will he live like his ancestors or go back to the city?

I liked the book very much. It has exciting hunting scenes, and it tells a lot about Eskimo life. I liked Jonas. He seemed very real to me. I felt sad for him at different times.

# Friendly Letter

- In a **friendly letter,** a writer sends greetings or news to someone he or she knows. A friendly letter has five parts.

### Writer's Guide: Friendly Letter

1. Write the heading in the upper right corner.
2. Write the greeting at the left margin.
3. In the body, write your message in paragraph form. Tell the person some news about yourself. Ask the person some questions about his or her life.
4. Use words that suit your purpose and audience. Be sure that your tone reflects the way you feel about your news.
5. Write the closing and your signature in line with the heading.

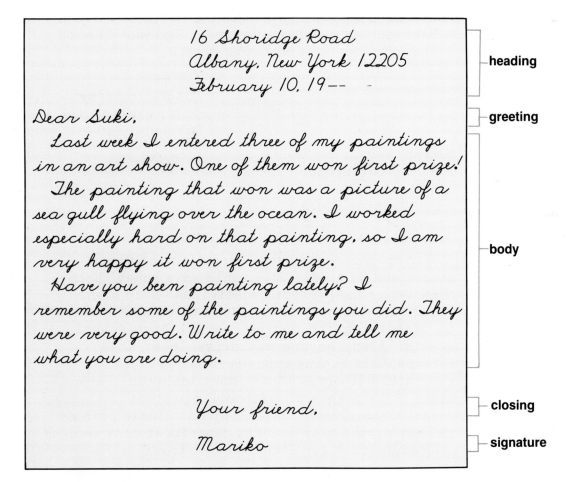

16 Shoridge Road
Albany, New York 12205
February 10, 19-- — heading

Dear Suki, — greeting

Last week I entered three of my paintings in an art show. One of them won first prize!

The painting that won was a picture of a sea gull flying over the ocean. I worked especially hard on that painting, so I am very happy it won first prize.

Have you been painting lately? I remember some of the paintings you did. They were very good. Write to me and tell me what you are doing. — body

Your friend, — closing

Mariko — signature

# Business Letter

**business letter**

- In a **business letter** a writer usually writes to someone he or she does not know. The purpose of a business letter may be to ask for information or to order something. In addition to the five parts of a friendly letter, a business letter has an **inside address.** It is the receiver's address.

---

### Writer's Guide: Business Letter

1. Write the heading in the upper right corner.
2. Write the inside address at the left margin.
3. Write the greeting under the inside address. Put a colon after the greeting.
4. Write the body in paragraph form. Tell why you are writing to the person or business. Use a polite tone.
5. Write the closing in line with the heading. In a business letter the closing is *Yours truly* or *Sincerely.*
6. Write your signature below the closing. Sign your full name. Then print your name below your signature.

---

**heading**

354 Eagle Street
Cody, Wyoming 82414
October 1, 19—

*School address*

**inside address**

Editor
The Cody Chronicle
756 Bison Drive
Cody, Wyoming 82414

**greeting**

Dear Editor:

**body**

   Our neighborhood needs stop signs at River Street and E Street. They would save money, help commuters, and protect pedestrians. Stop signs would save the city money. Now police must be used to direct traffic during special high-school events. Also, anyone who drives near this intersection during rush hours knows it is impossible to cross there. Most important, stop signs at this intersection would protect pedestrians, especially children. Please join me in letting the city traffic department know we need stop signs at River Street and E Street.

**closing**

Sincerely,

**signature**

*Ellen Singrossi*

Ellen Singrossi

# Invitation

- In an **invitation** a writer invites someone to come to a party or other event or to do something. An invitation has the same five parts as a friendly letter.

invitation

| Writer's Guide: Invitation |
|---|
| 1. Be sure to include a heading, a greeting, a body, a closing, and a signature. |
| 2. In the body, tell *who* is invited and *what* the invitation is for. |
| 3. Tell *when* and *where* the event or activity will take place and any other special information your guest must know. |

689 Lincoln Avenue
St. Paul, Minnesota 55105
April 22, 19—— — **heading**

Dear Mrs. Hendricks, — **greeting**

   Our class will be performing <u>Peter Pan</u> on Friday, April 30, at 11:00 A.M. in the Clark Elementary School auditorium. We know you worked very hard on the costumes, and we hope you will attend.
   We have reserved a special seat for you in the front row. — **body**

        Sincerely, — **closing**
        *Leslie Alcott* — **signature**

## Thank-You Note

thank-you note
- In a **thank-you note** a writer thanks someone for doing something. A thank-you note has the same five parts as a friendly letter.

| Writer's Guide: Thank-You Note |
|---|
| 1. Be sure to include a heading, a greeting, a body, a closing, and a signature. |
| 2. In the body, tell why you are thanking the person. |
| 3. If you have been a visitor somewhere, tell why you enjoyed yourself. |
| 4. If you received a gift, tell how you are using it. |

**heading**

50 South Oliver Street
Wichita, Kansas 65210
March 1, 19——

**greeting**

Dear Amanda,

**body**

Thank you so much for the dollhouse furniture. My little dolls seem very happy with their new tables, chairs, and beds. I hope you will come to visit me again soon. We could play with my dollhouse.

I was so glad that you could come to my birthday party. You helped to make the party very special for me.

**closing**

Your friend,

**signature**

Sabrina

WRITER'S HANDBOOK • Composition

# Envelope

- An **envelope** is used to send a letter or a note.

- The **mailing address** is the address of the person who will receive the letter. It is written toward the center of the envelope.

- The **return address** is the address of the person who writes the letter. It is written in the upper left corner.

- **Postal abbreviations** are used for state names.

- The **ZIP code** is written after the state abbreviation.

envelope

mailing address

return address

postal abbreviations

ZIP code

```
Lisa Boudet
24 Bay Avenue
Cape Coral, FL 33434



        Ms. Sharon London
        472 Lincoln Street
        Rochester, NY 14604
```

**return address**

**mailing address**

## Postal Abbreviations

| Alabama | AL | Kentucky | KY | North Dakota | ND |
|---|---|---|---|---|---|
| Alaska | AK | Louisiana | LA | Ohio | OH |
| Arizona | AZ | Maine | ME | Oklahoma | OK |
| Arkansas | AR | Maryland | MD | Oregon | OR |
| California | CA | Massachusetts | MA | Pennsylvania | PA |
| Colorado | CO | Michigan | MI | Rhode Island | RI |
| Connecticut | CT | Minnesota | MN | South Carolina | SC |
| Delaware | DE | Mississippi | MS | South Dakota | SD |
| District of | | Missouri | MO | Tennessee | TN |
| Columbia | DC | Montana | MT | Texas | TX |
| Florida | FL | Nebraska | NE | Utah | UT |
| Georgia | GA | Nevada | NV | Vermont | VT |
| Hawaii | HI | New Hampshire | NH | Virginia | VA |
| Idaho | ID | New Jersey | NJ | Washington | WA |
| Illinois | IL | New Mexico | NM | West Virginia | WV |
| Indiana | IN | New York | NY | Wisconsin | WI |
| Iowa | IA | North Carolina | NC | Wyoming | WY |
| Kansas | KS | | | | |

base word · A **base word** is a word to which other word parts may be added to form new words.

Even is the base word of uneven .

High is the base word of higher .

prefix · A **prefix** is a group of letters added to the beginning of a word. A prefix changes the meaning of a word.

| Prefix | Meaning | Example | Meaning |
|--------|---------|---------|---------|
| un | not | <u>un</u>happy | not happy |
| re | again | <u>re</u>open | open again |
| dis | not | <u>dis</u>agree | not agree |

Gary is unhappy about the test.

Liz will reopen her office.

The teams disagree about the score.

suffix · A **suffix** is a group of letters added to the end of a word. A suffix changes the meaning of a word.

| Suffix | Meaning | Example | Meaning |
|--------|---------|---------|---------|
| er | one who | farm<u>er</u> | one who farms |
| or | one who | visit<u>or</u> | one who visits |
| ful | full of | color<u>ful</u> | full of color |
| less | without | fear<u>less</u> | without fear |
| able | able to be | break<u>able</u> | able to be broken |

The singer has a sweet voice.

The director lost the script.

Lucy is a careful person.

Your directions are useless .

This old coat is wearable .

- A **synonym** is a word that has almost the same meaning as another word.

    The grass here is `tall` .     The grass here is `high` .

- An **antonym** is a word that has the opposite meaning from another word.

    The caterpillar crawled `up` .

    The caterpillar crawled `down` .

- **Homographs** are words that are spelled the same but have different meanings. Sometimes they have different pronunciations.

    You owe a `fine` for this overdue library book.

    She did a `fine` job cleaning up the backyard.

    Wash the `wound` and cover it with a clean bandage.

    I `wound` my watch too much. Now it's broken.

- **Homophones** are words that sound alike but are spelled differently and have different meanings.

    `Meet` me downtown at three o'clock at the `meat` market.

- A **compound word** consists of two or more words used as a single word.

- A **closed compound** is made up of two words written as one.

    raincoat     homework
    sunset       mailbox

- An **open compound** is a compound in which the words are written separately.

    fire engine      motor home
    sign language    bank account

- A **hyphenated compound** is a compound in which the words are connected by hyphens.

    high-rise     attorney-at-law
    two-faced     jack-in-the-box

# Study Steps to Learn a Word

**Say** the word. Recall when you have heard the word used. Think about what it means.

**Look** at the word. Find any prefixes, suffixes, or other word parts you know. Think about other words that are related in meaning and spelling. Try to picture the word in your mind.

**Spell** the word to yourself. Think about the way each sound is spelled. Notice any unusual spelling.

**Write** the word while looking at it. Check the way you have formed your letters. If you have not written the word clearly or correctly, write it again.

**Check** your learning. Cover the word and write it. If you did not spell the word correctly, practice these steps until the word becomes your own.

# Guidelines for Creating a Spelling Word List

You may want to keep your own spelling word list in a notebook. You can organize your spelling word list alphabetically, by subject areas, by parts of speech, or by other categories. Follow these guidelines.

**1.** Check your writing for words you have misspelled. Circle each misspelled word.

*a (vegatable) garden*

**2.** Find out how to spell the word correctly.
- Look up the word in a dictionary or a thesaurus.
- Ask a teacher or a classmate.

*vegetable*
*a (vegatable) garden*

**3.** Write the word in your notebook.
- Spell the word correctly.
- Write a definition, a synonym, or an antonym to help you understand the meaning of the word.
- Use the word in a sentence.

*vegetable—a plant used as food*
*Corn is a vegetable.*

**4.** When you write, look at your spelling word list to check your spelling.

*A beet's a vegetable.*

WRITER'S HANDBOOK • Spelling

WRITER'S HANDBOOK   Spelling   **51**

| | | | |
|---|---|---|---|
| accident | congratulated | kitchen | someone |
| against | connected | ladder | square |
| allowed | covered | language | staircase |
| answer | degrees | leaves | stairway |
| anymore | describe | leaving | steal |
| anyway | described | library | straight |
| assignment | description | maybe | struck |
| assignments | different | metal | studying |
| attention | disappointed | mind | supposed |
| audience | elevator | month | surprise |
| backwards | especially | myself | telephone |
| balloon | everybody | nervous | television |
| beginning | everyday | opposite | temperature |
| believe | everything | outside | themselves |
| believed | except | overtime | thermometer |
| break | excited | paid | title |
| business | exclaimed | pictures | tomorrow |
| catching | fault | position | touched |
| caught | field | principal | unknown |
| celebrate | finally | probably | unusual |
| central | forever | question | usual |
| championship | goal | realized | where |
| chicken | happened | reason | winner |
| circles | herself | remember | without |
| classroom | himself | signed | wondering |
| clothes | hungry | sincerely | written |
| clumsy | important | smiling | young |
| concentrate | invited | social | |

# Vowel Sounds

- The short vowel sounds are often spelled with one vowel letter.

> /a/ is spelled with **a,** as in *back*
> /e/ is spelled with **e,** as in *wet*
> /e/ can be spelled with **ea,** as in *bread*
> /i/ is spelled with **i,** as in *fit*
> /o/ is spelled with **o,** as in *top*
> /u/ is spelled with **u,** as in *cup*

- Here are five ways to spell the /ā/ sound.

> **a-consonant-e,** as in *rake*
> **ai,** as in *paid*
> **ay,** as in *stay*
> **ey,** as in *prey*
> **eigh,** as in *freight*

- Here are five ways to spell the /ē/ sound.

> **e-consonant-e,** as in *concede*
> **ea,** as in *clean*
> **ee,** as in *meet*
> **ei,** as in *receive*
> **ie,** as in *reprieve*

- When /ē/ comes at the end of a word of more than one syllable, it is usually spelled **y,** as in *pretty. Ski* is one of the few English words that has /ē/ spelled with **i.**

- Here are five ways to spell the /ī/ sound.

> **i-consonant-e,** as in *dime*
> **i,** as in *lion*
> **ie,** as in *tie*
> **igh,** as in *tight*
> **y,** as in *try*

- Here are five ways to spell the /ō/ sound.

> **o-consonant-e,** as in *phone*
> **o,** as in *go*
> **oe,** as in *hoe*
> **oa,** as in *toast*
> **ow,** as in *slow*

/o͞o/   ● Here are six ways to spell the /o͞o/ sound.

> **oo,** as in *boot*
> **ou,** as in *group*
> **o-consonant-e,** as in *move*
> **ew,** as in *flew*
> **u-consonant-e,** as in *crude*
> **ue,** as in *blue*

## Letter Combinations

*ie, ei*   ● The letters **ie** usually make the /ē/ sound. However, if the /ē/ sound follows the letter **c,** it is spelled **ei.** When these letters make the /ā/ sound, they are written **ei.**

> piece     deceive     neighbor

final /ər/   ● Here are three ways to spell the /ər/ sound.

> **ar,** as in *scholar*
> **er,** as in *better*
> **or,** as in *actor*

final /əl/   ● Here are four ways to spell the /əl/ sound.

> **le,** as in *circle*
> **al,** as in *medal*
> **el,** as in *shovel*
> **il,** as in *pencil*

## Syllable Division

compound words   ● Divide compound words into syllables between the two words.

> outgrow—out·grow     bulldog—bull·dog

two-syllable words   ● When a word has two consonant letters between two vowel letters, divide the word between the two consonants.

> danger—dan·ger     pudding—pud·ding

When a word ends with a consonant letter before *le,* divide the word before the consonant.

> handle—han·dle     eagle—ea·gle

- When a two-syllable word has a long vowel sound in the first syllable, divide the word before the middle consonant.

sofa—so·fa    baker—ba·ker

- When a two-syllable word has a short vowel sound in the first syllable, divide the word after the middle consonant.

cabin—cab·in    metal—met·al

- Some words contain syllables that are difficult to hear. When you spell these words, be sure to write each syllable.

**three-syllable words**

capital—cap·i·tal    mystery—mys·te·ry

## Verbs

Add *ed* to form the past tense of most verbs.

**past tense**

learn—learned    walk—walked    ask—asked

- To form the past tense of verbs ending in a consonant plus *e*, drop the *e* and add *ed*.

glance—glanced    like—liked    blame—blamed

- To form the past tense of verbs that end in a short vowel and a consonant, double the final consonant and add *ed*.

knit—knitted    mop—mopped    hum—hummed

- To form the past tense of verbs that end in a consonant plus *y*, change the *y* to *i* and add *ed*.

carry—carried    hurry—hurried    try—tried

- To form the past tense of verbs that end with a vowel plus *y*, add *ed*.

annoy—annoyed    destroy—destroyed    play—played

## Plurals

- Add *s* to form the plural of most nouns.

**nouns**

book—books    school—schools    table—tables

- Add *es* to form the plural of nouns ending in *s, ss, x, ch,* or *sh.*

    class—classes     fox—foxes
    wish—wishes     lunch—lunches

- Add *s* to form the plural of nouns ending in a vowel plus *y.*

    monkey—monkeys     day—days     toy—toys

- Change *y* to *i* and add *es* to form the plural of nouns ending in a consonant plus *y.*

    mystery—mysteries     baby—babies     family—families

- Change *f* or *fe* to *v* and add *es* to form the plural of most nouns ending in *f* or *fe.*

    wolf—wolves     life—lives     half—halves

- Add *s* to form the plural of some nouns ending in *f.*

    belief—beliefs     chief—chiefs

- Some singular nouns have irregular plural forms.

    woman—women     child—children     foot—feet
    man—men     tooth—teeth     mouse—mice     ox—oxen

- Some nouns have the same singular and plural forms.

    moose—moose     deer—deer
    sheep—sheep     series—series

## Contractions

- A **contraction** is a shortened form of two words.

pronoun
contractions

- Some contractions are formed by joining one of the pronouns *I, you, he, she, it, we,* and *they* and a verb. An apostrophe takes the place of the letter or letters that have been dropped to combine the two words.

    I + will = I'll
    you + are = you're
    he + is = he's
    she + has = she's
    it + is = it's
    we + would = we'd
    they + have = they've

- Some contractions are formed by joining a verb and the word *not*. **verb contractions**

> have + not = haven't    were + not = weren't
> should + not = shouldn't    must + not = mustn't

- The verb *will* forms a contraction in a special way.

> will + not = won't

## Possessive Nouns

- A singular possessive noun shows ownership by one person or thing. To form the possessive of a singular noun, add an apostrophe and an *s*. **singular nouns**

> Carol 's book    dog 's tail

- To form the possessive of a plural noun that ends with *s*, add an apostrophe. **plural nouns**

> friends ' letters    butterflies ' wings

- To form the possessive of a plural noun that does not end with *s*, add an apostrophe and an *s*.

> women 's club    mice 's whiskers

## Abbreviations

- An **abbreviation** is the shortened form of a word. Many abbreviations begin with a capital letter and end with a period. The abbreviation of a proper noun always begins with a capital letter. **proper nouns**

> December—Dec.    Doctor—Dr.    Wednesday—Wed.

- Words such as *Street, Avenue, Boulevard, North, South, East,* and *West* may be abbreviated in an address.

> 46 E. Main St.    5728 Lake Blvd.

- Postal abbreviations of state names are written with two capital letters. They do not have a period.

> Nevada— NV    New Jersey— NJ

# Adjectives That Compare

**er**
- To compare two things, add *er* to most one-syllable adjectives.

    small—smaller      tall—taller

**est**
- To compare more than two things, add *est* to most one-syllable adjectives.

    light—lightest      short—shortest

**final e**
- If the adjective ends in *e*, drop the *e* before adding *er* or *est*.

    blue—bluer—bluest

**short vowel + consonant**
- If a one-syllable adjective ends in a short vowel sound plus a consonant, double the last letter before adding *er* or *est*.

    mad—madder—maddest      fat—fatter—fattest

**consonant + y**
- If the adjective ends in a consonant plus *y*, change the *y* to *i* before adding *er* or *est*.

    silly—sillier—silliest

**special forms**
- Some adjectives that compare have special forms. The adjectives *good, bad, little,* and *many* have special forms for comparison.

    Rosa is a  good  swimmer.

    Roger is a  better  diver than Joe.

    Ruth is the  best  athlete in her class.

    The  bad  weather ruined our hike.

    The rain was  worse  than the wind.

    Tuesday was the  worst  day in the week.

    Carmen has  little  trouble understanding math.

    Tony has  less  trouble understanding math.

    Sandy has the  least  trouble in the subject.

    There are  many  members in the nature club.

    There are  more  members in the photography club.

    The computer club has the  most  members of all.

# Adverbs That Compare

- Adverbs can be used to compare two or more actions. When you compare two actions, add *er* to most short adverbs. When you compare three or more actions, add *est* to most short adverbs.

*er, est*

> Komiko always studies hard before a test.
>
> Her brother Isamu studies even harder .
>
> Their older sister, Kyoko, studies the hardest .

- Most adverbs that end in *ly* and have two or more syllables use *more* and *most* for comparison.

*more, most*

> Maria swam the length of the pool easily .
>
> Ron swam the length of the pool more easily than Maria.
>
> Linda swam the length of the pool the most easily of all.

- The adverbs *well* and *badly* have special forms for comparison.

*well, badly*

> The boy flew his kite well .
>
> His cousin flew her kite better than he did.
>
> The man flew his kite best of all.
>
> The performer acted badly in rehearsal.
>
> Her stand-in acted worse .
>
> She acted the worst of all the performers.

# Sentence Diagramming

**sentence diagram**

- A **sentence diagram** shows how the parts of a sentence work together.

**simple subject and simple predicate**

- The **simple subject** is the key word in the complete subject. The **simple predicate** is the verb in the complete predicate.

Steve won.

| subject | verb |
|---------|------|
| Steve | won |

**inverted word order**

- A sentence is in **inverted word order** when the verb or part of the verb comes before the subject. When you diagram a sentence with inverted word order, place the subject before the verb as usual, and capitalize any words that are capitalized in the sentence.

Is Robert going?

| subject | verb |
|---------|------|
| Robert | Is going |

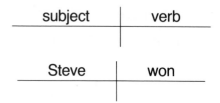

**four kinds of sentences**

- These diagrams show the simple subject and simple predicate in each kind of sentence.

Declarative: Rachael bakes muffins.

| Rachael | bakes |
|---------|-------|

Interrogative: Did Rachael bake muffins?

| Rachael | Did bake |
|---------|----------|

WRITER'S HANDBOOK • Sentence Diagramming

Imperative: Shut the door, please.

| _you_ (understood) | Shut |
|---|---|

Exclamatory: The storm is dangerous!

| storm | is |
|---|---|

● A **direct object** receives the action of the verb.

direct object

| subject | verb | direct object |
|---|---|---|

Carlos eats breakfast .

| Carlos | eats | breakfast |
|---|---|---|

● An **indirect object** tells to or for whom or to or for what the action of the verb is done.

indirect object

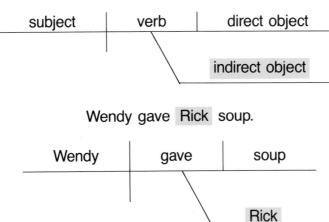

| subject | verb | direct object |
|---|---|---|
|  | indirect object | |

Wendy gave Rick soup.

| Wendy | gave | soup |
|---|---|---|
|  | Rick | |

predicate
nominative

● A **predicate nominative** is a noun or a pronoun that follows a linking verb and renames the subject of the sentence.

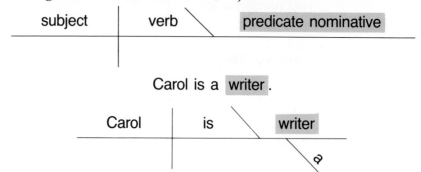

Carol is a writer .

adjective

● An **adjective** modifies a noun or a pronoun.

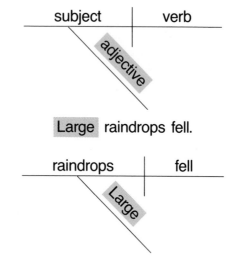

Large raindrops fell.

possessives and
articles

● **Possessive nouns** and **possessive pronouns** precede nouns to show ownership or possession. The **articles** *a, an,* and *the* always signal a noun.

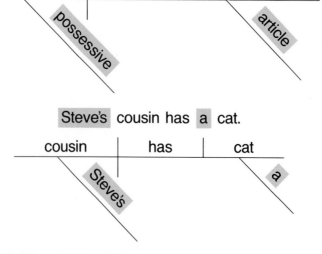

Steve's cousin has a cat.

- A **predicate adjective** follows a linking verb and describes the subject of the sentence.

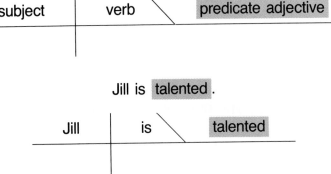

Jill is talented .

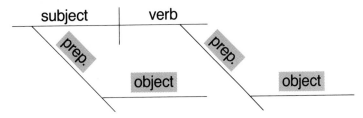

- A **prepositional phrase** is made up of a preposition (prep.), the object of the preposition, and all the words in between. The **object of the preposition** is the noun or pronoun at the end of the prepositional phrase.

The group of students walked to the field .

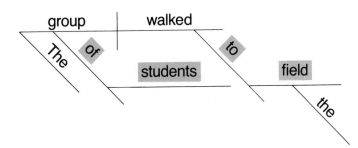

● An **adverb** modifies a verb, an adjective, or another adverb.

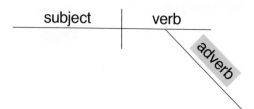

The boy spoke clearly.

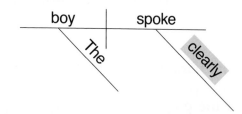

● A **compound subject** is two or more subjects that have the same verb. The subjects are joined by a conjunction.

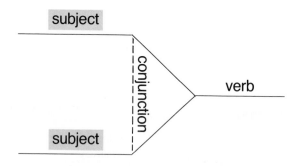

Ted and Mike played basketball.

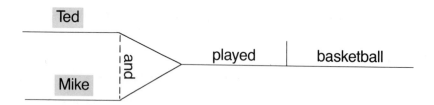

- A **compound predicate** is two or more verbs that have the same subject. The predicates are joined by a conjunction.

conjunction and a compound predicate

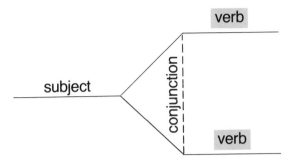

They passed the ball and dribbled it.

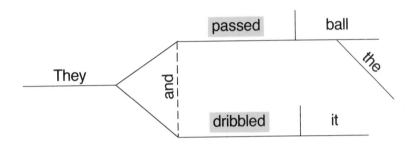

- A **compound sentence** contains two or more related simple sentences joined by a comma and a conjunction or by a semicolon.

conjunction and a compound sentence

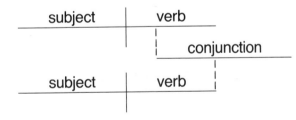

Ted won the game, but Mike played well.

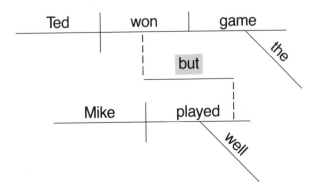

# GLOSSARY

## Contents

# GLOSSARY OF COMPOSITION AND LITERARY TERMS

## Composition Terms

**AUDIENCE**  *the reader or readers for whom a composition is written*  The audience for this business letter is Maria Lemmon, president of Tapco Games Company.

> Ms. Maria Lemmon, President
> Tapco Games Company
> 129 Sixth Avenue
> New York, NY 10010
>
> Dear Ms. Lemmon:

**COHERENCE**  *the quality of a composition in which ideas are presented in an orderly way*  Notice how the transitional words make this example easy to understand.

> The merry-go-round spun gaily in front of Albert. Behind him the roller coaster swooped and rattled. He heard screams from the House of Horrors on his right.

**DRAFTING**  *the actual writing of a composition, beginning with a rough version that will be revised later*  This girl is using a revised first draft to compose her final draft.

**EDITING** *the improving of a composition by changing its content, coherence, style, or tone* Notice the changes made here in style and tone.

> Dear Aunt May,
> Thank you for the ~~great~~ delicious dinner. The chicken was ~~yummy~~ so juicy and tender! ~~The artichokes were awful, though.~~ May I have the recipe for your wonderful strawberry shortcake, ~~please~~?

**EDITOR'S MARKS** *standard symbols for making changes when revising or proofreading* Note that each mark shows a different kind of change.

Use these marks when you revise.

| | |
|---|---|
| ↻ Move something. | ∧ Add something. |
| ⌅ Replace something | ✄ Cut something. |

Use these marks when you proofread.

| | | |
|---|---|---|
| ≡ Capitalize. | ∧ Add something. | ⊙ Add a period. |
| ⩖ Add quotation marks. | ⌅ Replace something. | ✄ Cut something. |
| ∿ Transpose. | ◯ Spell correctly. | ⋏ Add a comma. |
| / Make a lowercase letter. | | ¶ Indent paragraph. |

**FINAL DRAFT** *the final copy of a composition, ready to be published* This example shows the final draft of the letter to Aunt May.

> Dear Aunt May,
> Thank you for the delicious dinner. The chicken was so juicy and tender! May I have the recipe for your wonderful strawberry shortcake?

**FIRST DRAFT** *the first version of a composition, in which the writer tries to get his or her thoughts on paper* Notice that this draft is somewhat choppy.

> *The lake is beautiful. It is great in the fall. The red and yellow leaves are beautiful. I love the lake.*

**PREWRITING** *the first stage of the writing process, in which the writer gathers ideas and information and begins to organize them* This example shows a cluster as a way of organizing ideas.

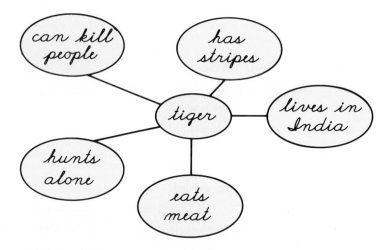

**PREWRITING STRATEGIES** *activities writers use to help them think of and organize ideas* Here are some examples.

- **brainstorming** *an activity in which an individual or a group tries to think of all possible ideas about a topic*

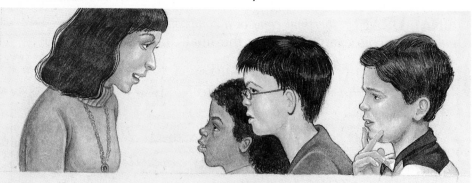

**Teacher:** *How can we save energy?*  **Students:** *Turn off lights. Recycle paper and bottles. Use cars less.*

- **charting**   *a way of writing and organizing facts or ideas in groups*

| Person | Birthday | Favorite Color | Favorite Activity |
|---|---|---|---|
| Charleen | July 22 | yellow | swimming |
| Tyrone | March 8 | red | cooking |
| Elvira | June 10 | blue | reading |

- **clustering**   *a way of organizing facts or ideas around a main idea or topic*   The topic of this cluster is "information found on maps."

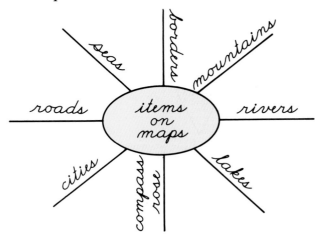

- **diagramming**   *a way of showing how ideas are related in time or space*

### Centers of an Ancient Greek City

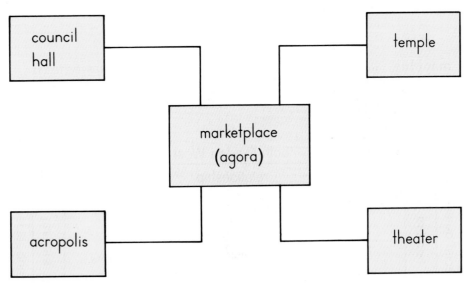

- **using an inverted triangle** *a way of organizing ideas to narrow a topic* Notice that the most general idea is at the top and the most specific idea is at the bottom.

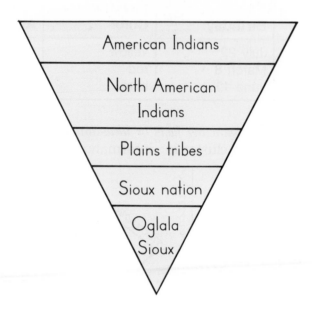

- **listing** *writing down one's own ideas or ideas that have been brainstormed by a group*

*Ways of Cooking*

| | | | |
|---|---|---|---|
| *baking* | *boiling* | *broiling* | *roasting* |
| *steaming* | *stewing* | *frying* | *stir-frying* |

- **mapping** *a way of organizing ideas to show relationships between them* This map shows relationships between the early settlers and the Indians

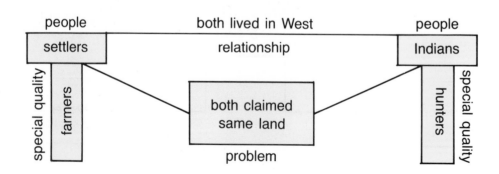

- **slotting** *brainstorming alone or with a group to find words to complete a sentence*

> *The mountain climber ___ up the last peak.*
> *climbed     struggled     bounded*
> *inched      strolled       ran*

**PROOFREADING** *reviewing a draft to correct mistakes in capitalization, punctuation, usage, grammar, and spelling* Notice the grammar change in this example.

> *Beverly and I* ~~was~~ *were ready for the party.*

**PUBLISHING** *sharing a final draft of a composition with others in one or more ways* This boy is putting his composition in a class notebook for others to read.

**PURPOSE** *the reason for writing a composition* The purpose of writing an advertisement, for example, is to persuade people to buy something.

**RESPONDING**   *a revising activity in which the writer answers questions asked about his or her composition. The questions may be asked by the writer himself or herself, or by a partner or group.*   The girl on the right is responding to the boy on the left.

**Boy:** Did you like what I wrote about Benjamin Franklin?

**Girl:** Yes, but I wish you'd put in more of the funny things he said.

**RESPONSE GROUP**   *a group of writers who help each other revise work by asking and answering questions about it*   These students are responding to a question about coherence.

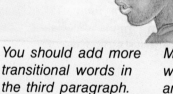

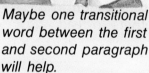

Do you think my composition is coherent?

You should add more transitional words in the third paragraph.

Maybe one transitional word between the first and second paragraph will help.

**REVISING**   *the process in which the writer thinks again about his or her writing, correcting errors in organization and language*   Notice this change in a revised draft.

Everything on the ground looked so small! Marian went up in a hot-air balloon. She had never done that before. "Now I know how a bird feels," she said.

**STYLE** *a writer's way of using varied sentences and vivid words to create a special tone* Notice how the style of this example shows Jennifer's excitement.

> What a shock! Jennifer couldn't help squealing when she came into the living room. She'd never dreamed her friends would give her a surprise birthday party!

**TASK** *a writing assignment or job* It was Bob's task to write a research report.

**TONE** *the feeling about the subject of a composition, shown by a writer's style* The tone in this example shows how much the writer dislikes the movie monster.

> The Trash Monster in the movie was slimy and disgusting. Its skin was gray and blue and green, like garbage that's been left in the trash can too long.

**UNITY** *the quality of a composition in which all the details tell about the same topic or main idea* Cutting out one sentence has improved unity in this example.

> Being an actor is hard work. Actors often have to rehearse for many hours. ~~They don't have to exercise as much as dancers, though.~~ They have to memorize lines and change costumes quickly.

**WRITING PROCESS** *the process of prewriting, drafting, responding and revising, proofreading, and publishing a composition* Writers go back and forth among the steps as needed while they write a composition.

# Literary Terms

**CHARACTERIZATION** *the ways in which writers present and develop characters to make the characters seem real* Writers develop their characters by
* describing how a character looks.

> **Mary Ellen's skin was the color of caramel. She made you think of candy in another way, too, because she wore what looked like a dozen bright-colored little ribbon bows in her hair.**

* letting the character speak.

> **"You . . . You can't scare me,"  Wendell said bravely, hoping his voice wouldn't crack, as Billy the Bully loomed over him.**

* telling the character's thoughts and feelings.

> **I was sweating, but my hands got colder and colder as Miss Walters read off the names of the contest winners. Third place, second place . . . not me. Had I won, or was I nothing?**

* telling what others think of the character.

> **Sarah walked by her giggling classmates without a word. "There goes Miss Stuck-up," one of them whispered.**

**CHARACTERS** *the people or animals in a story, poem, or play* Sometimes authors are concerned mainly with making their characters come alive. For example, in *Cracker Jackson,* author Betsy Byars gives us much information about this character. We learn what he thinks and feels and how he acts. The story is *about* him, not just about what happens to him. At other times, authors are concerned mainly with the plot.

**FICTION** *a story invented by a writer* A work of fiction may be based on real events, but it always includes made-up characters and experiences. A work of fiction may be brief, like a fable, a folk tale, or a short story, or it may be a book-length story, called a **novel.**

**FIGURATIVE LANGUAGE** *words used in unusual rather than literal (exact) ways* Whenever you say that someone looks like "the cat that swallowed the canary" or that you feel "all broken up" because something sad happened, you are using figurative language.

The most common forms of figurative language in literature are similes and metaphors.
* In a **simile** the words *like* or *as* are used to compare two very different things. For example, Author Cynthia Overbeck Bix says that the drops of liquid on the leaves of the sundew plant sparkle "like diamonds."
* A **metaphor** suggests a comparison by saying that one thing *is* another. For example, an author might write *An owl is a cat with wings* or *The full moon is a golden coin.*

Onomatopoeia and alliteration are two other kinds of figurative language.
* **Onomatopoeia** involves using words that sound like the thing or action they describe. *Bow-wow, boom,* and *snip* are examples of onomatopoeia.

- **Alliteration** is the repetition of the same consonant sound in several words. *Five giant giraffes jumped through the jungle* is an example of alliteration that repeats the /j/ sound.

**NONFICTION** *a piece of writing that describes things as they actually happened or that presents information or opinions about something* Cynthia Overbeck Bix's "Two Ways to Trap a Fly," for example, is a science **article** that tells facts about carnivorous plants. The **news story** is another kind of nonfiction. Jon Engellenner's news stories tell about "Humphrey," the humpback whale that swam up a California river. Other kinds of nonfiction are the **biography,** the written history of a person's life, the **travel story,** and the personal **journal** or **diary.**

**PLOT** *the action in a story* When you tell what happens in a story, you are talking about the plot. For instance, in Lloyd Alexander's *Westmark,* the plot tells how Mickle, a street child, and Theo, a runaway, work together to fight Cabbarus, Chief Minister of Westmark.

The most important part of the plot is **conflict,** a character's struggle to do the right thing. Sometimes a character struggles against nature, as when a young Indian girl in Scott O'Dell's *Island of the Blue Dolphins* must learn to live alone on an island. At other times, the character struggles with another character, as when Bilbo Baggins opposes the sneaky Gollum and the fearsome dragon Smaug in J.R.R. Tolkien's novel *The Hobbit.* Finally, the conflict is sometimes within the character's own mind, as in *Ghost Vision* by Jeanie Kortum, when Panipaq, an Inuit (Eskimo) boy, must decide what to do about the strange visions he sees.

**PUN** *a joke that depends on a word that has two different meanings or on two words that sound alike but have different meanings* For example, the pun in the funny title of James Howe's book *The Celery Stalks at Midnight* depends on the two meanings of the word *stalks.*

**QUATRAIN** *a poem or stanza that has four lines* Gelett Burgess's poem "The Purple Cow" is a quatrain.

> **I never saw a purple cow,**
> **I never hope to see one,**
> **But I can tell you, anyhow,**
> **I'd rather see than be one.**

**RHYME** *the repetition of ending sounds of words, especially at the ends of lines of poetry* These two lines from Richard Fonbuena's poem about Humphrey the whale make a rhyme.

> **Humphrey the humpback whale, a mighty whale was he.**
> **He swam into the Delta to see what he could see.**

*He* and *see* are the rhyming words in these two lines.

**RHYTHM** *the repeating pattern of stressed and unstressed syllables in a poem* The syllables can be marked with / over each loud syllable and ⌣ over each soft syllable. Notice how the rhythm is marked in the first two lines of "The Purple Cow."

> **I never saw a purple cow,**
> **I never hope to see one,**

**SETTING** *the time and place in which a story takes place* If you say, "Last August in Oregon, Simon rowed a boat up a river," you have given the setting of Simon's adventure. Authors may choose a wide variety of settings for a story. For instance, the setting of Patricia McLachlan's novel *Sarah, Plain and Tall* is the western prairie in the 1800's. The setting of Robert Heinlein's *Space Cadet,* on the other hand, is a training school in the distant future for spaceship pilots.

# WRITER'S THESAURUS

## Contents

# What Is a Thesaurus?

A **thesaurus** lists words and their synonyms. Like a dictionary, a thesaurus lists words in alphabetical order. Each of these words is called an **entry word.** A list of synonyms follows the entry word. Sometimes a thesaurus lists antonyms.

Look at the parts of this thesaurus entry for the word **interesting.**

The **entry word** is in color. It is followed by the part of speech and a definition. An **example sentence** shows how the word can be used.

> interesting *adj.* Having or arousing interest or attention. This book has an interesting plot.

*Synonyms* for the entry word are in italics. Each synonym is followed by a definition and an example sentence.

> *absorbing* Taking the full attention of; deeply involving. She finds her work challenging and *absorbing.*
> *appealing* Inviting; attractive. The casserole gave off an *appealing* smell.
> *engaging* Attracting attention in a pleasing manner. The politician had an *engaging* way of speaking.
> *fascinating* Very interesting. We saw a *fascinating* television program about kangaroos.
> *intriguing* Interesting in an unusual way. He has an *intriguing* and new approach to the problem.

If an **antonym** is given, it is printed in dark letters.

> **ANTONYMS: boring, dull, uninteresting**

# How to Use Your Writer's Thesaurus

Suppose you are writing a book report on a book about dinosaurs. When you read your first draft, you realize that you have overused the word interesting. You open your **Writer's Thesaurus** to find some synonyms. Here are the steps you should follow.

1. Look for the word in the **Index to Thesaurus.** The Index lists every word in the **Writer's Thesaurus.**

2. Find the word in the Index.

interesting *adj.*

You know that interesting is an entry word because it is printed in color.

3. Turn to the page in your **Writer's Thesaurus** on which interesting is printed in color. Read the entry carefully. Not every synonym may express exactly what you want to say. Choose the synonym that makes the most sense in your report.

**Remember:** Not every synonym will have the exact meaning you want. Look at the entry for interesting on page 13. Which synonyms fit your writing best?

◆ Sometimes a word is listed in the Index like this:

*fascinating* interesting *adj.*

This means you will find *fascinating* listed as a synonym under the entry word **interesting.** Since *fascinating* is not printed in color, it is not an entry word.

◆ You will also see some lines in the Index that look like this:

**boring** interesting *adj.*

This means that **boring** is listed as an antonym under the entry word interesting.

## Index to Thesaurus

fear courage *n.*
*fearful* **afraid** *adj.*
**fearless** afraid *adj.*
*feasible* **possible** *adj.*
*feast* **eat** *v.*
**feeble** strong *adj.*
*feeling* **idea** *n.*
**final** first *adj.*
*finest* **best** *adj.*
*first* *adj.*
*flag* **stop** *v.*
*flee* **run** *v.*
**flimsy** strong *adj.*
*flutter* **fly** *v.*
*fly* *v.*
*foremost* **first** *adj.*
*forest* *n.*
*form* **organize** *v.*
*frequently* **often** *adv.*
*friendly* *adj.*
*frightened* **afraid** *adj.*
*frisky* **lively** *adj.*
*frosty* **cold** *adj.*
**frown** smile *v.*
*fry* **cook** *v.*

*gallop* **run** *v.*
*gentle* **tender** *adj.*
*gigantic* **large** *adj.*
*gist* **sense** *n.*
*give* *v.*
*glide* **fly** *v.*
*glimpse* **see** *v.*
**go** come *v.*
*good* *adj.*
*gorgeous* **beautiful** *adj.*
*great* **good** *adj.*
*grin* **smile** *v.*

*halt* **stop** *v.*
*handsome* **beautiful** *adj.*
*happy* *adj.*
**hard** tender *adj.*
**harsh** enjoyable *adj.*

**heartbroken** happy *adj.*
*hesitate* *v.*
*highway* **road** *n.*
*hit* **strike** *v.*
**homely** beautiful *adj.*
*homey* **cozy** *adj.*
*hop* **jump** *v.*
**hostile** friendly *adj.*
**hot** cold *adj.*
*house* **building** *n.*
*hover* **fly** *v.*
*huge* **large** *adj.*
*hum* *v.*

*idea* *n.*
*immense* **large** *adj.*
**impossible** possible *adj.*
**inactive** lively *adj.*
**infrequently** often *adv.*
**inhibition** courage *n.*
*intelligent* **clever** *adj.*
*interesting* *adj.*
*intriguing* **interesting** *adj.*

*joyful* **happy** *adj.*
*jubilant* **happy** *adj.*
*jump* *v.*
*jumpy* **nervous** *adj.*
*jungle* **forest** *n.*

*kind* **friendly** *adj.*
*kind* **tender** *adj.*
*knock* **strike** *v.*

L

*large* *adj.*
**last** first *adj.*
*laugh* **smile** *v.*
*lavish* **give** *v.*
**lazy** lively *adj.*

*leading* **first** *adj.*
*leap* **jump** *v.*
**leave** come *v.*
**leisurely** fast *adj.*
**lifeless** lively *adj.*
*likely* **possible** *adj.*
**listless** lively *adj.*
**little** large *adj.*
*lively* *adj.*
*look* **see** *v.*
**lose** win *v.*
**loud** silent *adj.*
*lovely* **beautiful** *adj.*
**lowest** best *adj.*

*mammoth* **large** *adj.*
*matchless* **best** *adj.*
**mean** friendly *adj.*
*meaning* **sense** *n.*
**meaninglessness** sense *n.*
*meditate* **think** *v.*
*mighty* **strong** *adj.*
**miniature** large *adj.*
**minute** large *adj.*
*moan* **sigh** *v.*
**modern** old *adj.*
*monstrous* **large** *adj.*
*motion* **move** *v.*
*move* *v.*
**muddle** organize *v.*
*munch* **eat** *v.*
*murmur* **hum** *v.*

**nasty** friendly *adj.*
*nasty* **unpleasant** *adj.*
*nervous* *adj.*
**new** old *adj.*
*nibble* **eat** *v.*
*nice* **good** *adj.*
**noisy** silent *adj.*
**nonsense** sense *n.*
*notion* **idea** *n.*

**O**

*observe* see *v.*
*often* adv.
*old* adj.
*open* friendly adj.
*opinion* idea *n.*
*opt* pick *v.*
*ordinarily* often adv.
*organize* v.

**P**

**painful** enjoyable *adj.*
*path* road *n.*
*pause* hesitate *v.*
*pick* v.
**plain** beautiful *adj.*
*pleasant* enjoyable *adj.*
**pleasant** unpleasant *adj.*
*pleased* happy adj.
**pleasing** unpleasant adj.
**plod** run *v.*
*point* sense *n.*
*ponder* think *v.*
*possible* adj.
**pout** smile *v.*
*powerful* strong adj.
*present* give *v.*
*pretty* beautiful adj.
**proceed** hesitate *v.*
*pronounce* say *v.*
*provide* give *v.*
*purr* hum *v.*

**Q**

*quick* clever adj.
*quick* fast adj.
*quiet* silent adj.
*quit* stop *v.*

**R**

*race* run *v.*
*rapid* fast adj.
**rarely** often adv.

*reach* come *v.*
*reason* think *v.*
**recede** come *v.*
**receive** give *v.*
**recent** old adj.
*reflect* think *v.*
*regularly* often adv.
**relaxed** nervous adj.
*repeatedly* often adv.
*restful* cozy adj.
*restless* nervous adj.
*road* n.
*roast* cook *v.*
*route* road *n.*
*run* v.

**S**

**sad** happy adj.
*sail* fly *v.*
*sapling* tree *n.*
*say* v.
*scamper* run *v.*
*scared* afraid adj.
*see* v.
*seedling* tree *n.*
**seldom** often adv.
*select* pick *v.*
*sense* n.
**senselessness** sense *n.*
*sharp* clever adj.
*shock* v.
*sigh* v.
*significance* sense *n.*
*silent* adj.
**simple** clever adj.
*skip* jump *v.*
*skyscraper* building *n.*
**slight** strong adj.
**slow** clever adj.
**slow** fast adj.
**sluggish** fast adj.
**sluggish** lively adj.
**small** large adj.
*smart* clever adj.
*smash* strike *v.*
*smile* v.
*snug* cozy adj.

*soar* fly *v.*
*sob* sigh *v.*
*soft* tender adj.
*speak* say *v.*
*speechless* silent adj.
*speedy* fast adj.
*spring* jump *v.*
*sprint* run *v.*
*spry* lively adj.
**start** stop *v.*
*startle* shock *v.*
*state* say *v.*
**steal** give *v.*
*still* silent adj.
*stop* v.
*street* road *n.*
*stride* walk *v.*
*strike* v.
*stroll* walk *v.*
*strong* adj.
*structure* building *n.*
*strut* walk *v.*
*stun* shock *v.*
**stupid** clever adj.
*sturdy* strong adj.
*succeed* win *v.*
*supreme* best adj.
*sureness* courage *n.*
*surprise* shock *v.*
**surrender** win *v.*
*suspect* doubt *v.*
*sweep* move *v.*
*swift* fast adj.
*systematize* organize *v.*

**T**

**take** give *v.*
*tease* annoy *v.*
*tell* say *v.*
*tender* adj.
*tense* nervous adj.
**terrible** good adj.
*think* v.
*thought* idea *n.*
*thrilled* happy adj.
*timber* tree *n.*
*timberland* forest *n.*
*timid* afraid adj.

**tiny** large *adj.*
**tired** lively *adj.*
*top* best *adj.*
*tree n.*
*triumph* win *v.*
*trot* move *v.*
*trouble* annoy *v.*
*troublesome* unpleasant *adj.*
*truck* vehicle *n.*
**trudge** run *v.*
*trudge* walk *v.*
**trust** doubt *v.*

**ugly** beautiful *adj.*
**unattainable** possible *adj.*
**uncomfortable** cozy *adj.*
**undisturbed** nervous *adj.*
*uneasy* nervous *adj.*
**unenjoyable** enjoyable *adj.*
**unfriendly** friendly *adj.*
**unhappy** happy *adj.*
**unheard-of** possible *adj.*

**uninteresting** interesting *adj.*
**unkind** friendly *adj.*
**unkind** tender *adj.*
**unlikely** possible *adj.*
**unpleasant** *adj.*
**unpleasant** enjoyable *adj.*
**unsettle** organize *v.*
**unthinkable** possible *adj.*
**unwise** clever *adj.*
**upset** organize *v.*
*used* old *adj.*
*usually* often *adv.*

*van* vehicle *n.*
*vehicle n.*
*view* idea *n.*
*view* see *v.*
*vivid* lively *adj.*

*wait* hesitate *v.*
*walk v.*
**warm** cold *adj.*

*warm* friendly *adj.*
*watch* see *v.*
**weak** strong *adj.*
*well-meaning* friendly *adj.*
*whisper* sigh *v.*
*wilderness* forest *n.*
*win v.*
*wise* clever *adj.*
**withdraw** come *v.*
*wonder* doubt *v.*
*woods* forest *n.*
*workable* possible *adj.*
*worn* old *adj.*
**worst** best *adj.*

**young** old *adj.*

*zoom* move *v.*

WRITER'S THESAURUS

## A

**afraid** *adj.* Scared. Are you **afraid** of the dark?

*alarmed* Filled with strong fear; frightened. The *alarmed* children ran when they heard the siren.

*fearful* Frightened; full of fear. The dog looked *fearful* during the storm.

*frightened* Filled with sudden fear; scared. The man soothed the *frightened* baby.

*scared* Fearful. The *scared* animal hid in the bushes.

*timid* Fearful or shy. Don't be *timid* when you read your report.

**ANTONYMS: bold, brave, courageous, fearless**

**annoy** *v.* To bother. Does the loud music **annoy** you?

*badger* To nag; to pester; to tease. The children *badger* their mother for a treat.

*bother* To annoy or trouble. Don't *bother* me while I'm studying.

*disturb* To break in on or interrupt, especially with noise or disorder. Latecomers can *disturb* the audience at a concert.

*tease* To pick on or fool a person or an animal for fun. It is wrong to *tease* people for failing when they have done their best.

*trouble* To make or become upset, annoyed, worried, or ill. I do not want to *trouble* my parents by coming home late.

## B

**beautiful** *adj.* Lovely; pretty; full of beauty. This evening we saw a **beautiful** sunset.

*attractive* Interesting; tempting; pleasing. That shop always has *attractive* window displays.

*fair* Pleasant. The weather was *fair* for our whole vacation.

*gorgeous* Brilliant; dazzling; very beautiful. That is the most *gorgeous* dress I've ever seen!

*handsome* Pleasing in appearance, especially in a stately way. You look *handsome* in your new suit.

*lovely* Very pretty; pleasant. Nina has *lovely* brown hair.

*pretty* Pleasing; cute; winning. The child has a *pretty* smile.

**ANTONYMS: homely, plain, ugly**

**best** *adj.* Superlative form of the word *good;* superior to all others; most excellent. Kim is the **best** soccer player in the school.

*choicest* Of the highest quality. Sue sent us a basket of the *choicest* fruits.

*finest* Most elegant; most desirable. He wore a jacket of the *finest* soft wool.

*matchless* Without peer or equal. Her paintings are *matchless* works of art.

*supreme* Highest in quality, power, or ability. The Constitution sets forth the *supreme* law of the land.

*top* In the highest position; most accomplished. Carol is the *top* debater on our team.

**ANTONYMS: lowest, worst**

**building** *n.* A structure that is used as a shelter. This **building** has six floors.

*edifice* A large, imposing building. The ancient Romans erected a magnificent *edifice* on this site.

*house* A building designed to be lived in. My *house* is on Elm Street.

*skyscraper* A very tall building. Many companies have offices in this *skyscraper.*

*structure* Something that has been built, such as a building. The campers made a simple *structure* of rocks and branches.

# C

**clever** *adj.* Bright; good at solving problems. If you are **clever,** you can solve this mathematics puzzle.

*alert* Mentally quick and aware. The *alert* reader will notice the clues in this mystery.

*cunning* Clever or tricky. The *cunning* spy took the picture and escaped without being seen.

*intelligent* Having or showing intelligence; smart. Amy is *intelligent* and understands things quickly.

*quick* Swift to learn or understand; alert. Juan is *quick* with math problems.

*sharp* Quick-witted; clever; shrewd. A *sharp* mind is a great asset for a trial lawyer.

*smart* Intelligent; bright; not foolish. A *smart* student prepares well for tests.

*wise* Having or showing good judgment, knowledge, or experience; full of wisdom. The old man had a *wise* face.

**ANTONYMS: simple, slow, stupid, unwise**

**cold** *adj.* Low in temperature. Autumn nights are **cold** in the mountains.

*brisk* Cool; nippy. A *brisk* wind was blowing across the water.

*cool* Slightly cold. After the game, we had a *cool* drink.

*frosty* Cold enough for frost, or ice crystals, to form. Dress warmly on this *frosty* morning.

**ANTONYMS: hot, warm**

**come** *v.* To move in the direction of (something or someone); to approach. After two miles, you will **come** to a crossroad.

*advance* To move ahead or onward. The general ordered his troops to *advance.*

*approach* To come near to (something or someone). Trains slow down as they *approach* a station.

*arrive* To get to a place. The package will *arrive* at your office tomorrow.

*reach* To arrive at or extend to. This television program will *reach* millions of viewers.

**ANTONYMS: depart, go, leave, recede, withdraw**

**cook** *v.* To prepare food for eating by using heat. What shall we **cook** for dinner?

*bake* To cook in a heated oven. Darryl loves to *bake* bread.

*boil* To cook in very hot, or boiling, water. Gail will *boil* the vegetables for a few minutes.

*broil* To cook under a flame. Pour sauce over the chicken before you *broil* it.

*fry* To cook in hot oil or fat. Gary will bread the fish and then *fry* it.

*roast* To cook by heat in an oven or over a fire. We will *roast* a turkey for Thanksgiving dinner.

**courage** *n.* Bravery; strength of will. It takes **courage** to stand up for what is right.

*bravery* The quality of being brave or daring. The soldier was honored for his *bravery* in the war.

*confidence* Faith or trust. If you have *confidence* in yourself, you will not be afraid to try new things.

*sureness* Certainty. Tim guided his horse with strength and *sureness.*

**ANTONYMS: fear, inhibition**

**WRITER'S THESAURUS**

**cozy** *adj.* Warm and comfortable. The attic room was very **cozy**.

*comfortable* Giving comfort and ease. I love to sit in a *comfortable* chair and read a good book.

*homey* Homelike; simple and comfortable. My father's kitchen is small, but it is *homey*.

*restful* Relaxing. We had a *restful* week at the seashore.

*snug* Closely and comfortably covered or sheltered. The campers were *snug* in their sleeping bags.

**ANTONYM: uncomfortable**

**D**

**disagree** *v.* To fail to agree; to argue. The two candidates **disagree** on almost everything.

*argue* To disagree openly; to discuss differing opinions. Our family likes to *argue* about politics.

*debate* To give reasons for or against; to consider. To *debate* well, you must think and speak clearly.

**ANTONYM: agree**

**doubt** *v.* To be unsure or uncertain about. Do you **doubt** the truth of what he says?

*distrust* To have little confidence in. I *distrust* long-range weather forecasts.

*suspect* To have doubts about; to believe (something bad). We *suspect* that the cat broke the pitcher.

*wonder* To be doubtful or curious about something; to want to know. I *wonder* what time it is.

**ANTONYMS: accept, trust**

**E**

**eat** *v.* To take food into oneself. It's healthful to **eat** a good breakfast.

*chew* To grind with the teeth. Do you *chew* your food well?

*consume* To take in; to use up. Whales *consume* large amounts of algae.

*dine* To eat dinner or another important meal. We like to listen to music while we *dine*.

*feast* To eat a large and lavish meal. At the banquet, we will *feast* on many delicious foods.

*munch* To chew noisily; to eat as a snack. I love to *munch* on a crisp apple.

*nibble* To eat a small amount delicately and quickly. We watched the rabbit *nibble* a lettuce leaf.

**enjoyable** *adj.* Pleasant; fun. We spent an **enjoyable** evening at the theater.

*agreeable* Pleasant; comfortable. It is *agreeable* to relax in the shade on a hot day.

*delightful* Giving joy or pleasure. This has been a *delightful* party.

*pleasant* Giving pleasure; nice. He has a friendly, *pleasant* smile.

**ANTONYMS: bitter, harsh, painful, unenjoyable, unpleasant**

**F**

**fast** *adj.* Moving or able to move quickly. Maria is a **fast** runner.

*quick* Taking very little time; speedy. We had a *quick* lunch before leaving.

*rapid* Very fast. There is a *rapid* current in the middle of the river.

*speedy* Very fast. The messenger promised *speedy* delivery of the letter.

*swift* Moving rapidly, directly, and with ease. He mounted his horse in one *swift* motion.

**ANTONYMS: leisurely, slow, sluggish**

**first** *adj.* Before all others. Carl is always **first** in line.

*chief* Leading; most important. The *chief* crop of many Asian nations is rice.

*foremost* First in time or place. Einstein was the *foremost* physicist of his day.

*leading* Ahead of all others. Her book has been accepted by a *leading* publisher of children's picture books.

**ANTONYMS: final, last**

**fly** *v.* To move through the air. In the winter, many birds **fly** south.

*flutter* To flap the wings without actually flying; to fly clumsily. We watched the birds *flutter* in the birdbath.

*glide* To coast or move without using power. The trapeze artists *glide* gracefully through the air.

*hover* To remain in or near one place in the air. Traffic helicopters *hover* over the highway.

*sail* To move, glide, or float. Try to make your kite *sail* over the trees.

*soar* To rise high into the air. Two black hawks *soar* over the peaceful valley.

**forest** *n.* A large area of land covered by trees. The **forest** is home to many animals.

*jungle* A thick, often tropical, forest. Many rare plants grow in the *jungle.*

*timberland* An area that is covered with trees. The loggers worked all winter in the *timberland.*

*wilderness* An area that is wild and unchanged by humans. At one time, much of our country was *wilderness.*

*woods* A small forest thick with trees. I love to walk in the *woods* on a winter day.

**friendly** *adj.* Of or like a friend; showing kindness. The librarian gave us a **friendly** smile.

*amicable* Having goodwill; friendly and open. The two countries have always had *amicable* relations.

*kind* Caring and considerate; sympathetic. We always try to be *kind* to animals.

*open* Generous; frank and straightforward; without deception. They had an *open* and honest discussion of the problem.

*warm* Affectionate and kind. Our new neighbors gave us a *warm* welcome.

*well-meaning* Showing good intentions or goodwill. She had *well-meaning* but interfering relatives.

**ANTONYMS: cold, hostile, mean, nasty, unfriendly, unkind**

## G

**give** *v.* To offer or present. What will you **give** your sister for her birthday?

*donate* To give as a gift to a charity or a cause. We will *donate* our old piano to the music school.

*lavish* To give generously or too generously. Tommy's grandparents *lavish* gifts on him.

*present* To award or offer. Mrs. Chin will *present* the prize for the best essay.

*provide* To supply. Niki will *provide* potato salad for the picnic.

**ANTONYMS: receive, steal, take**

WRITER'S THESAURUS

**good** *adj.* Having positive qualities. I like to read a **good** book before going to bed.

*excellent* Very good. Jorge has written an *excellent* science report.

*great* Among the best; very good. Edgar Allan Poe was a *great* writer.

*nice* Enjoyable; pleasant. Mindy had a *nice* visit with her aunt.

**ANTONYMS: awful, bad, terrible**

**happy** *adj.* Showing joy or pleasure. Wendy was very **happy** to see her friends again.

*carefree* Without worries; happy. We are having a relaxed and *carefree* vacation.

*elated* Full of joy or pride, as over success or good fortune. Jim was *elated* when he heard he had won the contest.

*joyful* Full of joy; very happy. *Joyful* singing filled the hall.

*jubilant* Expressing great joy; exultant. The students were *jubilant* when their team won the play-offs.

*pleased* Satisfied; showing pleasure. We are *pleased* that the meeting went so smoothly.

*thrilled* Feeling great emotion or excitement. The audience was *thrilled* by the singer's performance.

**ANTONYMS: depressed, dissatisfied, heartbroken, sad, unhappy**

**hesitate** *v.* To feel doubtful; to pause. I **hesitate** to call them at this late hour.

*delay* To go slowly; to linger; to cause to be late. The storm will *delay* our flight.

*pause* To stop temporarily. Hikers often *pause* here to admire the view.

*wait* To stay until something happens. I will *wait* for you to come home.

**ANTONYMS: continue, proceed**

**hum** *v.* To make a low, steady sound. At night, I can hear the refrigerator **hum.**

*buzz* To make a harsh, steady sound such as that a mosquito or a bee makes. She heard a mosquito *buzz* near her ear.

*croak* To make a deep, throaty sound. The frogs in the pond *croak* at night.

*drone* To make a steady, deep, even sound. Some machines *drone* endlessly through the night.

*murmur* To make a low, muffled sound. Voices *murmur* in the next room.

*purr* To make a low, humming sound, such as that a contented cat makes. Tigers *purr* very loudly.

**idea** *n.* A thought or an opinion. Ian has a good **idea** for a story.

*belief* Something that someone thinks is true. It is my *belief* that Bigfoot really exists.

*feeling* An opinion or an emotion. I have a *feeling* that we will see each other again.

*notion* An idea or an opinion. I've never heard such a strange *notion*!

*opinion* A belief; a judgment about the value of something. What is your *opinion* of that movie?

*thought* The result of thinking; an idea or a judgment. I have had a new *thought* about the matter since we last talked.

*view* An opinion or judgment; a way of looking at something. Your *view* of the situation is different from mine.

**interesting** *adj.* Having or arousing interest or attention. This book has an **interesting** plot.

*absorbing* Taking the full attention of; deeply involving. She finds her work challenging and *absorbing.*

*appealing* Inviting; attractive. The casserole gave off an *appealing* aroma.

*engaging* Attracting attention in a pleasing manner. The politician had an *engaging* way of speaking.

*fascinating* Very interesting. We saw a *fascinating* television program about kangaroos.

*intriguing* Interesting in an unusual way. He has an *intriguing* new approach to the problem.

**ANTONYMS: boring, dull, uninteresting**

## J

**jump** *v.* To spring or leap into the air. Kathy can **jump** higher than anyone else in our class.

*bounce* To jump up and down or to jump suddenly. Michelle loves to *bounce* on the trampoline.

*hop* To move in short jumps; to jump on one foot. Kangaroos *hop* from place to place.

*leap* To rise from the ground; to jump. Deer sometimes *leap* over the fence into our lot.

*skip* To move by making little, rhythmic hops and steps. The children *skip* home from school.

*spring* To jump up rapidly. When the alarm sounds, the firefighters *spring* onto the truck.

## L

**large** *adj.* Great in size, amount, or extent. The United States is a very **large** country.

*big* Large; great in size. Cleaning out the attic will be a *big* job.

*gigantic* Huge; giant. A *gigantic* ocean liner was docked at the pier.

*huge* Very large. We drove through *huge* fields of corn.

*immense* Very large; seeming to be endless. A glacier is an *immense* expanse of ice.

*mammoth* Huge; enormous. Repairing the highways of our state is a *mammoth* project.

*monstrous* Abnormally large; overwhelming in size. The country's *monstrous* debt is a great burden.

**ANTONYMS: little, miniature, minute, small, tiny**

**lively** *adj.* Full of life; spirited. The polka is a **lively** dance.

*active* Showing action; busy. The parents' association is very *active* in our school.

*frisky* Lively or playful. The *frisky* puppies jumped out of their box.

*spry* Quick and agile; active. My grandmother keeps limber and *spry* by riding her bicycle.

*vivid* Full of life or seeming very much alive. Gina is the most *vivid* character in the book.

**ANTONYMS: inactive, lazy, lifeless, listless, sluggish, tired**

## M

**move** *v.* To go or make go from one place to another. Please **move** that table against the wall.

*climb* To go up. Squirrels *climb* the tree outside my window.

*dance* To move in time, usually to music. My parents *dance* together every weekend.

**WRITER'S THESAURUS**

*motion* To signal; to make a movement that shows meaning. The traffic officer will *motion* to us when it is safe to cross the street.

*sweep* To move or pass swiftly or with force. Express trains *sweep* by this station without stopping.

*trot* To run at medium speed. Graceful horses *trot* around the circus ring.

*zoom* To move very quickly, often with a low humming sound. The high-speed airplanes *zoom* by at three hundred miles per hour.

**nervous** *adj.* Tense; uneasy. Eric was **nervous** before the big game.

*anxious* Worried; uneasy. News of an approaching hurricane made us *anxious.*

*jumpy* Nervous; uneasy; overly active because of nervousness. Our dog becomes *jumpy* when he is kept inside all day.

*restless* Unable to rest or be still; nervous; uneasy. Jan was *restless* and could not sleep.

*tense* Nervous; strained. The mood at the space center was *tense* before lift-off.

*uneasy* Restless; uncomfortable; nervous. Myrtle was *uneasy* about riding the bicycle without a light.

**ANTONYMS: calm, relaxed, undisturbed**

**O**

**often** *adv.* At frequent intervals; over and over. I **often** play softball after school.

*frequently* Often; again and again. Our car breaks down *frequently.*

*ordinarily* Normally; commonly; as a matter of course. We *ordinarily* eat dinner at 6:00 P.M.

*regularly* Usually; in a scheduled manner. Mrs. Morales *regularly* writes a column for the Sunday paper.

*repeatedly* Over and over; several times. You have been late for class *repeatedly.*

*usually* Commonly or customarily; normally. There are *usually* many children at the Saturday afternoon movie.

**ANTONYMS: infrequently, rarely, seldom**

**old** *adj.* Not new. Sometimes **old** clothes are the most comfortable of all.

*ancient* Very old. The *ancient* scroll was surprisingly well preserved.

*used* Having belonged to another person. You should be careful when buying a *used* car.

*worn* Damaged by much use. The sofa was faded and *worn.*

**ANTONYMS: modern, new, recent, young**

**organize** *v.* To put in order; to form; to get together, as a group of people. The class will **organize** a committee to plan the party.

*arrange* To put in a particular order. Minna will *arrange* the flowers in a vase.

*classify* To separate into classes or groups. When books arrive at the library, the staff must *classify* them as fiction or nonfiction.

*establish* To bring into being and give a permanent form to. The leader wanted to *establish* a true democracy.

*form* To give shape to; to create. My friends and I plan to *form* a stamp-collecting club.

*systematize* To organize in an orderly manner. Computers have helped us to *systematize* our bookkeeping.

**ANTONYMS: confuse, disarrange, disorganize, muddle, unsettle, upset**

**pick** *v.* To choose one from a number of possibilities. I hope the coach will **pick** me to pitch the game.

*choose* To decide on; to select. Some people *choose* to work at night.

*elect* To choose by voting. We *elect* a President every four years.

*opt* To choose; to decide in favor of something. Many high school graduates *opt* to go on to college.

*select* To choose one in preference over others. In our school cafeteria, we can *select* one of two main courses.

**possible** *adj.* Capable of happening or being done. It is **possible** that we will have a snowstorm today.

*attainable* Reachable. Are the goals of this plan *attainable*?

*conceivable* Possible. It is *conceivable* that there is life on other planets.

*feasible* Capable of being done or accomplished. Now that we have more money, our plan to put on a show is *feasible*.

*likely* Tending to be; probable. It is *likely* that we will need more milk for breakfast.

*workable* Capable of being done or worked out. Your plan is not perfect, but it is *workable*.

**ANTONYMS: absurd, impossible, unattainable, unheard-of, unlikely, unthinkable**

**road** *n.* A cleared way along which people and vehicles can travel. Is this the **road** to town?

*avenue* A broad road or street. There are many elegant shops along the *avenue*.

*highway* A main road or route. That *highway* goes all the way across the state.

*path* A small road, usually meant for walking. We followed a winding *path* through the woods.

*route* The road or course followed in traveling from one place to another. Take the most direct *route* from here to there.

*street* A road in a city or town, often with sidewalks. The Davidsons live on a quiet, shady *street*.

**run** *v.* To move quickly on foot. The athletes **run** around the track.

*dash* To move with sudden speed, usually over a short distance. I'll *dash* to the corner and buy a paper.

*flee* To move swiftly to get away from something. As the floodwaters rose, some people had to *flee* their homes.

*gallop* To run fast, as a horse does at top speed. Wild horses *gallop* along the seashore.

*race* To run or move swiftly, as in a competition. I'll *race* you to the playground.

*scamper* To run playfully. Two chipmunks *scamper* across the grass.

*sprint* To run at top speed for a short distance. Mr. Evans had to *sprint* to catch his bus.

**ANTONYMS: crawl, creep, dawdle, plod, trudge**

## S

**say** *v.* To express something by speaking. Sometimes it is hard to **say** what you mean.

*assert* To state clearly and firmly; to declare. I *assert* my right to speak at this meeting.

*express* To communicate a thought or an idea in words. You can *express* all your feelings in a diary.

*pronounce* To produce the sounds of a word. When you talk on the telephone, *pronounce* your words carefully.

*speak* To talk. The President will *speak* on television tonight.

*state* To make a clear declaration; to say plainly. The senators must *state* their reasons for supporting the bill.

*tell* To relate or narrate; to say to. I won't *tell* you how the movie ends.

**see** *v.* To receive images through the eye. Can you **see** the ship on the horizon?

*glimpse* To catch sight of for a moment. Did you happen to *glimpse* the headlines of the newspaper?

*look* To turn the eyes toward with the intention of seeing. Please *look* at the chalkboard.

*observe* To watch carefully; to take notice of. With this telescope, we can *observe* distant stars.

*view* To see or watch. Nan traveled to New England to *view* the fall colors.

*watch* To observe over a period of time. We went down to the field to *watch* the ball game.

**sense** *n.* Meaning, as of a word. In that sentence, the **sense** of the word *hide* is "animal skin."

*gist* The main point or idea. The *gist* of the report is that we must conserve water.

*meaning* Significance or sense. Please explain the *meaning* of your remark.

*point* The main idea. The author's *point* is that exercise is important.

*significance* Meaning or importance. That book has great *significance* for the future of education.

**ANTONYMS: meaninglessness, nonsense, senselessness**

**shock** *v.* To cause to feel surprise, terror, or disgust. The destruction caused by the earthquake will **shock** you.

*startle* To frighten, surprise, or excite suddenly. Loud noises can *startle* a baby.

*stun* To shock; to astonish. The beautiful costumes in our show are sure to *stun* the audience.

*surprise* To affect someone with something unexpected. Let's *surprise* Mom by cleaning the garage.

**sigh** *v.* To draw in the breath and let it out with a sound that expresses an emotion such as weariness, sadness, or relief. We can only **sigh** when we see how much work remains to be done.

*breathe* To take in and let out air. I love to *breathe* clean mountain air.

*moan* To make a low, prolonged sound that expresses sadness or pain. I heard her *moan* when she saw her bad grades.

*sob* To cry or weep in a way that can be heard. The child began to *sob* when his toy was taken away.

*whisper* To speak very softly, hardly using the vocal cords. If you must speak in the library, please *whisper.*

**silent** *adj.* Remaining quiet; not speaking. The people became **silent** when the judge entered the courtroom.

*dumb* Speechless; unable to speak. We were struck *dumb* by the shocking news.

*quiet* Having or making little noise. It's *quiet* in the house after my little brother goes to sleep.

*speechless* Not speaking; unable to speak. Iris was *speechless* with delight at her surprise birthday party.

*still* Making no sound or movement; silent. You must remain *still,* or you will scare the birds away.

**ANTONYMS: loud, noisy**

**smile** *v.* To show pleasure or happiness by turning up the corners of the mouth. The clown's antics made us **smile.**

*grin* To smile broadly and show the teeth. At Halloween, jack-o'-lanterns *grin* in the windows.

*laugh* To smile and make a sound that shows amusement or happiness. The children always *laugh* at Grandpa's jokes.

**ANTONYMS: cry, frown, pout**

**stop** *v.* To come or bring to a halt. The buses **stop** in front of the school.

*flag* To stop by signaling. Walk to the curb and *flag* a taxicab.

*halt* To stop; to stop temporarily. We will have to *halt* construction until more money can be raised.

*quit* To give up an activity; to stop. We *quit* playing when Mom calls us for dinner.

**ANTONYMS: begin, start**

**strike** *v.* To hit sharply. The percussion player will **strike** a cymbal.

*crash* To hit or break noisily. The firefighters had to *crash* through the blocked door.

*hit* To strike or give a forceful blow to. I *hit* my head on the edge of the cabinet door.

*knock* To strike a sharp blow. Please *knock* on the door before you enter the room.

*smash* To hit with great force. *Smash* that ball over the fence!

**strong** *adj.* Powerful; forceful. A **strong** wind blew down the sign.

*mighty* Extremely strong or powerful. The king's *mighty* army defeated the town's small group of poorly-trained soldiers.

*powerful* Having great power or physical strength. The alligator's jaws are *powerful.*

*sturdy* Solidly made. This *sturdy* table will not break.

**ANTONYMS: feeble, flimsy, slight, weak**

**tender** *adj.* Gentle and loving. The mother gave her child a **tender** kiss.

*gentle* Kind and tender; not rough. The *gentle* dog likes to play with children.

*kind* Willing to help; gentle; friendly; sympathetic. Our *kind* neighbors helped us unload packages from the car.

*soft* Tender; kind; sympathetic. His *soft* smile and reassuring words made us feel less anxious.

**ANTONYMS: cruel, hard, unkind**

**think** *v.* To make use of the mind; to form ideas. You'll have to **think** hard to solve this problem.

*consider* To give careful thought to. We must *consider* all sides of the question.

*meditate* To think quietly and deeply. I like to walk in the woods and *meditate* upon the meaning of life.

*ponder* To carefully think over a problem. Ecologists *ponder* the question of how to save endangered species.

*reason* To think in a logical way; to try to persuade someone with logic. It is often difficult to *reason* with someone who is upset.

*reflect* To meditate or think quietly. My grandmother likes to *reflect* on how things have changed since she was a girl.

**tree** *n.* A woody plant with a central trunk from which branches grow. This elm is a beautiful shade **tree.**

*sapling* A tree not yet fully grown. This *sapling* bends in the breeze.

*seedling* A tree younger than a sapling and grown from a seed. We bought a *seedling* at the nursery and planted it in our yard.

*timber* Trees; the wood of trees. There is a lot of *timber* on our property.

**unpleasant** *adj.* Not agreeable; not pleasant. I am sorry about the **unpleasant** argument we had.

*annoying* Troublesome; irritating. The loud hum of the ceiling fan was *annoying.*

*disgusting* Arousing disgust; offensive. The smell of rotten eggs is *disgusting.*

*nasty* Offensive or disgusting. The cough medicine has a *nasty* taste.

*troublesome* Causing trouble or worry. I found that math problem very *troublesome.*

**ANTONYMS: agreeable, pleasant, pleasing**

**vehicle** *n.* A piece of equipment meant to carry things or people. No **vehicle** can travel faster than 50 miles an hour on this stretch of the road.

*automobile* A motorized vehicle with four wheels, designed to carry a small number of people; a car. The neighbors bought a new *automobile* for their cross-country drive.

*bus* A motorized vehicle with seats for many passengers. Tamara takes the *bus* to work every morning.

*conveyance* A means of transporting something from one place to another. In some Asian countries, a cart called a rickshaw is a commonly used *conveyance.*

*truck* A motor vehicle used for carrying heavy loads. A large *truck* was being unloaded near the warehouse.

*van* An enclosed motor vehicle with a somewhat boxlike shape, used for moving and carrying things or people. We rented a *van* to move our furniture.

walk *v.* To go on foot, advancing by steps. Many people **walk** for exercise.

*amble* To walk in an easy, relaxed way. On Sunday afternoons, we *amble* over to the park.

*stride* To walk in an energetic way, with long steps. We saw an angry customer *stride* out of the store.

*stroll* To walk in a casual, idle way; to ramble. Many sightseers *stroll* along the main avenue.

*strut* To walk in a proud or pompous way. The peacock likes to *strut* around in its cage.

*trudge* To walk in a tired, plodding way. The weary travelers *trudge* toward their hotel.

win *v.* To gain a victory in a contest or a struggle. We hope our team will **win** the game.

*conquer* To win control by force. The ancient Romans were able to *conquer* most of the known world.

*defeat* To conquer or triumph over an opposing force. The Lions were able to *defeat* the Jets in the play-offs.

*succeed* To achieve something worked for and desired. We hope to *succeed* in cleaning up the harbor.

*triumph* To be victorious, with a sense of joy and celebration. It was wonderful to see him *triumph* over his long illness.

**ANTONYMS: fail, fall, lose, surrender**

**WRITER'S THESAURUS**

# INDEX

# INDEX

with direct quotations, 428–429, EP65
with interjections, 374–375
in letters and on envelopes, 418–420,
421–423, EP61, EP62
within sentences, 412–413, EP58
in a series, 315, 412–413, EP58
Common nouns, 94–95, 110, 115, 439, EP16,
WH5
Comparative. *See* Adjectives; Compare and
contrast.
Compare and contrast, 161, 166–167, 168,
170–181, 182, 183, WH26, WH27
comparison with adjectives, 282–283,
284–285, 286–287, 295, 342, 442,
EP44, EP45, EP46, WH12, WH58
comparison with adverbs, 322–323, 336,
EP48, WH13, WH59
Composition, WH24–47. *See also* Writing
process.
glossary of terms, G2–9
Compound sentence, 50–51, 61, 113, 132, 177,
EP11, WH3
Compound words, 104–105, 107, WH49
closed, 104–105
hyphenated, 104–105
open, 104–105
Confusing words. *See* Homographs;
Homophones; Verbs.
Conjunctions, 372–373, 378, 379, 380, 383,
**443, EP55, WH15**
Conklin, Kenna Elise, 118–119
Connecting ideas
main ideas and details, 72
Context clues, 54–55, 57
Contractions, 192–193, 196, 198, 201,
WH56–57
Cooperative learning, 17, 26, 29–30, 32, 55, 56,
71, 84, 105, 106, 122, 134–135, 145, 151, 153,
154, 167, 168, 181, 195, 196, 211, 212, 221, 225,
226, 243, 244, 257, 258, 267, 271, 277, 285,
289, 290, 291, 304, 305, 314, 331, 332, 333,
349, 350, 351, 358, 363, 375, 377, 378, 395,
402, 429, 431, 432, 433
Cross-curriculum writing
art, 364
fine arts, 32, 318
health, 136, 226, 272, 364
history, 364
language arts, 364
literature, 136, 226, 272, 318
mathematics, 32
music, 86

physical education, 86, 136, 182, 226, 272, 364
reading, 182
science, 32, 86, 182, 226, 318, 364
social studies, 32, 86, 136, 182, 226, 318
Cumulative review, 112–115, 202–205,
338–343, 438–443

Days of the week. *See* Capitalization.
Deck, Sally Elizabeth, 118–119
Declarative sentences, 36–37, 44–45, 59,
410–411, EP4, WH3
Demonstrative adjectives, 276–277, 294, EP41,
WH11
Descriptive paragraph, 251–255, 260–271, 273,
WH29
analyzing a, 256–257
Details
to create good characters, 395
using to explain, 19
main idea and, 72
in spatial order, 258, 262–263
Dialogue, 395, 428–429, 437, EP65, WH30
Dictionary, 446–448
Direct objects, 188–189, 197, 198, 200, 205, 340,
WH4
Directions. *See* How-to paragraph.
Double negative, 326–327, 337, EP50, WH13,
WH23
Drafting, 6, 24, 78, 129, 174, 219, 265, 312, 356,
400, G2
Dramatize, 407

Editor's marks, 25–26, 28, 79–80, 82, 130–131,
133, 175–176, 178, 220–221, 223, 266–267,
269, 313–314, 316, 357–358, 360, 401–402,
404, G3
Encyclopedia, 454–455
Engellenner, Jon, 207–209
Enrichment activities
language, 56, 57, 106, 107, 154, 155, 196, 197,
244, 245, 290, 291, 332, 333, 378, 379,
432, 433
Entertain, writing to, 161–165, 251–255,
385–391, 400
Envelopes, 421–423, EP62, WH47

**T**

**U**

**V**

*continued from page IV*

UNIT 3: 116, HBJ Photo/Richard Haynes; 124, HBJ; 128, HBJ Photo; 134(l), HBJ Photo; (r), HBJ Photo; 135, HBJ Photo; 142(t), HBJ Photo/Rodney Jones; (b), HBJ Photo/Rodney Jones.

UNIT 4: 160, HBJ Photo/Richard Haynes; 161, Jill Jepson; 170, HBJ Photo; 179, HBJ Photo/Mark Cunningham; 180(t), HBJ Photo/Mark Cunningham; (l), HBJ Photo/Mark Cunningham; (r), HBJ Photo/Mark Cunningham; 181(l), HBJ Photo/Mark Cunningham; (r), HBJ Photo/Mark Cunningham.

UNIT 5: 206, Mark Reinstein/Tony Stone Worldwide; 207, Michael Williamson; 214, HBJ Photo/Tom O'Neal; 218, HBJ Photo/Tom O'Neal; 224(t), HBJ Photo/Tom O'Neal; (l), HBJ Photo/Tom O'Neal; (r), HBJ Photo/Tom O'Neal; 225(l), HBJ Photo/Tom O'Neal; (r), HBJ Photo/Tom O'Neal.

UNIT 6: 250, HBJ Photo/Richard Haynes; 251, Harper & Row; 260, HBJ Photo; 264, HBJ Photo; 270(t), HBJ Photo; (b), HBJ Photo; 271(l), HBJ Photo; (r), HBJ Photo; 280, HBJ Photo/Wiley & Flynn.

UNIT 7: 296, HBJ Photo; 297, Sandra Hansen/William Morrow & Company; 307, HBJ Photo; 311, HBJ Photo; 317, HBJ Photo; 326, NASA.

UNIT 8: 344, HBJ Photo; 352, HBJ Photo; 361, HBJ Photo; 362(t), HBJ Photo; (l), HBJ Photo; (r), HBJ Photo; 363, HBJ Photo.

UNIT 9: 384, HBJ Photo/Richard Haynes; 385, Larry Murphy; 396, HBJ Photo; 405(t), HBJ Photo; (b), HBJ Photo; 406(l), HBJ Photo; (r), HBJ Photo; 407, HBJ Photo.

1
2
3
F 4
G 5
H 6
I 7
J 8